The Ultimate Unofficial Rainbow Loom® Guide

The Ultimate Unofficial Rainbow Loom® Guide

Everything You Need to Know to Weave, Stitch, and Loop Your Way Through Dozens of Rainbow Loom Projects

Sky Pony Press
New York

Skypony Press books may be purchased in bulk at special discounts for sales promotion, corporate gifts, fund-raising, or educational purposes. Special editions can also be created to specifications. For details, contact the Special Sales Department, Skyhorse Publishing, 307 West 36th Street, 11th Floor, New York, NY 10018 or info@skyhorsepublishing.com.

Sky Pony is a registered trademark of Skyhorse Publishing, Inc. ®, a Delaware corporation.

Visit our website at www.skyponypress.com

10 9 8 7 6 5 4 3 2

Manufactured in the United States of America, October 2014
This product conforms to CPSIA 2008

Library of Congress Cataloging-in-Publication Data is available on file.

Print ISBN: 978-1-63220-240-6
Ebook IBSN: 1-63220-248-2

Disclaimer:

This book is intended to offer general guidance. It is sold with the understanding that every effort was made to provide the most current and accurate information. However, errors and omissions are still possible. Any use or misuse of the information contained herein is solely the responsibility of the user, and the author and publisher make no warrantees or claims as to the truth or validity of the information. The author and publisher shall have neither liability nor responsibility to any person or entity with respect to any loss or damage caused, or alleged to have been caused, directly or indirectly, by the information contained in this book. Furthermore, this book is not intended to give professional dietary, technical, or medical advice. Please refer to and follow any local laws when using any of the information contained herein, and act responsibly and safely at all times.

TABLE OF CONTENTS

THE BASICS

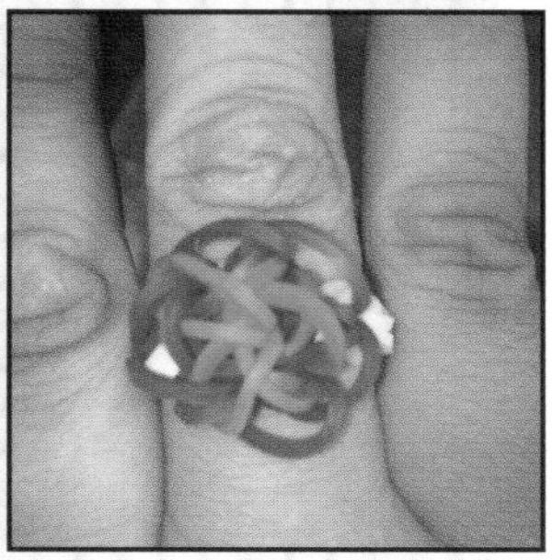

FANCY JEWELRY

CHARMS

MAKE STUFF OUT OF RAINBOW LOOM JEWELRY

IMPROV LOOMING

HELPFUL TIPS & IDEAS

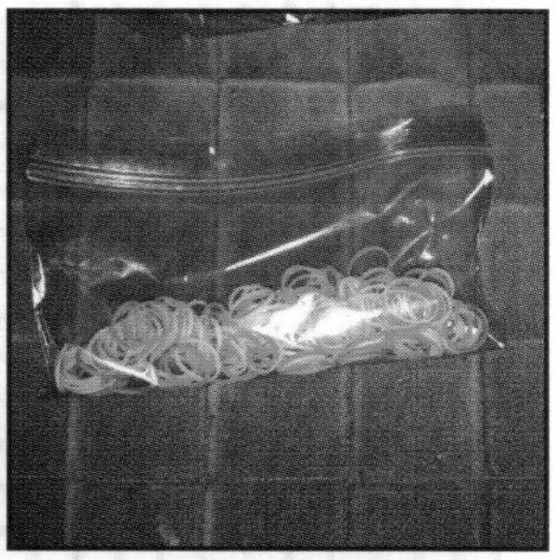
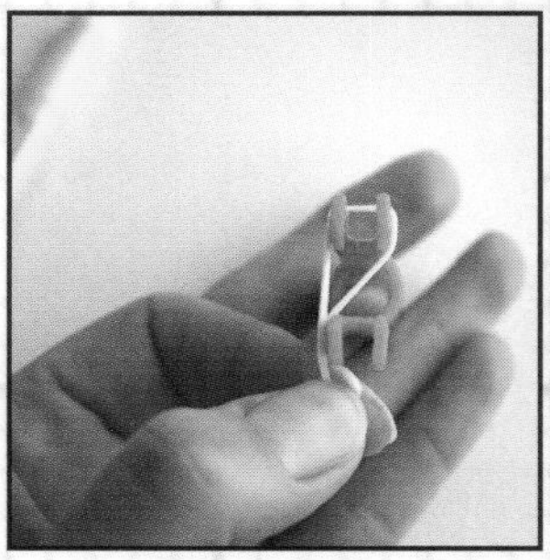

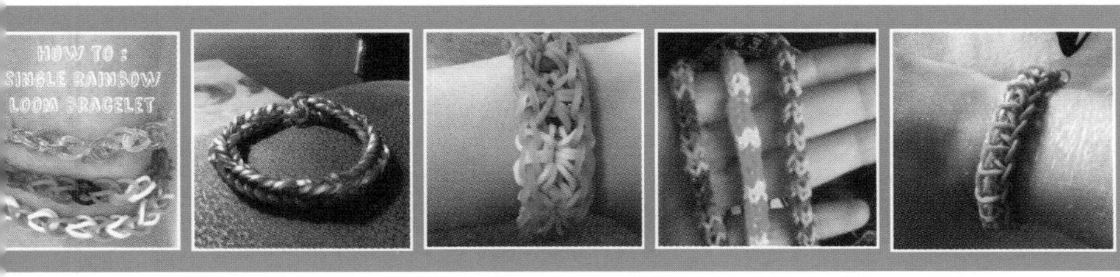

The Basics

Basic Bracelet

By Jessy Ellenberger (jessyratfink)
(http://www.instructables.com/id/single-rainbow-loom-bracelet/)

This is the quickest and easiest Rainbow Loom (rubber band) bracelet you can make! It's a great place to start if you've just gotten a Rainbow Loom. It took me only a few minutes to make my first single Rainbow Loom bracelet, and I've gotten even faster since then.

Step 1: What You'll Need

- A Rainbow Loom kit or other rubber band loom
- Bands
- C-clips
- Loom hook or a small crochet hook

If you buy the Rainbow Loom kit pictured, you will get the hook shown, some c-clips, and some bands—you won't need to buy anything else!

Step 2: Lay Down the Bands

Turn the loom so that the red arrow is facing away from you and the loom pieces. It should be arranged so that the middle piece is one notch lower than the two side pieces. Place one rubber band around the bottom middle and the bottom left pegs. Place another rubber band so that it goes from the bottom left to the second middle peg. Make sure this band lies on top of the previous band. Place a band that goes from the second middle peg to the second left peg. Repeat all the way up the loom, making sure that each band you're putting on the loom sits on top of the previous one. Check the photos for additional help.

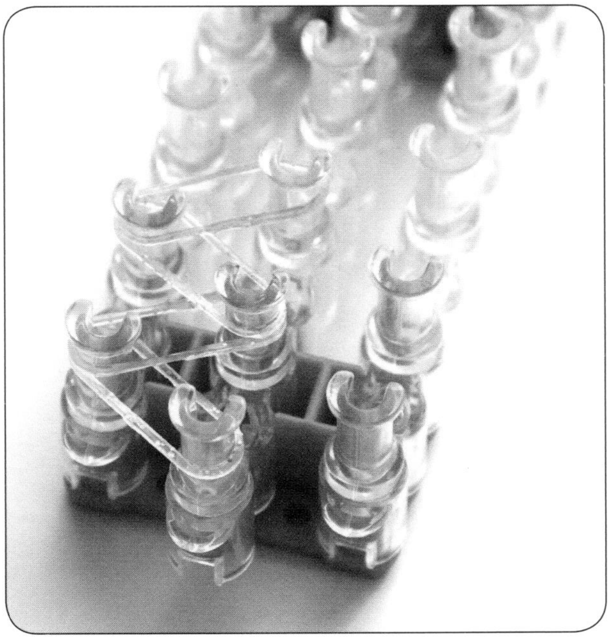

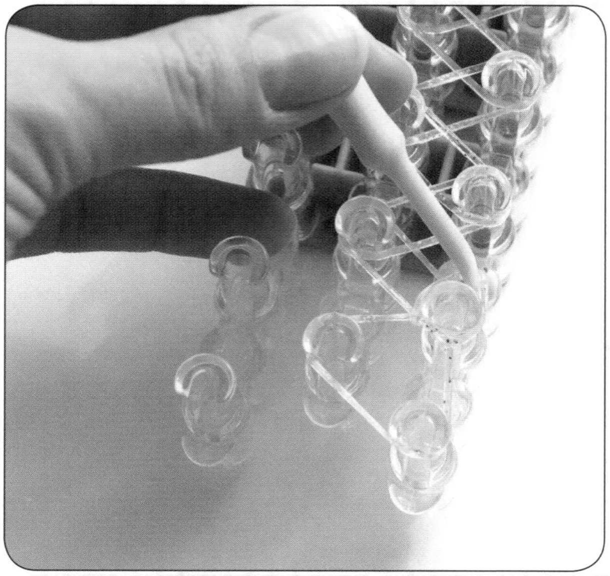

Step 3: Loop the Bands

Now we're going to learn how to loop the bands over one another to give the finished bracelet the right look.

Turn the loom so the arrows are facing you. Insert your hook under the orange band that is stretched between the first middle and second right pegs. Pull that band up and over so it sits only on the second right peg. Now have a look at the second right peg; there's a pink band going from that to the second middle peg. Insert your hook and grab the pink band only, then pull it up and over so it's sitting entirely on the second middle peg. Continue looping the bands over as shown in the fourth photo, always grabbing the lone band under the one you just looped. In the next step I'll explain how to finish looping once you get to the other end of the loom.

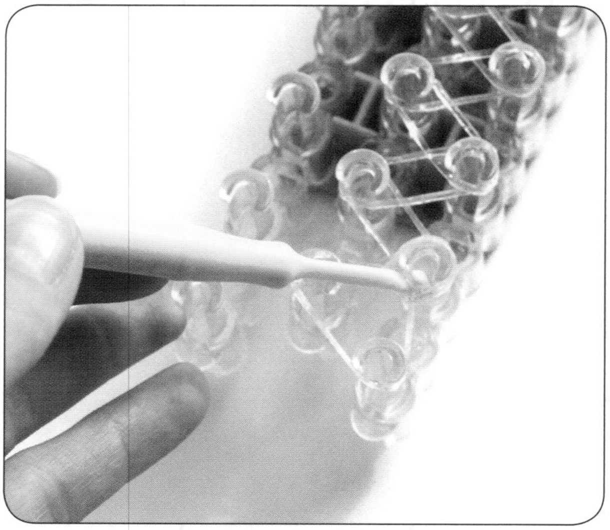

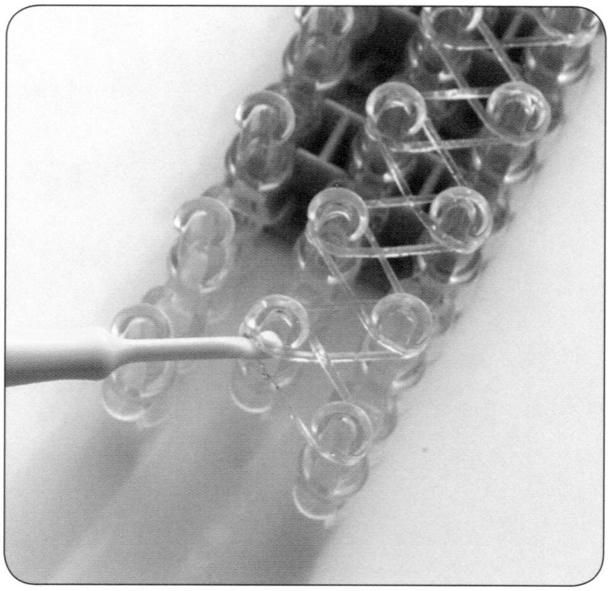

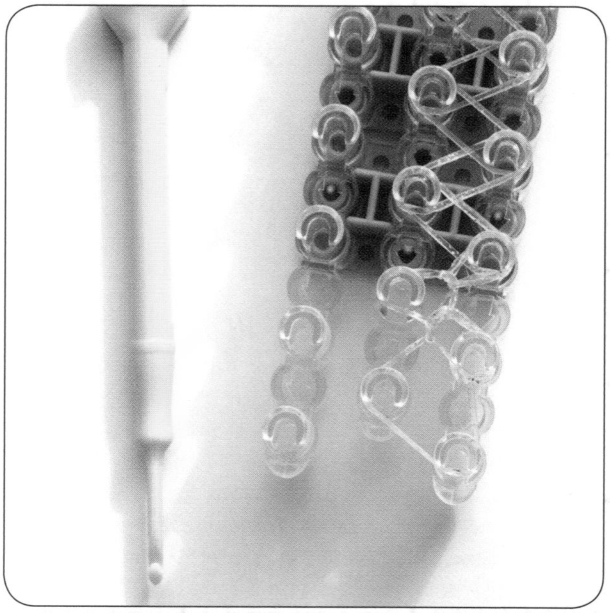

Step 4: Finish Looping and Start Securing

Once you make it to the other end of the loom, it will look like the photo. Pull off the end loop (mine is orange) and loop a c-clip onto the band. Make sure both sides of the band go into the c-clip.

Step 5: Pull the Band Off and Finish It

Once the c-clip is holding the end farthest from you securely, you can start pulling the bracelet off the loom. Do this by pulling up and towards yourself. When you get to the end, you'll have one bigger rubber band loop (mine is green). Pop that big loop into the same c-clip you used to secure the other end (see photo). Congrats! Now go make hundreds of them.

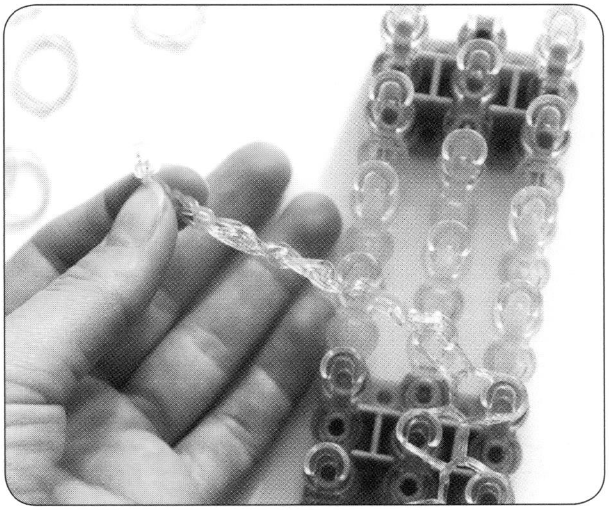

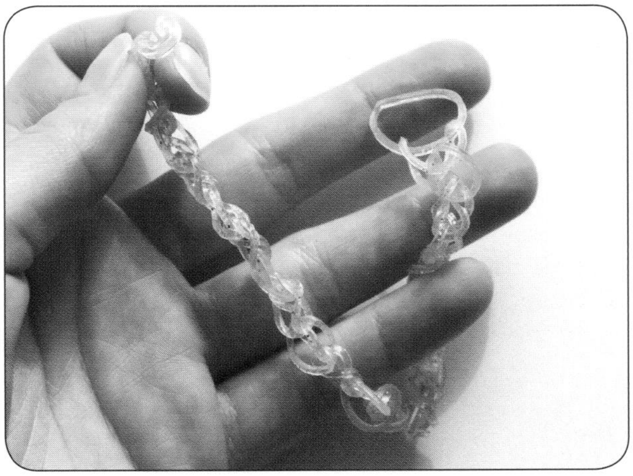

Double Bracelet

By Jessy Ellenberger (jessyratfink)

(http://www.instructables.com/id/double-rainbow-loom-bracelet/)

This double Rainbow Loom (rubber band) bracelet is slightly trickier than the single Rainbow Loom bracelet and is a good one for trying to learn how to manage looping more and more bands.

This bracelet is chunkier and more complex than the single Rainbow Loom bracelet and fits better, too—a little less loose. Your patterns will depend on the colors you choose. You can change the way it looks just by changing up the colors!

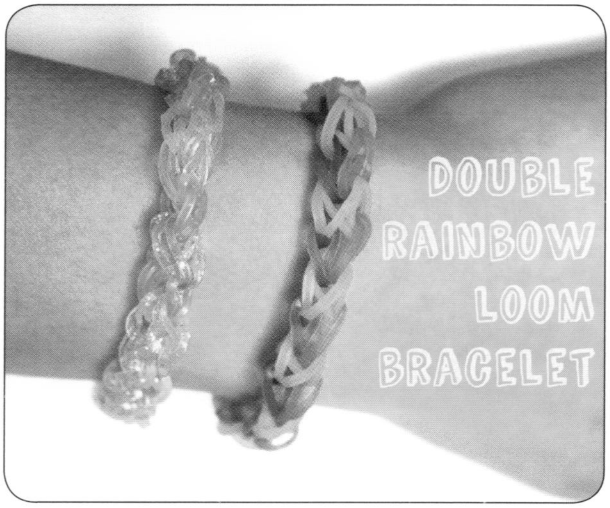

Step 1: What You'll Need

- A Rainbow Loom kit or other rubber band loom
- Bands
- C-clips
- Loom hook or a small crochet hook

Step 2: The Pattern

This is pretty easy—you're just going to be forming a diamond shape with the bands. Place the Rainbow Loom on your work surface with the arrows pointing away from you and the pieces aligned as shown in the photos. Put your first band on over the bottom middle and bottom left pegs. Put your second band on over the bottom middle and bottom right pegs. Put your third band on over the bottom left and second middle pegs. Put your fourth band on over the second middle and bottom right pegs.

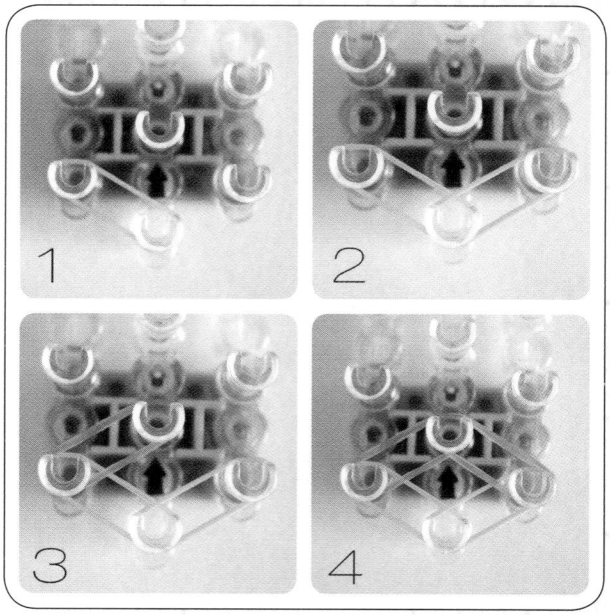

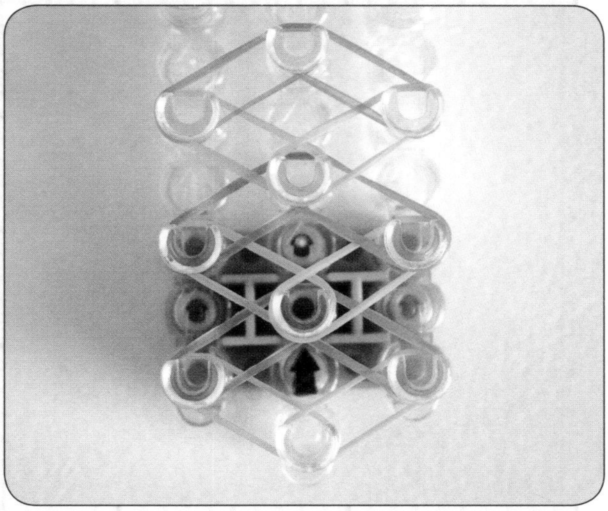

Step 3: Keep Putting the Bands On

Keep making the same diamond pattern all the way up, making sure each new layer of bands sits on top of the previous layer.

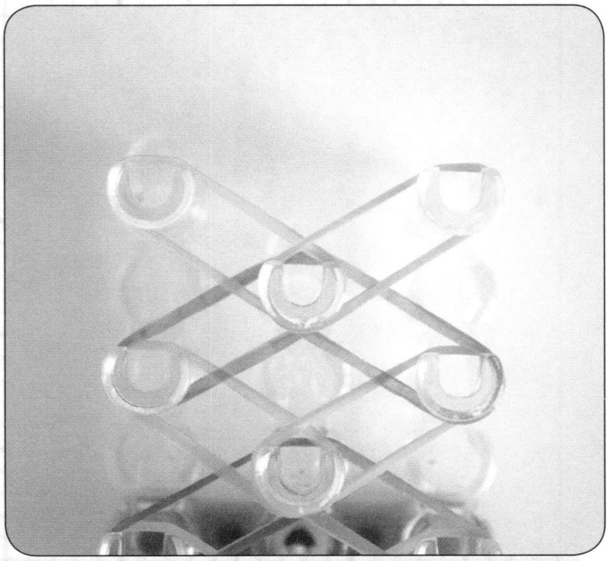

Step 4: Looping the Bands

Turn the loom so the arrows are facing you and have a look at the middle bottom peg. This is where you'll start! Because this is a little more confusing than the single Rainbow Loom bracelet, I'll be calling the bands by their color; see the photos to follow along!

Ignore the bottom two bands on each side—they're staying where they are. We'll be grabbing the top band (the blue one) on the middle peg and looping it up and over to the left. Then grab the purple band that's still on the middle peg and loop it up and to the right. Now we'll grab the yellow band that's under the purple one and loop it to the middle peg. To complete this set of loops, grab the green band on the second left peg and loop it over the middle. Repeat! A simplified way to think of this: loop left, loop right, loop right, loop left. If you keep up that pattern you'll do fine!

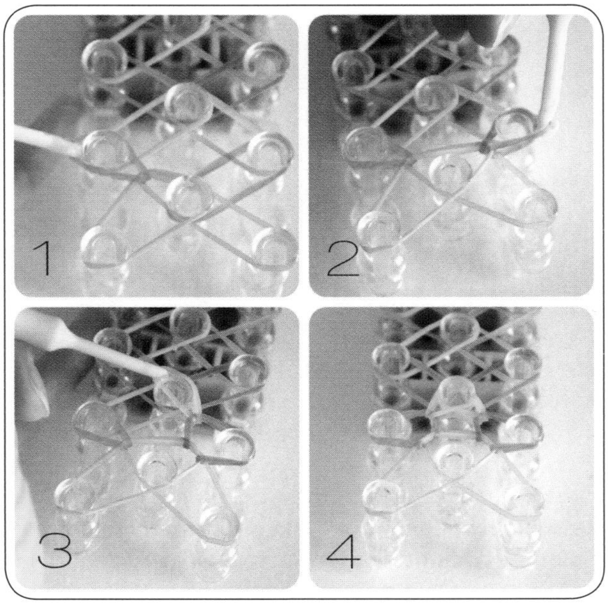

Step 5: Final Loops

Once you get to the end of the loom, loop both of the end rubber bands around the middle peg—first the right side and then the left.

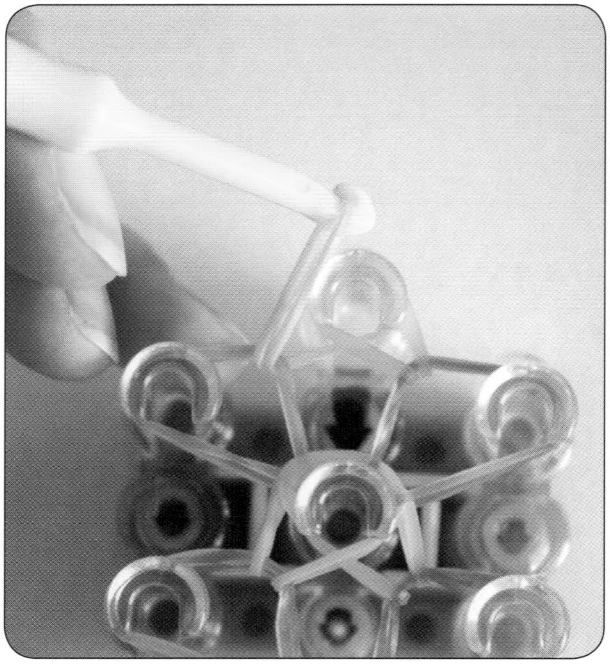

Step 6: Securing and Removing the Bracelet

Put your hook under the last bands you looped at the very end and slide a c-clip onto them. Make sure you've got both of them inside the clip! Pull the band gently off the loom—up and toward you. When it's entirely off, hold it by the two large rubber band loops at the other end.

Step 7: Finishing the Bracelet

Slip the c-clip over the two rubber band loops, making sure you've got all the ends inside it. Now you're ready to wear it.

Rainbow Fishtail Bracelet Two Ways

By rayray9889
(http://www.instructables.com/id/Rainbow-Loom-Fishtail-Bracelet-1/)

I'm going to show you two different ways to create the fishtail.

Step 1: Things You Need

- Rubber bands C-clips
- Loom and hook (version 1)
- Your fingers (version 2)

Step 2: Put a Twisted 8-Shape Rubber Band on Two Pegs

Step 3: Put Two More Rubber Bands on Top

Step 4: Grab the Bottom Band

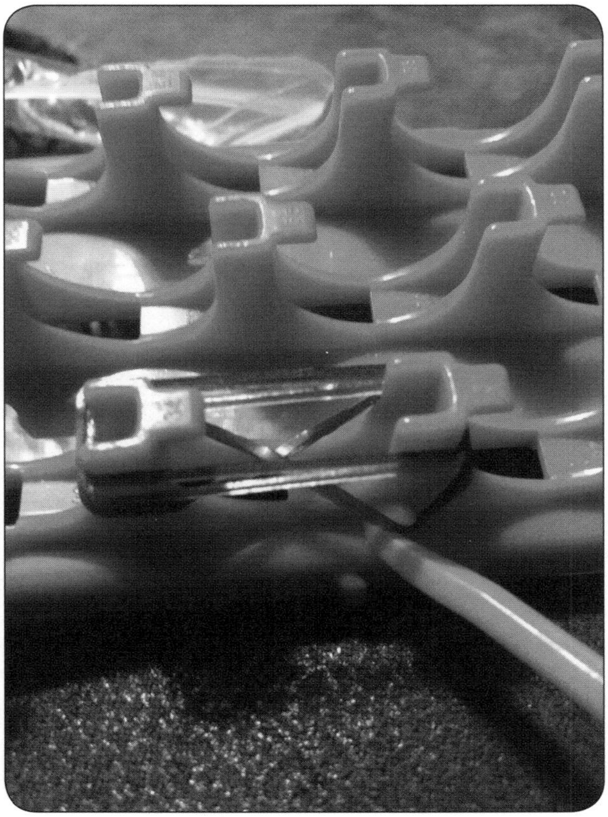

Step 5: Pull It Over on Top Do the Same on the Other Side

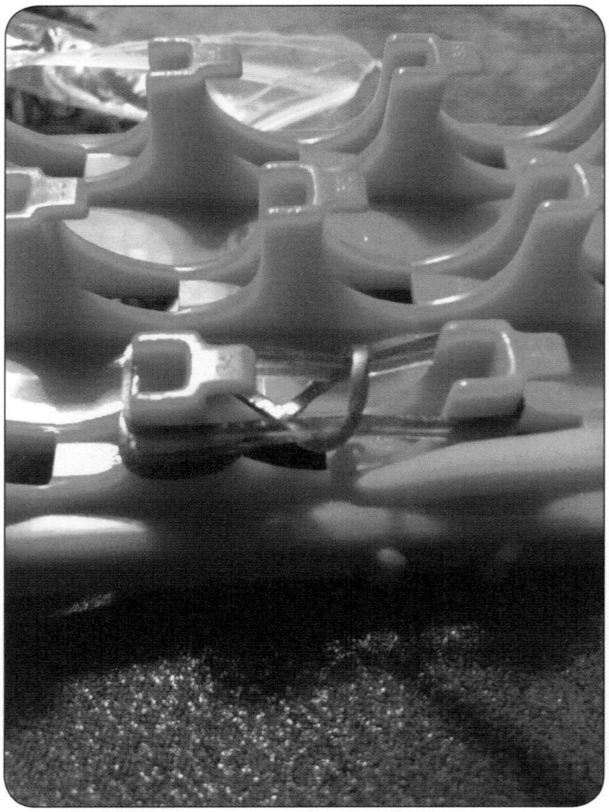

Step 6: Add Another Rubber Band on Top

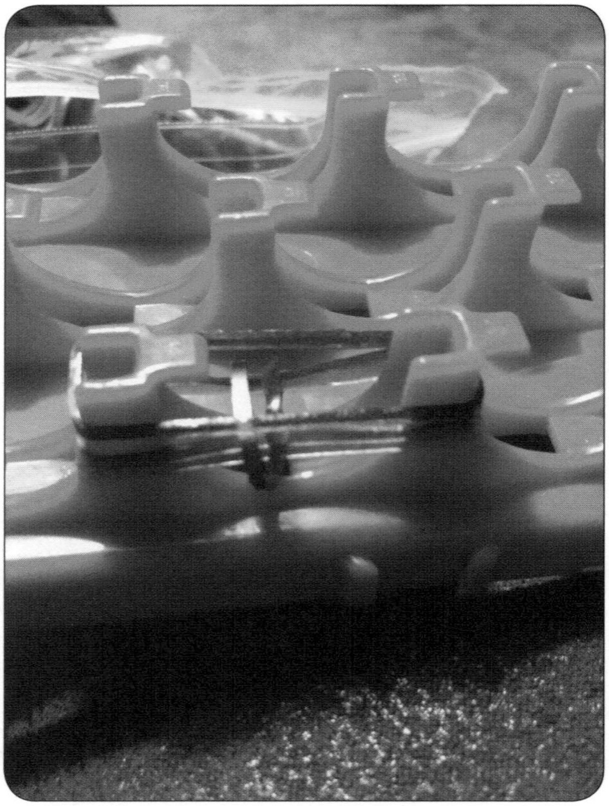

Step 7: Grab the Bottom Band

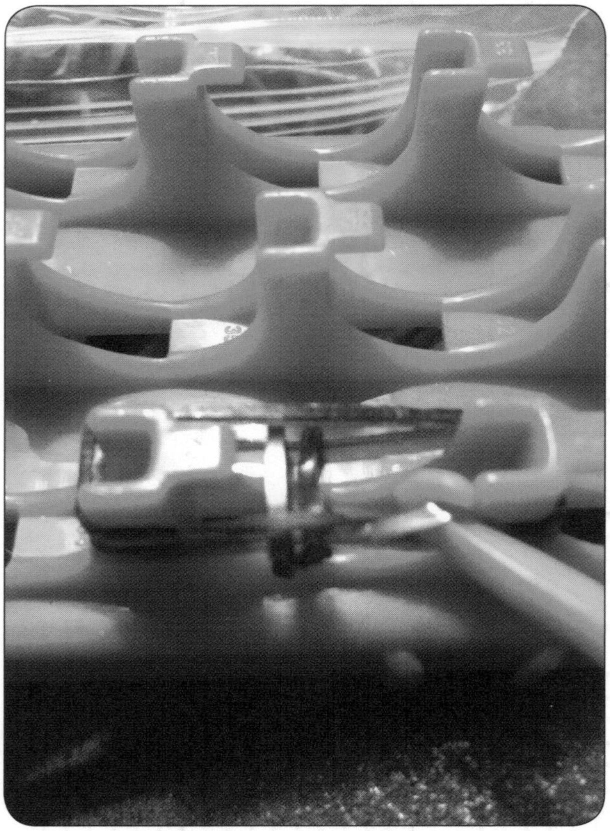

Step 8: And Pull It Over

Step 9: Continue to Length You Want

Step 10: When You Are Done, Only Have Two Bands On the Pegs

Step 11: Pull the Bottom Band Over on Both Sides As Before

Step 12: Put The Last Band on Your Hook

Step 13: Put on Clip to Fix Together

Step 14: Version 2!

Put an 8-shaped band on your pointer and middle fingers.

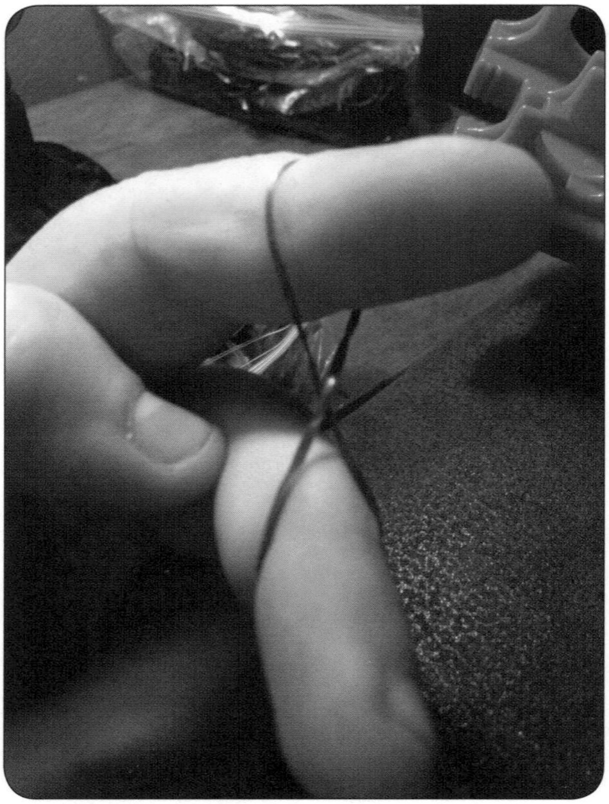

Step 15: Add Two More Bands on Top

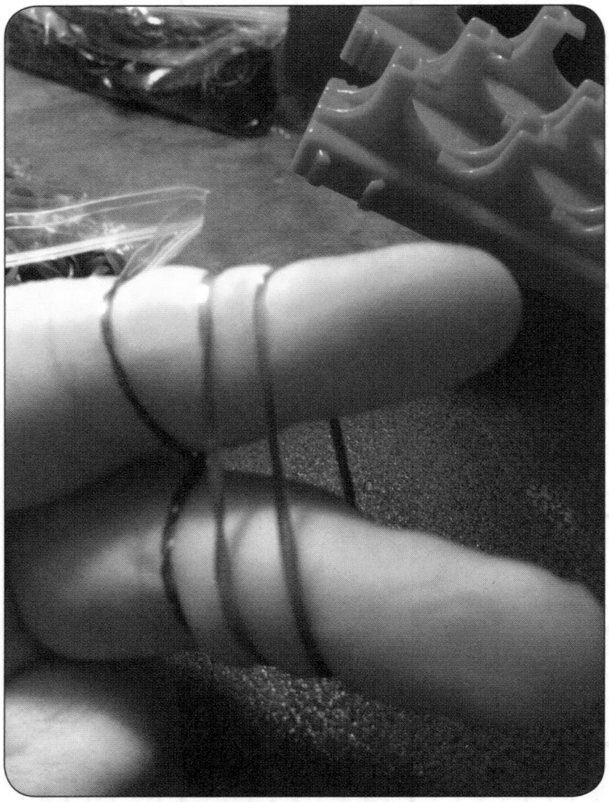

Step 16: Pull the Bottom Band Up on One Side and Do the Same for the Other Side

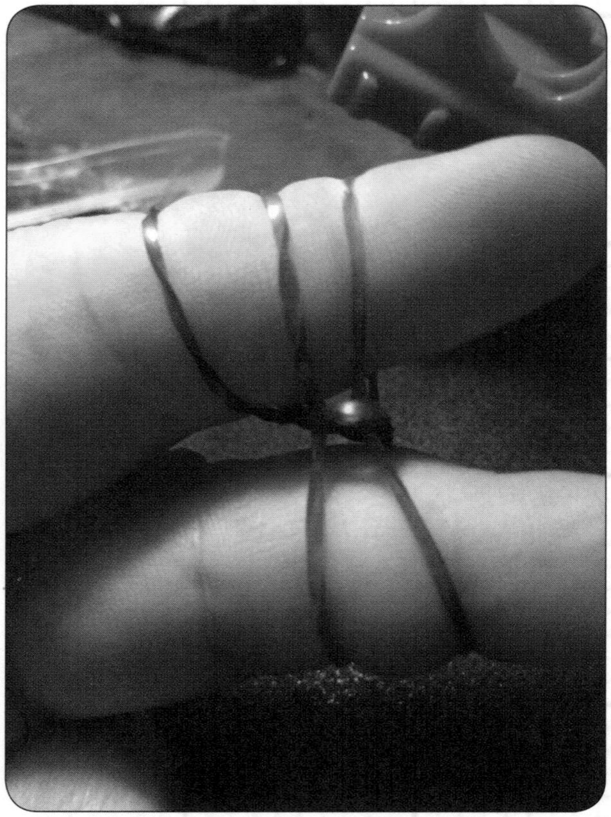

Step 17: Place Another Band on Your Fingers

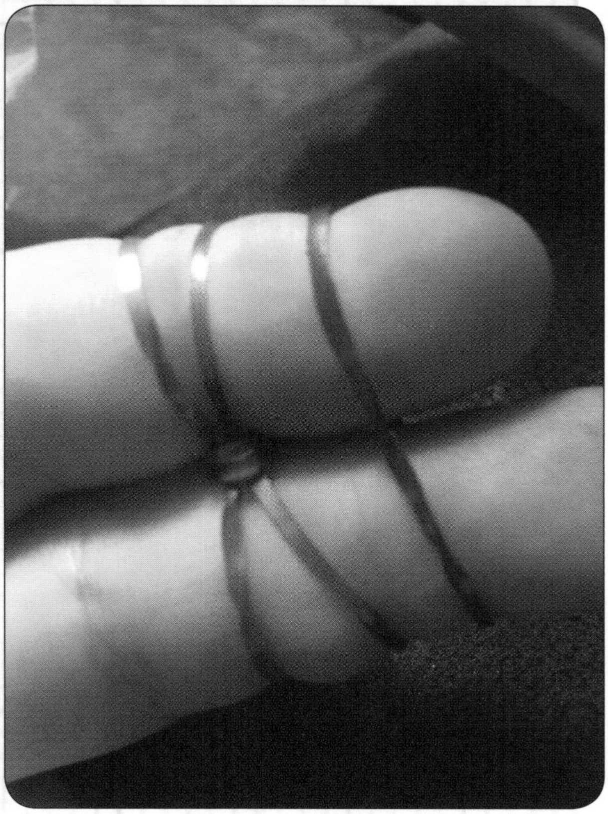

Step 18: Pull the Bottom Bands Up

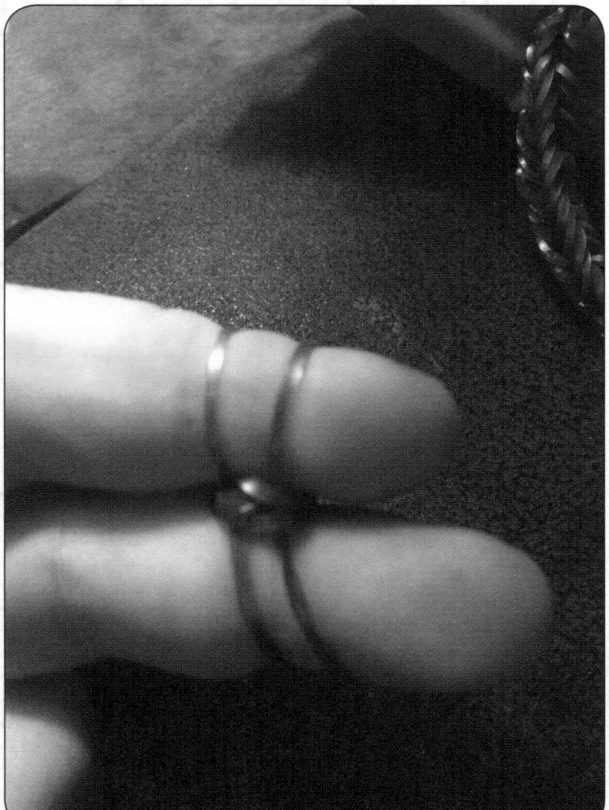

Step 19: Only Have Two Bands When You Reach Your Desired Length

Step 20: Pull Bottom Band Over on Top

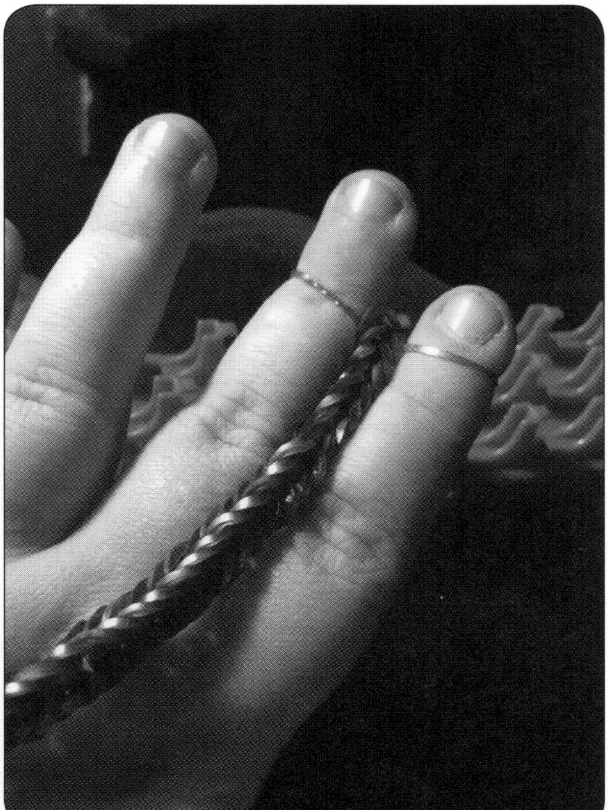

Step 21: You Can Put the Last Band on Your Hook or Single Finger

Step 22: Attach Clip to Both Ends

Step 23: Enjoy Your Bracelet!

Triple Single Bracelet

By Cindy02

Step 1: What You Need

- Rainbow Loom kit or other rubber band loom
- Hook
- Rubber bands in colors of your choice
- C- or S-clip

Step 2: Bands

Grab twelve bands of your first color and make sure the loom arrow is facing away from you. Start by placing your bands on the left side. Go all the way up. Do that for *all* three rows.

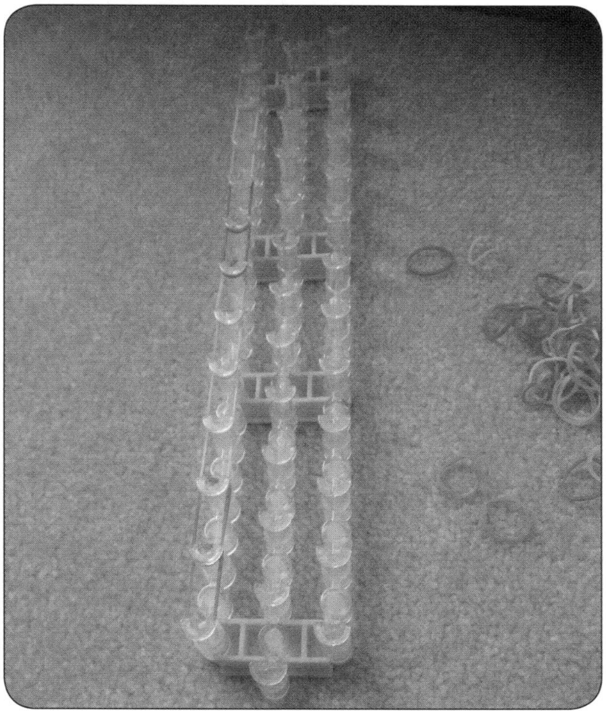

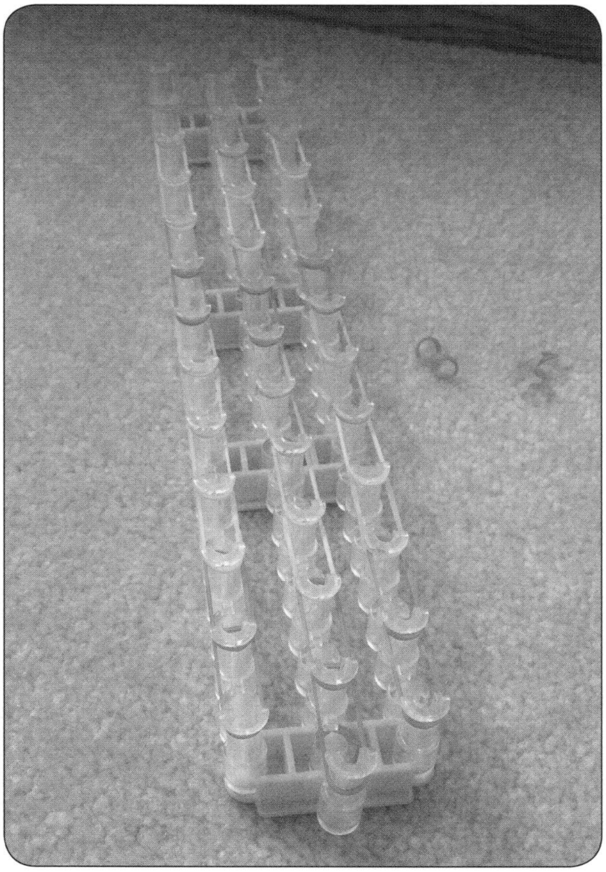

Step 3: Bands Going Across

With more bands, make an upside down triangle going all the way up the loom, skipping the first three pegs closest to you.

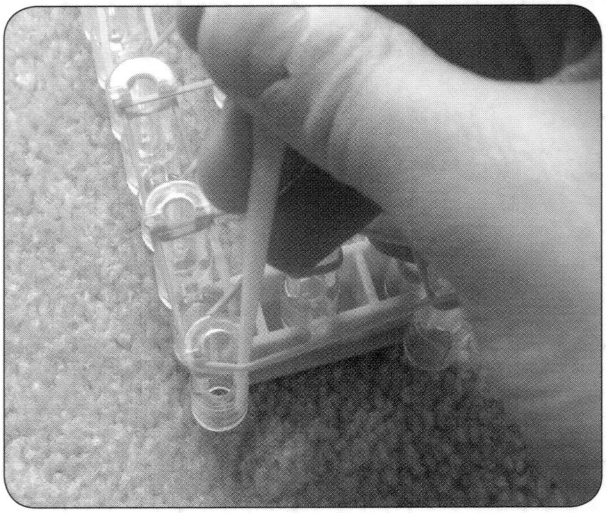

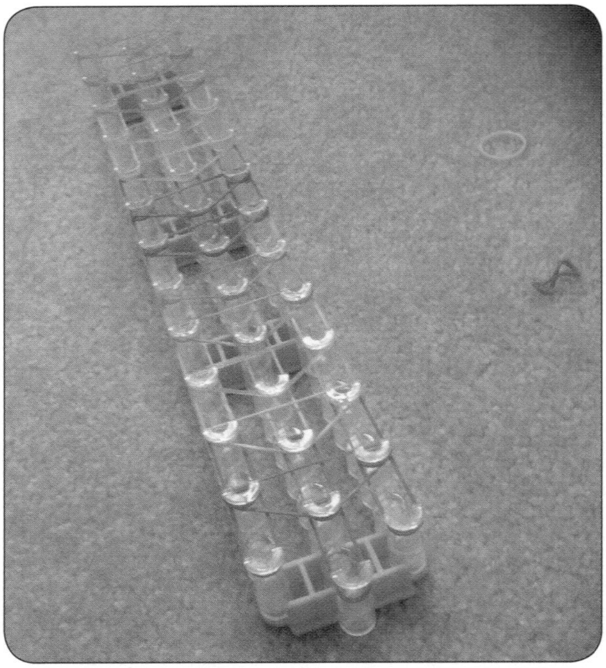

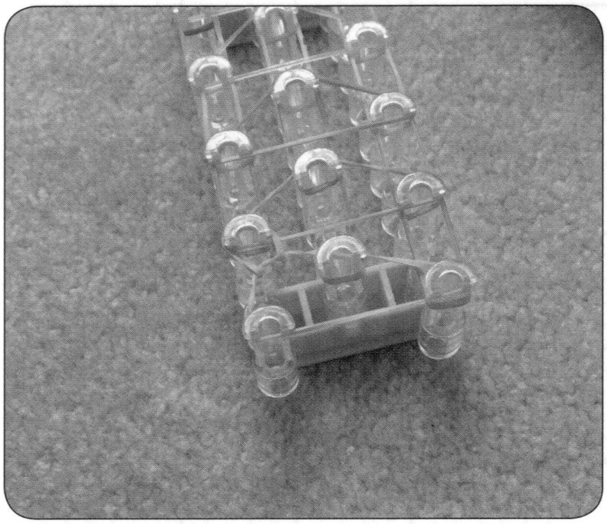

Step 4: Hooking

Now, spin your loom around. Grab your hook and start hooking the left row. Reach all the way down, grab the band, and place it around the next peg. Do that the entire way up. Do that same step for the middle and right rows.

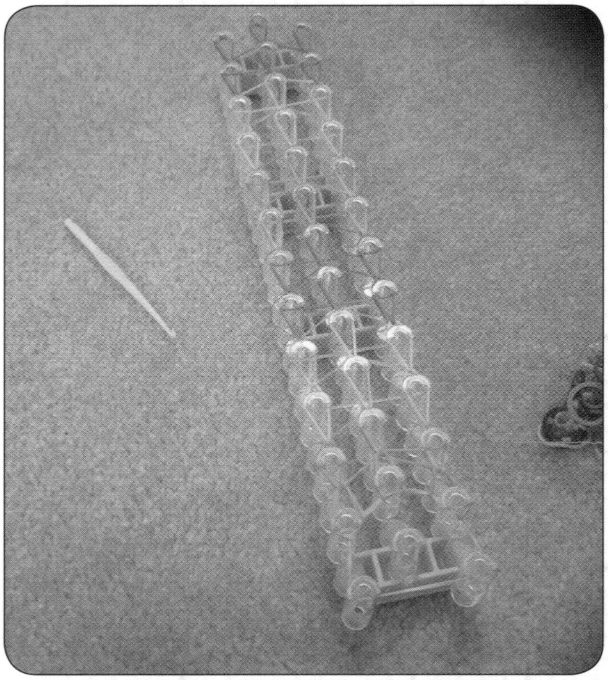

Step 5: Hooking the Three

At the top, there are three hooked bands not attached. Grab the left band and place it onto the middle peg, then do the same with the right. Be *very* careful—do not let go of your bracelet as it could fall apart.

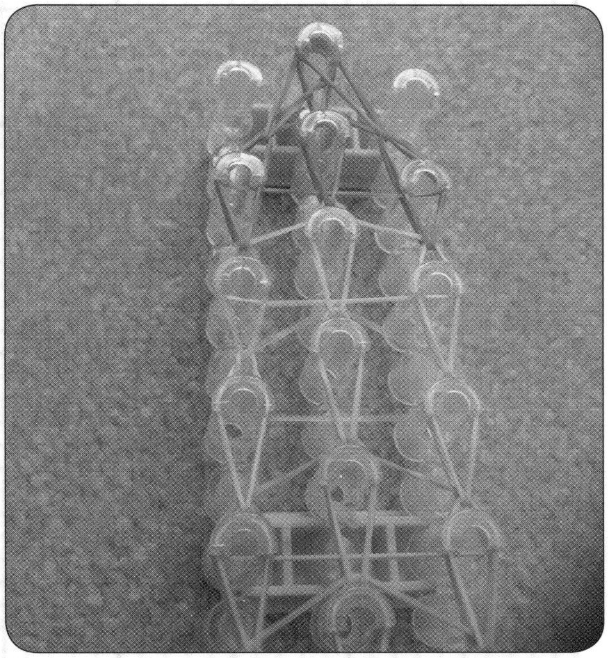

Step 6: Taking It Off

Take another same color band, place it on your hook, and pull it through all the bands at the top. Take half of the band and place it on the hook. Put your bands on the thicker part of the hook and *carefully* pull off your bracelet. Be gentle so you don't snap any bands.

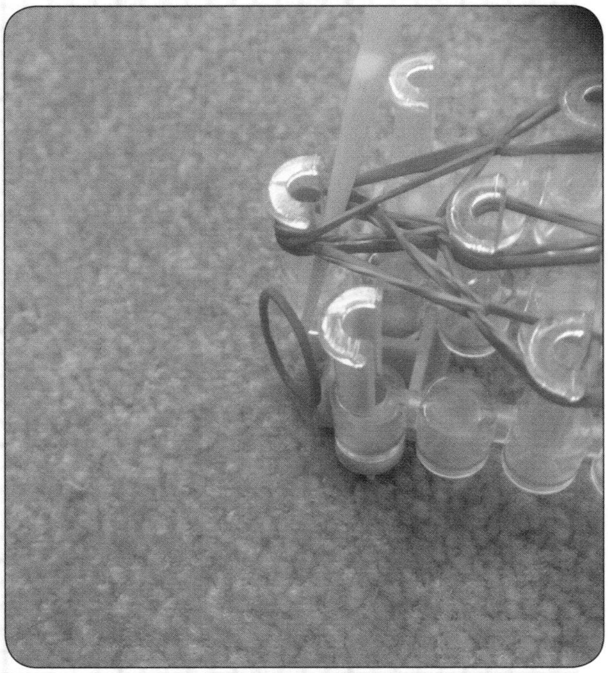

Step 7: Extension

It's probably not long enough for your wrist, so you are going to take some more bands and loop them through the bands on your hook. Do that until it is long enough for your wrist. Then take a C- or S-clip and attach it to both ends.

Step 8: Finished!

You are now finished with your bracelet! Enjoy!

Starburst Bracelet

By SumSum_101

(http://www.instructables.com/id/How-To-Make-A-Rainbow-Loom-Starburst-Bracelet/)

Step 1: Gather Your Supplies

For this starburst, I'm using yellow as the starburst, navy blue as the border, and clear for the alternations, like the cap bands and whatnot. Next, you will need your loom and your hook. Then, you need a place to sit and your imagination.

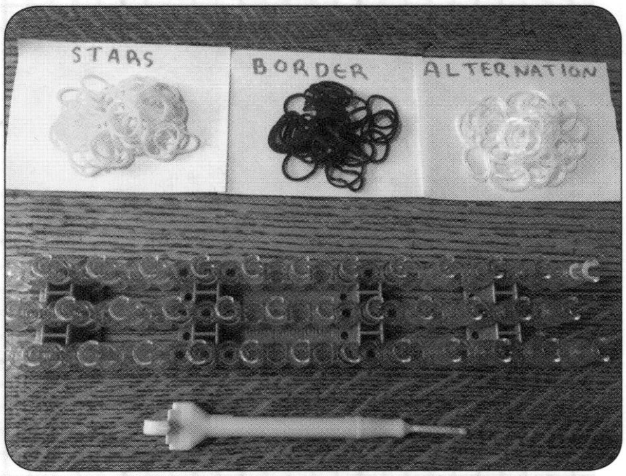

Step 2: Placing the Bands

Take your loom and make sure the arrows are pointing away from you. Next, take your navy blue band and place it from the center peg to the second peg on the left.

Step 3: Keep Going

Then, take another navy blue band and stretch it from the second left peg to the peg in front of this. Continue until you are at the end of the loom.

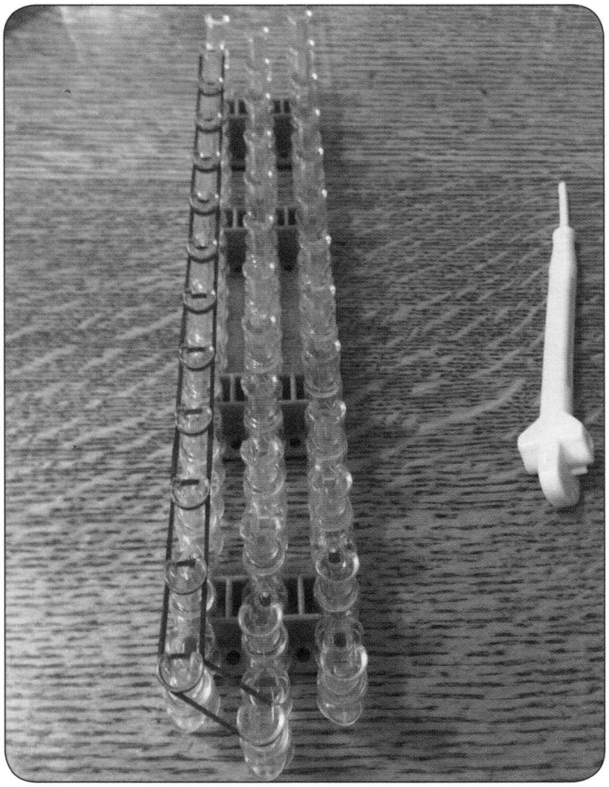

Step 4: Continue

Now, take another navy blue band and place it from the left peg to the center top peg of the loom. Do the same thing to the other side of the loom.

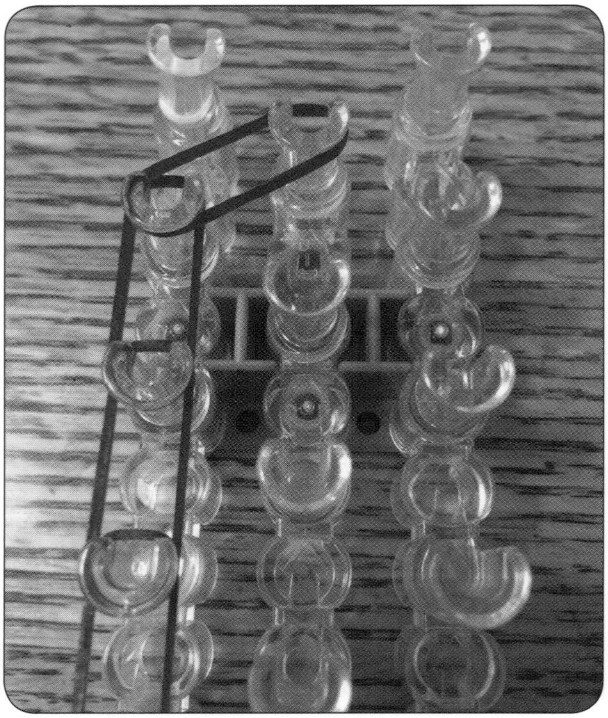

Step 5: Start Yellow

Now that you have finished with the border, take a yellow band and stretch it from the second center peg of the loom to the second peg on the right. Do this to the end of the loom.

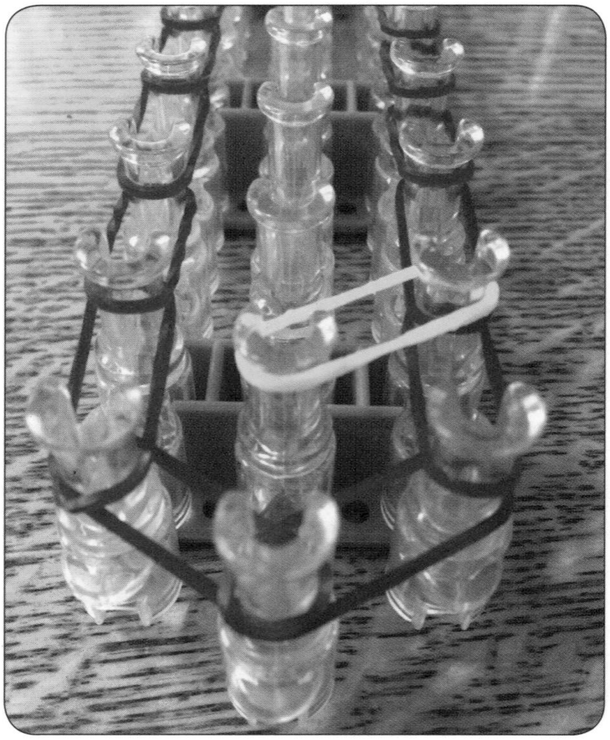

Step 6: More Yellow

Then, take another yellow band and place it on the center peg to the first right peg of the loom. Continue clockwise until done.

Step 7: Clear Bands

When you are done with that, take a clear band and make a double cap band with it. To do this, take your band and make a figure eight with it. Place it over the top of the loom. Do this to every center peg of every star until you are at the bottom.

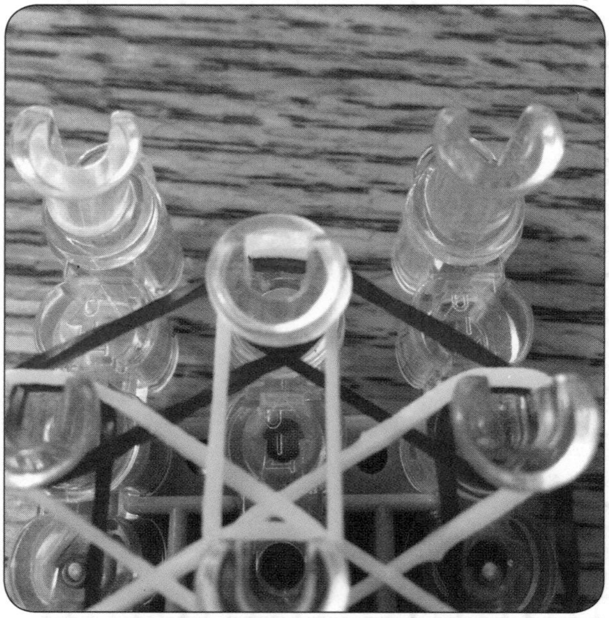

Step 8: Ready to Loop

Now that you are done with the cap bands, you are ready to loop the bands.

Step 9: Looping the Bands

First, turn your loom around so that the arrows are pointing toward you. Then, take your hook and loop the first center peg to the middle. Continue counterclockwise until at the end of the loom.

Step 10: Border Bands

When you are done looping the bands, you are ready to loop the border bands.

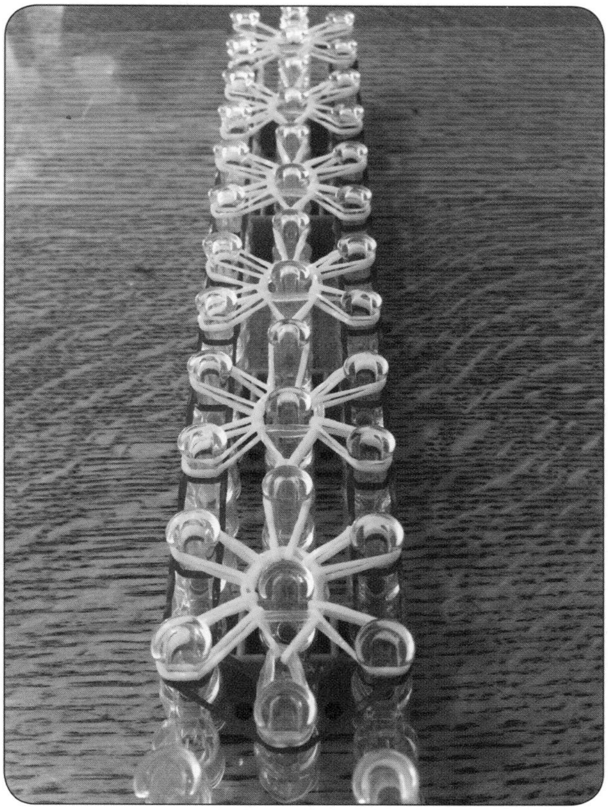

Step 11: Loop Navy Blue

Now, take your hook again and loop the navy blue band on the bottom. Do this to every band on the loom.

Step 12: A Visual

Your loom should look like this:

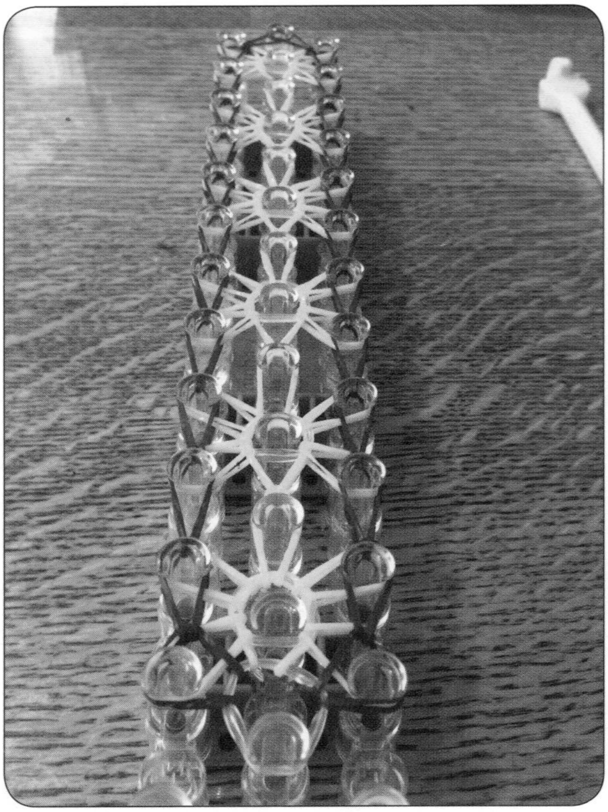

Step 13: Ready to Pull It Off

Now you are ready to pull it off! First, take a navy blue band and pull your hook through the top bands like you would with a triple single.

Step 14: Pull It Off!

Now just pull it off!

Step 15: Making an Extension

Now, to make an extension, you want to put navy blue bands all the way to the top of the loom in a straight line.

Step 16: Place Bracelet

Then, put your bracelet with the open end on the loom over the first band.

Step 17: Loop

Loop them like you would with a single, and then pull it off.

Step 18: C-Clip

Pull it off, then attach a C-clip to it and you're done! Congratulations! You have made your first starburst!

Diamond-Pattern Bracelet

By Jenny Nguyen (nngân)
(http://www.instructables.com/id/Rainbow-Loom-Diamond-Pattern-Bracelet/)

Step 1: What You Need

- A loom
- A hook
- Rainbow bands
- Clip

The perfect storage solution to store and protect your craft projects.

Step 2: Starting!

Make sure (if you're using the Rainbow Loom) your arrow is pointing AWAY from you! Place your first rainbow band from the bottom peg in the middle row to the bottom peg in the left row. Do the same to the right!

Step 3: More Bands

Now place another rubber band from your first rubber band to the middle row, going diagonally.

Step 4: Repeat

Now repeat steps 2 and 3 until you reach the top.

Step 5: Take a Band Off

Now take one of the top rubber bands off (either one works; it doesn't matter).

Step 6: Now to Start Looping

Now flip your loom over so that your arrow is pointing AT you.

Step 7: Looping

Now reach into your last rubber band and pull the top rubber band, looping it over to the peg to the left, then do the same to the right.

Step 8: More Looping

Now reach into the rubber band you looped first. Pull the rubber band and loop it on the middle peg diagonally. Do the same to the other side.

Step 9: Keep Looping

Do the same until you reach the top of the loom!

Step 10: Use the Hook

Now reach into the top rubber band and place a rubber band on the hook. Then pull the rubber band so that the rubber band is half in the rubber band it's in and half out.

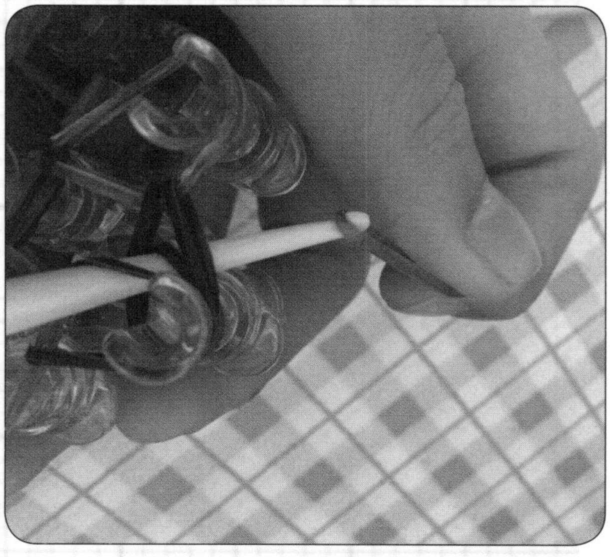

Step 11: Pull Off

Now pull the rubber bands off and place a hook on one end of the rubber bands. Then connect the clip to the other end.

Step 12: Done!

Now you're done!

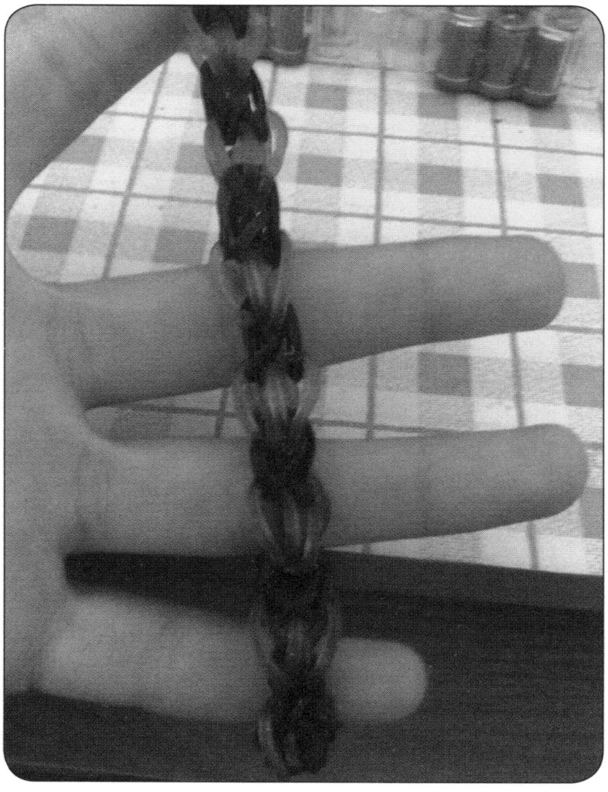

Valentine's Day Inverted Fishtail

By Elizabeth Jane Nutter (creativity123)

http://www.instructables.com/id/DIY-V-Day-Inverted-Fishtail-Bracelet/

This one is very fun and simple to do, so let's begin.

Step 1: What You Need

- Rainbow Loom rubber bands (pink, red, and purple)
- Rainbow Loom kit (I am using Fun Loom) Hook and C-clip should be bulleted on separate lines

Step 2: Starting Your Bracelet

To start your bracelet, place your first band (I am using pink) like a figure eight on two pegs. Then just simply place two rubber bands over it. (The order of rubber band colors is pink, purple, and then red.) Then, to loop the bands, pull back the purple band with your hook and grab the pink rubber band and pull it up and off that peg. Then do the same thing on the other side of the pink band. Check the pictures for guidance.

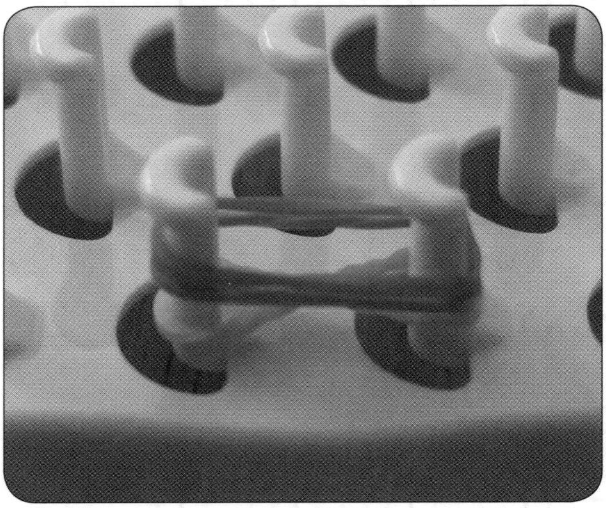

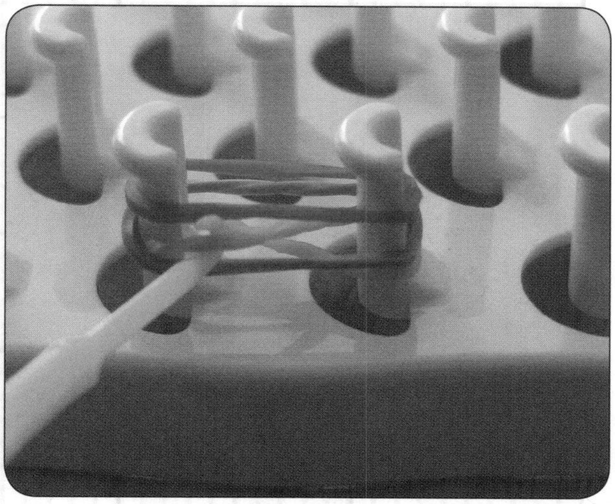

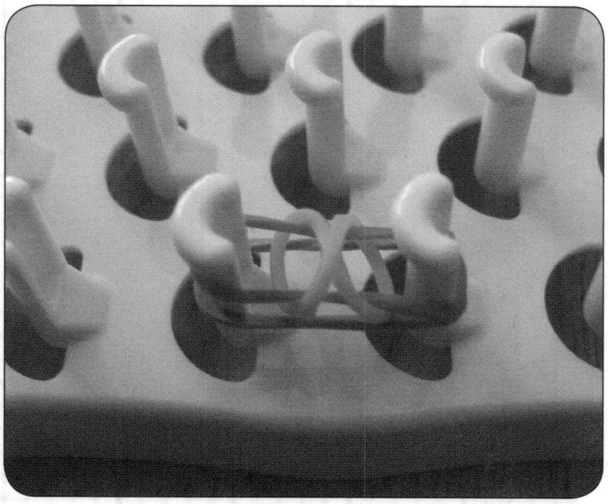

Step 3: Looping More Rubber Bands

Once you have looped the pink band off in step 2, it's time to place a pink rubber band on top. Go in and pull back the red band, then grab the purple band and loop it off like in step 2. Here's how to loop it off again: Pull back the red and grab the purple band with your hook. Then pull it up and around off the peg. Then just repeat on the other side of your purple band. Then repeat this process, alternating colors, until your bracelet is the length you want.

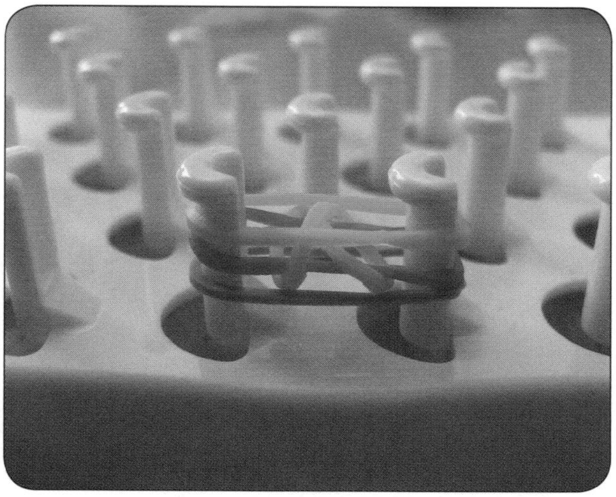

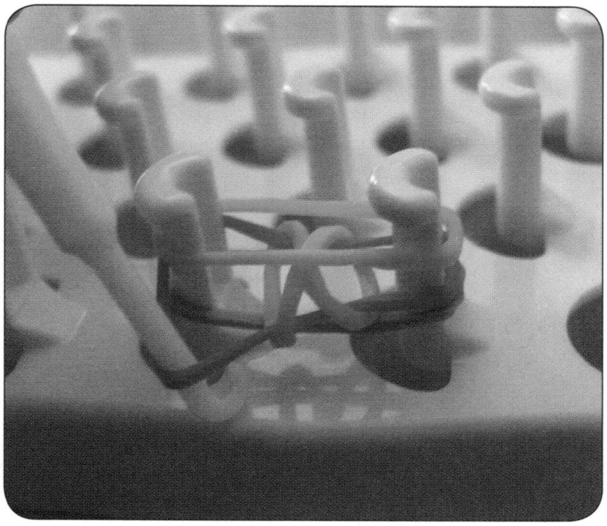

Step 4: Finishing

Once you've made the bracelet long enough for your wrist, it's time to clip it all together. Take your bracelet off the loom and transfer it to your fingers, just as if your fingers are the pegs. Simply add a C-clip and get the other end to clip both ends together. Ta-da! You're done! Enjoy wearing your new bracelet!

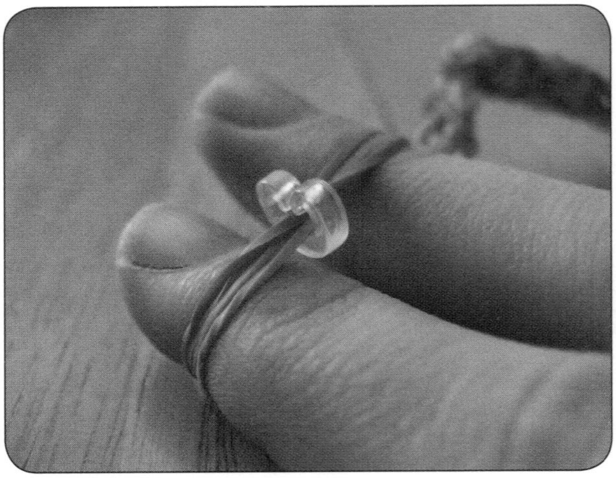

Hexagon Bracelet

By aqua 12

(http://www.instructables.com/id/The-Hexagon-Rainbow-Loom-Bracelet/)

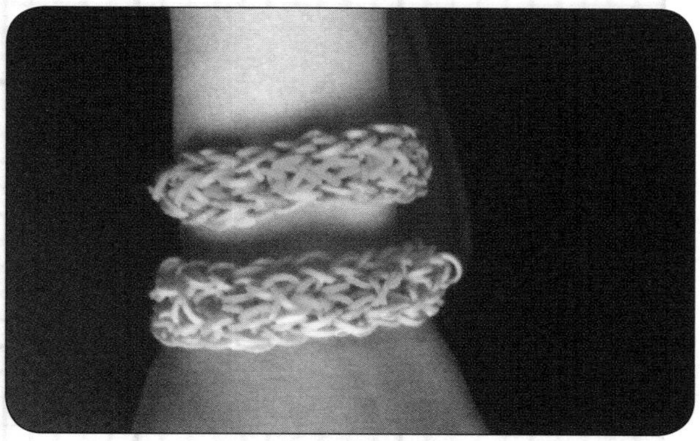

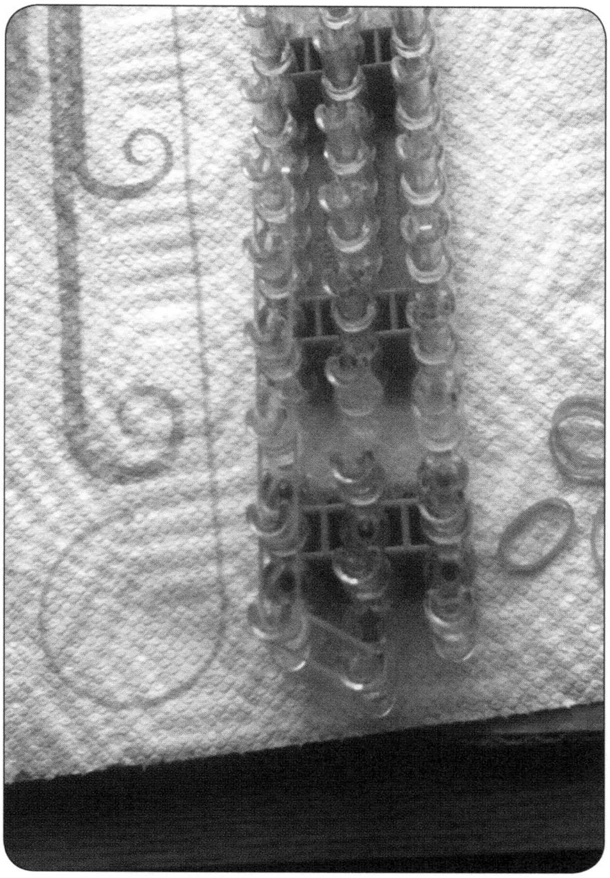

Step 1: What you need

- Rubber bands in colors of your choice
- Loom
- Hook
- C-clip

Step 2: Border

You're going to start from the bottom, where the arrow is facing away from you, and place one band from the end peg over to the left and keep going straight. You should end up one peg away from the end of the loom. Do the same thing on the other side.

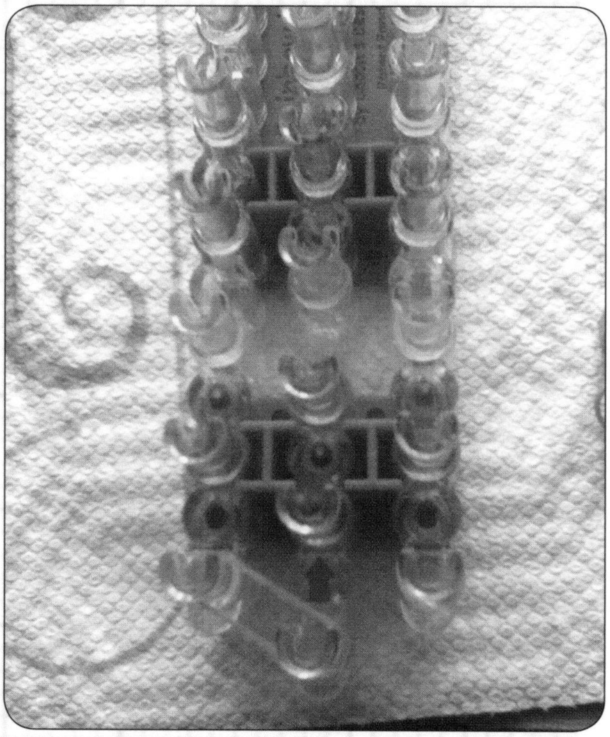

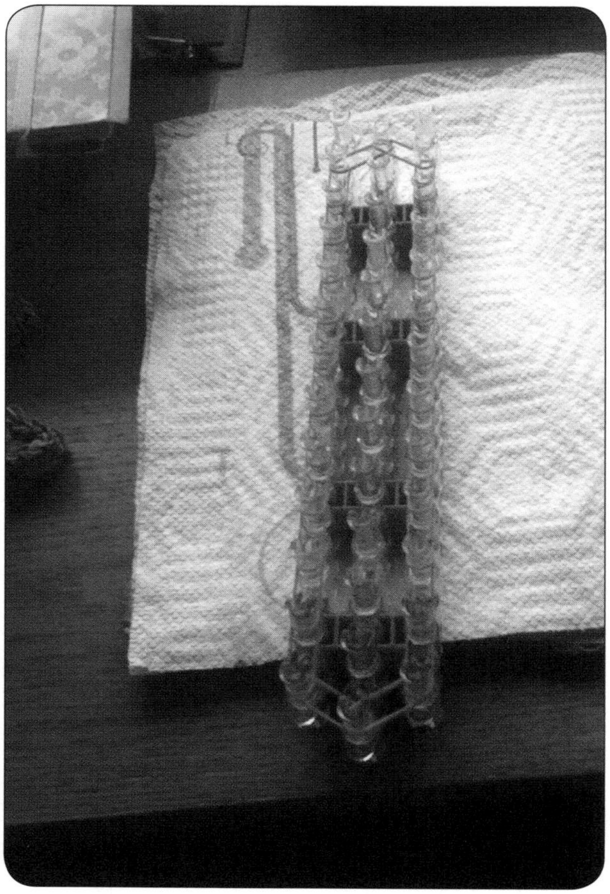

Step 3: Hexagon

Now start from the middle peg on the bottom and put a band straight to the next peg. Then put one band on the second peg in the middle and stretch it to the left peg and same for the right peg. Then put two straight, and then two to the middle from the sides, and then put one from the 4 peg straight. Do the same hexagon pattern all the way through. When you're done with that, put a rubber band on the top peg in the shape of a triangle.

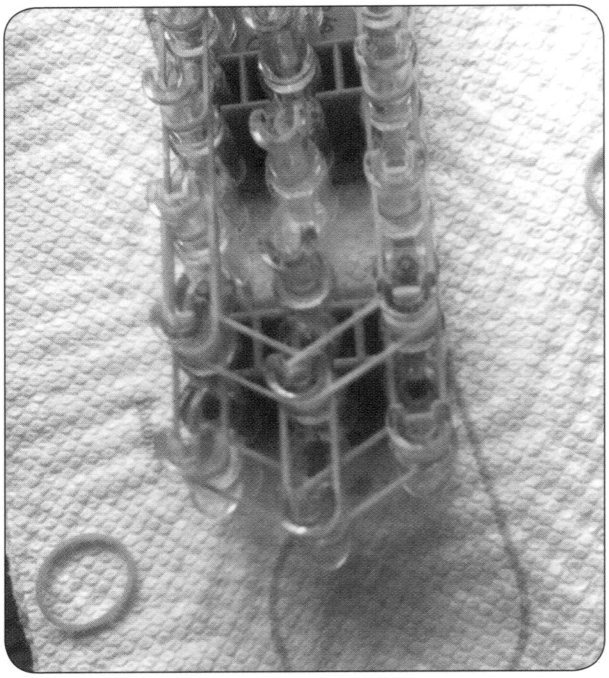

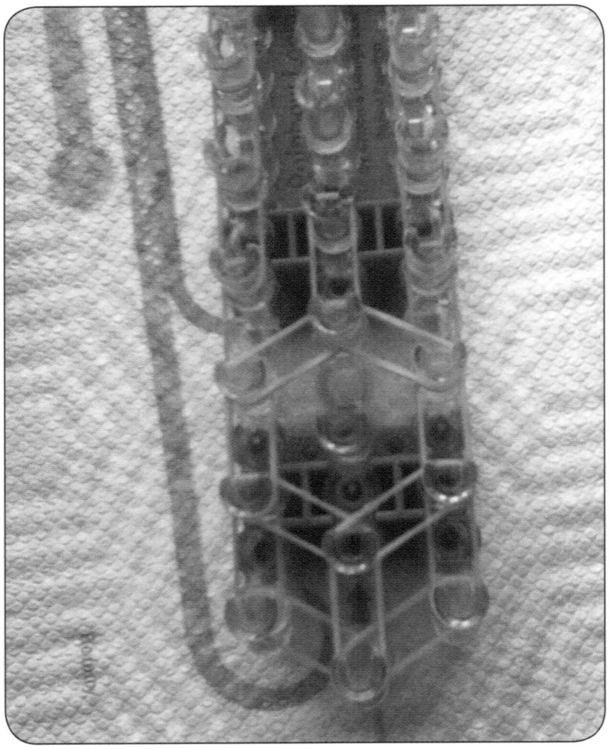

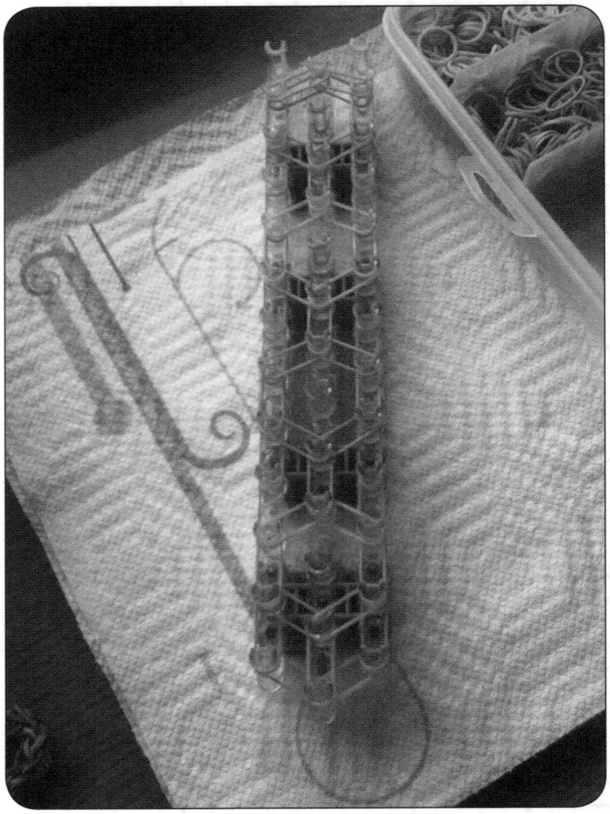

Step 4: Hexagon Stitching

Turn the loom around so the arrow is now facing you, then grab the orange band and stretch it to the right. Then take the other orange band and put it to the left, and put the other two straight. Stretch the last one to the middle like a hexagon, and do this pattern until the end.

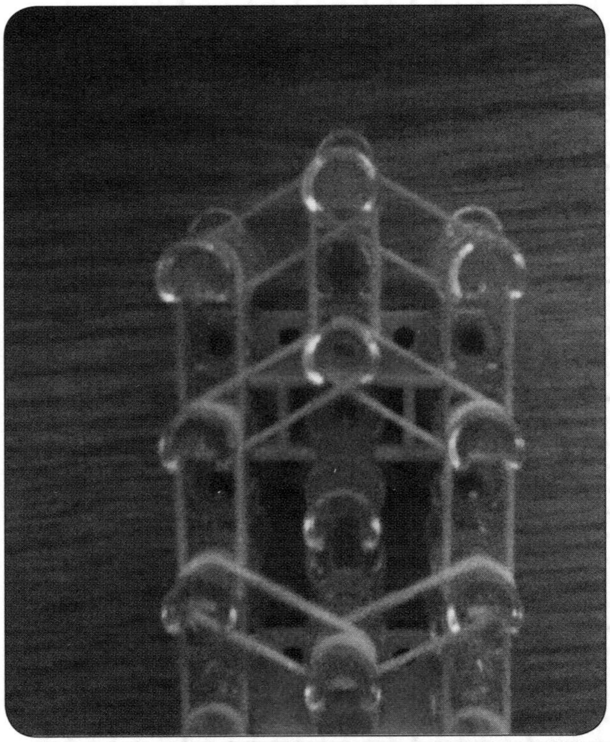

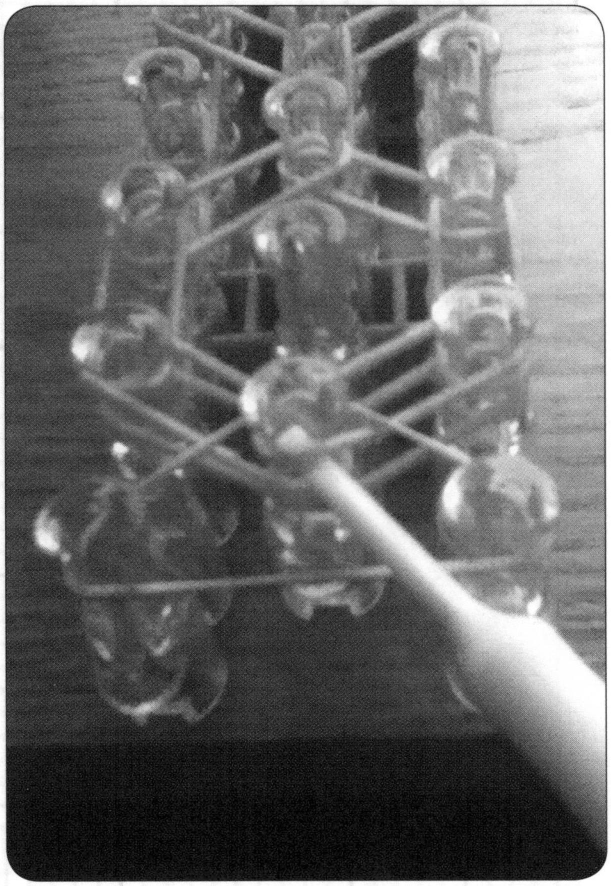

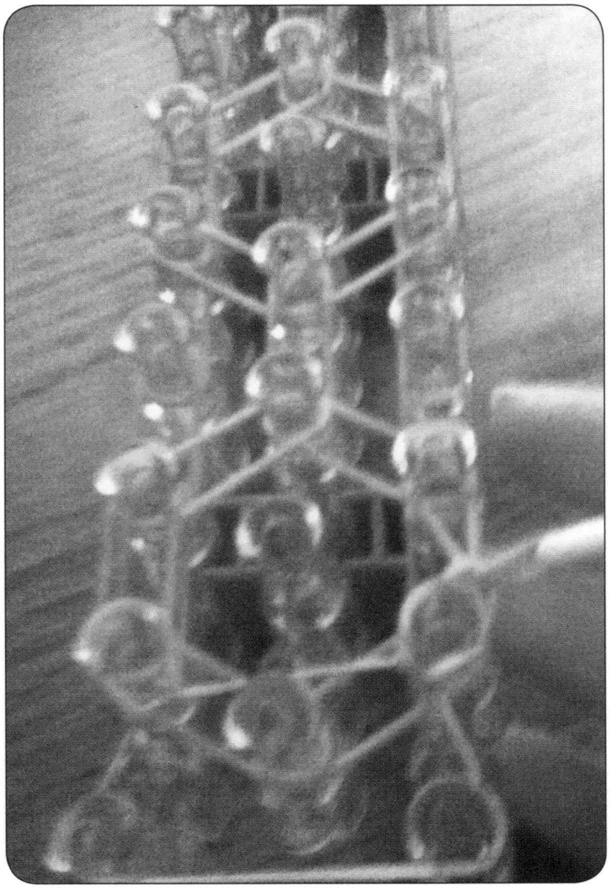

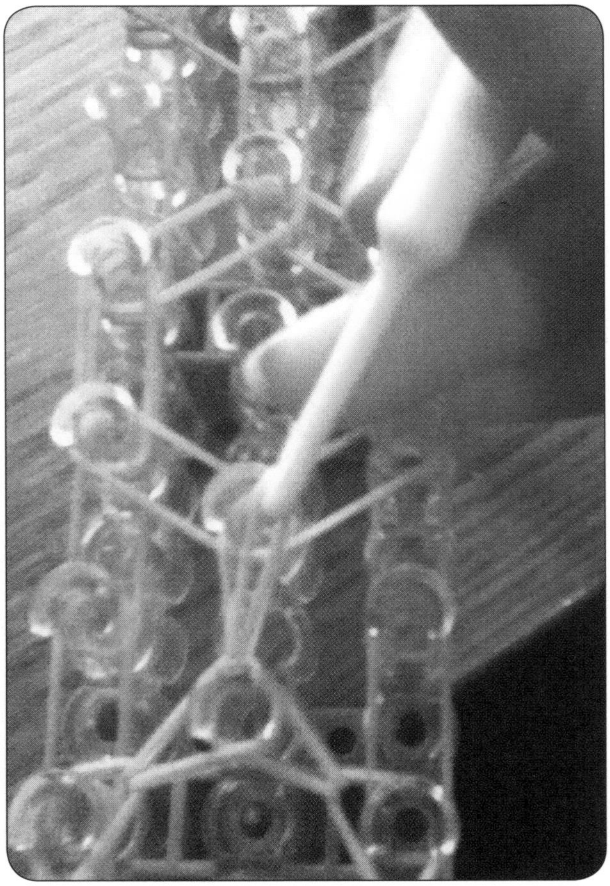

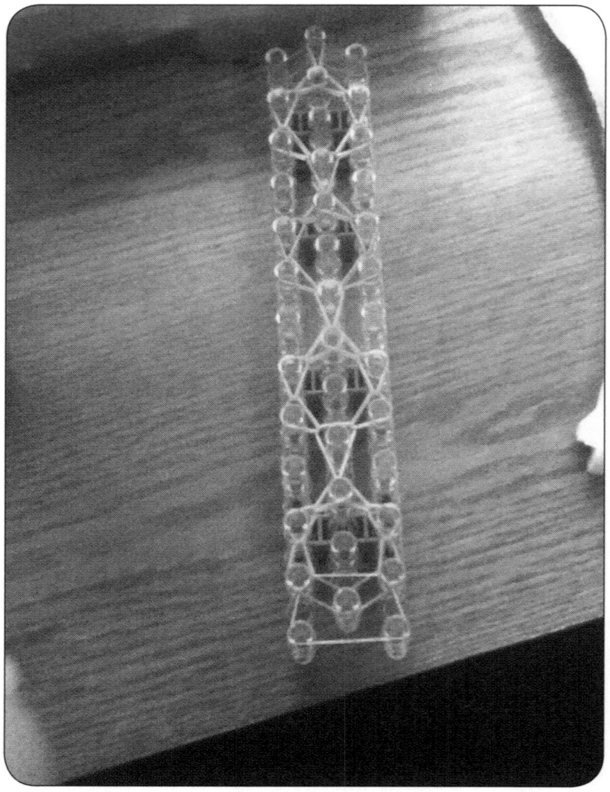

Step 5: Base

While still having the arrow facing you, take the top pink one and put it toward the left. All you are doing here is taking the very bottom one and putting it forward, and then doing the same for the other side.

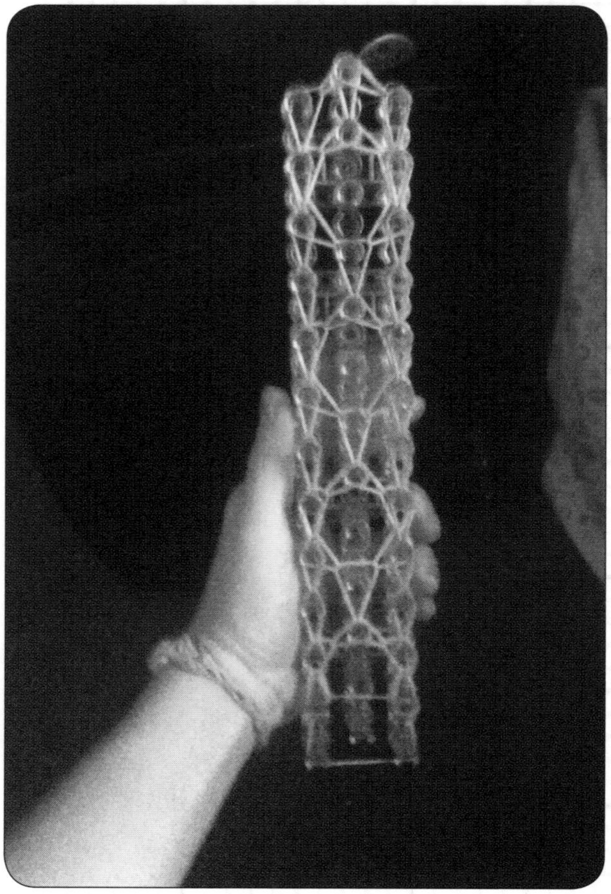

Step 6: Extension

Once you put the hook through all the rubber bands on top, carefully remove your bracelet from the loom. Add any extension in the normal way if needed, and don't forget to add a c-clip! And you're done!

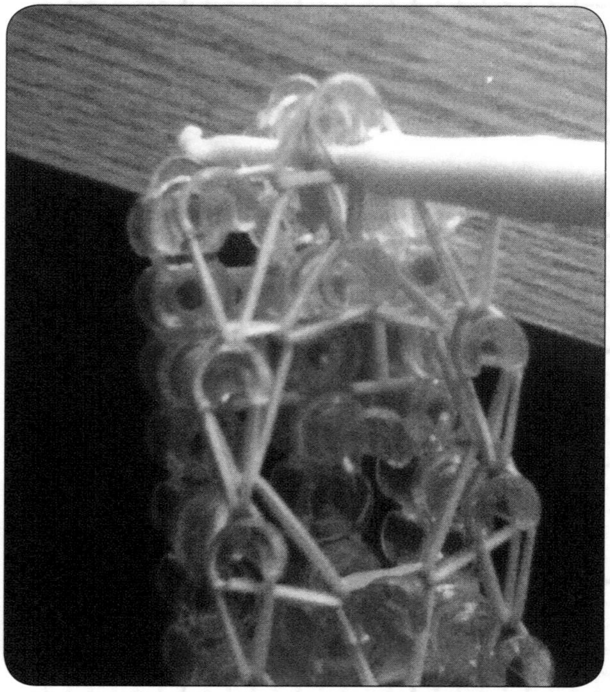

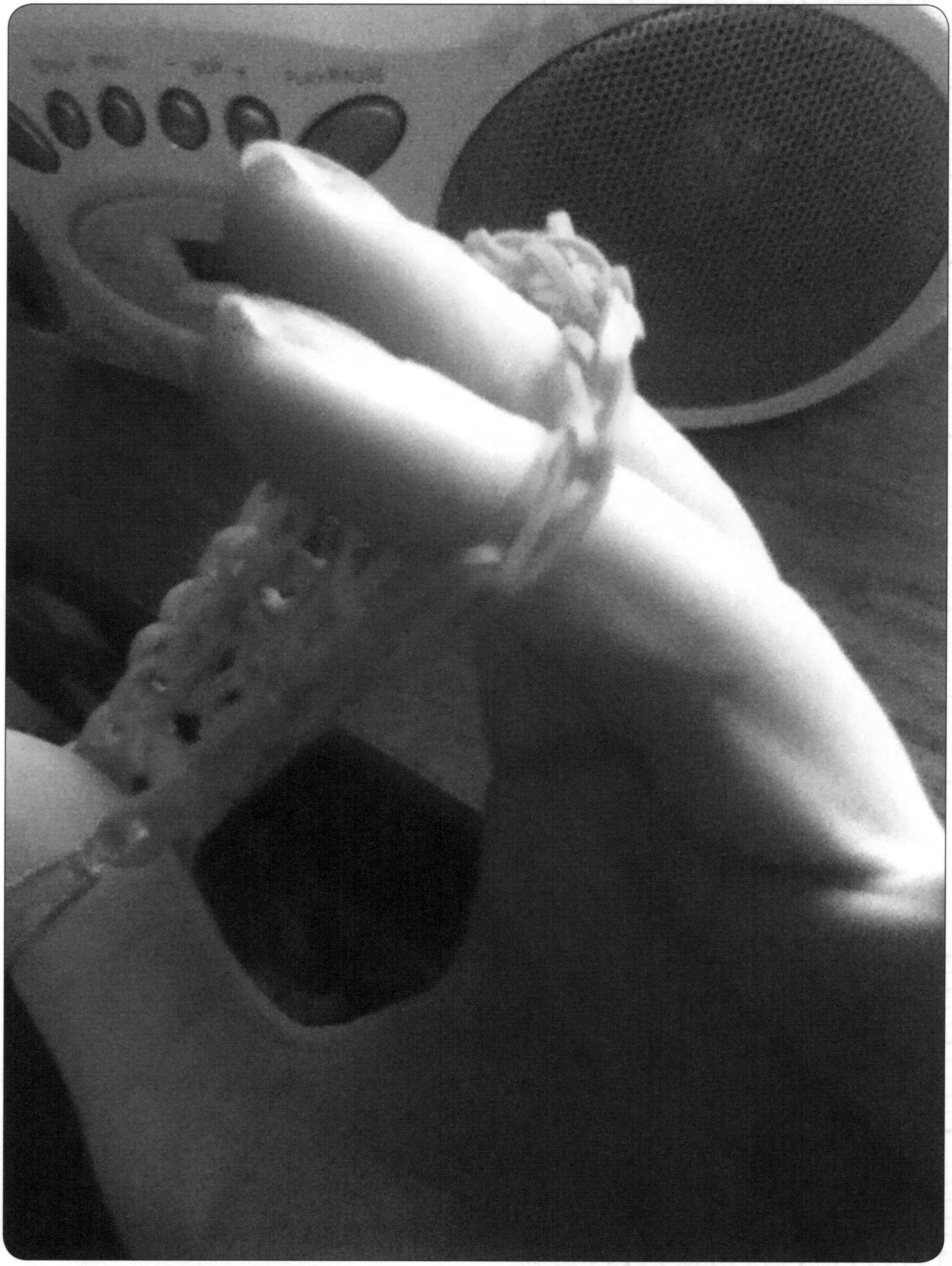

Six-Band Hexafish

By Jessy Ellenberger (jessyratfink)
(http://www.instructables.com/id/hexafish-rainbow-loom-bracelet/)

This is my favorite of all the Rainbow Loom bracelets—the hexafish! It's much chunkier and more complex and looks more like a bangle. I made mine a bit larger than my wrist so I could wear it like a bangle, too.

And the best part? While it's a little time consuming, it's really not that complicated! This hexafish bracelet probably took me a couple hours over a few days, and the end result is perfect.

Note: I really recommend making the original Rainbow Loom fishtail bracelet before tackling the hexafish. The hexafish bracelet is just like the fishtail bracelet times six.

Step 1: What You'll Need

- Rainbow Loom kit or other rubber band loom
- Rubber bands
- C-clips
- Loom hook or a small crochet hook
- Scissors

Step 2: Starting the Bracelet

To start the bracelet, remove one of the pieces of the loom (so you've only got two rows of pegs) and make sure the pegs are squared up. Now, take your first band and loop it like a figure eight from pegs 1 to 2. Then place a band from 2–3, 3–4, 4–5, 5–6, and 6–1 as shown in the photo. These bands can be any color you want, as we'll be cutting them away at the end. I used black so I wouldn't waste any of the colors I use more often.

Step 3: Making the Foundation

Stretch two bands all the way around the six pegs. Use your hook and pull the figure eight bands over the top bands, going from the outside in. It should look like photo #4. I like to go from left to right on each row of pegs, but it's not really important which order you do it in.

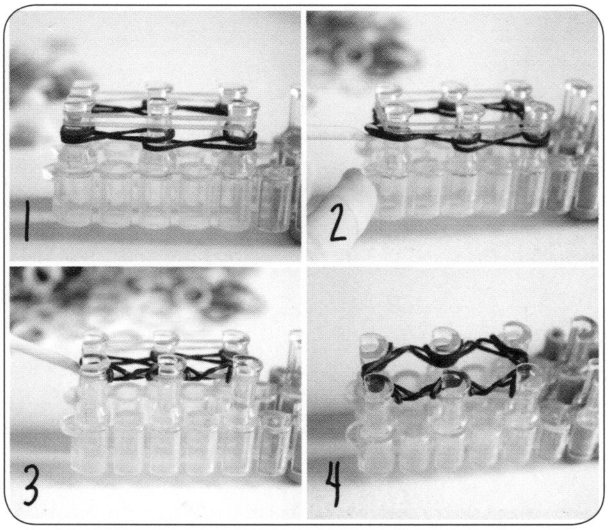

Step 4: Add Additional Bands

At this point, your foundation is done! Now you can really get to work. You will want three bands on the loom at all times while building the bracelet: one band stretched across all six pegs and two bands below on each peg. For each layer, add a new band around all six pegs and then take the very bottom band and stretch it up and over the two top bands on each peg. Add another band around all six pegs and repeat the process.

Step 5: It's Growing!

This hexafish bracelet will come out of the bottom of the loom, so you'll get to see it grow while you work. Keep adding additional bands until it reaches the length you want. (I'll show you how to finish the loom end on the next two steps!) The bracelet will be flat and strange looking as it comes out of the loom, but pulling the end will tighten it up and get it into the proper shape.

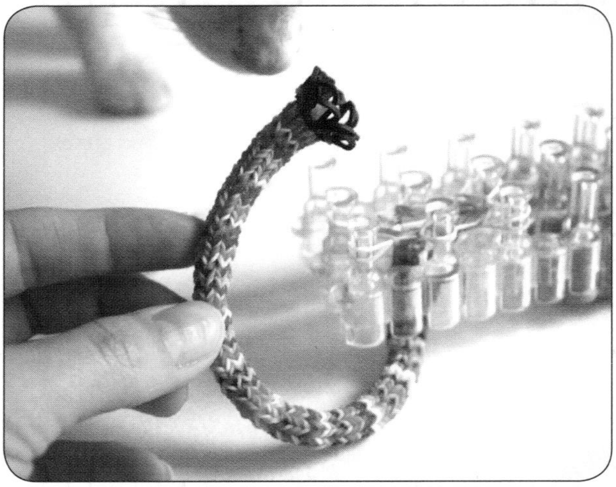

Step 6: Finish the Loom End, Part 1

Once you've reached the length you want, loop over all the extra bands on the pegs until you're left with one each. Now you'll want to loop the bands over so they're only on three pegs as the photos show. I take the loop on peg 3 and move it to peg 2, peg 1 to peg 6, and peg 5 to peg 4 (going by the way the pegs are labeled on step 2).

Step 7: Finish the Loom End, Part 2

Once you've got the original loops on three pegs, put another band around all three of those so it forms a triangle. Pass the two bottom bands on each peg over the top. Now take the three loops left on the pegs and consolidate them onto the middle peg closest to you. Clip these three bands together and you can pull it off the loom. Now one end is done! Pull the bracelet again at this point to make sure it's all the right shape. As you can see in the second photo, it looks really silly before you stretch it.

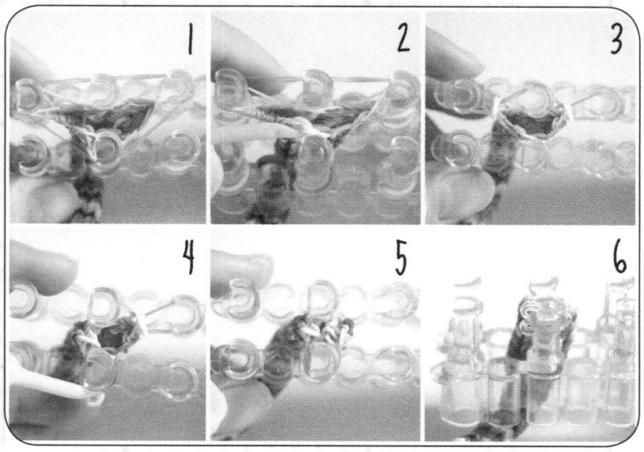

Step 8: Put the Bracelet Back on the Loom

The is the absolute trickiest part of the hexafish bracelet, but it's important for a nice finish. Leaving it like this makes for a bulky mess that's hard to fit in a C-clip. At the end of the bracelet, you'll see lots of large loops held in place by six sets of two bands. You're going to transfer six sets of bands back onto the loom. Make sure to get both bands. The last set is the hardest to get, but keep digging with the hook and you'll get under it. Once all six loops are back on the loom and you double check to make sure you've got two bands on each peg, you can cut away the excess looped bands on the end. This will leave you with two bands on each peg, so loop over the bottom one on each so you end up with one band on each of the six pegs. Now we'll finish like we did the other end!

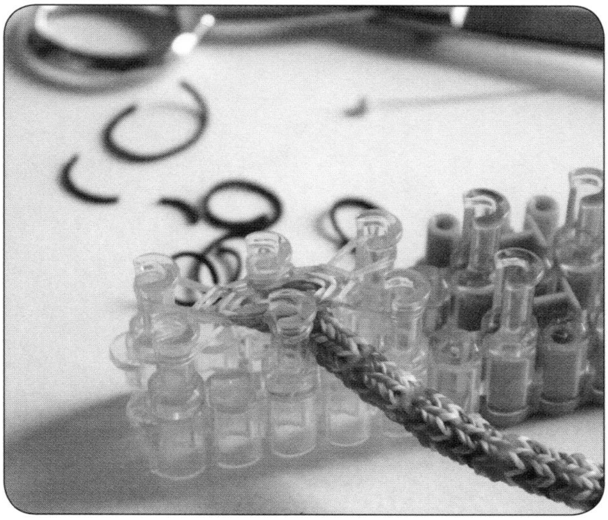

Step 9: Finishing the Other End

Now we'll finish the other end of the bracelet just like we did in step 7. Condense the bands to three pegs, add a band around them, and bring over the bottom bands. Put all the bands on one peg and attach to the other end of the bracelet with the C-clip. Remove from the loom and BAM! You just created the most wonderful Rainbow Loom hexafish bracelet ever.

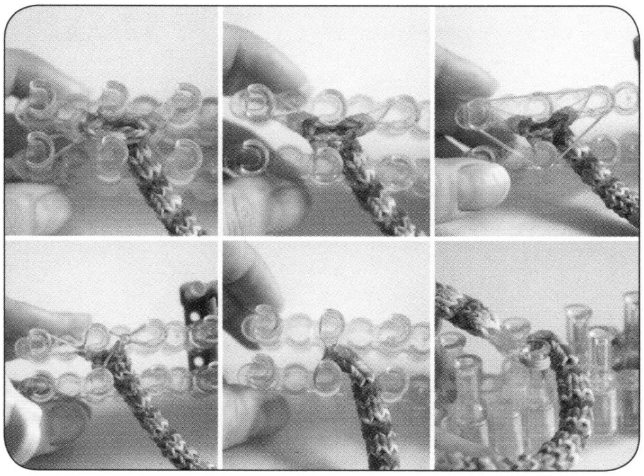

Step 10: More Photos

I am so in awe of this thing that I have to share more photos.

Single Rhombus

By socksmonkeysduckstape
(http://www.instructables.com/id/Rainbow-Loom-Single-Rhombus/)

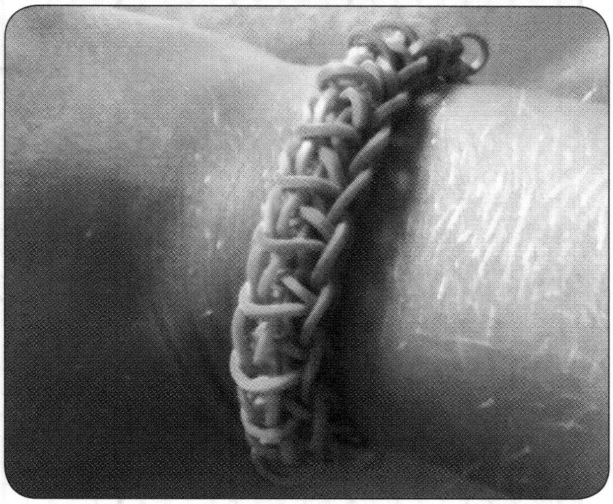

Step 1: Supplies

- Rainbow Loom
- Hook
- Rubber bands
- C-hook

Step 2: The Base

Place one band in the middle going up, then another next to it going diagonal, then up, then diagonal. Repeat this process until those two lines are done to the top

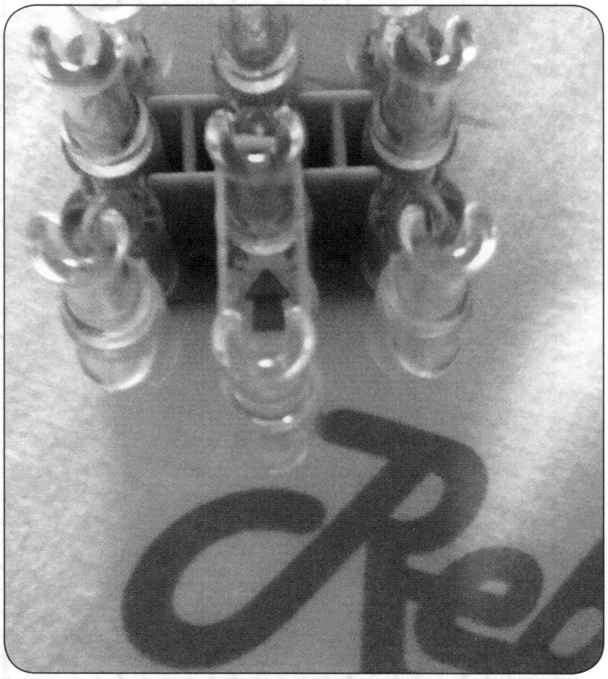

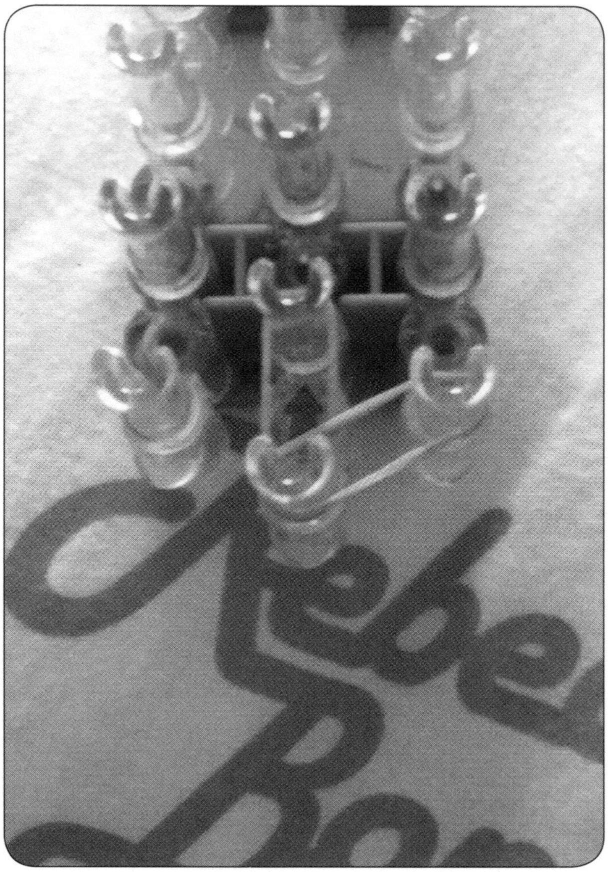

Step 3: Hook and Repeat!

Flip the loom around and start where it's blue and purple. Go through the pegs and hook the purple, then go up and put on forward peg. Repeat on the opposite peg for the pink. Do the same for blue. Repeat until it's done.

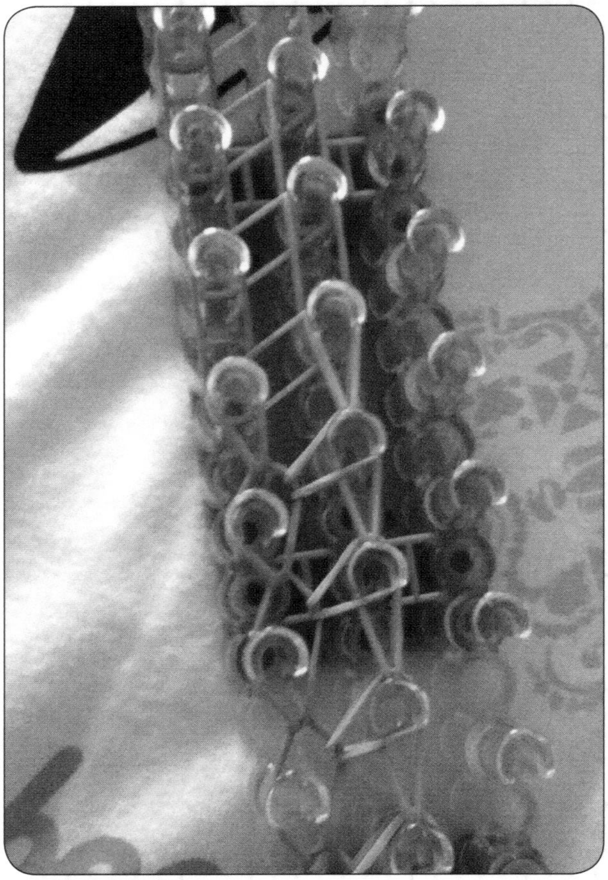

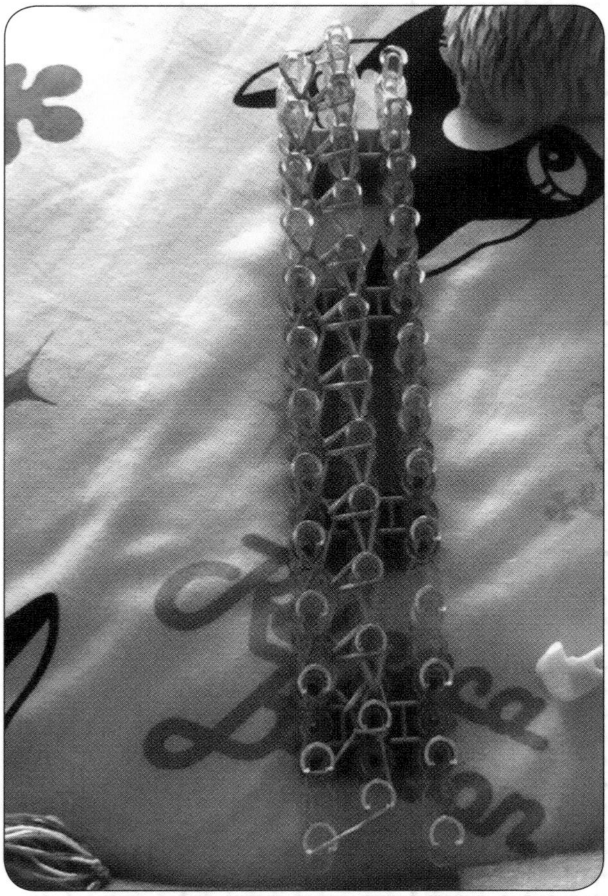

Step 4: C-Clip and Pull

Go to where the arrow is and put a C-clip on those two bands. Pull from that side off.

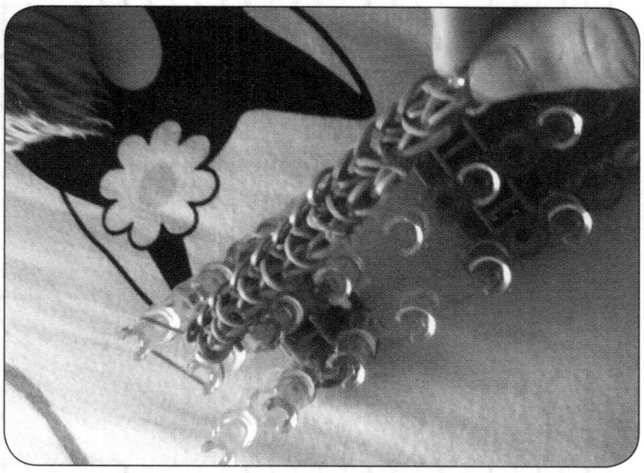

Step 5: Hook

Put your hook through the last two pinks and blues where the C-clip was placed. Pull through a blue band and reattach it to hook.

Step 6: Make It Longer!

Add blue bands onto the loom normally. Only go about halfway or a little more. Add the bracelet to the last peg of the blues. Hook them. Add a C-clip onto the last blue you hooked. Pull.

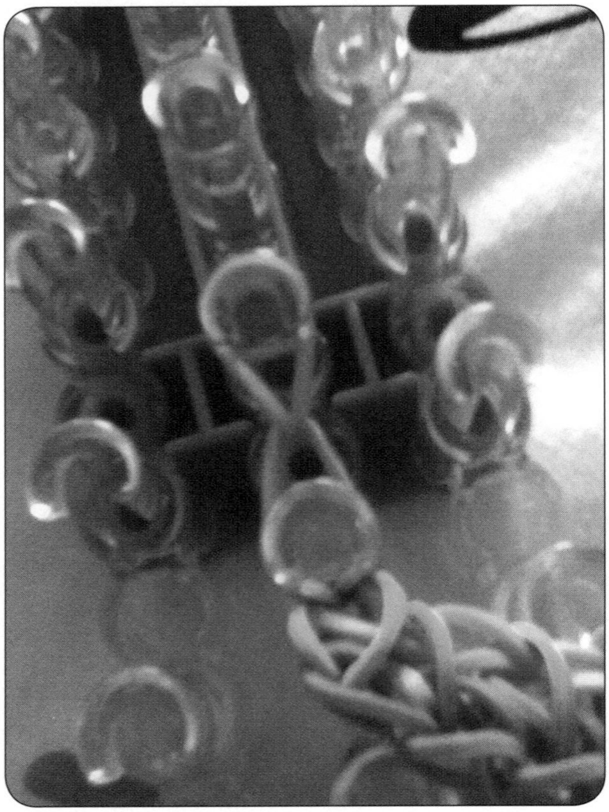

Step 7: Attach And Done!

Attach the C-clip onto the other side of the bracelet. You are done!

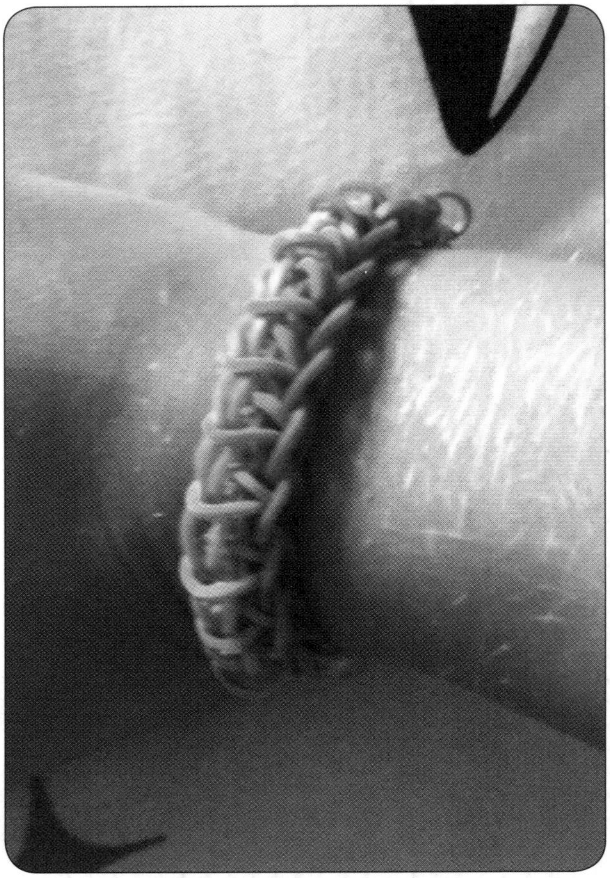

Triple-Braid Bracelet

By vanessanmajer
(http://www.instructables.com/id/Triple-Braid-Rainbowloom/)

Step 1: Materials

- 1 or 2 looms (depends on how long you want it)
- 3 piles of different colored rubber bands
- Hook C- or S-clip

Step 2: Adding the Bands

Use two bands each time! Red will be my outside color, and black and blue will be my inside colors. Continue this pattern till you reach the end of your loom(s).

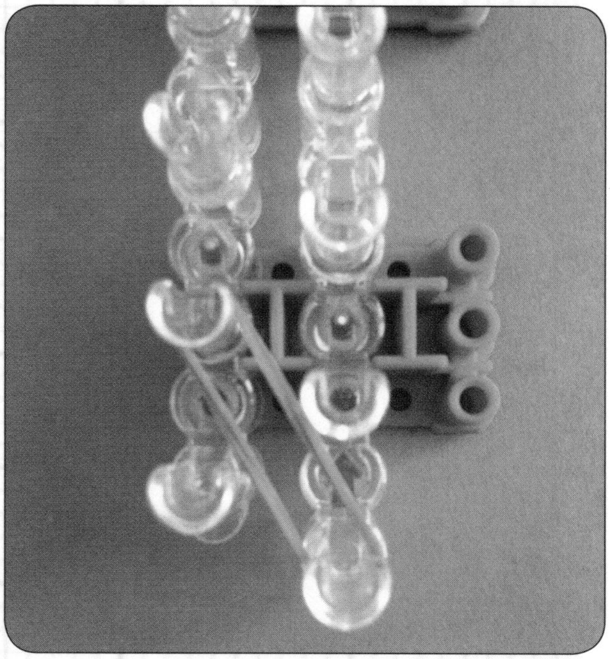

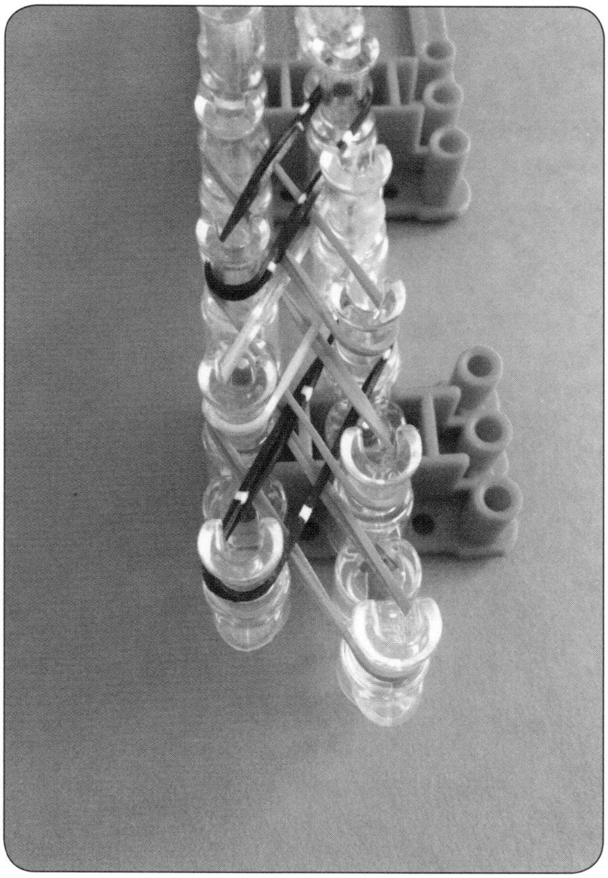

Step 3: When You're Done

It should look like the photo. Then flip the loom around.

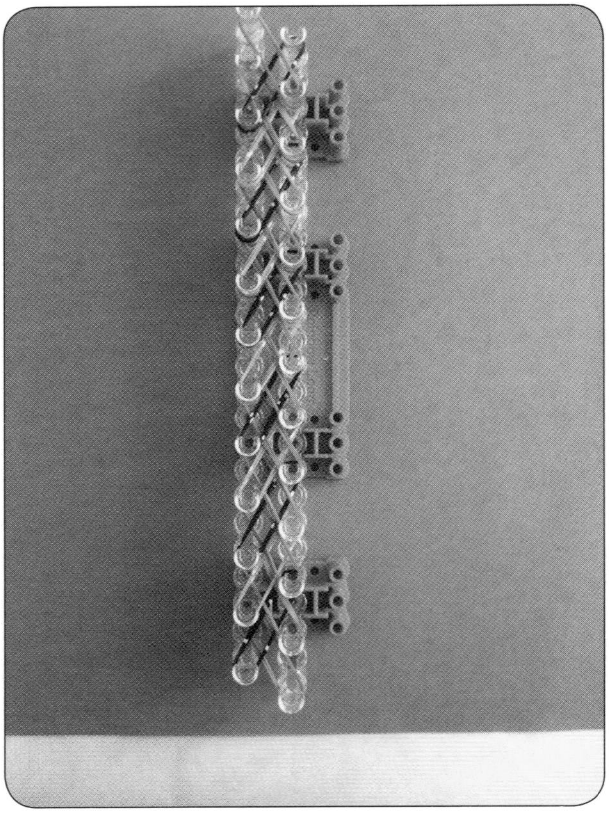

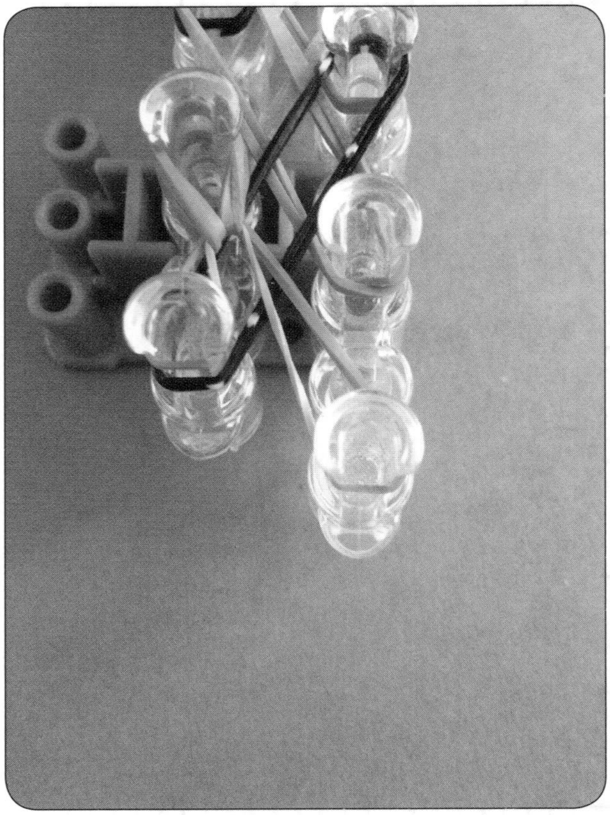

Step 4: Hooking

Take your outside color and hold it like shown in the picture. Hook the rubber bands back to where they have come from. Continue this pattern.

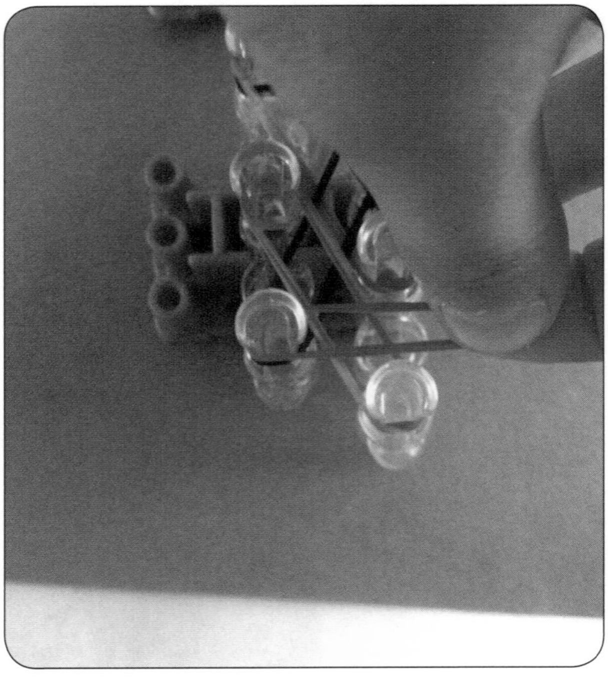

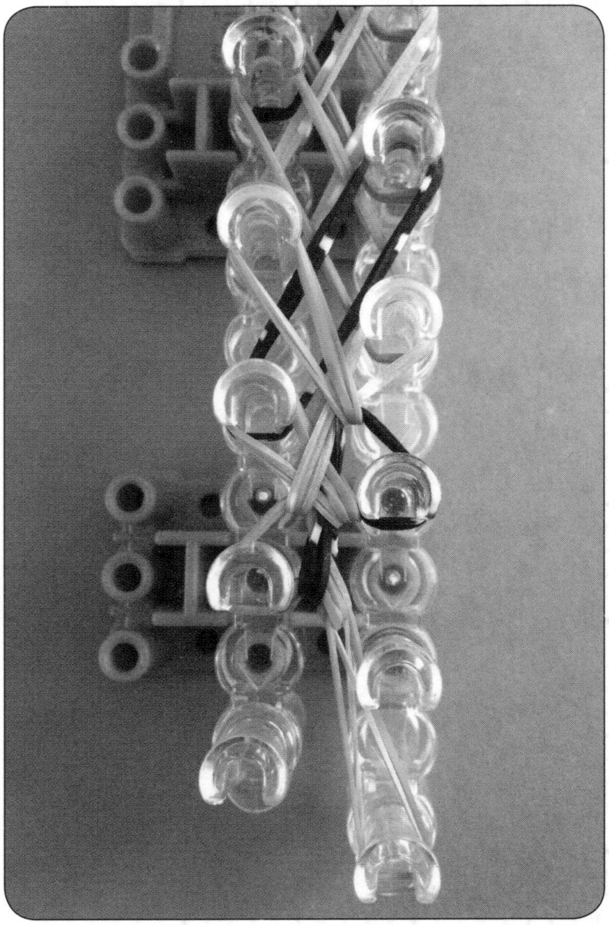

Step 5: Hooking the End

Take the rubber bands off the top peg, then add it to the one below it. Next, take the rubber bands off the peg below the one we just added the bands to and put those on it too. Put your hook inside all the rubber bands and add an extension piece to it.

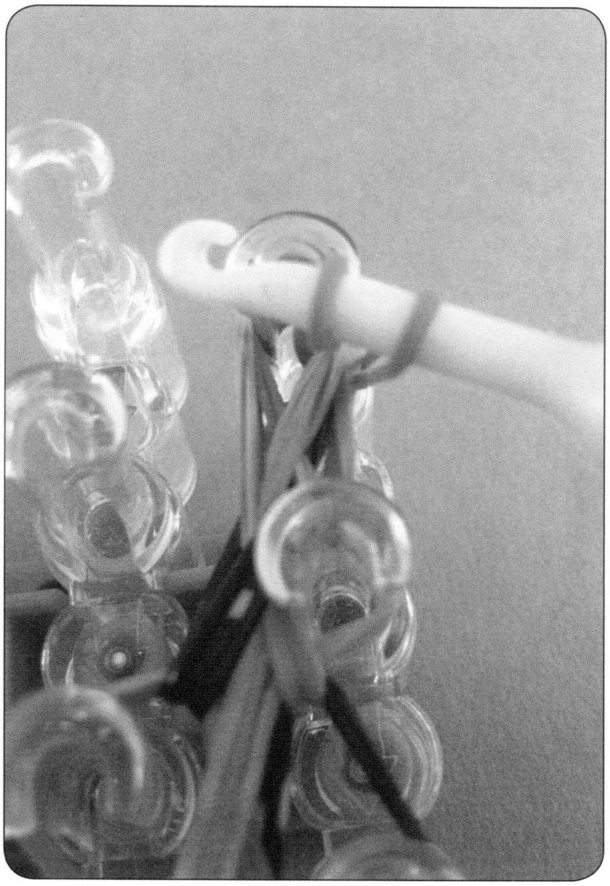

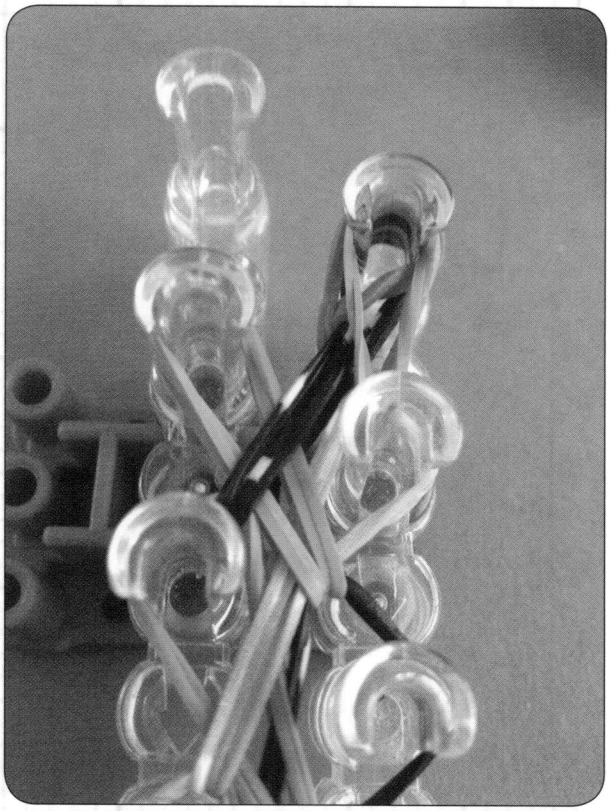

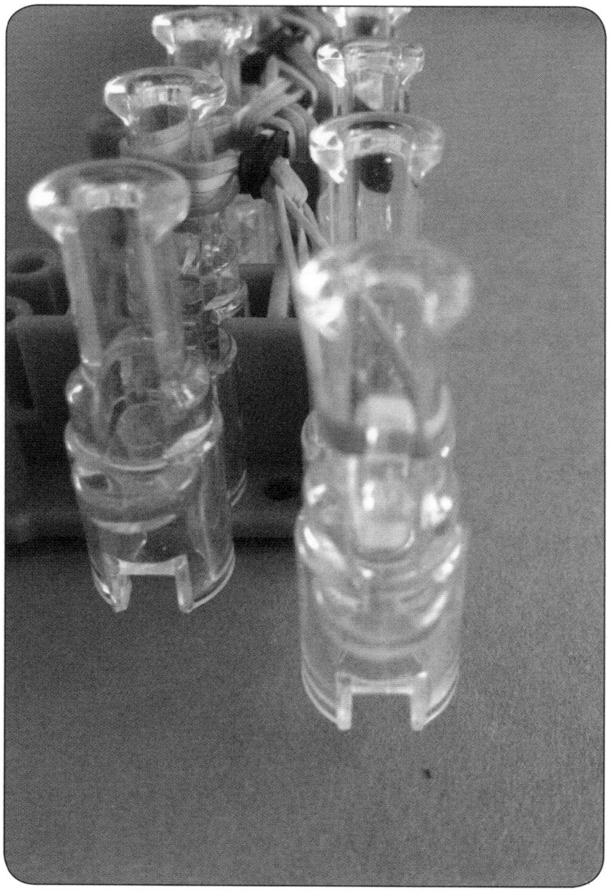

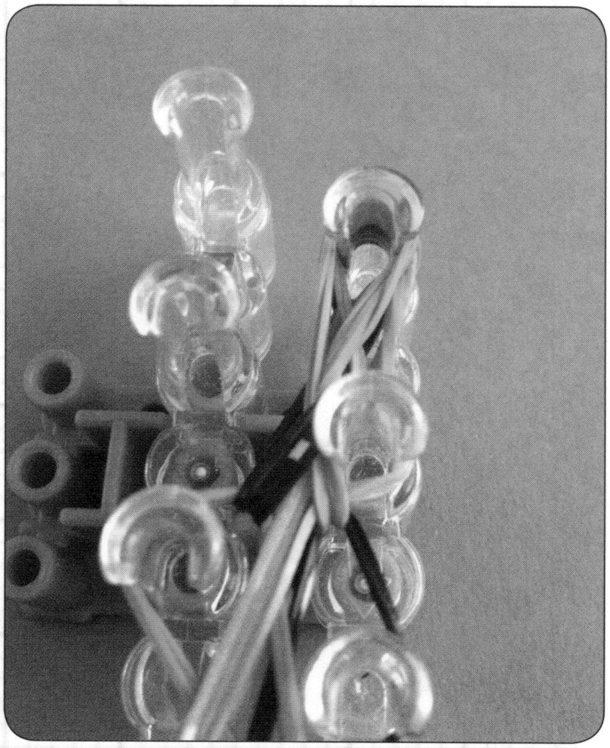

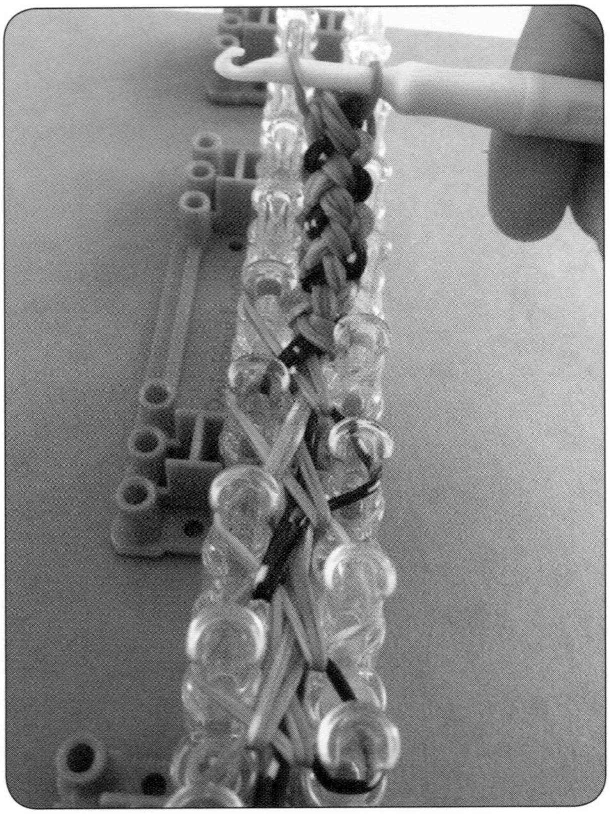

Step 6: Ending Your Bracelet

Use the C- or S-clip to close the bracelet.

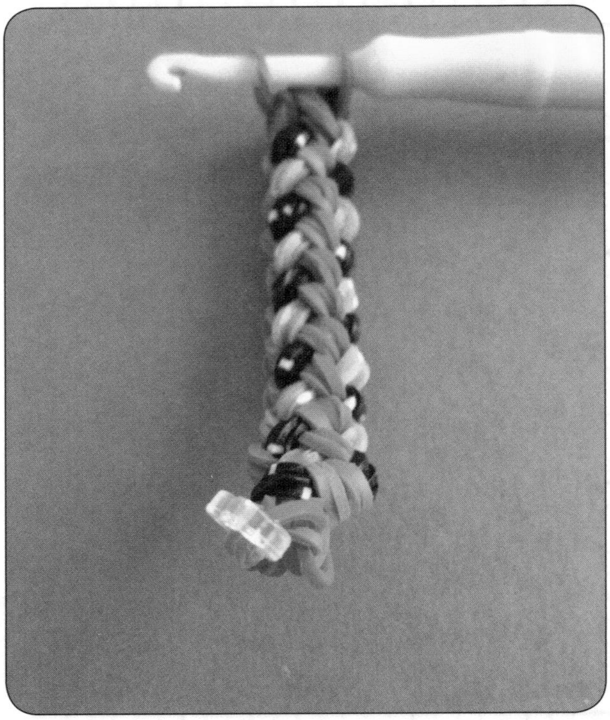

Taffy-Twist Bracelet

By mclare50

(http://www.instructables.com/id/Taffy-Twist-Rainbow-Loom-Tutorial/)

This bracelet is so cool and pretty easy to make, too! I would say this is a intermediate level design just because you have to work with a lot of bands.

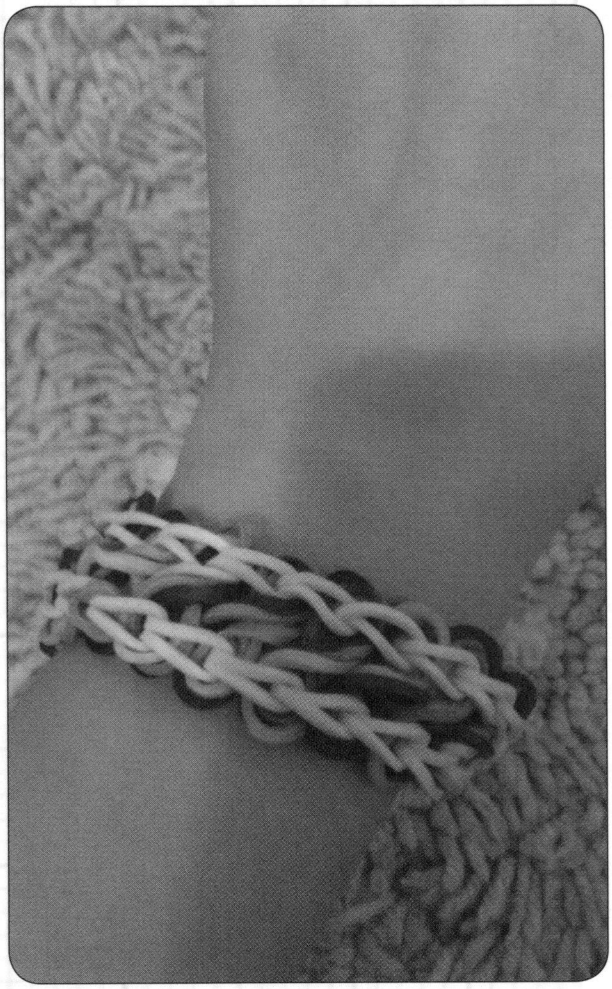

Step 1: Supplies

- Rainbow Loom
- Four rubber band colors
- Hook
- Clip

Step 2: Placing the Bands

Start with your Rainbow Loom in the normal configuration. Start with the red arrow facing away from you and place the first band diagonally out to the left. Now go in a straight chain up until the second-to-last pin. To end this, take one more band and bring it into the middle. Do the same on the right.

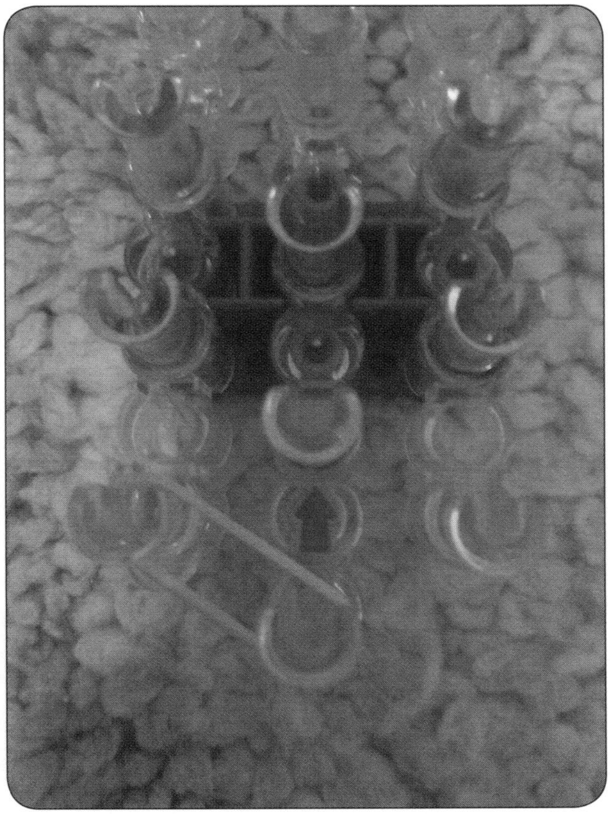

Step 3: Cap Band

When you're done, it should look like the photos. Now, place a cap band on the last peg.

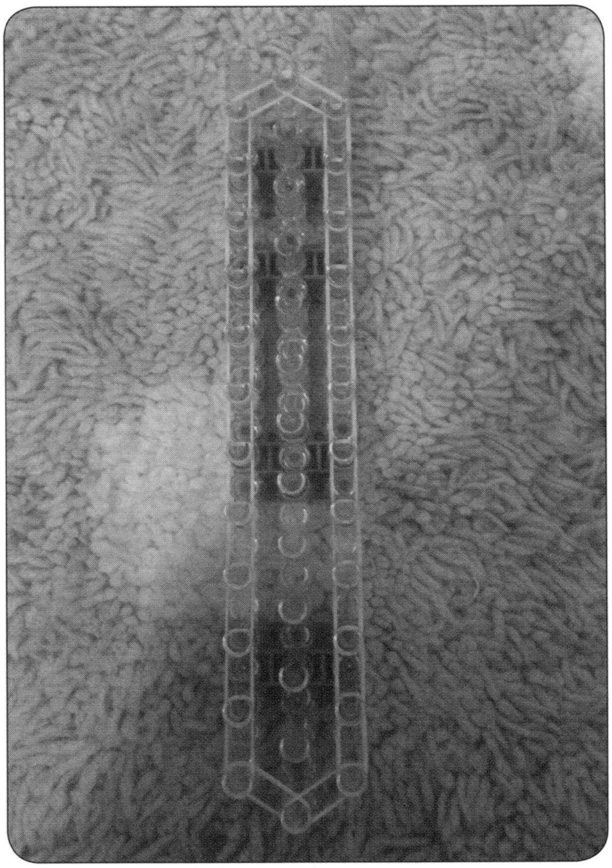

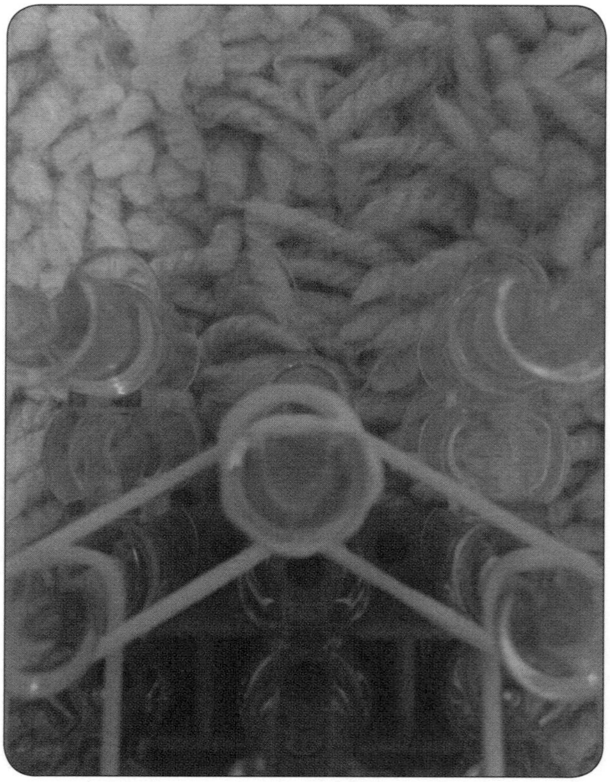

Step 4: Adding the Twists

The twists will go horizontally across the loom. To do this, take three different colors of bands and twist them together into a figure-eight shape. Place this across the loom on the pegs, as the picture shows. Continue this all the way up the loom.

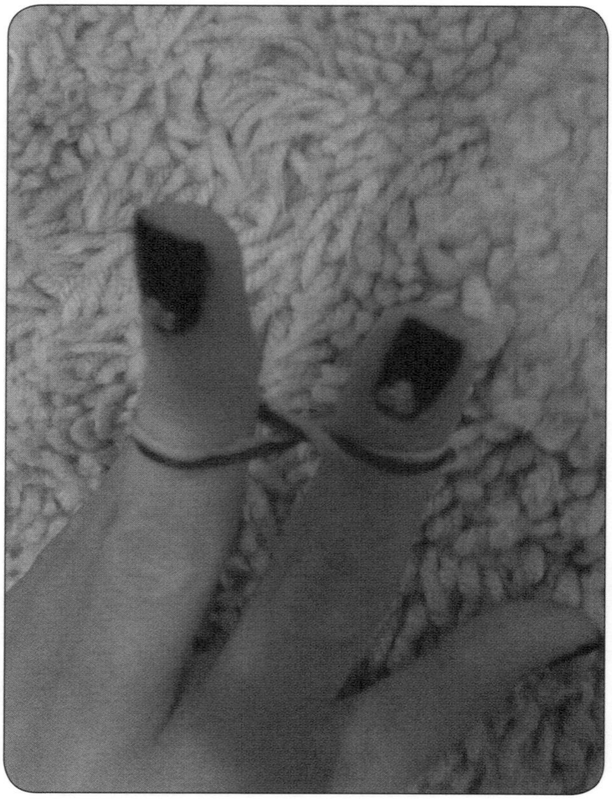

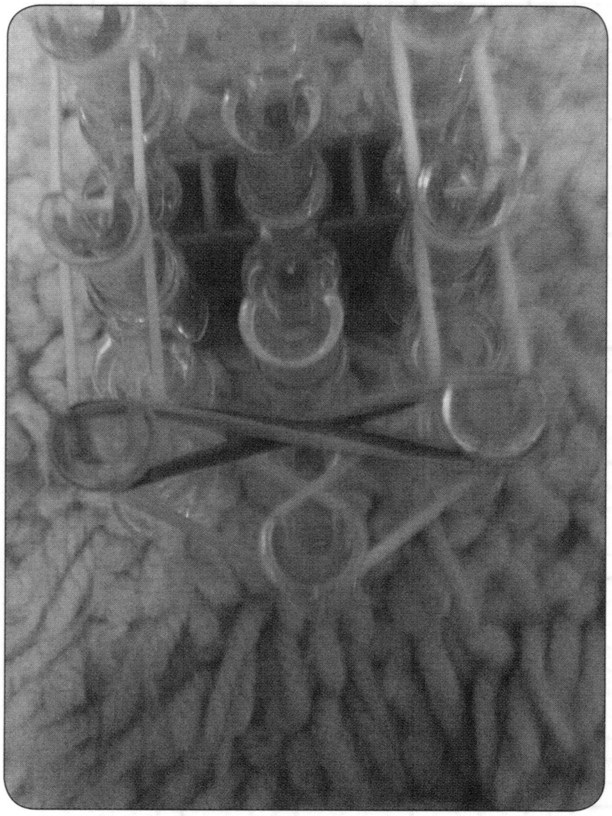

Step 5: A Visual

It should look like the photo when you have finished.

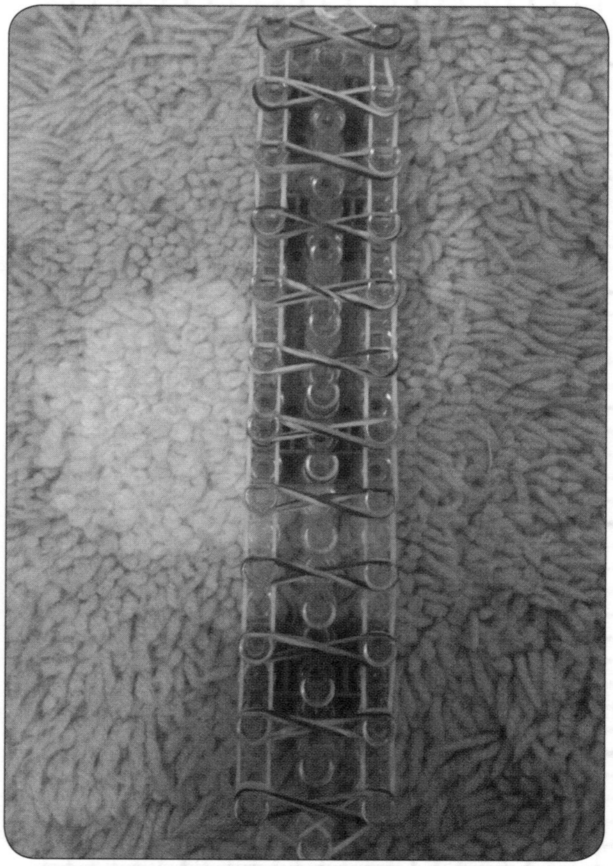

Step 6: Flip the Loom

Flip the loom over so that the arrow is facing you and put a cap band on the first pin on the top.

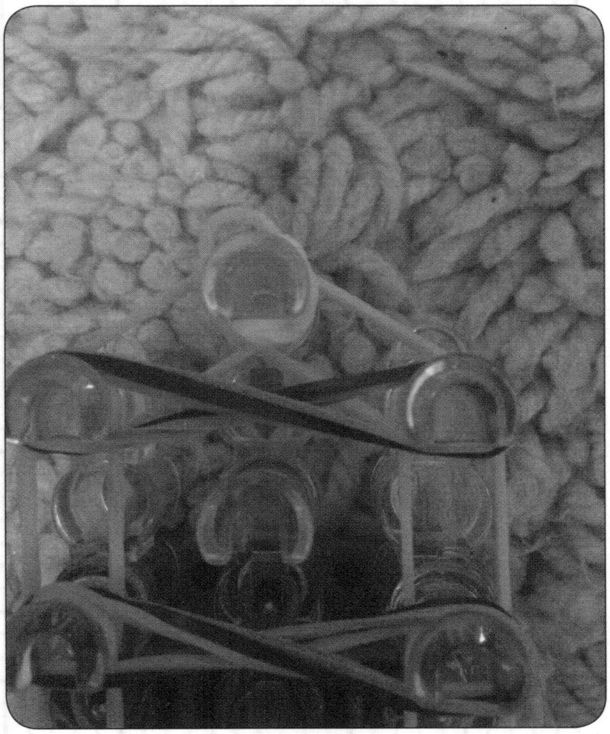

Step 7: Looming the Bands

To start looming, go under the cap band and grab the first yellow band. Hook it to the left. Reach under and grab the right band and bring it to the right.

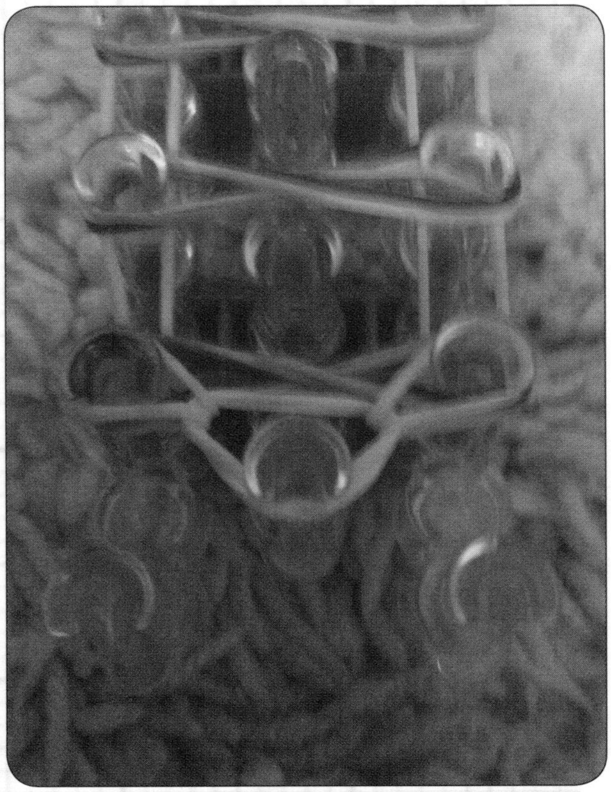

Step 8: A Straight Chain

Now you will be working in a straight chain up the loom. Once you have reached the end, bring the last band into the middle. Do the same thing with the right side. Make sure you're not grabbing the twist bands!

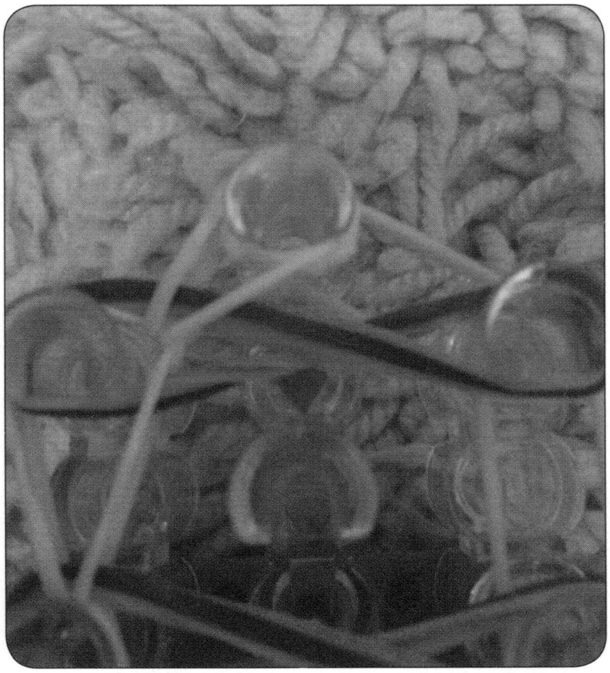

Step 9: A Visual

Your loom should look like the photo when you have finished.

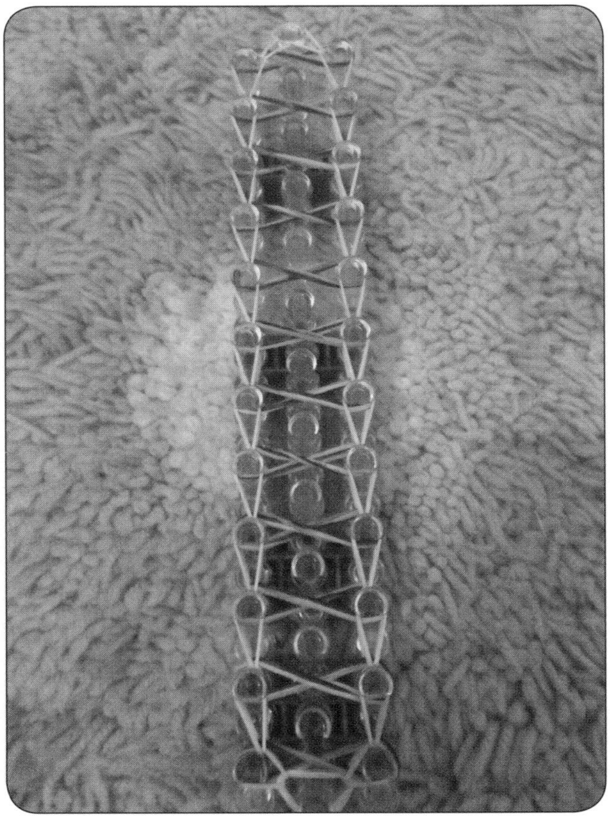

Step 10: Extension/Finishing

To finish your bracelet, stick the hook through the last pin and feed a rubber band through it. Make an extension using the single-chain method. Add a clip when you have finished.

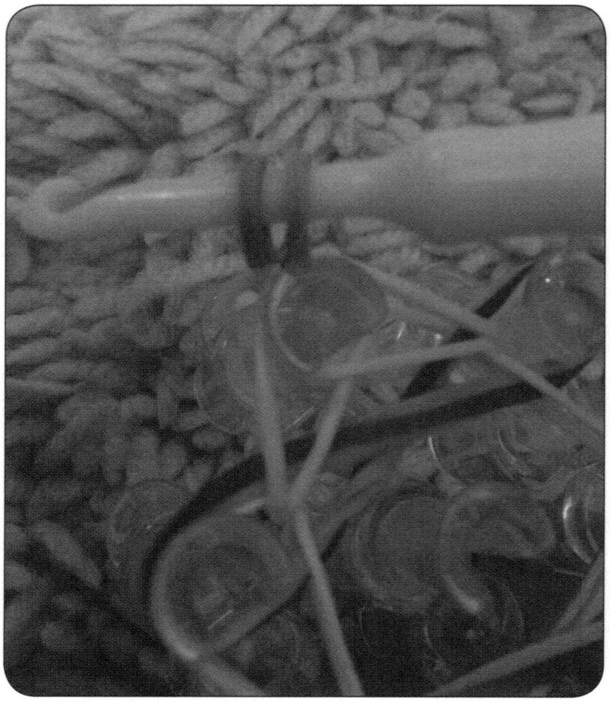

Step 11: Yay, All Done!

We're done! Pull your bracelet off of the loom and attach the clip to the cap band on the other side.

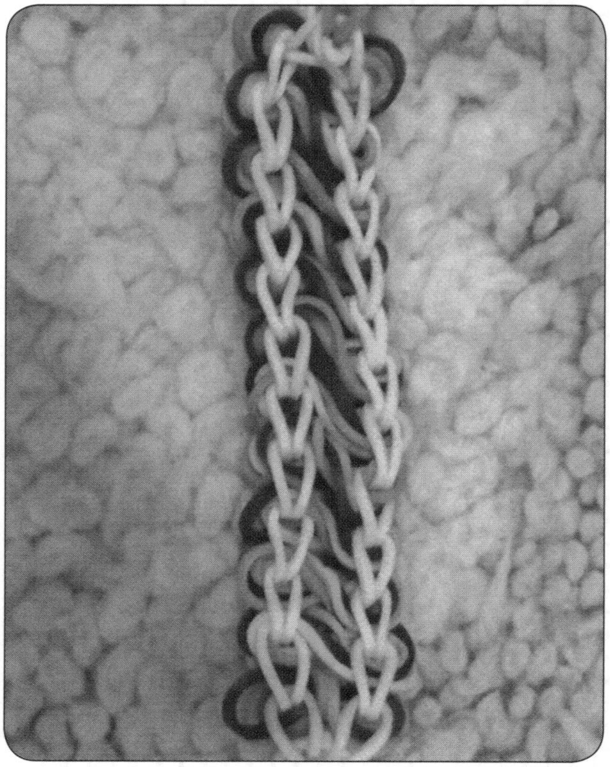

Double-Cross Bracelet

By crazymustacheluver
(http://www.instructables.com/id/How-to-make-Rainbow-Loom-bracelet-double-x-cross-I/)

Step 1: What You Need

- Rainbow Loom kit or other rubber band loom
- Green, blue, and yellow rubber bands
- Hook
- C-clip

Step 2: Place Rubber Bands

First, place a rubber band (green) onto the middle peg and stretch it diagonally upward to the left, and then do the same thing to the right. Next, go to the left peg and put a rubber band diagonally upward to the middle peg, and the same to the right. Continue all the way to the top, alternating between your three colors.

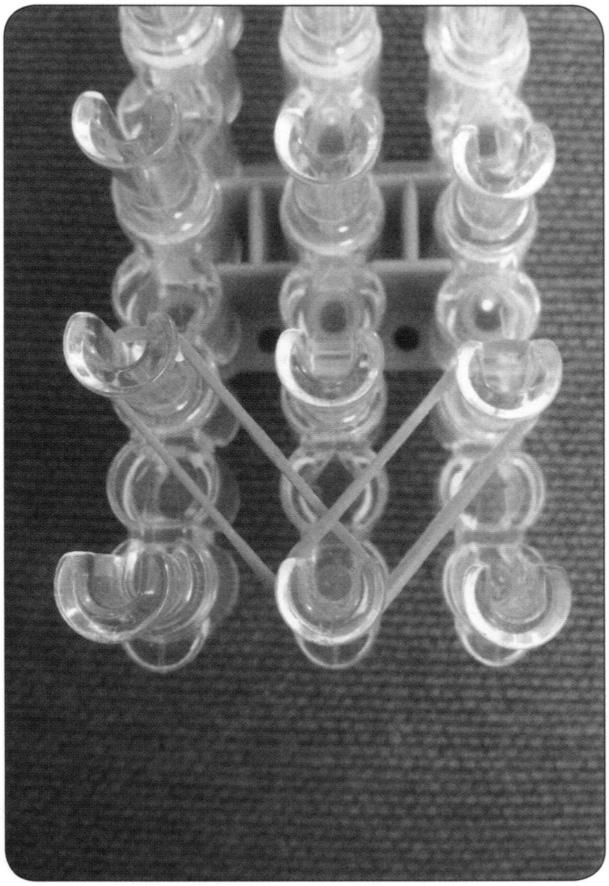

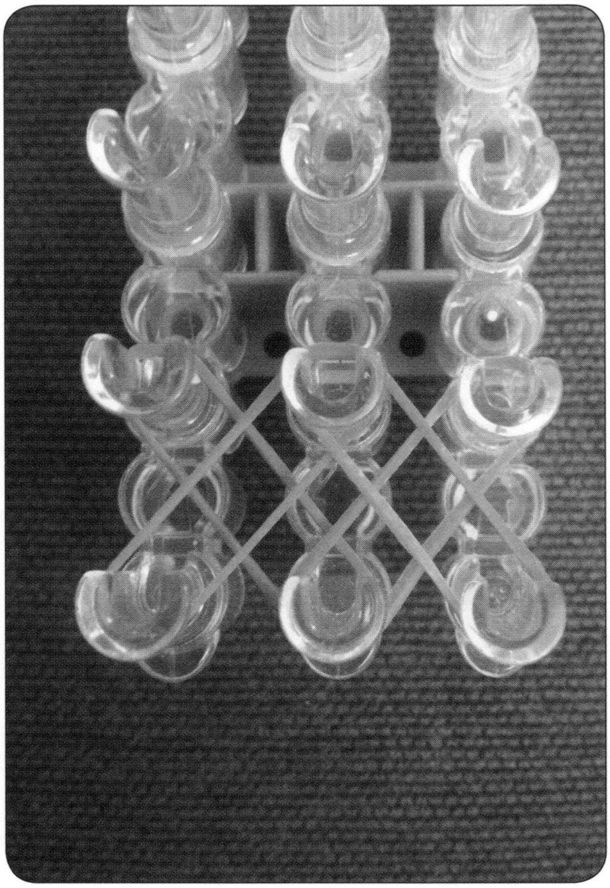

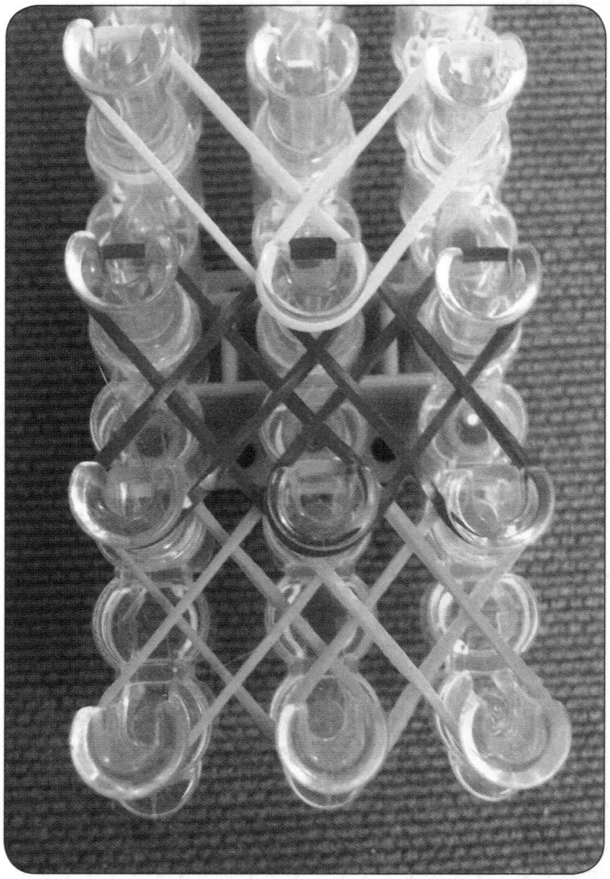

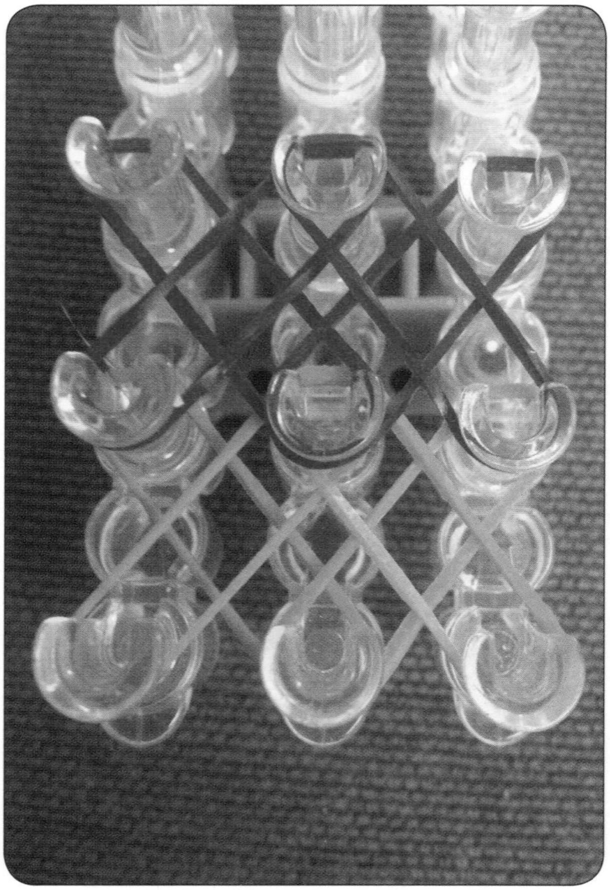

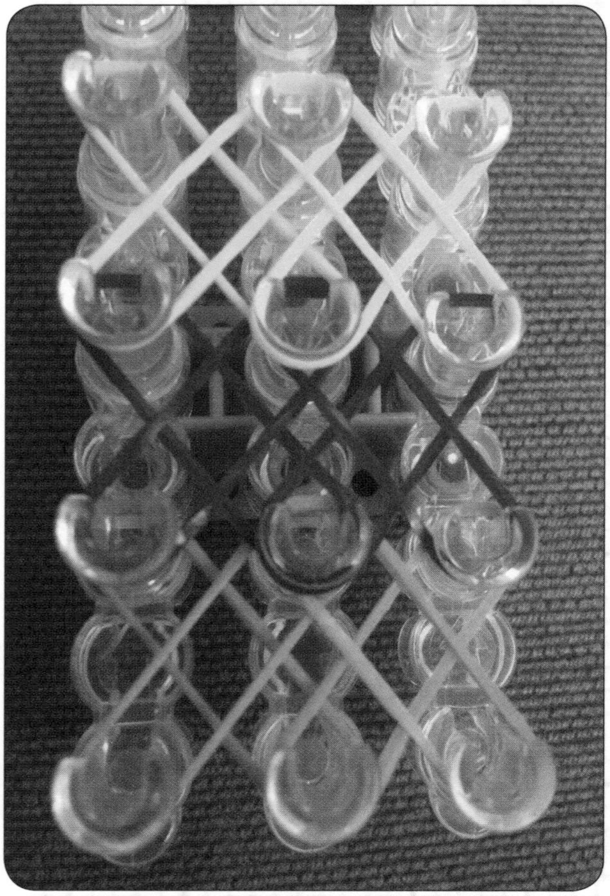

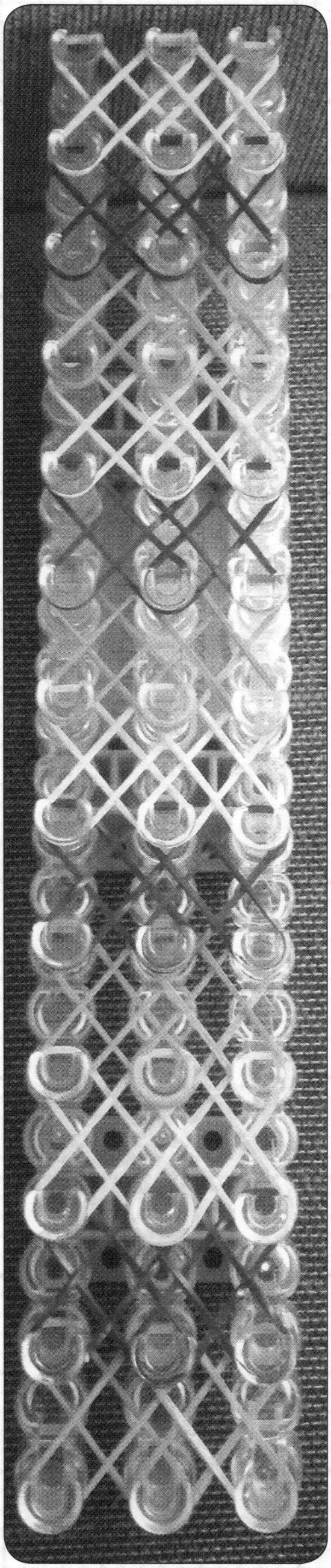

Step 3: Looping

Turn your loom around. Go to the middle peg and stretch the (yellow) rubber band diagonally upward to the left, and then do the same to the right. Do this to the next two rubber bands. Go to the middle peg and stretch the (blue) rubber band diagonally upward to the left, then do the same to the right. Go to the left peg and take the rubber band and stretch it to the middle peg; do the same to the right. Repeat this all the way to the top.

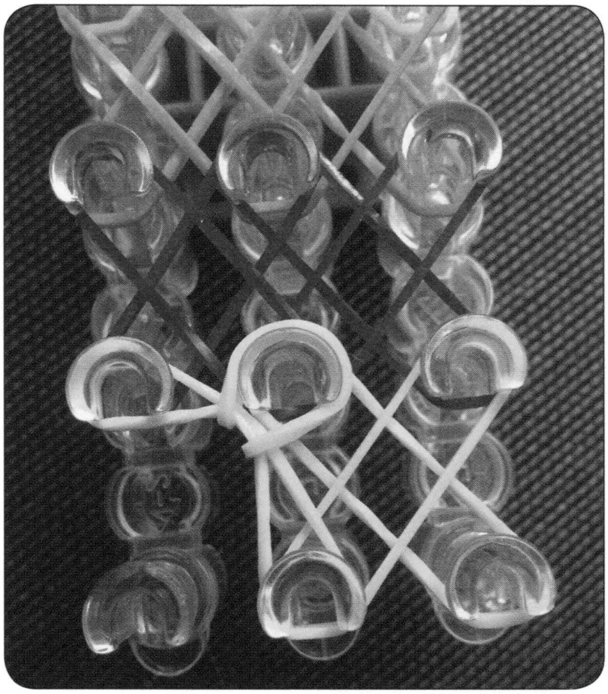

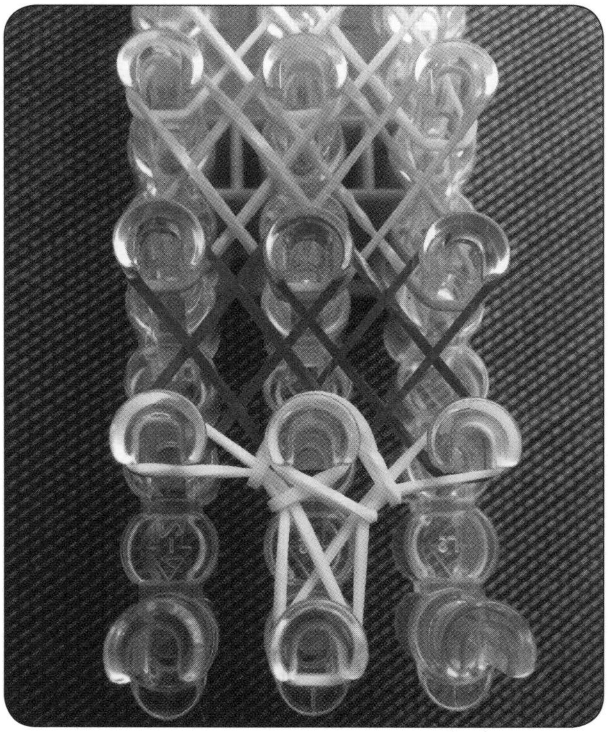

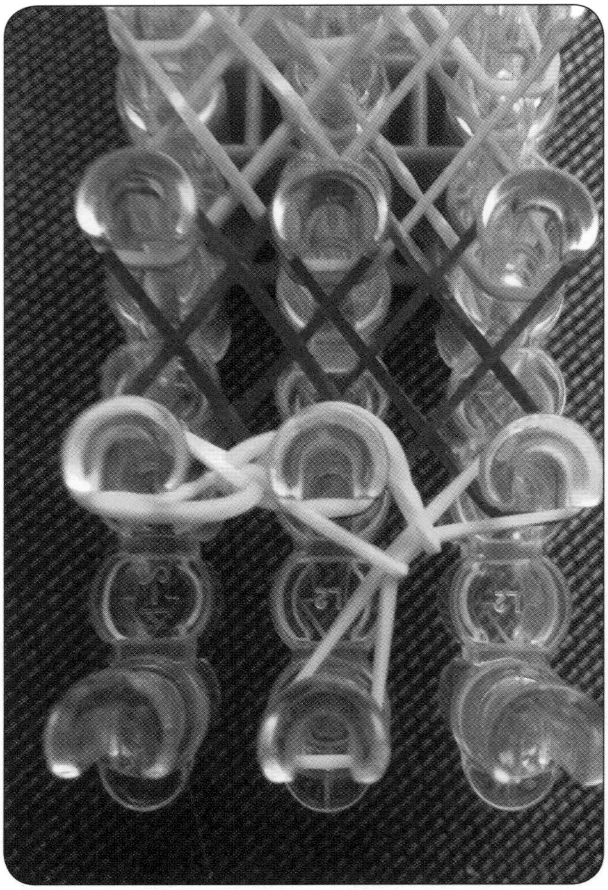

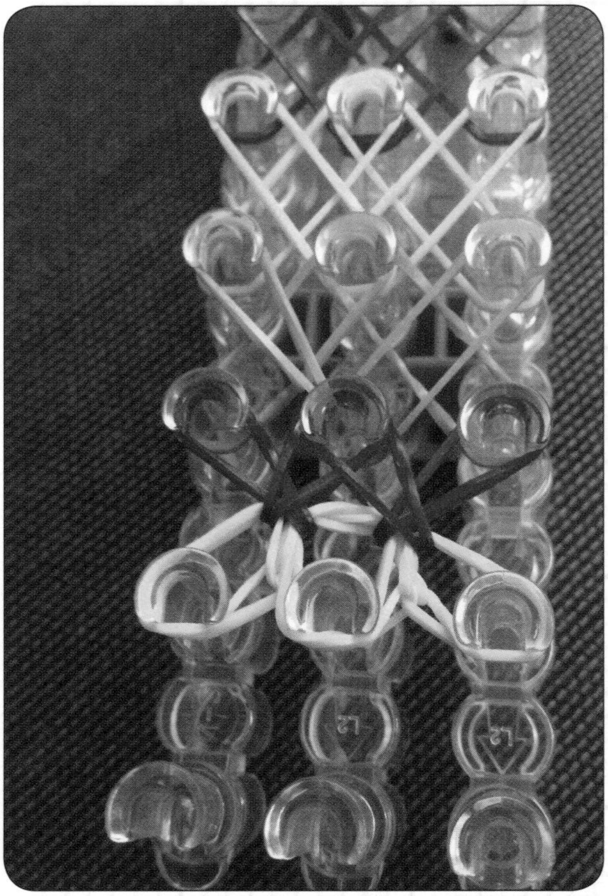

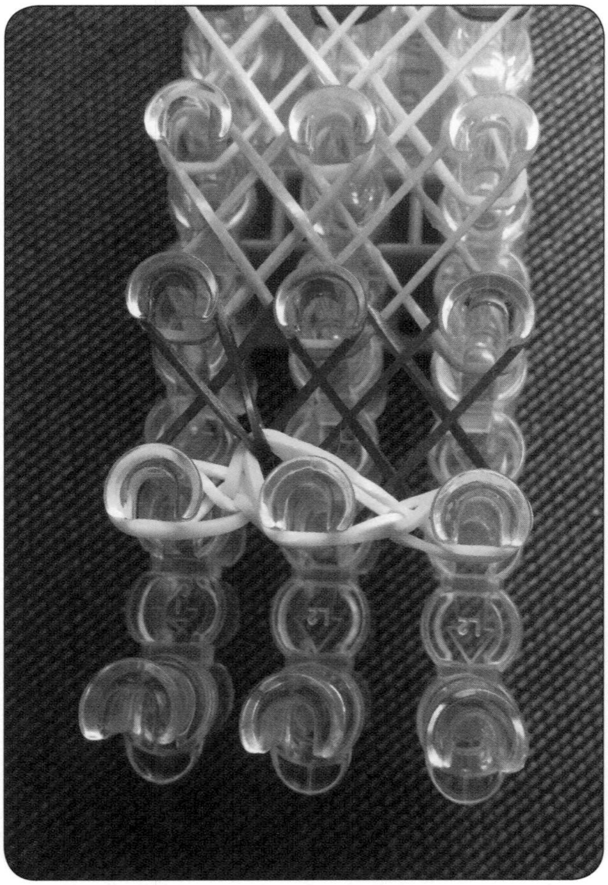

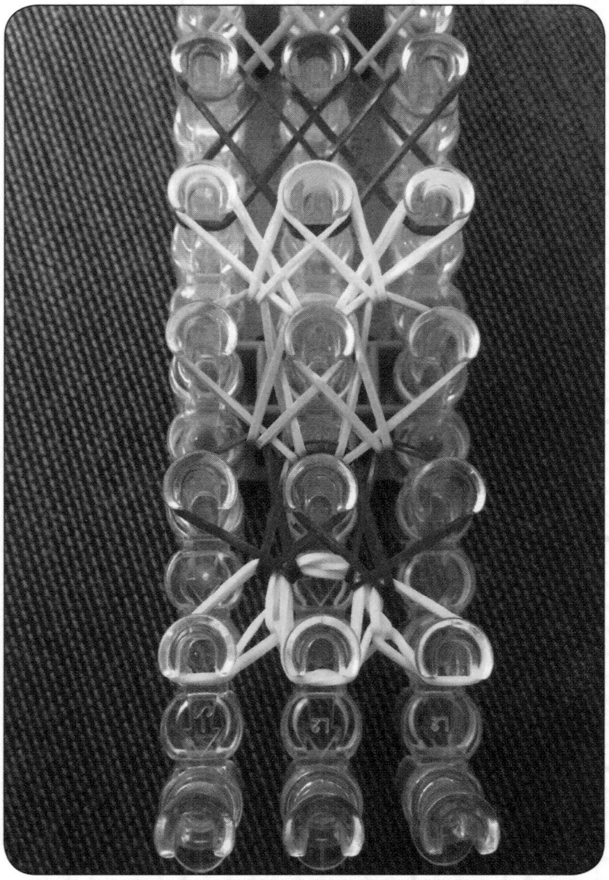

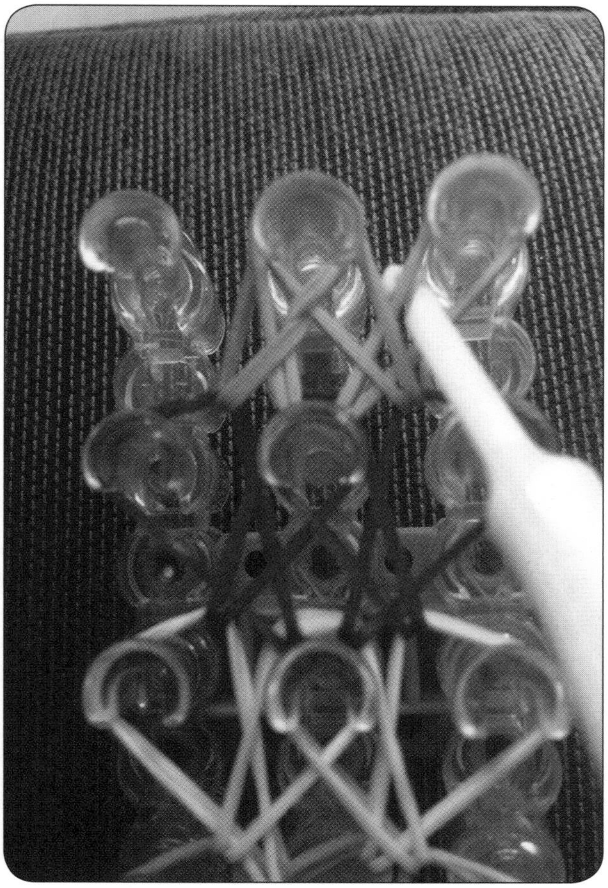

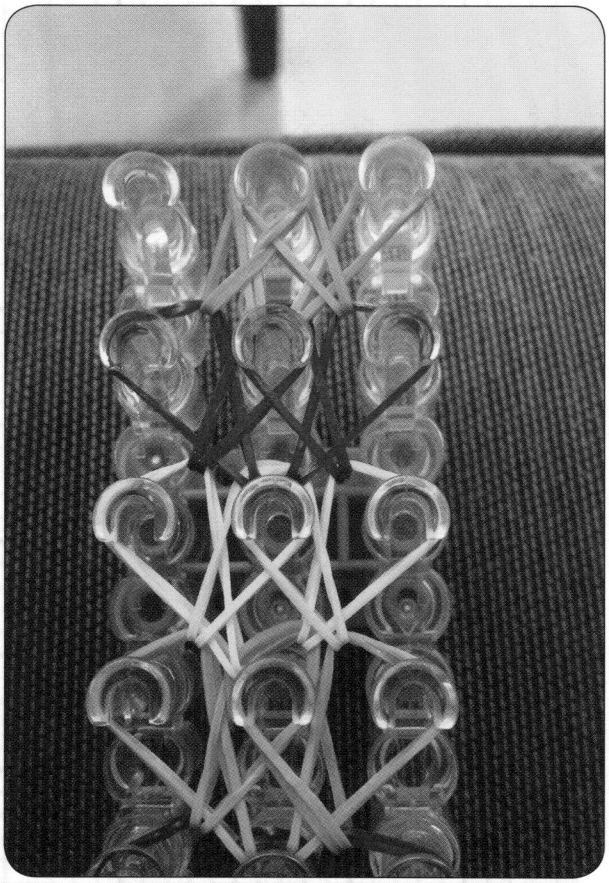

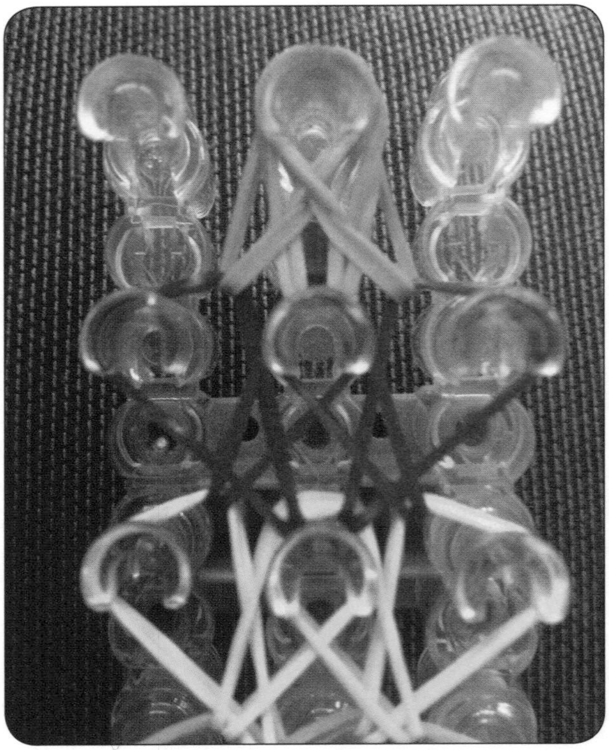

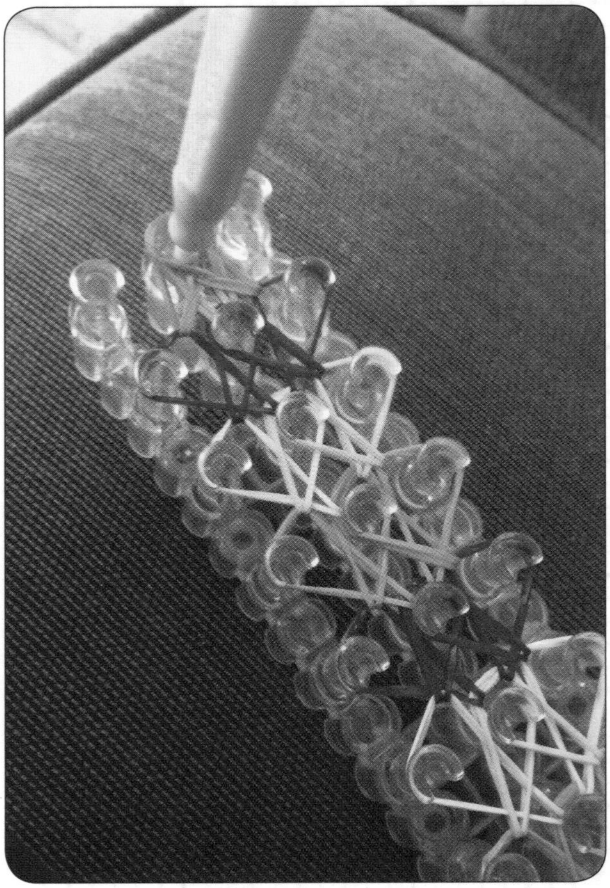

Step 4: Pulling Off the Bracelet

Go to the last left side peg and pick up all the rubber bands on the peg. Stretch them to the middle peg. Do the same on the right. Put your hook down your last middle peg and drag a rubber band through it. Gently pull off .

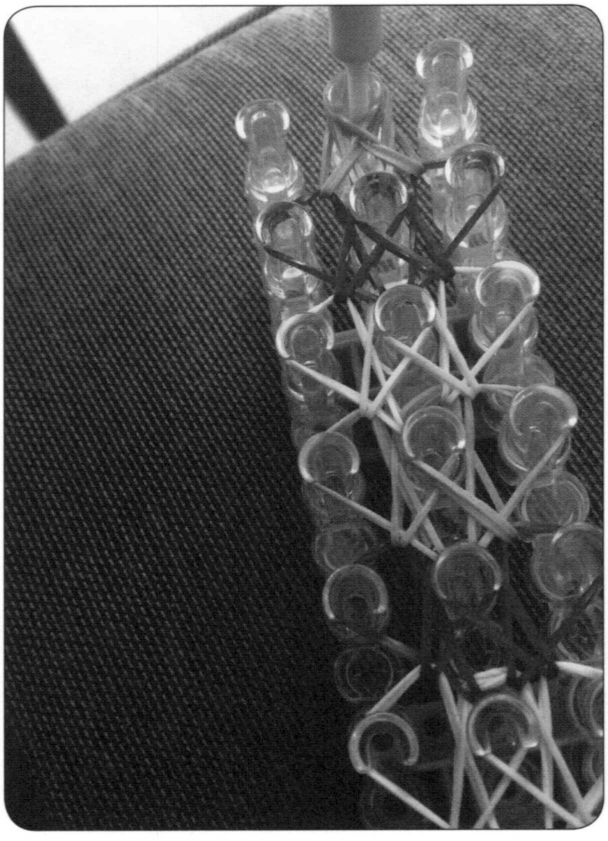

Step 5: Last Step

Put six rubber bands straight up one side of the loom. Then connect your bracelet. Loop straight. Pull off then connect with C-clip.

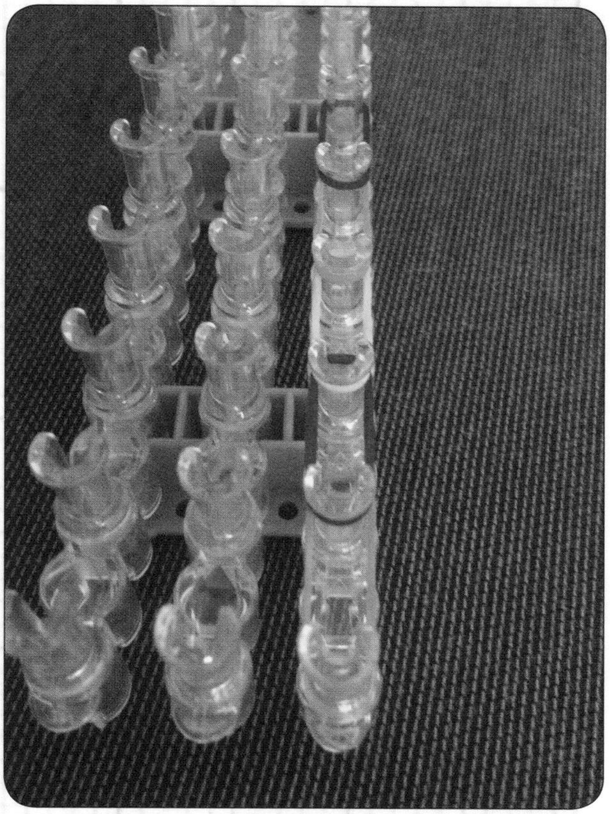

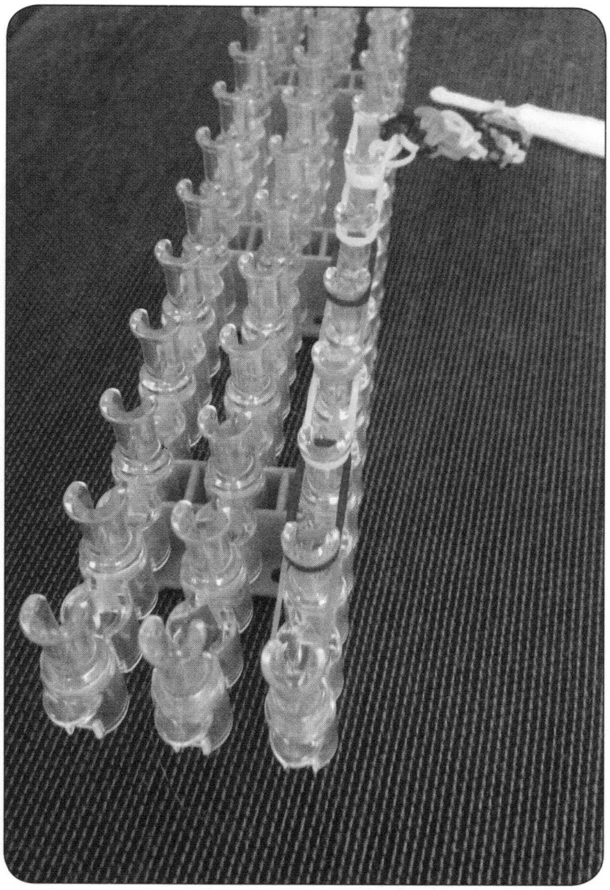

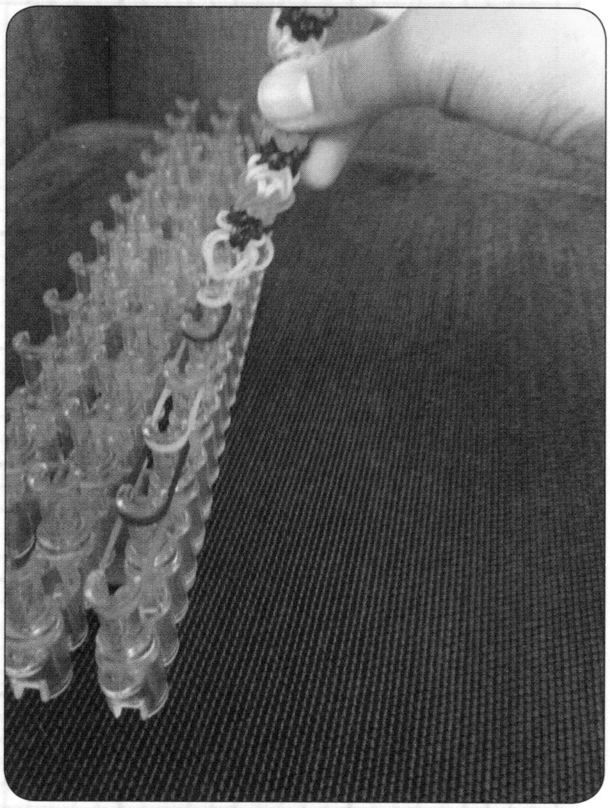

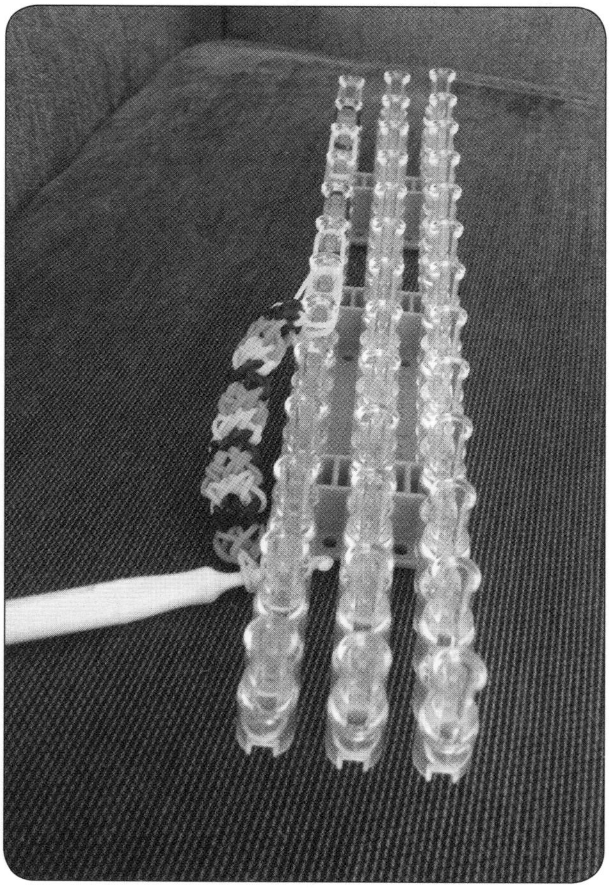

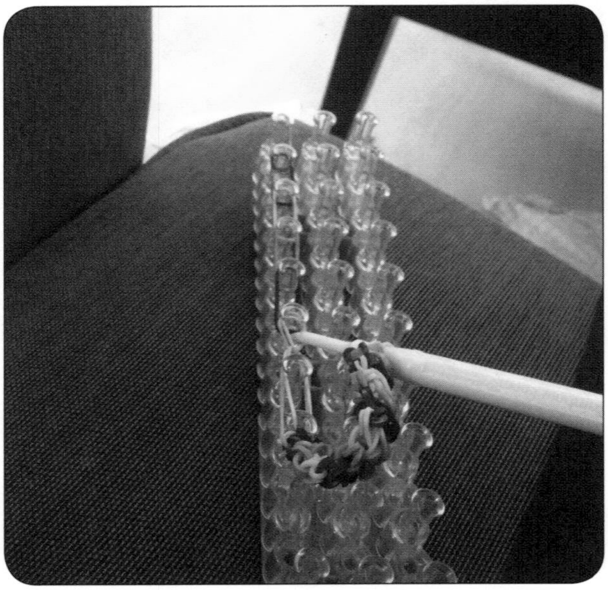

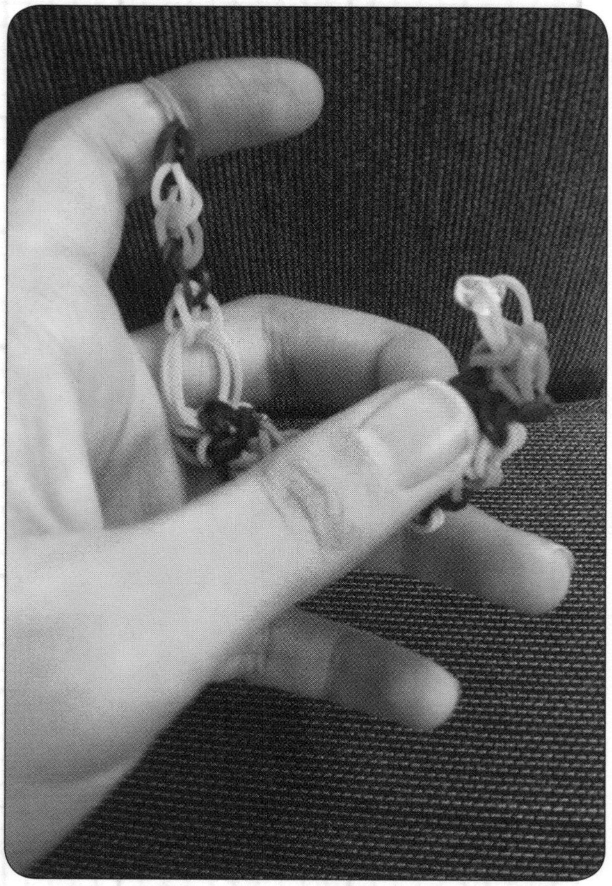

Ladder Bracelet

By shan_2004

(http://www.instructables.com/id/Rainbow-Loom-Ladder-Braclet/)

This is a very easy and fun bracelet to make. I hope you enjoy!

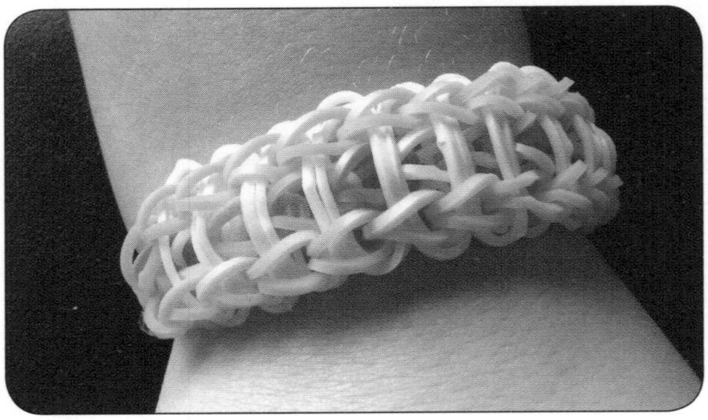

Step 1: Materials

- Loom
- Hook
- Elastics
- C-clip

Step 2: Placing the Elastics

First, pick three colors and start at the center peg. Put your outside color out to the left and right pegs. Now with the same color, go straight all the way up the sides of the loom.

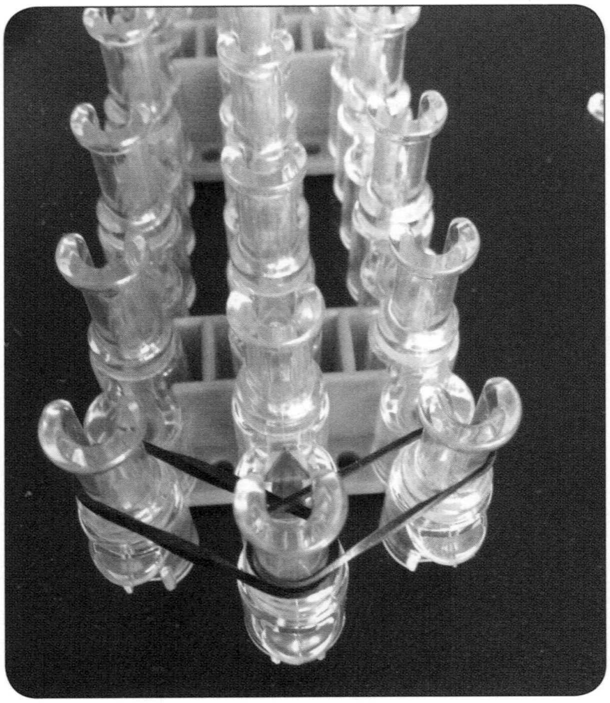

Step 3: The Ladder, Part 1

Place a different color on the second pegs and go all the way up like a ladder.

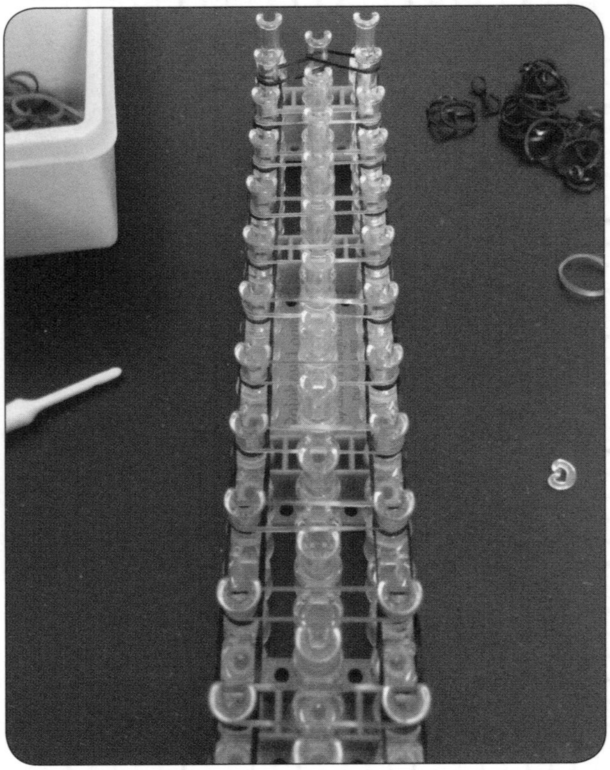

Step 4: Middle

Now choose a different color and place it on the first and second pegs on the middle row. Then continue this straight pattern all the way up the middle row.

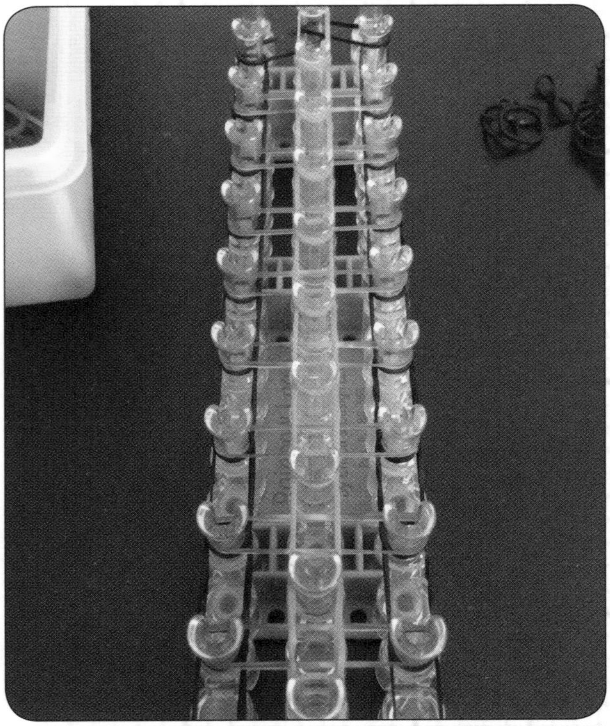

Step 5: Hooking

Now you're going to turn your loom around and put a capping band on the center peg. Then you get your hook and get the blue elastic and bring it to the peg in front of it. Hook the blue elastics all the way up the middle.

Step 6: The Ladder, Part 2

Now you're going to take the color of the ladder and place the elastics in the same spots as you did on the last ladder.

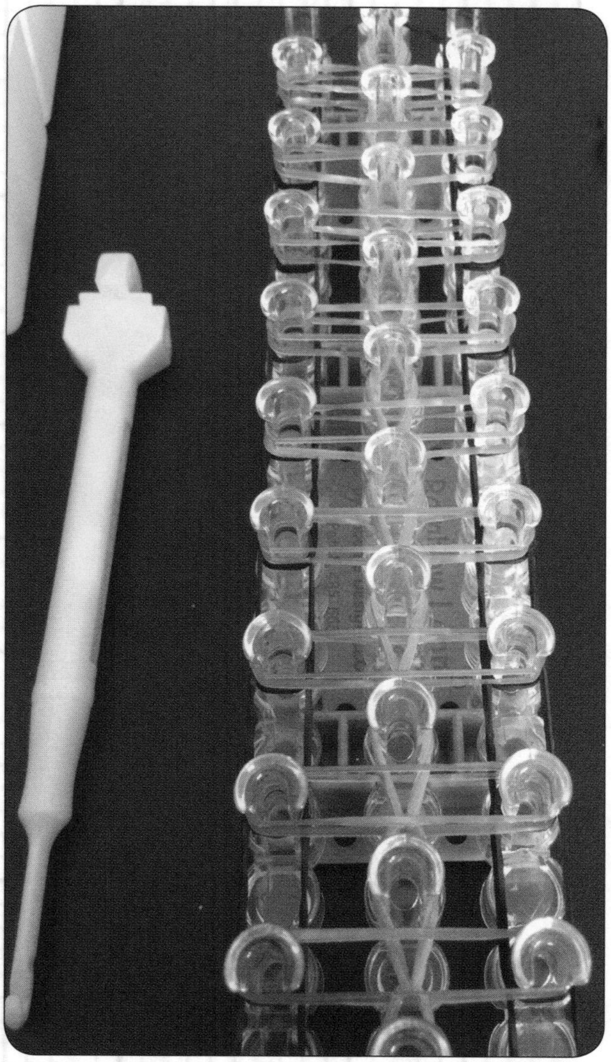

Step 7: Hooking the Perimeter

Get under the capping band and hook the first elastic to the side and go all the way up on both sides.

Step 8: Taking the Bracelet Off

Now you're going to put your hook through the center peg, take a colored band, and pull it through. Now you can pull your bracelet off the loom.

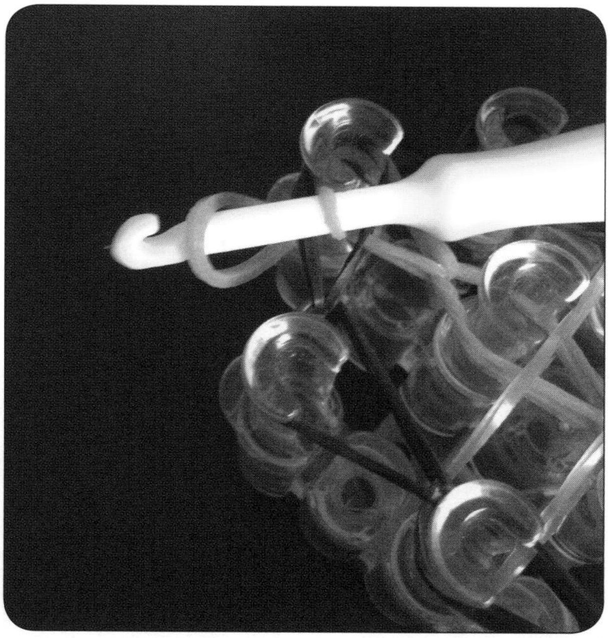

Step 9: Finishing the Bracelet

Now take your extension color and place the elastics all the way up the loom. Now put the elastic that you pulled through all the elastics and place it on the loom. Now turn your loom around and hook the blue elastics all the way up. Then put the C-clip on the elastic and pull it off. Now hook the C-clip to the black capping band. Your bracelet is all done!

Zippy Chain Bracelet

By l_cokkinos

(http://www.instructables.com/id/Rainbow-Loom-Zippy-Chain-Bracelet/)

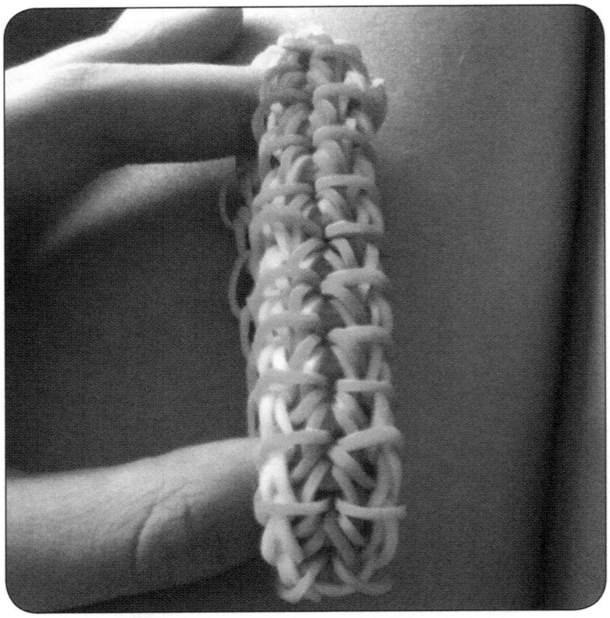

Step 1: Supplies

You will need a starting kit for Rainbow Loom and some rubber bands in the colors of your choice.

Step 2: Placing the Bands

Start by placing a border color. Don't start putting it up the whole thing, as you have to do it in patterns.

Step 3: Placing the Bands

Next, put one elastic in the middle between the first two bands. Now put one rubber band of another color in the middle between the first two bands.

Step 4: Placing the Bands

Put a color from the middle to the border, then start the pattern again. Take another color and put one from the middle to the border; do the same on the other side. Then start the pattern again, beginning with the border color.

Step 5: Continue placing the Bands

Continue the steps.

Step 6: Placing the Cap Bands

Place one cap band on the first peg when you flip it.

Step 7: Looping the Bands

Start by taking the bands under the cap bands and looping them to the outside.

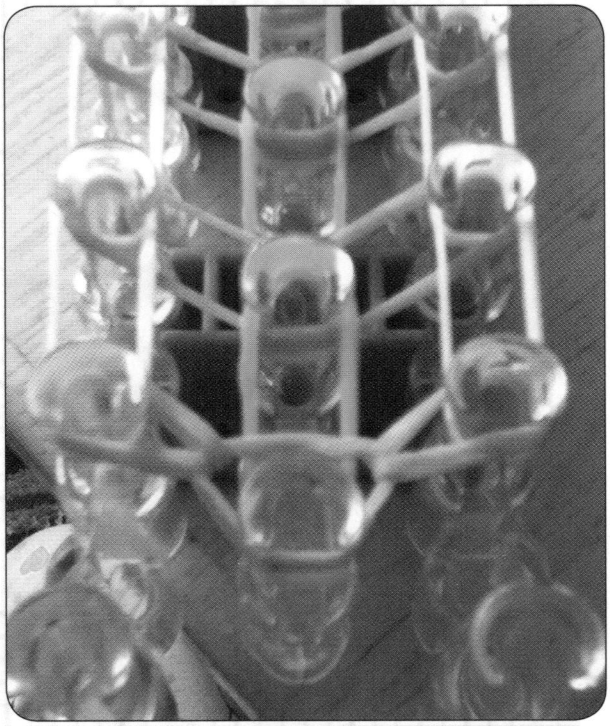

Step 8: Looping the Bands

Next, loop the middle elastic up to the middle peg above it.

Step 9: Looping the Bands

You have to loop up the borders in the order that the steps show you.

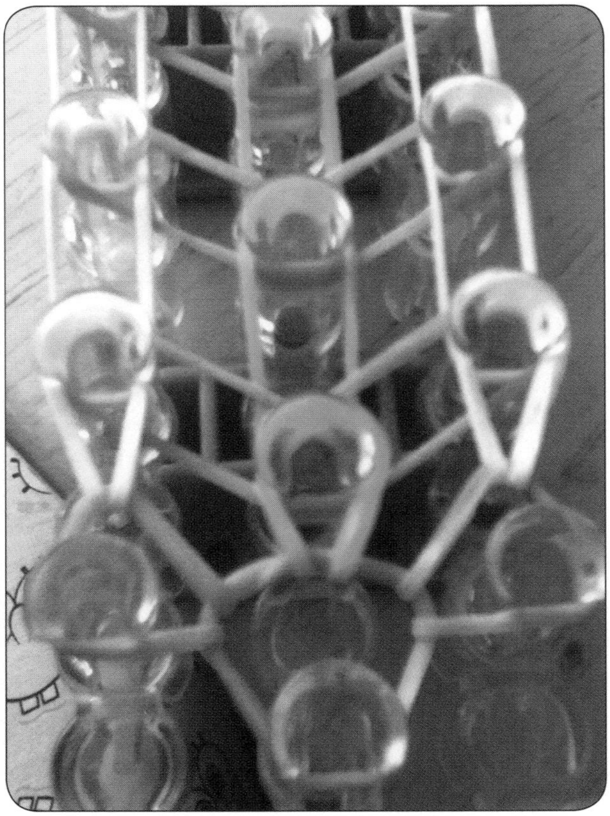

Step 10: Looping the Bands

Next, take the middle rubber band and put it to the outside and do the same thing on the other side.

Step 11: Looping the Bands

Then you have to take the middle band and move it up to the next peg.

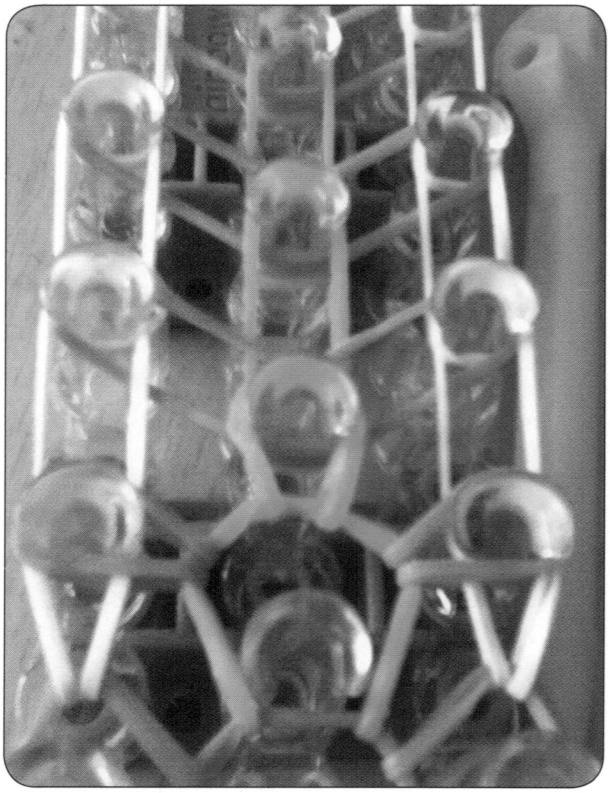

Step 12: Looping the Bands

Near the end, loop the ending border band to the middle peg.

Step 13: Finishing Up the Bracelet

Now, stick your looping hook down the end of the board. Take any color elastic and put it on the hook and pull it through. Do the same thing to the other side and pull off.

Step 14: Finishing Up the Bracelet

Once you pull off it off the Rainbow Loom, your bracelet should look like this!

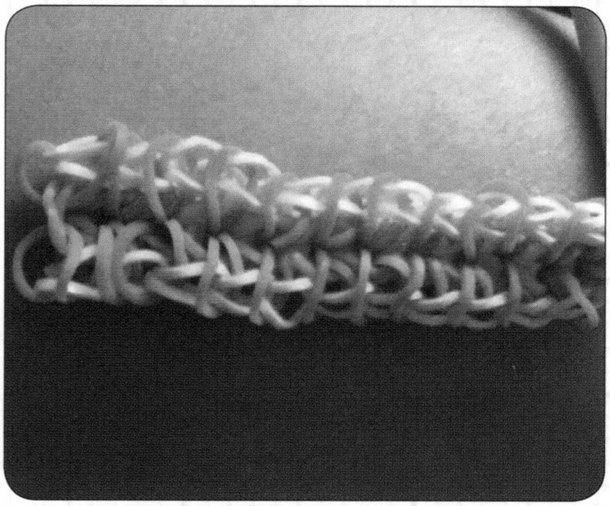

Dragon-Scale Bracelet

By RAWR Its Gracie
(http://www.instructables.com/id/How-To-Make-A-Dragon-scale-Loom-Bracelet/)

This can be an eight-peg bracelet. The one I've done is a six-peg bracelet, but you can make it as many pegs long as you like.

Step 1: Items You'll Need

- 1 Rainbow Loom
- 1 hook
- 2 or more colors of bands
- 2 to 6 C-clips or S-clips

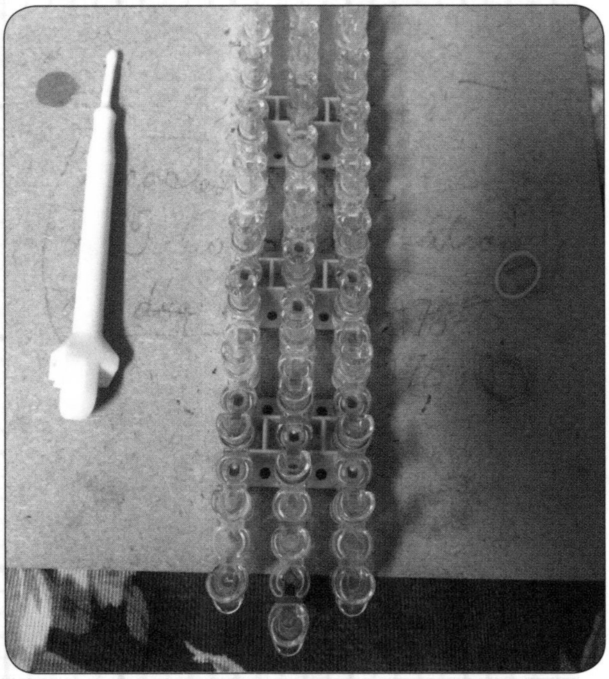

Step 2: Placing Bands

Place rubber bands on the loom as shown in the images below.

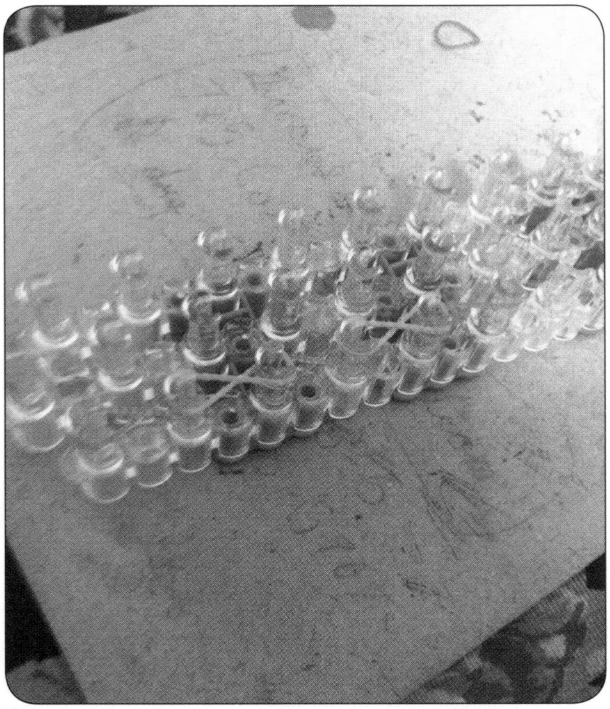

Step 3: Looping Bands

Loop the band over the band on top. Make sure the band is twisted. If it's not, take it off and twist it. Keep looping the bands over top of the bands on top. Once they are looped, place three more blue bands on. Continue looping until your bracelet is long enough.

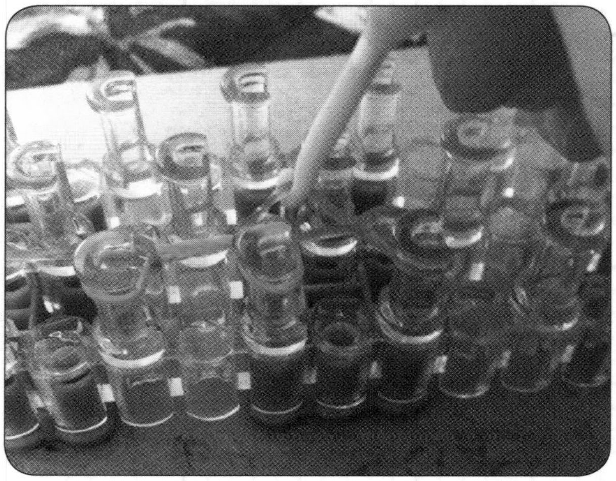

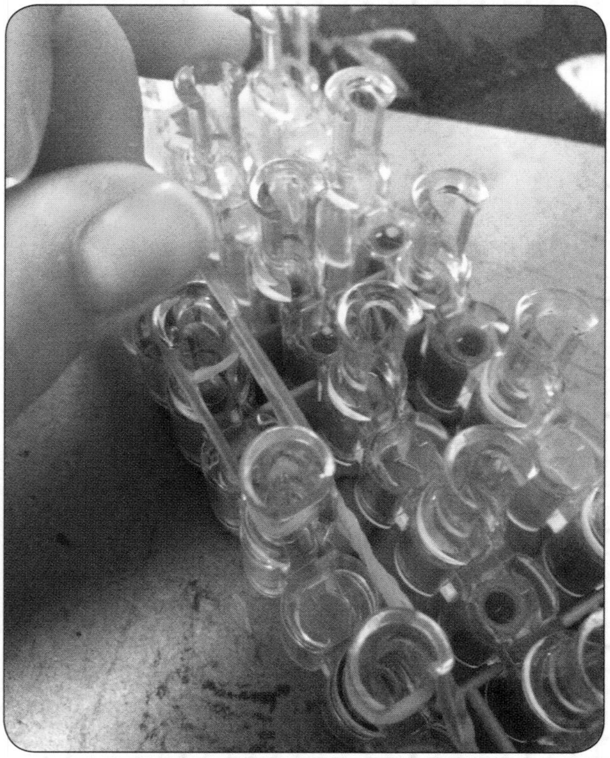

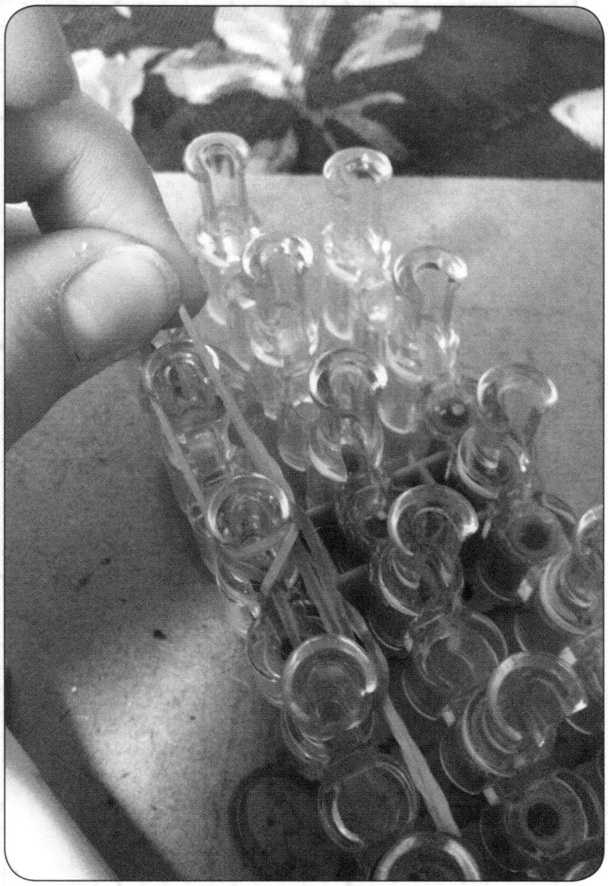

Step 4: Finishing the Bracelet

Your bracelet should look somewhat like the photos. Take the left end band and put it onto the peg next to it. Take the right end band and put it onto the peg beside it. Take one of the middle bands (it doesn't matter which one) and put it on to the peg next to it. Then attach your C-clip or S-clip. Take your bracelet off of the loom and attach both ends.

Step 5: Wearing the Bracelet

Now you can wear your bracelet!

Loopy Stripe Bracelet

By Nadia Braun (Nadflick)

(http://www.instructables.com/id/Loopy-Stripes-Rainbow-Loom-Bracelet/)

The thing I wanted so bad for Christmas was a Rainbow Loom. So when I opened my present and got just what I wanted, I immediately got to work making bracelets that I'd watched videos about. Ever since I started watching those videos, I've had ideas in my head for my very own Rainbow Loom bracelets. One of them was what I call the Loopy Stripe Bracelet. Through work and failures I have finally perfected my bracelet. Enjoy!

Step 1: What You Need

- 28 "A" (black) colored bands
- 6 "B" (green) colored bands
- 6 "C" (blue) colored bands
- Rainbow Loom with the hook
- C-clip

Step 2: Single Chain

First, make sure the red arrow is pointing away from you. Then, take your "A" colored band and stretch it from the bottom pin to the left pin above it. Then take another band and stretch it to the next pin. This is also known as the "single chain" and is very easy to do. Once you've reached the second-to-end pin of that row, stretch your next band from the end to the center top pin. Now go all the way back to the bottom of the loom and do the exact same thing except on the right side of the loom. It should kind-of look like a tall hexagon.

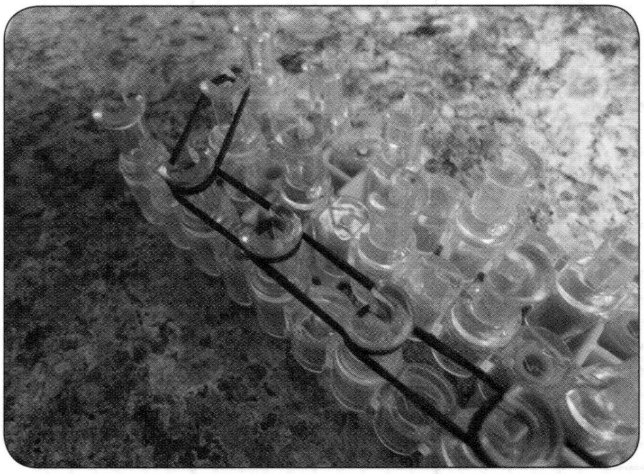

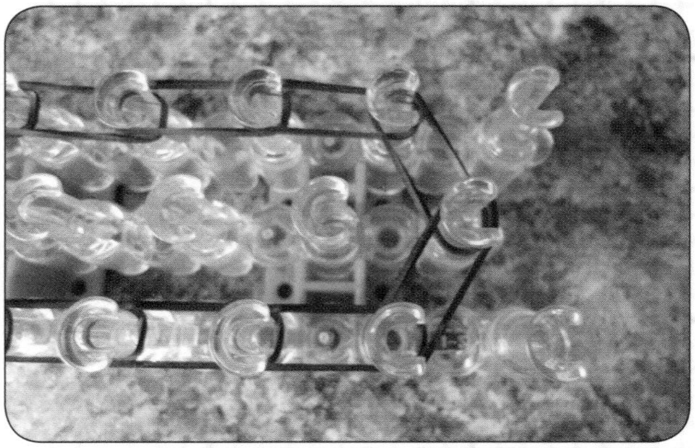

Step 3: Triangles!

On to the next step. This is the unique part of this bracelet. First, take your "B" colored band and stretch it onto the bottom pin on the left and the bottom pin on the right. Then, stretch the top of the band onto the center pin above the other two. This should form a triangle shape. Now take a "C" colored band and do the exact same thing on the pins above the triangle you just made. Do this pattern until the end of the loom, where you can't go any further.

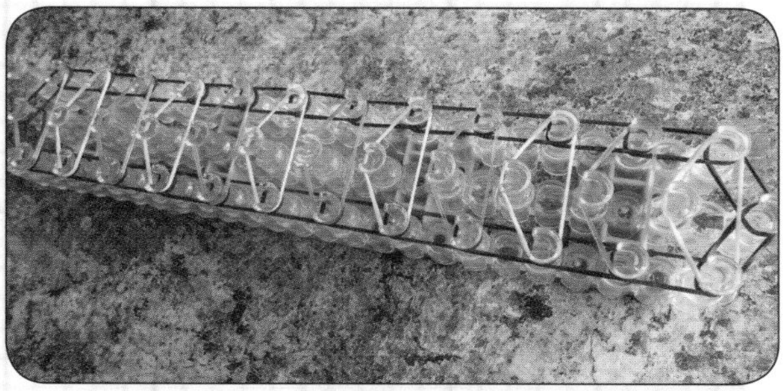

Step 4: Cap Band

This part is quite simple. First, take an "A" colored band and twist it into a figure eight. Now bring one loop of the figure eight onto the finger with the other loop. In other words, turn it back upon itself. Then place it onto the far center pin, the one that is not near the red arrow.

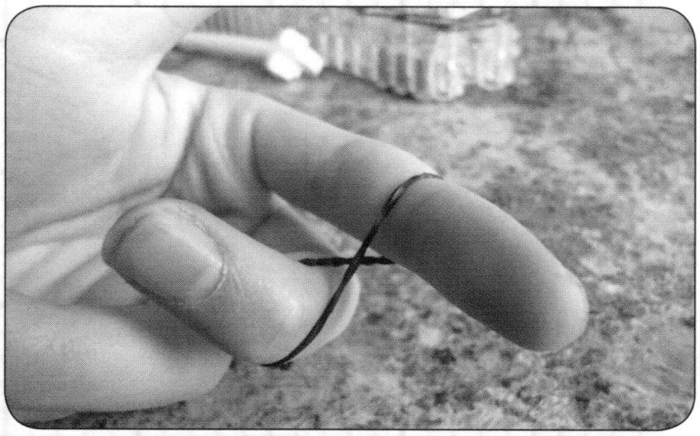

Step 5: Looping, Part 1

It's now time to loop! We're going to start by single-chaining (if that's even a word) the left side first. With your hook, push back the cap band and the triangle band and grab the first "A" band. Pull it over and attach it to the pin on the left. Now do your average single chain up the left side of the loom by always grabbing the bottom "A" band and bringing it over and looping it to the one above. Once you've done the left side, loop your last band onto the center pin. Now do the exact same thing on the right side, push back the cap band and the triangle band, and grab the bottom "A" band and bring it up, over, and onto the pin on the right. Then single chain all the way up the right side of the loom. Once you get to the end, loop your last band onto the center pin.

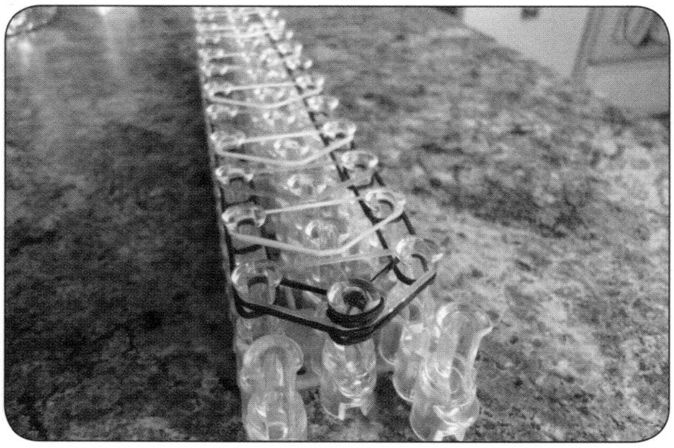

Step 6: Looping! Part 2

Now that you've done the single-chaining, you need to loop the triangles. This is a very unique process. Start at the bottom of the loom. With your hook, push back the cap band and grab the "C" colored triangle band. Pull the band over to the next center pin above it. Then grab the "B" colored band under the band you just looped and pull it over onto the center pin above it. Make sure that the bands are not caught on the pins and are going up the middle. Now repeat this process until you can't loop anymore.

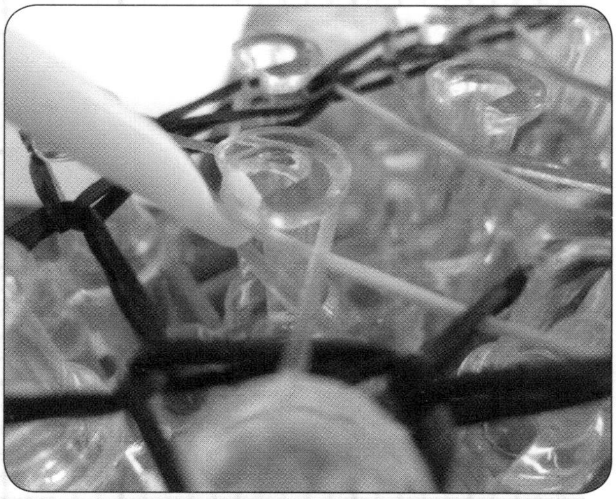

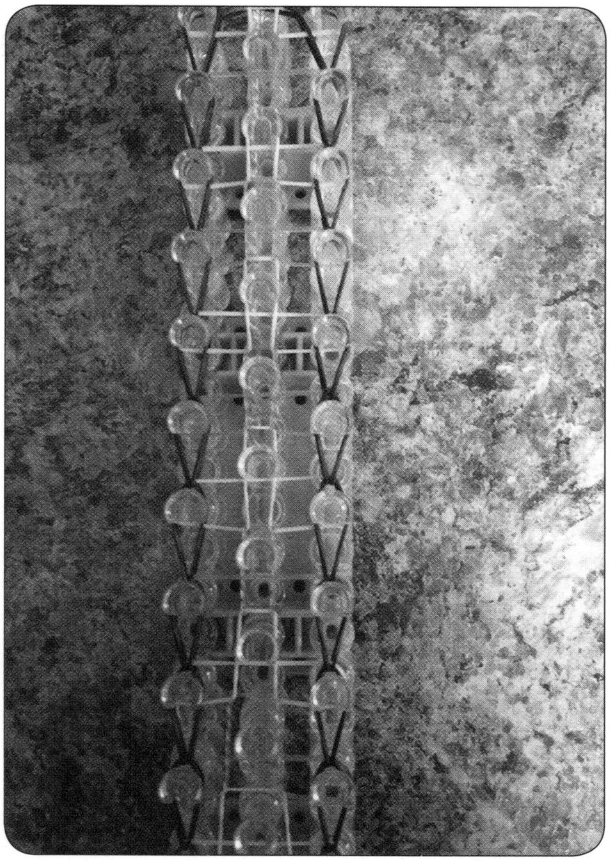

Step 7: Pulling Off

Once you've looped the last triangle you're almost ready to pull it off. Simply put your hook into the last pin and tilt it out to the side. Make sure that all the bands are on the hook. Then take an "A" colored band and hook it onto the end. While holding the other end of the band, pull the hook under and through the bands and connect the two ends of the "A" colored band onto the hook. Then just slide it up, onto the thickest part of the hook, and pull the bracelet off! Be careful while pulling and help it along with your fingers because if you pull too hard, a rubber band might break.

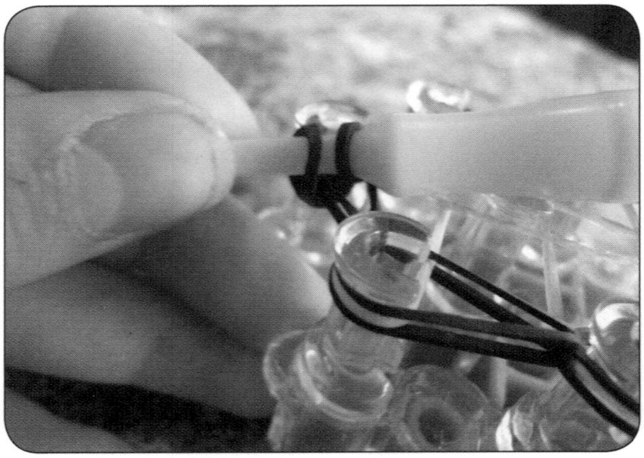

Step 8: Expanding

Once you have pulled the bracelet off, you will notice that there is a loose band—you can just cut that off. This bracelet is not big enough to fit a wrist yet, so we need to extend it. To extend it, have the red arrow pointing away from you and put down about five or six "A" colored bands in a single-chain pattern. Then locate your cap band on your bracelet and stretch it over the last band and the one behind it. Now you can do the single chain looping until the end. Once you get to the end, stretch that band onto the center pin. Now you can attach a C-clip to the outer band. Once this is all done, you can pull the extension off. To finish the bracelet , slide your two fingers into the band that is attached to the hook and pull the hook away, then simply attach the C-clip to the band in your fingers. You're finally done now!

Step 9: Wear and Enjoy!

Wear your bracelet on your wrist and enjoy!

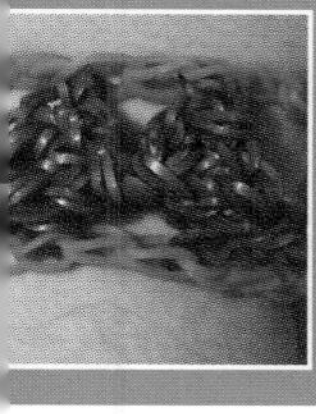

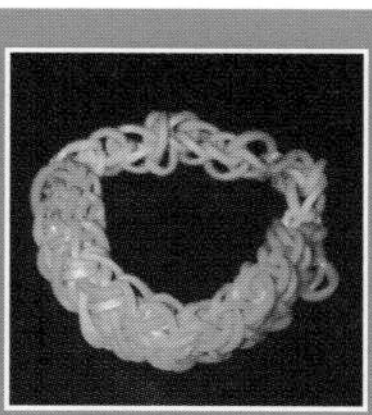
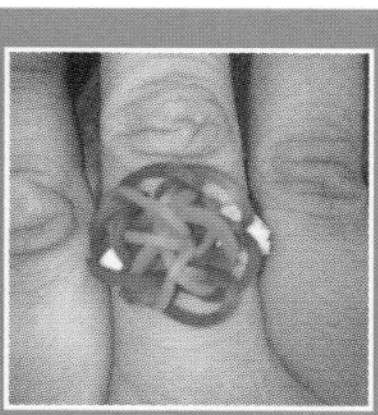

Fancy Jewelry

Mustache Bracelet

By Rose Winchester

(http://www.instructables.com/id/Large-Mustache-BraceletRainbow-Loom/)

I have a weird obsession with mustaches that I can't explain, so I decided to make a mustache bracelet! Enjoy!

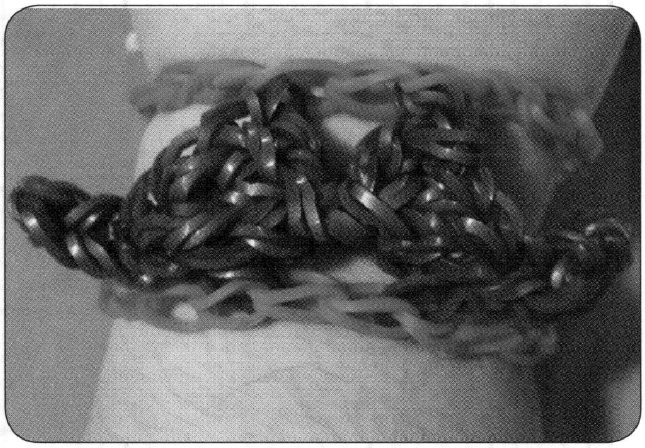

Step 1: Supplies

- Two colors of bands (one for the mustache, one for the bracelet bands around your wrist)
- Hooking tool
- Loom
- Two S-clips or two C-clips

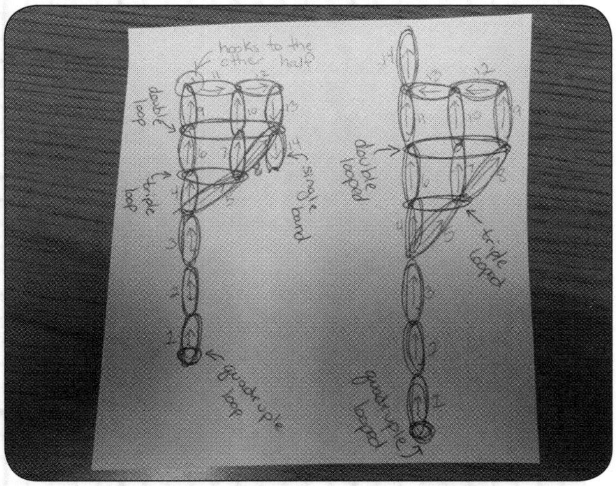

Step 2: Placing the Bands

To start, we make the first half of the mustache. We will be placing two bands between each peg to add stability and tension to the design. Please note the grid-style labeling for the pegs. In an attempt to avoid confusion, I will refer to pegs by these grid indicators (for example A1 is the peg in the top left corner of the picture). Stretch two bands between A3 and B3. Stretch two bands between B3 and B2. Stretch two bands between B2 and B1. This should form a backwards L pattern (see picture).

Stretch two bands between B1 and C1. Stretch two bands between B2 and C2. Stretch two bands between B3 and C3 (see picture). Stretch two bands diagonally between C1 and D2. Stretch two bands between C2 and D2 (see picture). Stretch two bands between C3 and D3. Stretch two bands diagonally between D2 and E3. Stretch two bands between D3 and E3. Stretch two bands between E3 and F3. Stretch two bands between F3 and G3. Stretch two bands between G3 and H3 (see picture). Take a single band and stretch it over C1, C2, and C3. Still holding the band, twist it and double it back over the same three pegs. This band should be wrapped twice over the pegs. Take another single band and wrap it three times over D2 and D3 in the same manner. Take a final single band and wrap it four times around H3 (see picture). You're now ready to hook. Follow the purple arrows in the pattern in the previous step (the pattern on the right side). Once you get to the end, slide your hook through the final two bands (four loops) on A3 and remove it from the loom. You now have one half of a wonderful mustache! (see picture)

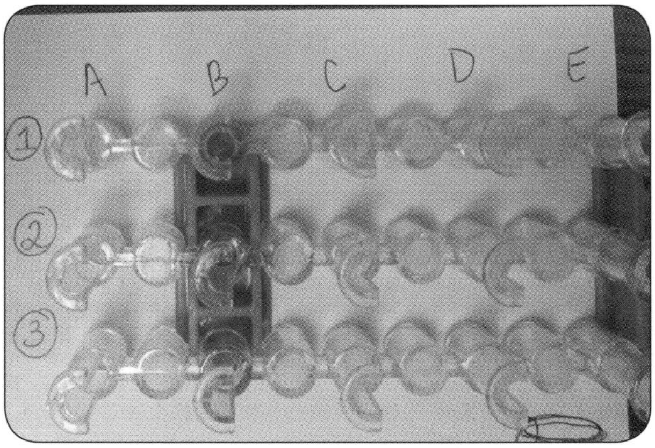

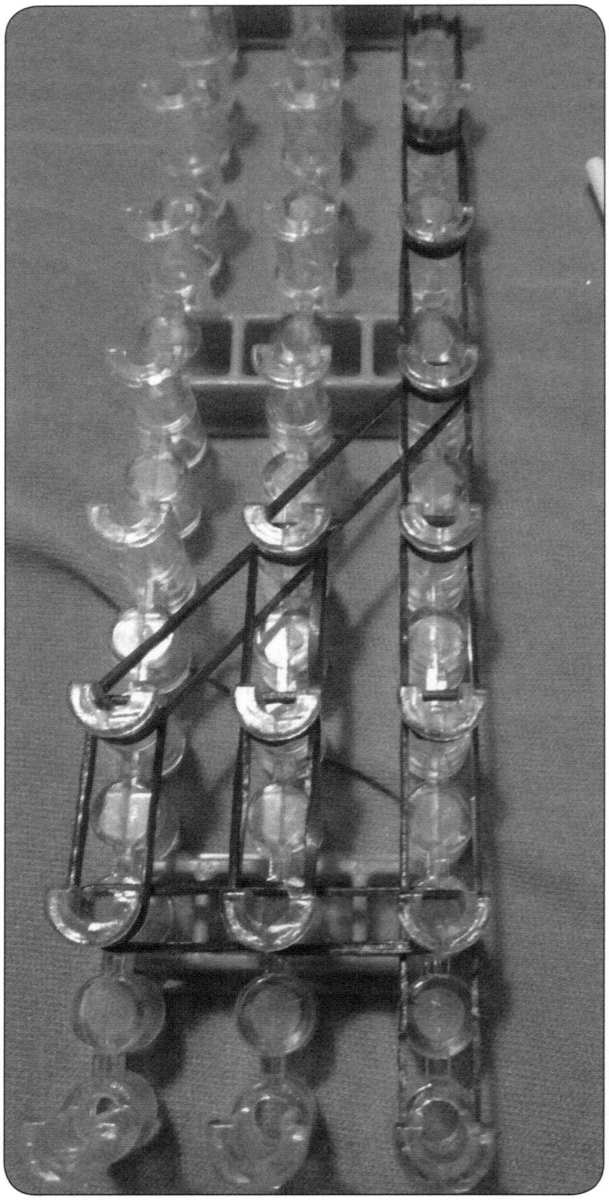

Step 3: More Bands

Now we'll work on the second half of your mustache. Place one band between D1 and C1. Place two bands between C1 and B1. Place two bands between B1 and A1. Stretch two bands between A1 and A2. Stretch two bands between A2 and A3 (see picture). Stretch two bands between A2 and B2. Stretch two bands between A3 and B3 (see picture). Stretch two bands diagonally between B1 and C2. Stretch two bands between B2 and C2. Stretch two bands between B3 and C3 (see picture). Stretch two bands diagonally between C2 and D3. Stretch two bands between C3 and D3. Stretch two bands between D3 and E3. Stretch two bands between E3 and F3. Stretch two bands between F3 and G3 (see picture). Stretch a single band over B1, B2, and B3, then twist it and stretch it over them again. You should have a single band looped twice over three pegs. Stretch a single band over C2 and C3 and loop it twice more. You should have a single band looped three times over two pegs. Loop a single band over G3 four times (see picture). Carefully slide the first half of your mustache off of your hooking tool and loop the ends over A3 (see picture). Follow the purple arrows in the original diagram (left side of the page) for hooking. Once you reach the last band (the single band stretched between B1 and C1), hook it from B1 to C1 and through itself. Once you remove the bands from the loom, you can pull on this loop and it should cinch tight over itself, leaving a loop sticking up from your mustache (see picture).

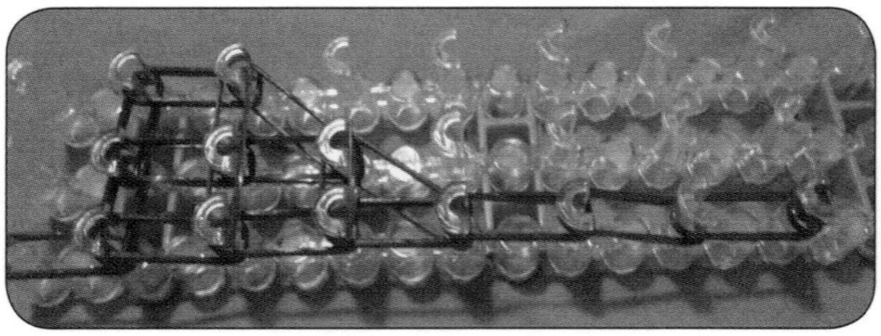

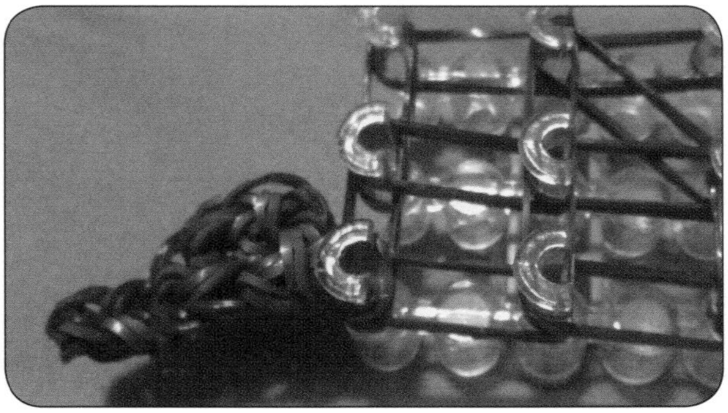

Step 4: The Rest of the Bracelet

Now that your mustache is done, we will make the rest of the bracelet, which will consist of two bands. One will attach to the top of the mustache in two places, and the other will attach to the bottom in two places. Make a single line of bands down the long edge of the loom in whatever color you want the band of your bracelet to be (see picture). Take the loop sticking out of the top of your mustache (the last one you cinched on itself) and carefully slide it out from underneath itself so that you have both ends of the band sticking out. Using your hook, weave another band through the other side of the top of the mustache, mirroring the first one. Slip these two loops over two pegs along your single chain of bands, leaving a peg between them (see picture). Hook the chain just like a single chain on the loom (see picture). If you need to, simply use your hook to add more bands until it is long enough to reach around your wrist. Secure with an S-clip. Do the same for the bottom of your mustache, linking the two bands through the lowest-most spots. Make another chain to whichever length you need and secure it with an S-clip (see picture).

Step 5: Done!

You're done! It's easy to adjust the size of the bracelet, should you need to. I hope you enjoy your mustache bracelet!

Turtle Bracelet

By craftmachine
(http://www.instructables.com/id/Turtle-Bracelet/)

This Turtle Shell bracelet is made on one Rainbow Loom and is very easy to make! Enjoy!

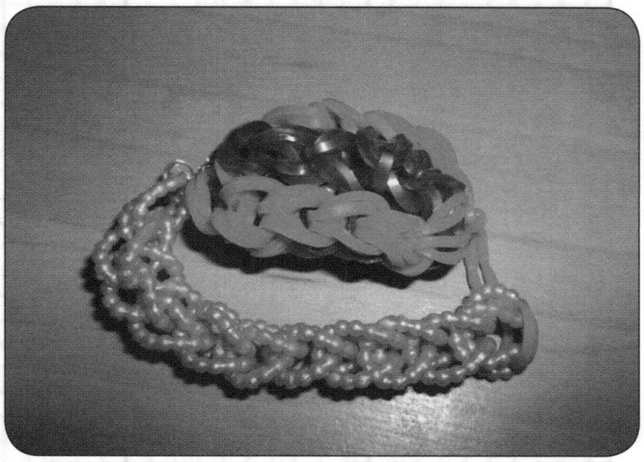

Step 1: Gather Supplies

- Rainbow Loom hook or any hook that works to loop rubber bands.
- Rainbow loom Several rubber bands of various colors
- C-clip or S-clip

Step 2: Placing the Bands

Start out by placing one rubber band (green) on the first two pegs vertically. Make sure that the arrow is pointing away from you. This is a single band, meaning that only one band is placed on the loom.

Step 3: Placing the Bands

This step requires two green rubber bands that are placed diagonally to the left from the first peg. It is important to place two bands instead of one to make the creation more sturdy.

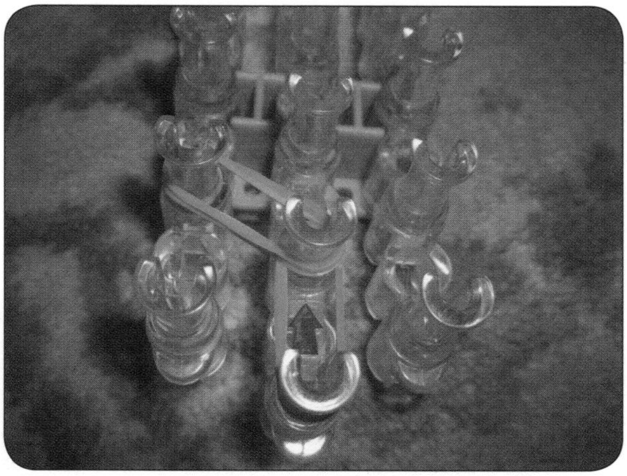

Step 4: Continue Placing the Bands

On the left-hand side of the loom (two bands at a time) place the bands for four rows. This will be how long the creation will be in the end.

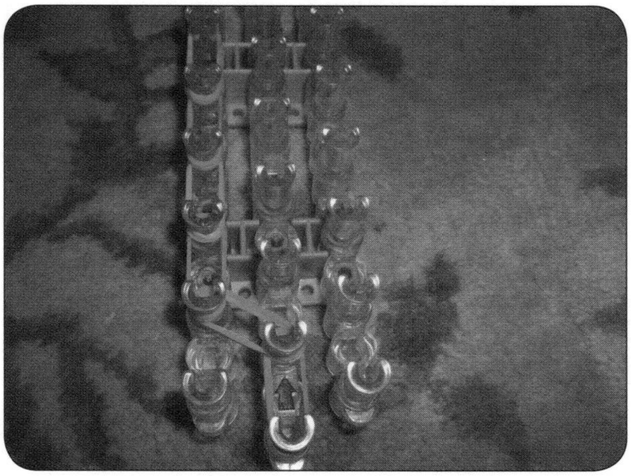

Step 5: Placing the Bands

At the fourth band place another band into the center diagonally. Remember to use two bands at a time. Repeat on the right side. Start at the beginning and not at the top where you placed your last diagonal band.

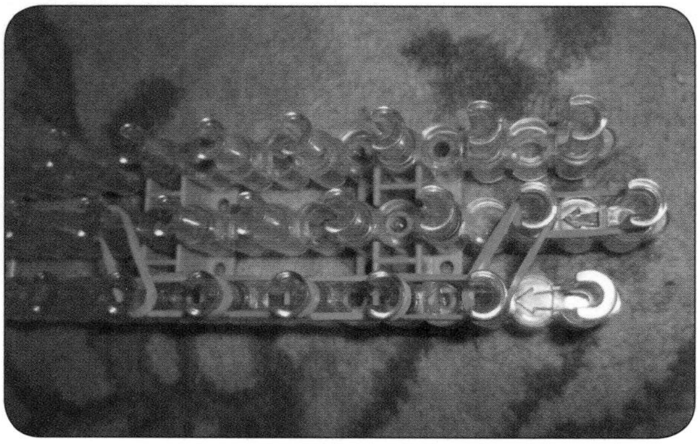

Step 6: Placing the Bands

Place the dark green bands from the center pin closest to the arrow. Again use two bands at a time and continue up the loom.

Step 7: Placing the Bands

Place only one band (not two at a time) horizontally in the center of the outline. You should complete this step three times.

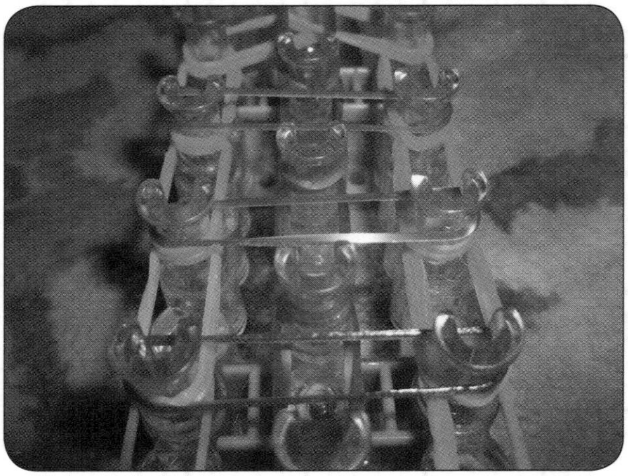

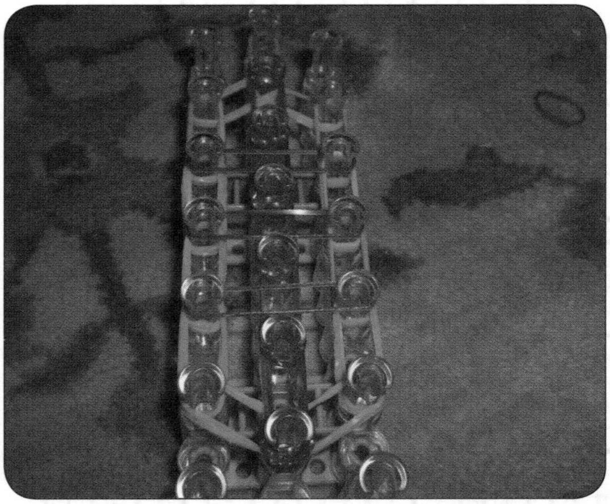

Step 8: Cap Bands

Put cap bands on each one of the middle pegs. This is important to make sure the shell does not fall apart. This done by making a figure eight on your finger and folding the band upon itself. Pull back the cap band with your hook and loop the first two dark green bands forward. Pull back the cap band each time and continue up the loom until the end.

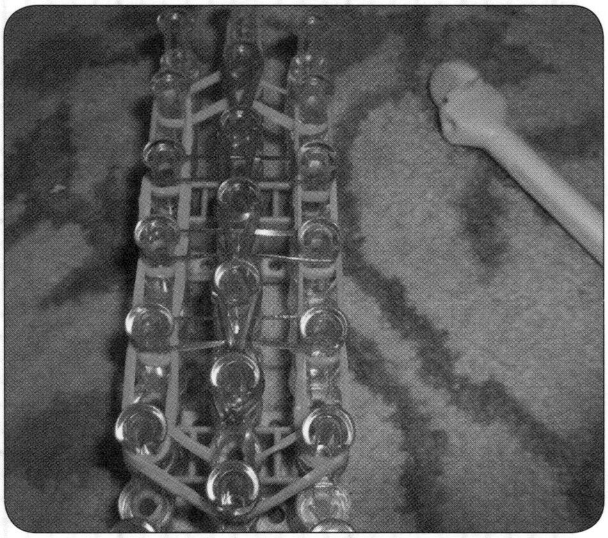

Step 9: Cap Bands

Pull the cap band back and bring the light green rubber bands to the left. Pull back that band and pull the bottom bands forward. This step is similar to in the center. On the last bands the rubber bands should be pulled diagonally to the opposite peg on the right side of the shell center.

Step 10: Finishing Up

Place your hook under all of the bands to hook the remaining band. Take those bands off the hook and take the outside band and pull it over the front band so a knot will be created.

Step 11: Pull Bands Off

Take the bands off the loom. Hopefully everything will be connected!

Step 12: Making the Bracelet Band

Depending how big or small your wrist is, the band length may vary. I used the total length of the loom to create mine. Start by placing the bands up the center of the loom. On the last peg where you would normally place your last rubber band, place the turtle.

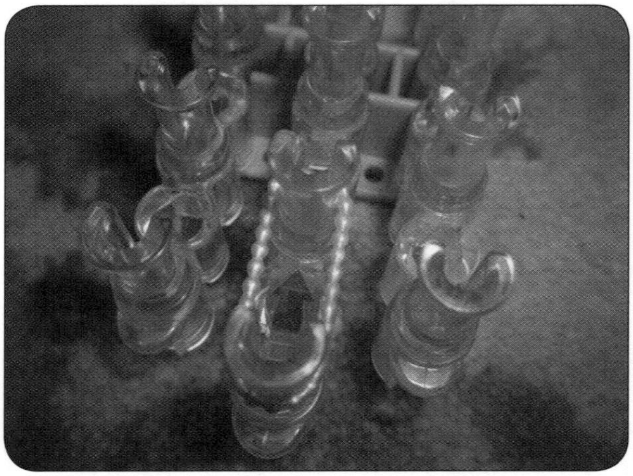

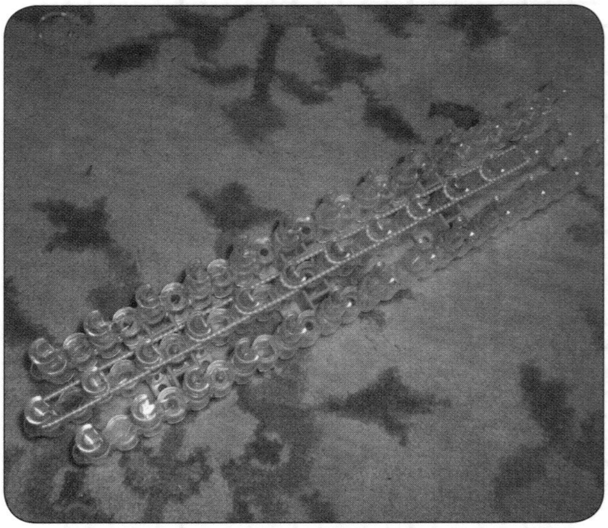

Step 13: Looping

Turn your loom over and start to loop forward. Complete until the last band. Take the bands off the loom. Place a C-clip or an S-clip on the end of the shell and connect it to the other side of the shell.

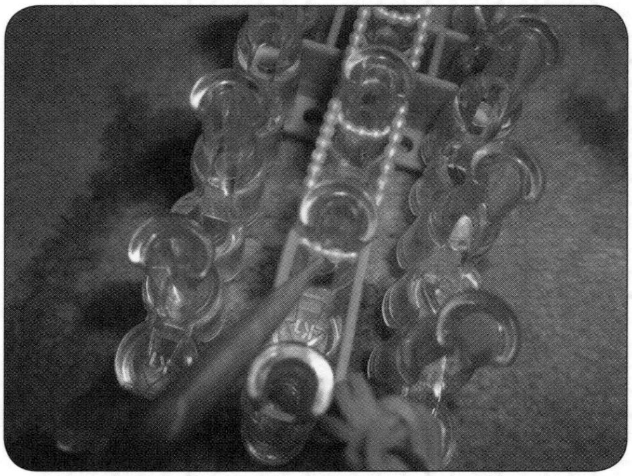

Q Bracelet

By aevans-mcbride

(http://www.instructables.com/id/Q-Bracelet/)

I don't really know what to call this design, so it's the "Q" for questionable. You can call it whatever you like!

Step 1: Materials:

- Rubber bands
- Loom
- Hook
- C-clip

Step 2: Layering the Bands

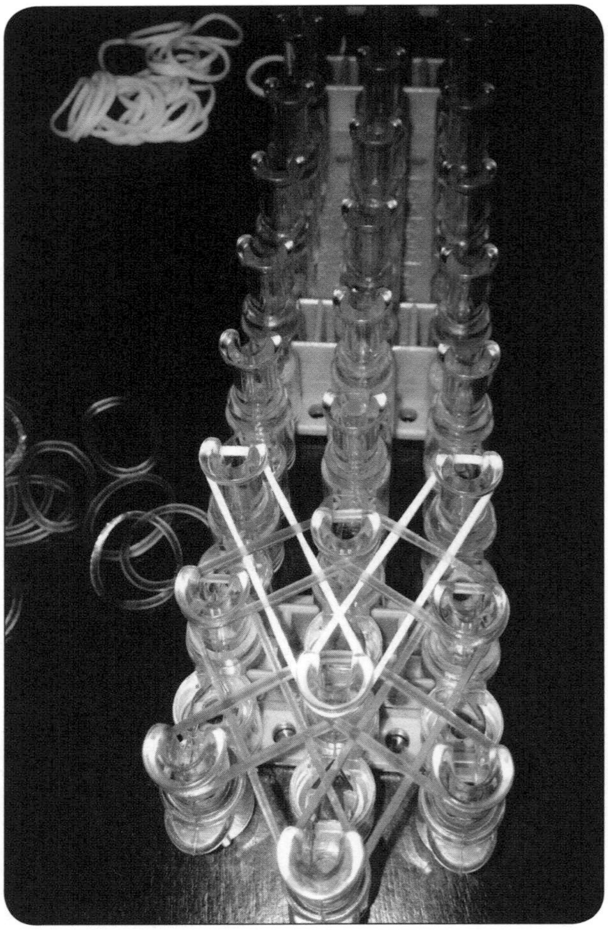

Step 3: Bands

Place the bands according to pictures.

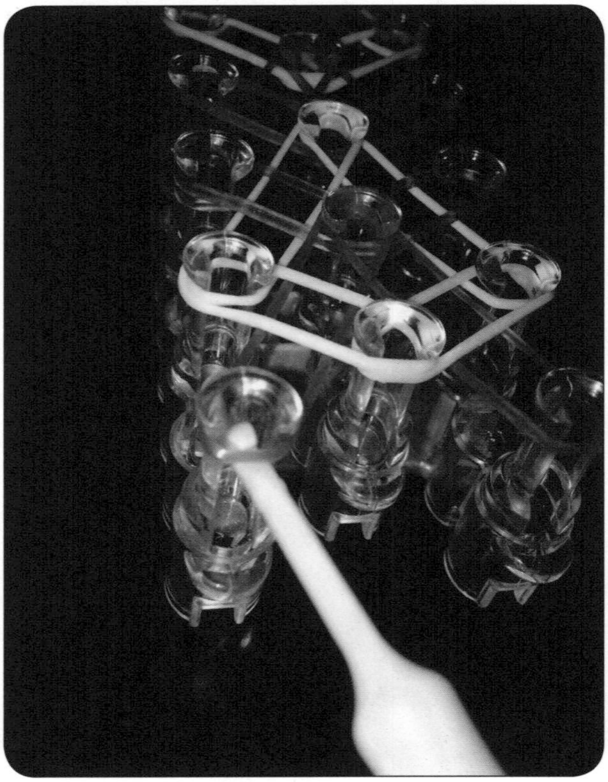

Step 4: First Chain

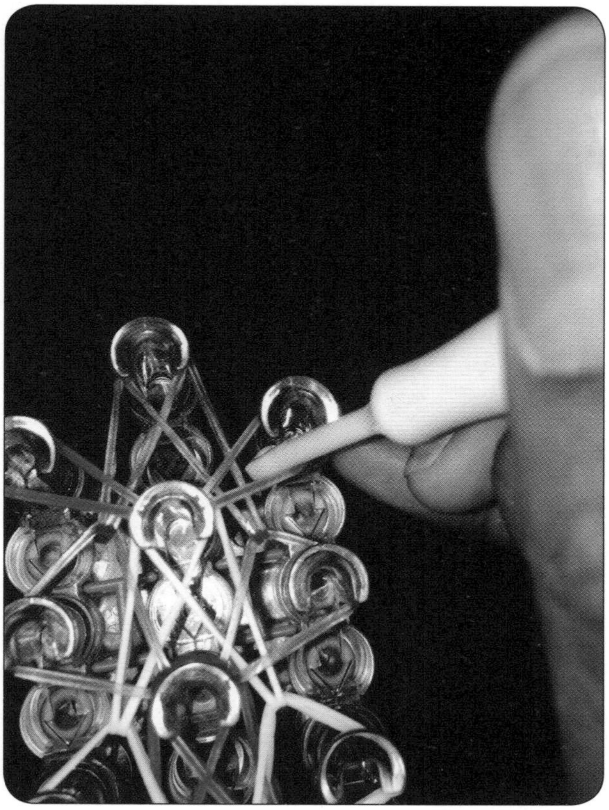

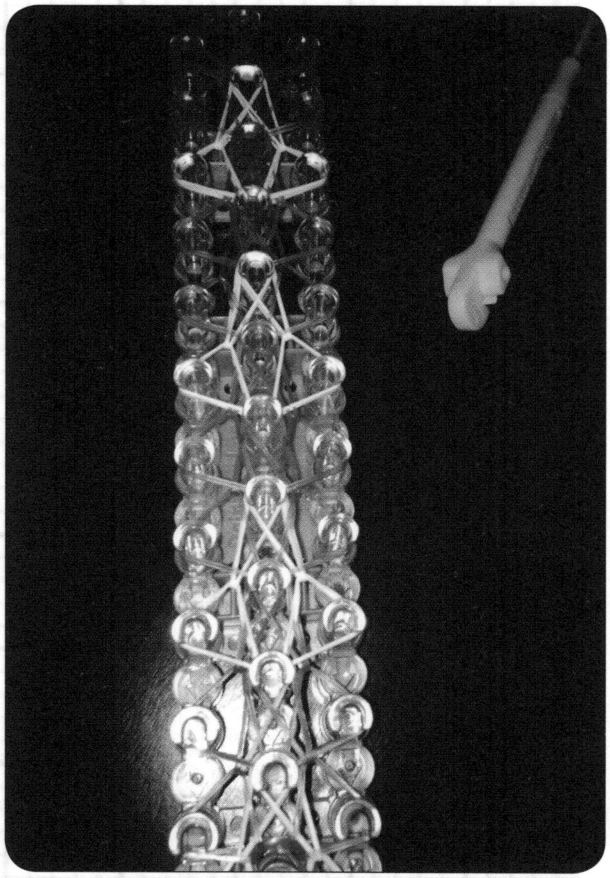

Step 5: Second Chain

Step 6: Finished Product

Flower Bracelet

By FrecklesMagee

(http://www.instructables.com/id/Flower-Rainbow-Loom-Bracelet/)

To keep up with the growing Rainbow Loom trend, I created a pattern that I just love! The Flower Rainbow Loom bracelet is cheerful, colorful, and customizable. Not to mention, pretty! This is not a pattern for beginner loomers. I would wait until you've at least made the single loom bracelet, which should be included in the instruction manual in your box! Now let's get this party started!

Step 1: Get Your Bands!

Let's get our stuff! For this bracelet, we're going to need:

- 25 green Rainbow Loom bands
- 25 yellow Rainbow Loom bands
- Rainbow Loom
- Rainbow Loom hook
- S-clip

Step 2: Shall We Begin?

Okay! Now, find the end of your loom and diagonally place one green band, as shown in the photo.

Step 3: And Again!

Take another green band and create the V shown in the photo. Continue with this pattern until you reach the other end!

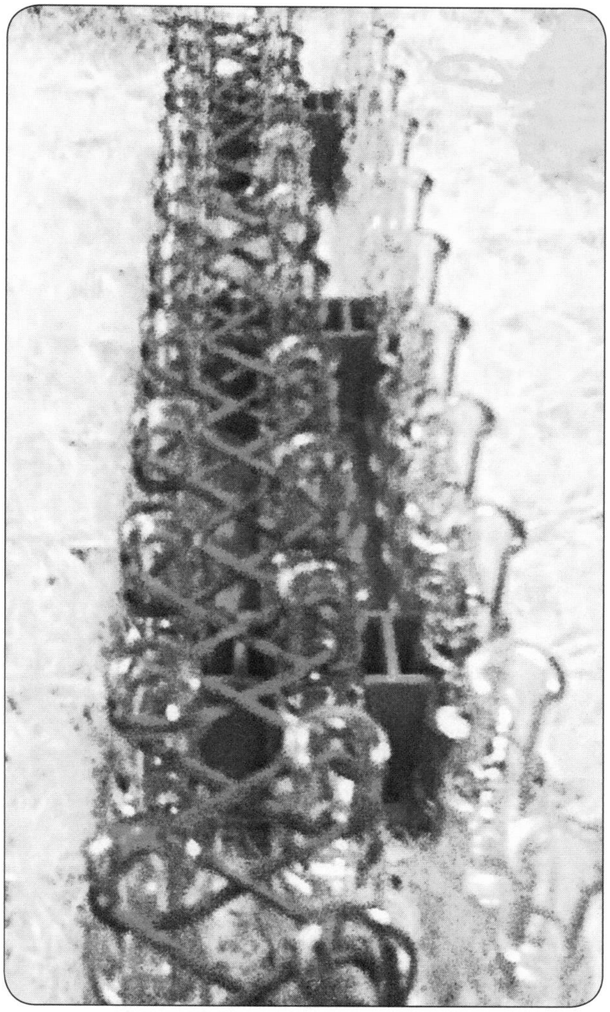

Step 4: Yellow!

Taking the yellow bands, create the same V, across from the green, forming an X. Continue with this until you reach the end. Lots of letters and numbers when it comes to looming!

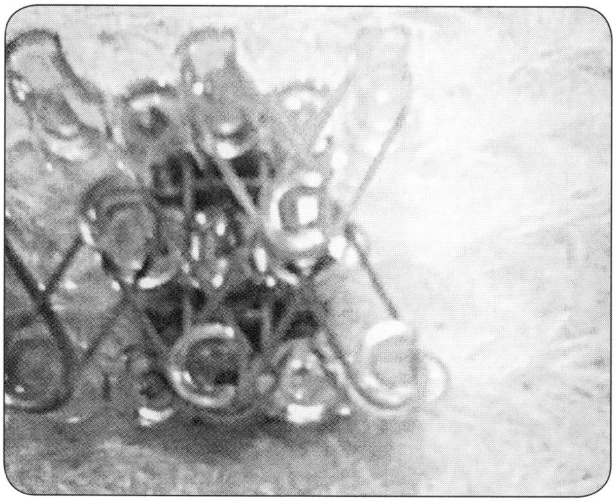

Step 5: "Band" Together!

At the end of the loom, take your looming hook and place it under the second green band, pulling it over the other ones, and place it over the second yellow band. Continue this pattern until you reach the other side.

Step 6: Almost Done!

Now, like a true loomer, form a slip knot twice at one end of the flower bracelet and slip it into an S-clip. Carefully peel the bracelet off of the loom. Two bands will fall off—no big deal! Connect the other side with the clip and you're almost ready!

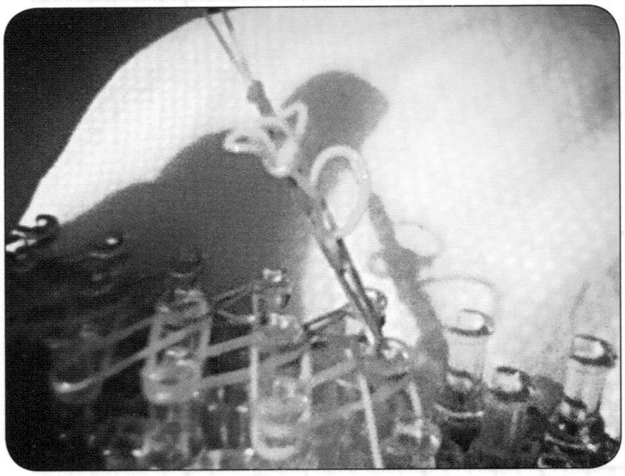

Step 7: How Beautiful!

Now admire your bright and beautiful flower bracelet! Slip it around your wrist and wear it all the time! This bracelet is both unique and trendy; it fits in and stands out! Enjoy!

Flower Ring

By jsowinski1
(http://www.instructables.com/id/Rainbow-Loom-Flower-Ring/)

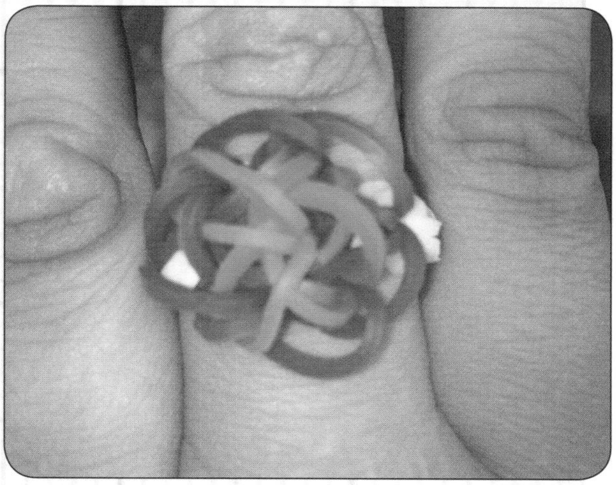

Step 1: What You Need

- Rubber bands in colors of your choice
- Rainbow Loom kit or other rubber band loom

Step 2: Add Bands

Add two rubber bands to the loom to begin the ring.

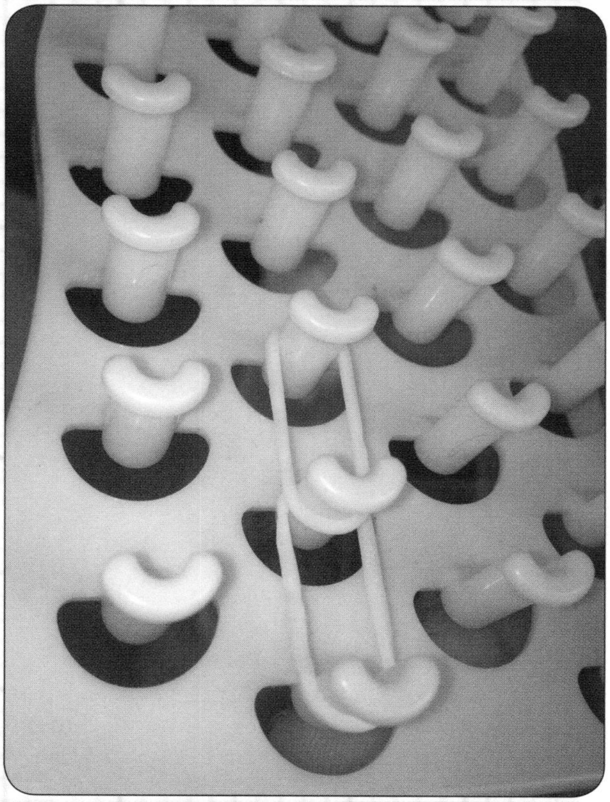

Step 3: Add Bands

Place the first two loops that begin the flower, first the left and then the right one.

Step 4: Add Bands

Place the next two bands, starting with the right and then the left one.

Step 5: Add Bands

Place the next two bands on the loom—order is not important here. Continue adding bands as shown in the picture.

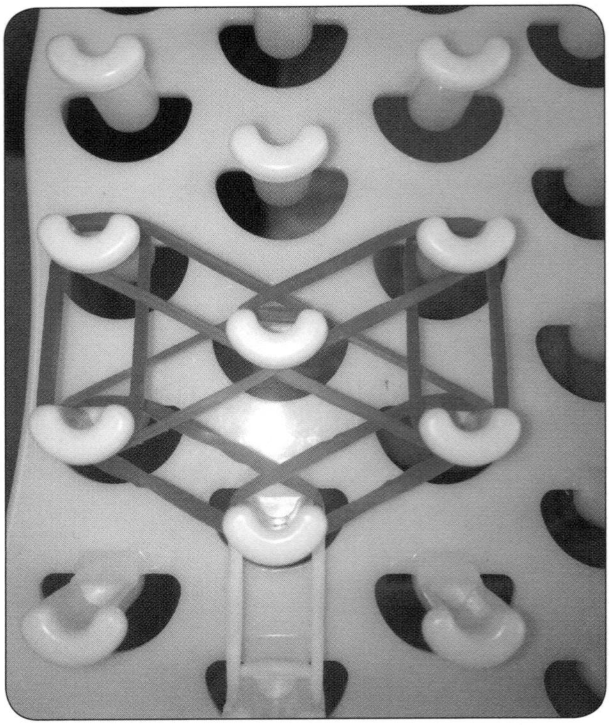

Step 6: Add Bands

Place the next two bands—right and then left. Then add three single bands to the end. This will form the rest of the ring portion that will go around your finger.

Step 7: Looping

Working from the end with the three single bands on the bottom, loop the second and third ones upward.

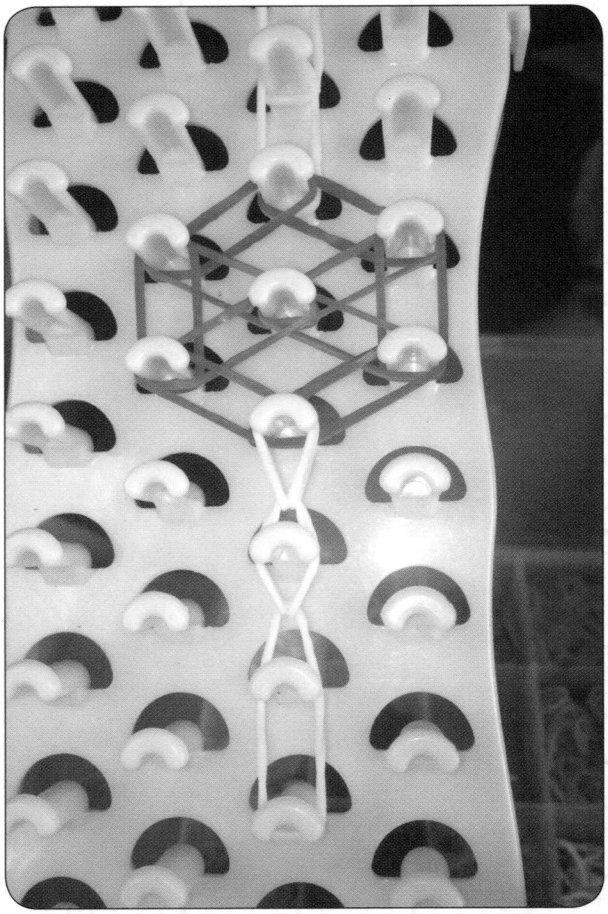

Step 8: Looping the Flower

Now you can start looping the flower portion. Make sure the two single loops are on the bottom when you start this. Loop the one to the left first and then the one to the right.

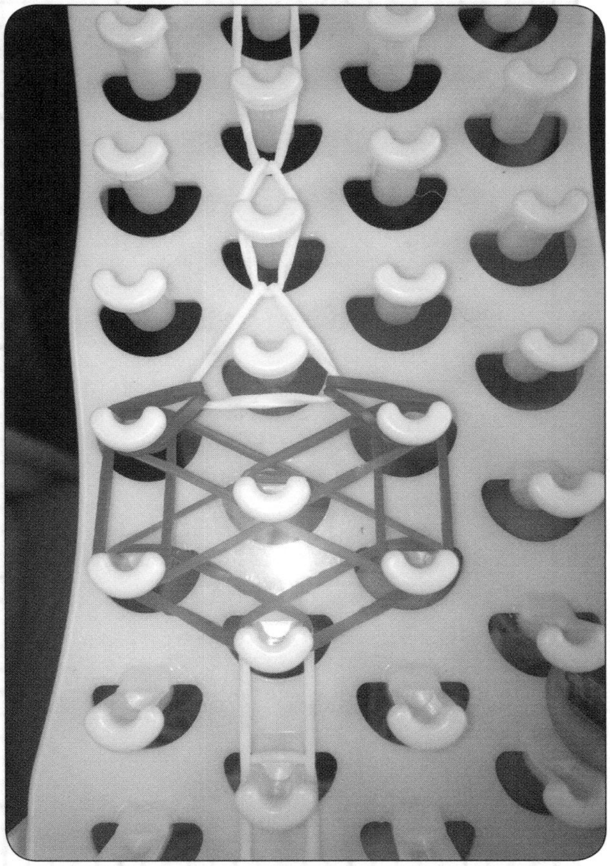

Step 9: Looping

Loop the two inner bands on the top, first looping in from the left to the right, and then right to left.

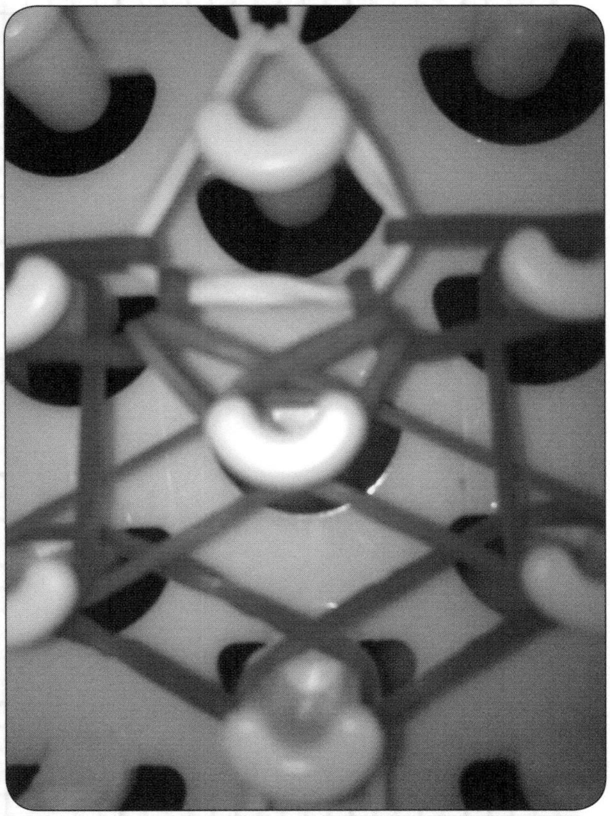

Step 10: Looping

Now loop the side bands downward; order is not important here.

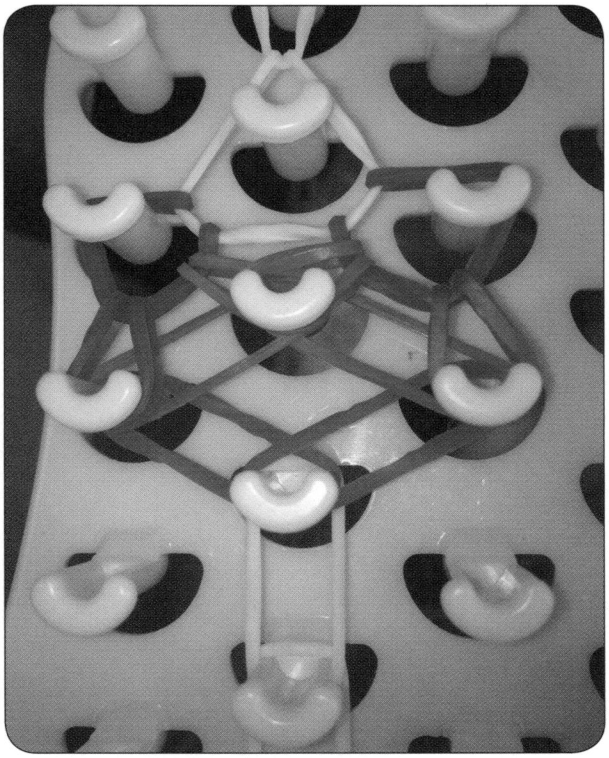

Step 11: Looping

Looping the inner bands on the bottom is a little different. Working from the middle pin, loop the one toward the left first, and then toward the right.

Step 12: Looping

Loop the two bottom bands—left inwards and then right inwards.

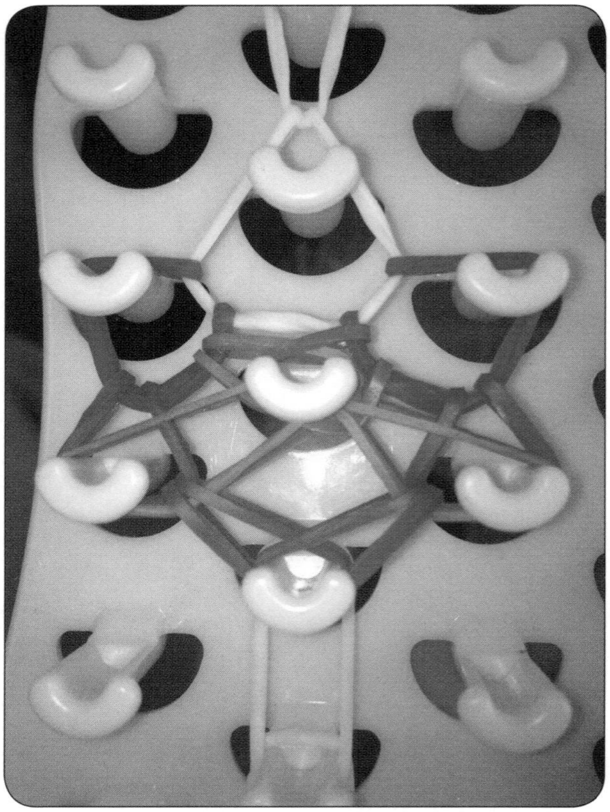

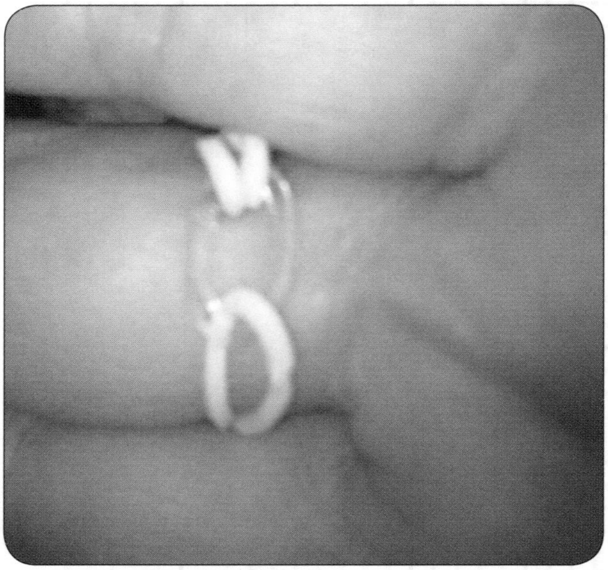

Step 13: Finish Looping

I forgot to take a picture of this step, but remember to loop the last two single bands that will complete the ring for your finger. Attach a clip to this end BEFORE taking the ring off the loom. This will prevent it from falling apart when you remove it. Attach the other end to the clip and you have your finished product!

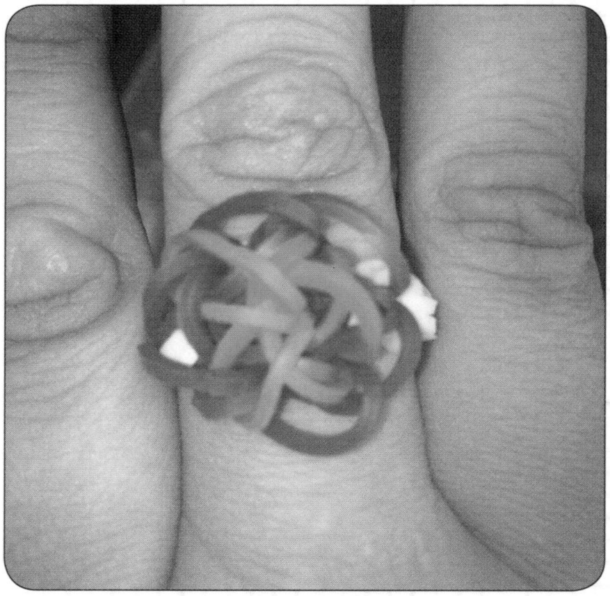

Olympic Bracelet

By mclare50

(http://www.instructables.com/id/Olympic-Rings-Rainbow-Loom-Tutorial/)

Here is my Olympic ring Rainbow Loom bracelet tutorial. I wanted to do something to get ready for the Winter Olympics, and the Olympic ring bracelet was born! This is a spin on the zigzag pattern, so if you know how to do that then you will be able to do this for sure. This is an intermediate-level bracelet.

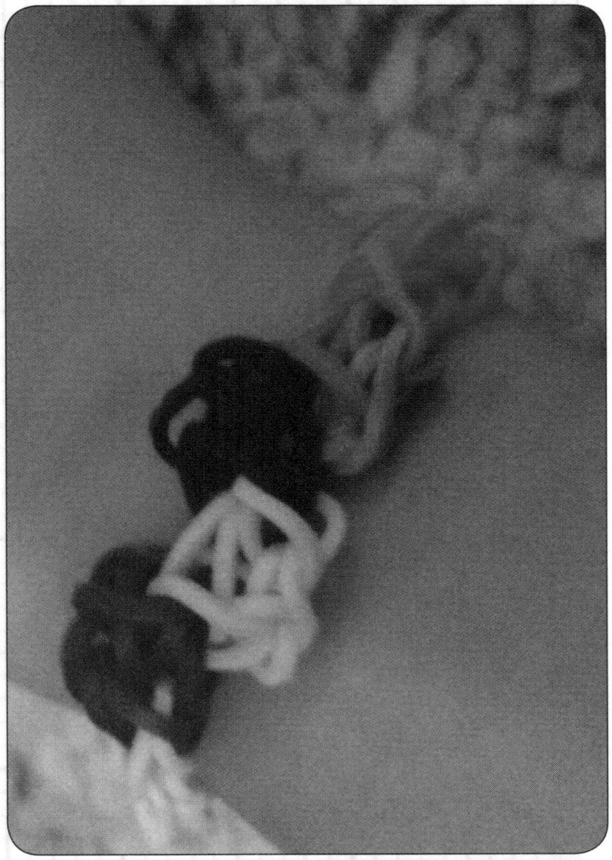

Step 1: Supplies

- Blue, yellow, black, green, red, and white bands
- One Rainbow Loom
- Hook
- Clip

Step 2: Placing the Bands

First, set up your loom in the rectangular configuration. Place a white band from the right row into middle, then place a navy band next to it. Then take another navy band and go up from the first navy band's beginning. Take another navy band and put that opposite of the last blue band you put down, and take one more band and put it on top.

Step 3: Placing the Bands

You will place the yellow bands on the opposite side of the navy bands. First go forward, then sideways to the right, then up, then across. Do this for the rest of the loom, switching sides in this order—navy, yellow, black, green, red.

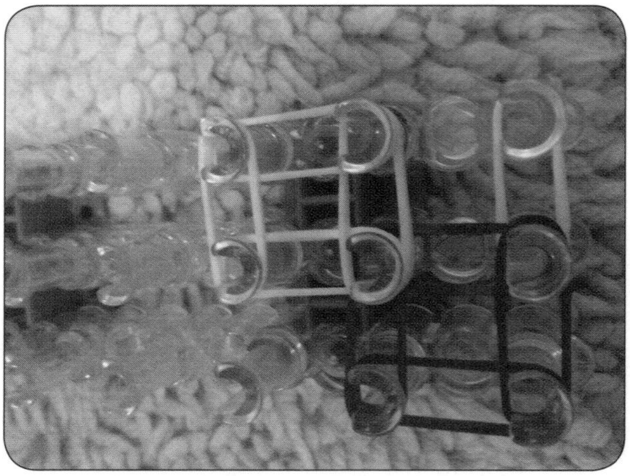

Step 4: A Visual

The loom should look like this photo when you are done:

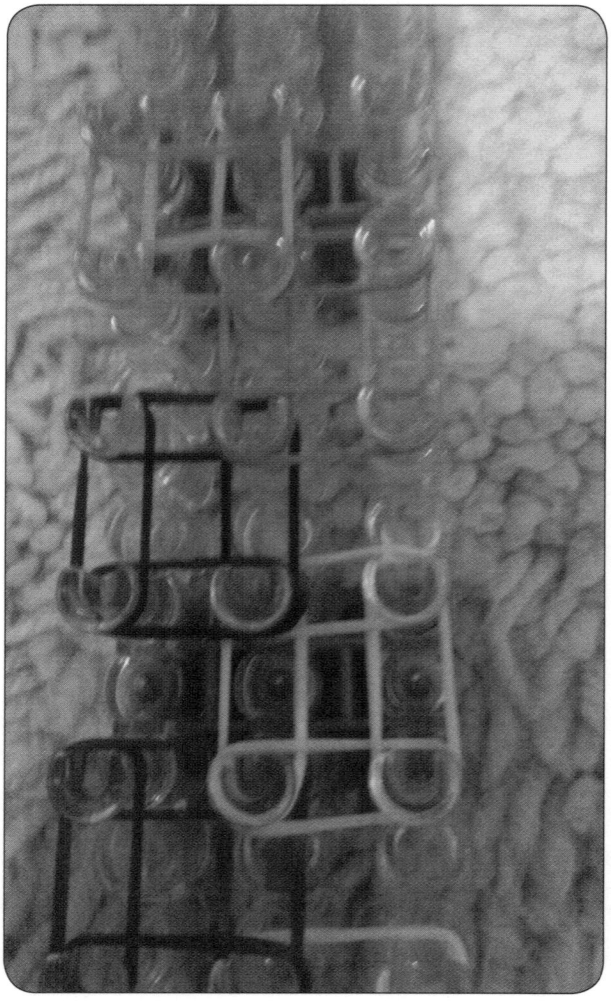

Step 5: Cap Band

Place a cap band on the last left band of the red ring.

Step 6: Looping the Bands

To start looping, flip your loom over so that the arrows are facing you. Take the first red band and loop it to the left. Go back to that first pin and take the band under the cap band and bring that forward. Go back to the pin on the left and bring the bottom band forward, then bring the band under that to the side.

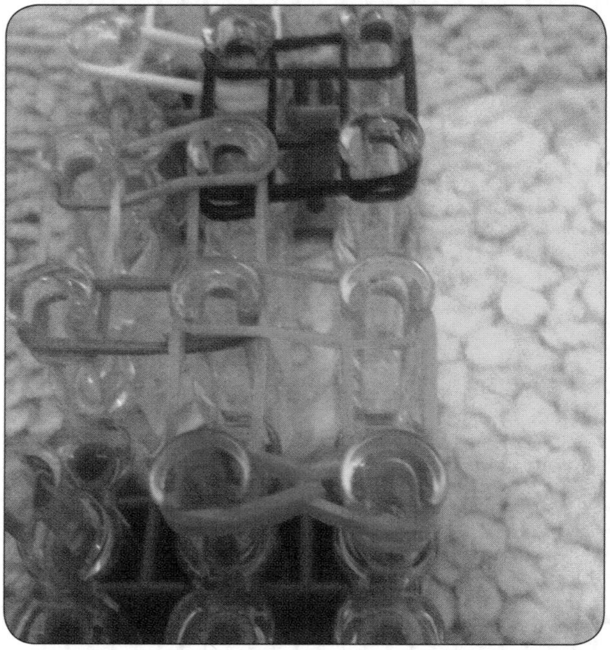

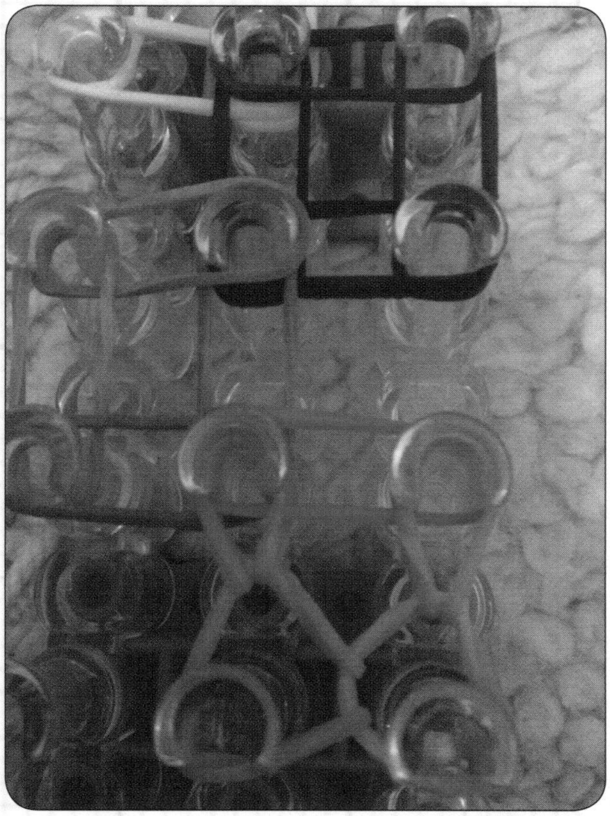

Step 7: Looping the Bands

Doing the bands on the left side is a bit different. Take the first green band and bring it to the left. Go back to the pin that band came from and bring that band forward. Go to the leftmost band and bring that forward, and bring the band next to it sideways. Do this, switching sides until the end of the loom.

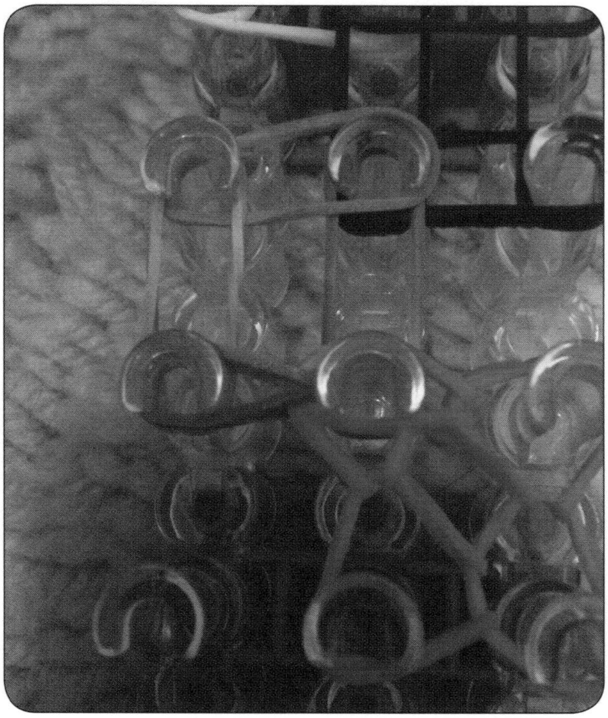

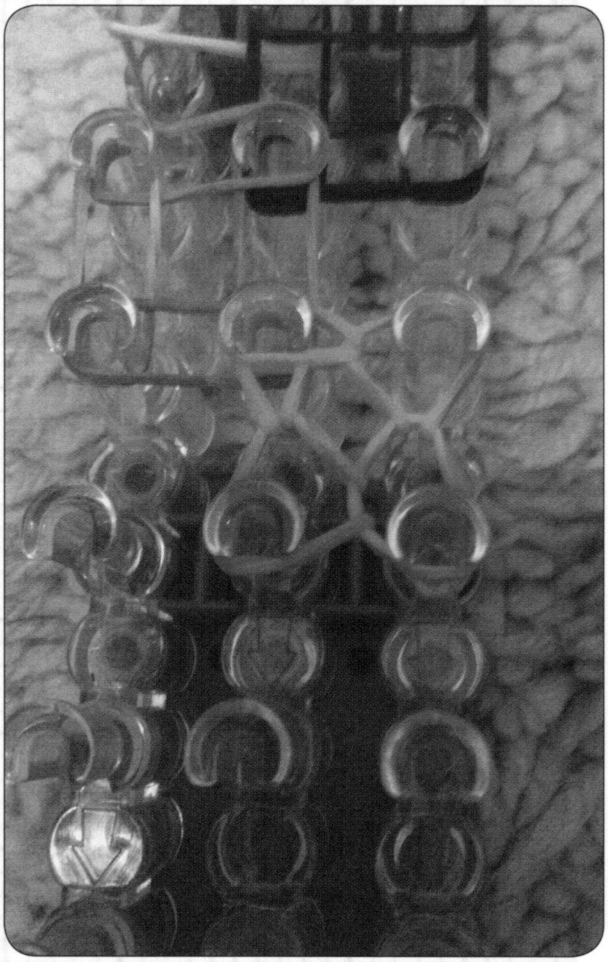

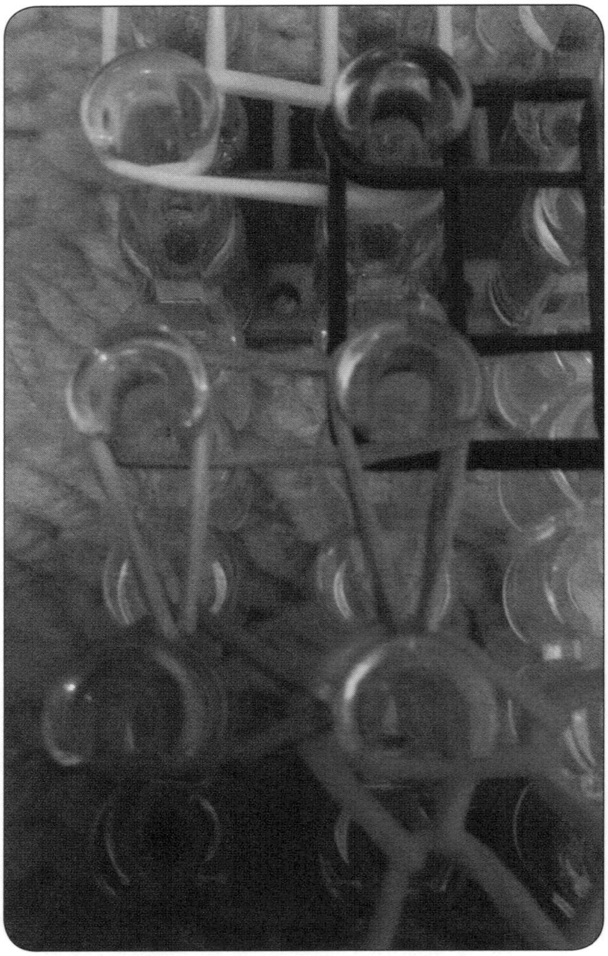

Step 8: White Band

When you have finished, there should be a white band at the end—bring that to the left.

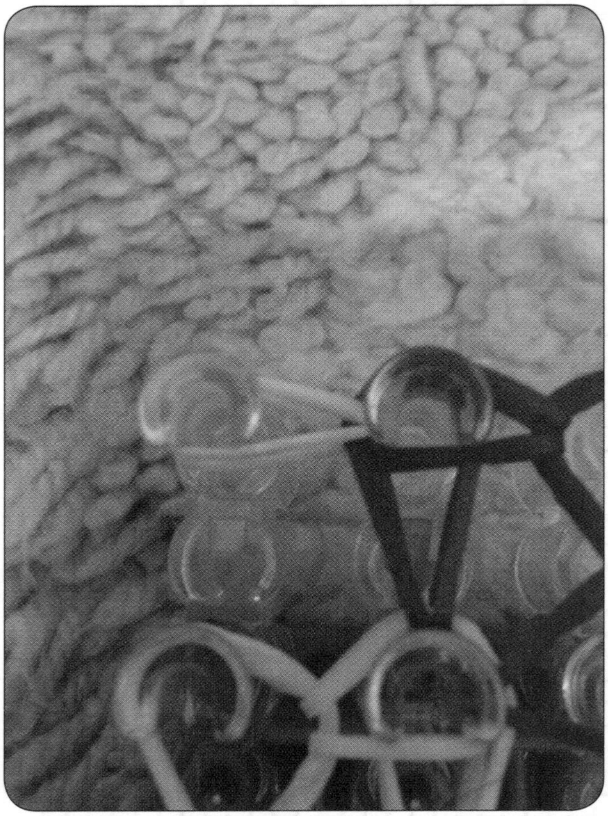

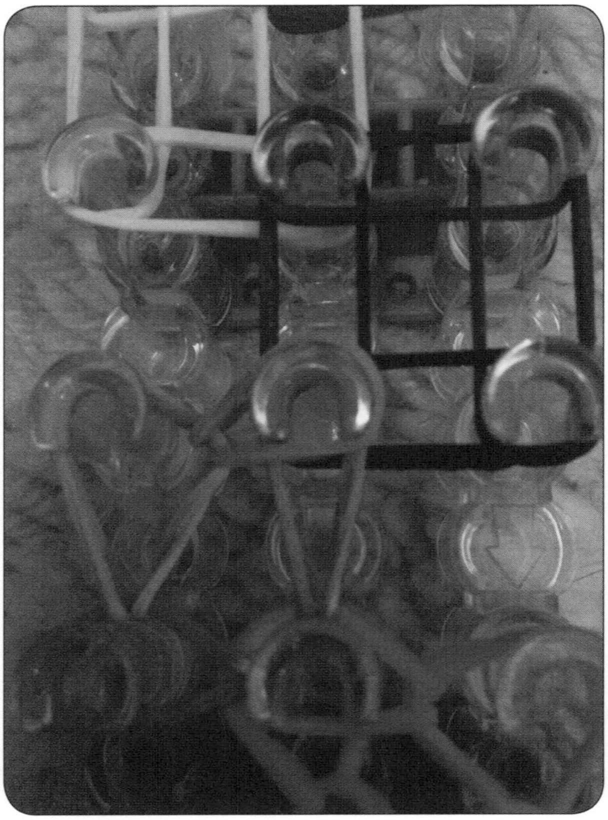

Step 9: Extension

Go under that white band and make an extension of about 5–7 bands and place a clip.

Step 10: Hook

Go to the red cap band and place your hook under and do the same thing—make an extension of 5–7 bands. When you have finished, pull off the loom and attach to the clip.

Step 11: All Done!

You're done with your Olympic ring bracelet!

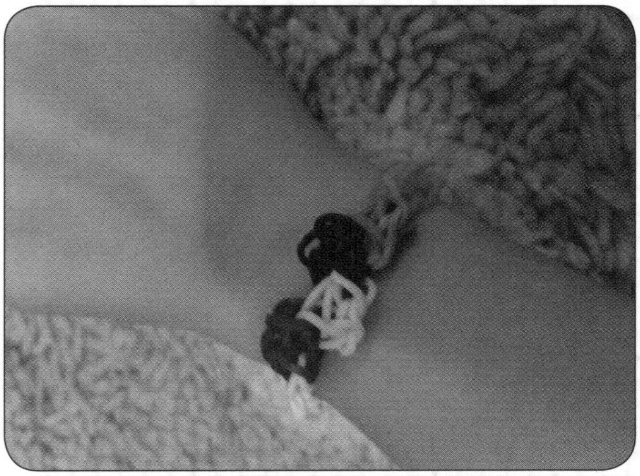

Rainbow Caterpillar Bracelet

By kellechu

(http://www.instructables.com/id/Rainbow-Loom-Caterpillar-Bracelets/)

These last few evenings, I decided to reverse engineer a bracelet I saw my daughter wearing. It looked like a cute caterpillar wrapping itself around her wrist. I loved the cute simplicity of the neon green caterpillar on the solid black bracelet, but wouldn't it be neat, I thought, if I could make a caterpillar that resembled the monarch caterpillar in nature? And then on the other end of the spectrum, what about creating the fictitious "Very Hungry Caterpillar" with all his foodie charms hanging off the bracelet as well!

Step 1: Choose Your Caterpillar and Bracelet Colors

I found a loom bracelet design on the Internet called the "Single Rhombus." This is the basis of the caterpillar bracelet. It is considered an easy pattern by the band-looming community. It took some trial and error to figure out which part of the design became the caterpillar's body and head and which became the bracelet, so I created a couple of layouts to show how to arrange your colors on the loom if you want to create a neon green caterpillar, or a monarch caterpillar, or even the "Very Hungry Caterpillar" (V.H.C. for short). Feel free to choose different caterpillar designs/colors than those in my examples. They are just for you to see which part of the loom becomes which part of the bracelet. For this tutorial, I will be using the V.H.C. color scheme to lead you through the example bracelet.

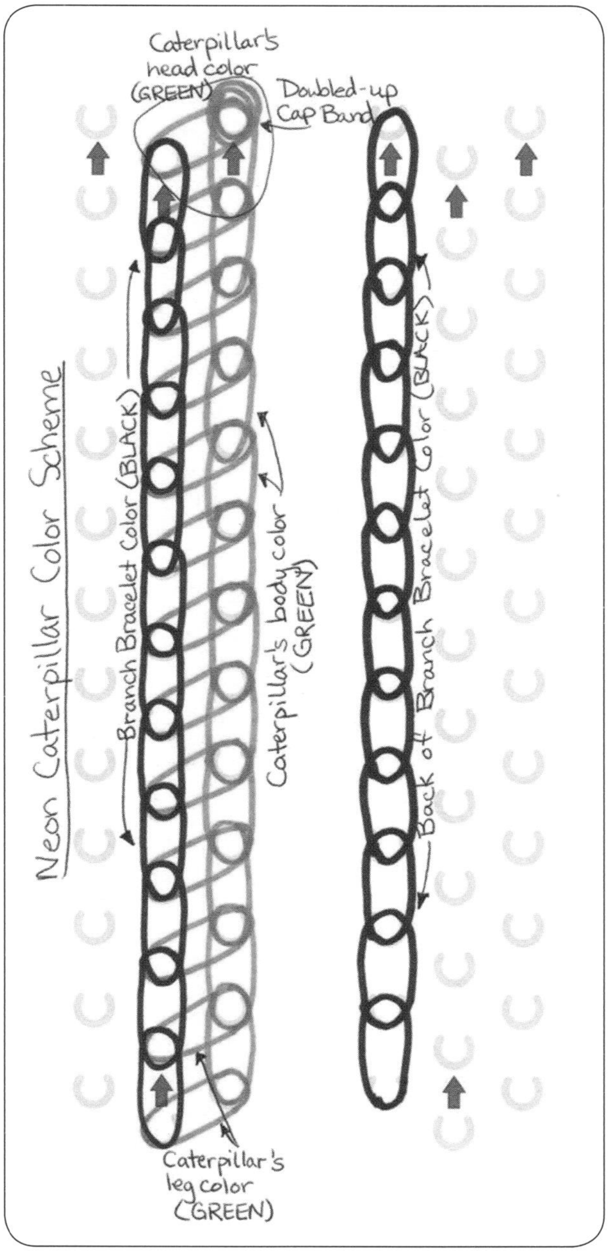

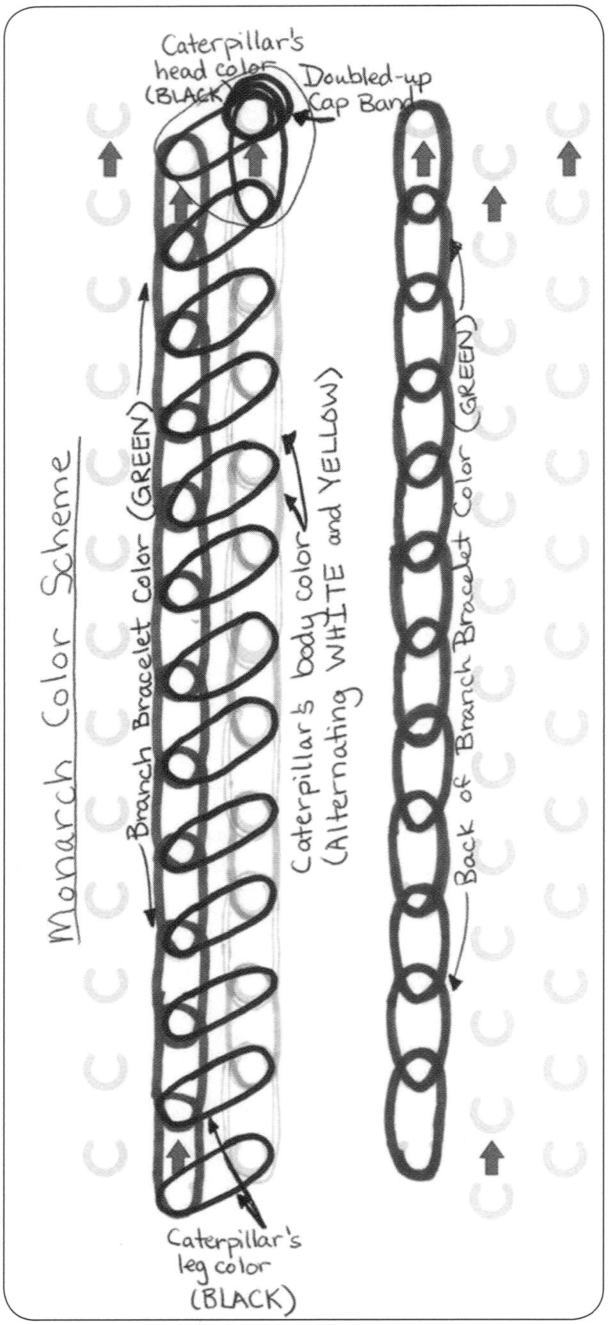
Caterpillar's head color (BLACK)
Doubled-up Cap Band
Monarch Color Scheme
Branch Bracelet Color (GREEN)
Caterpillar's body color (Alternating WHITE and YELLOW)
Back of Branch Bracelet Color (GREEN)
Caterpillar's leg color (BLACK)

V.H.C's head color (RED)
Doubled-up Cap Band
"V.H.C." Color Scheme
Branch Bracelet Color (WHITE)
V.H.C.'s body color (Alternating light and dark GREENS)
Back of Branch Bracelet Color (WHITE)
V.H.C's leg color (TEAL)

Step 2: Placing Rubber Bands on the Loom

Hopefully by using my pictures, you can see how to place the bands on the loom in the correct order. With the loom arrows pointing away from you, place your bands in a simple left to right diagonal, left vertical, right vertical repeating pattern that makes up the Single Rhombus bracelet design. The branch side of the bracelet is on the left vertical column, the caterpillar's body markings are on the right vertical column, and the caterpillar's feet are the diagonals that connect the two vertical columns. The caterpillar's head is made up of the last bands placed on the loom (the last right vertical band, the last diagonal band, and a doubled-up cap band. This doubled-up cap band is a single band twisted in the middle and folded back on itself to form two loops that go on top of the last peg. This cap band will ultimately turn into your caterpillar's antennae, so keep its color in mind if you want your caterpillar to have a different colored antennae than its head color.

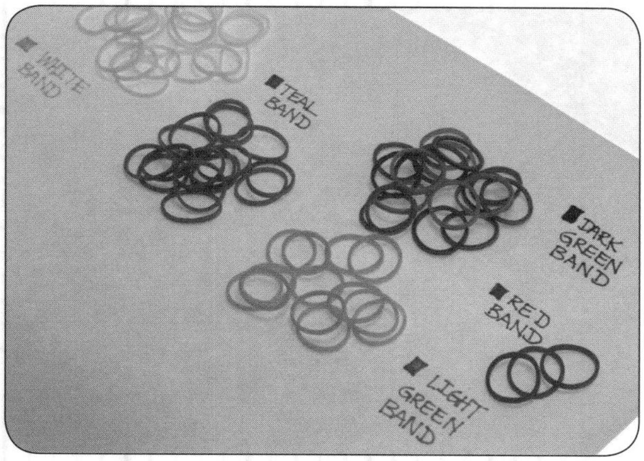

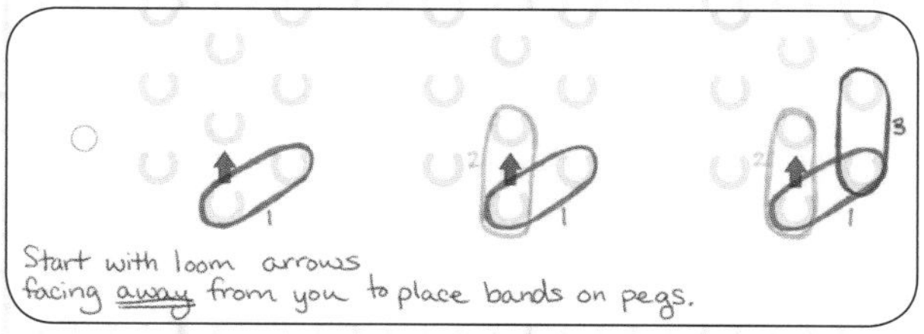

Start with loom arrows facing away from you to place bands on pegs.

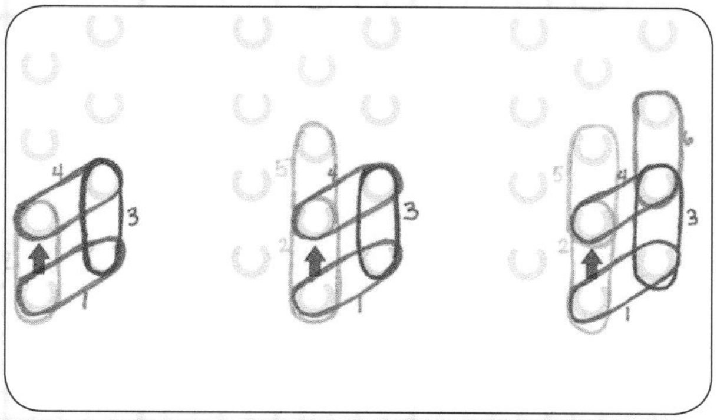

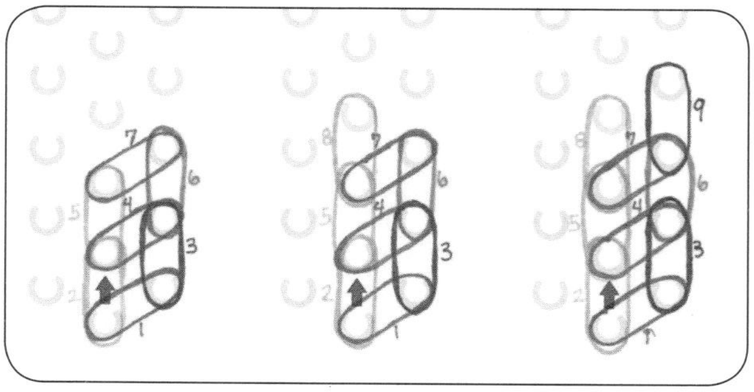

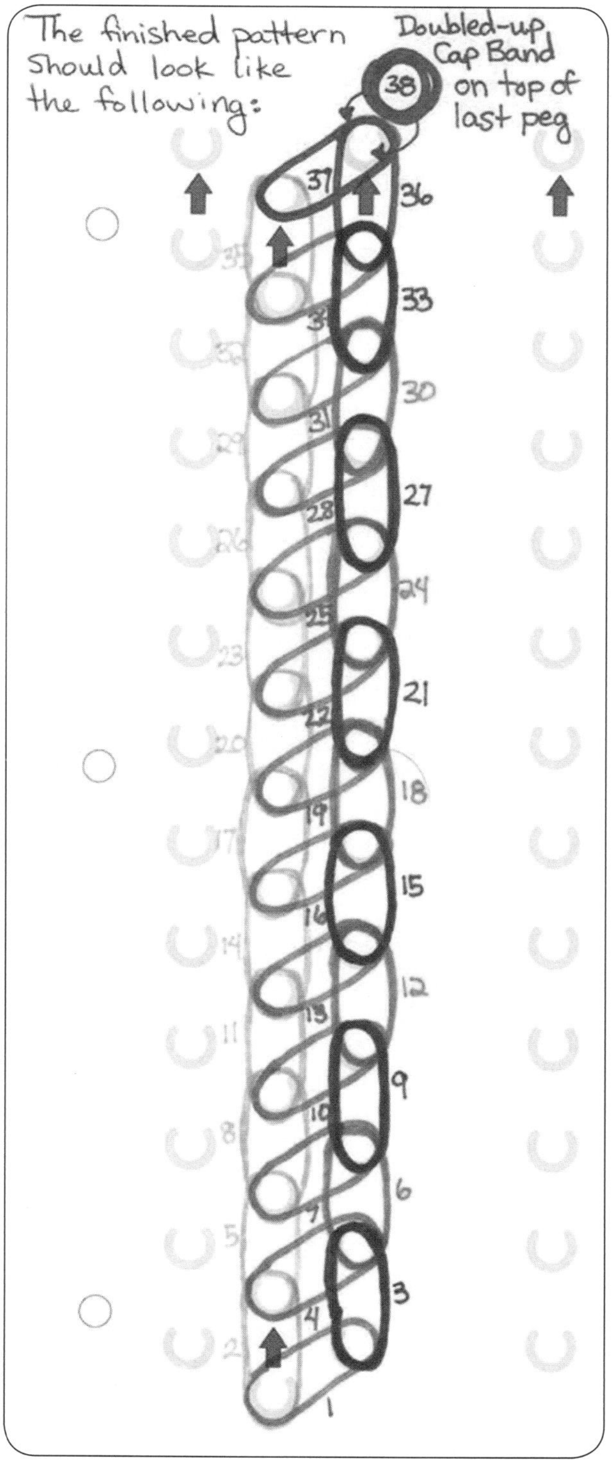

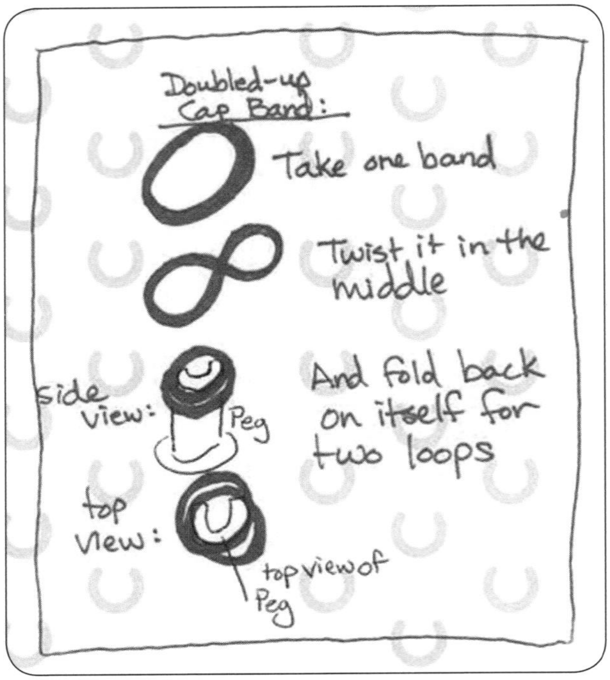

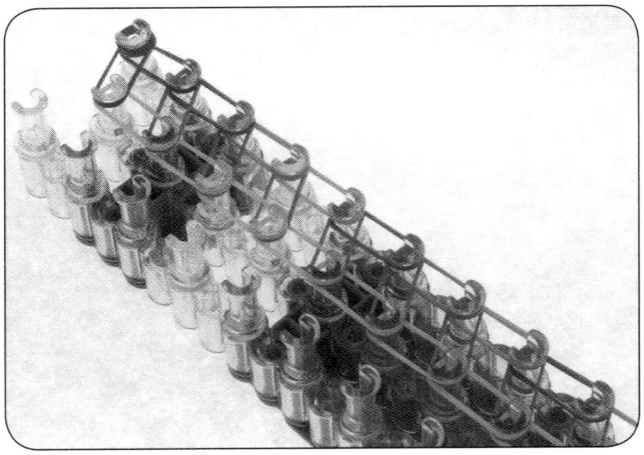

Step 3: Looping Bands Back onto Their Original Pegs

Flip the loom over so the arrows are now facing towards you. Holding down the last band you placed (the red, doubled-up cap band), pull the diagonal red band from under it and out and place it back on its original peg. Now pull the other red band, the vertical one on the left-side peg, out from under the red cap bands and place it back on its original peg. Pull the white vertical band from the right-side peg, out from under the red bands and place it back on its original peg. Repeat this pattern of pulling up first the diagonal band out and placing back on its original peg, then the left vertical band up and out and back on its original peg, and then the right vertical band up and out and back on its original peg, until you make your way to the end of the loom where your first bands were placed.

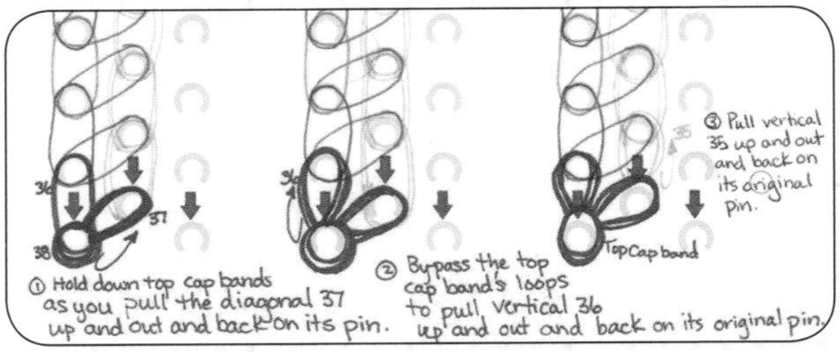

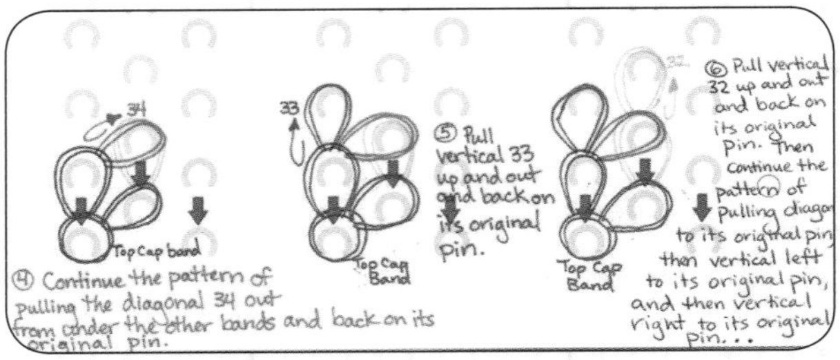

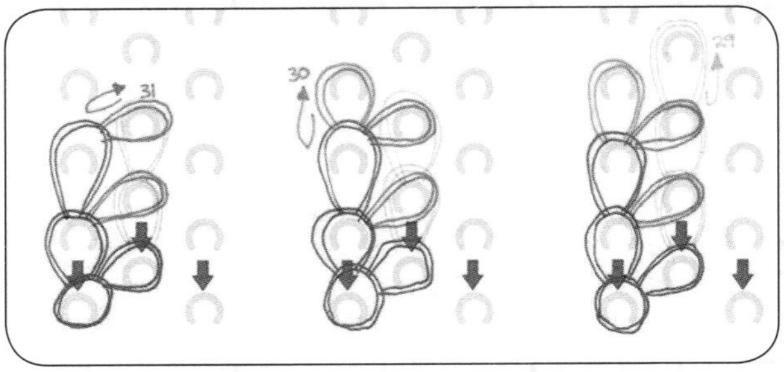

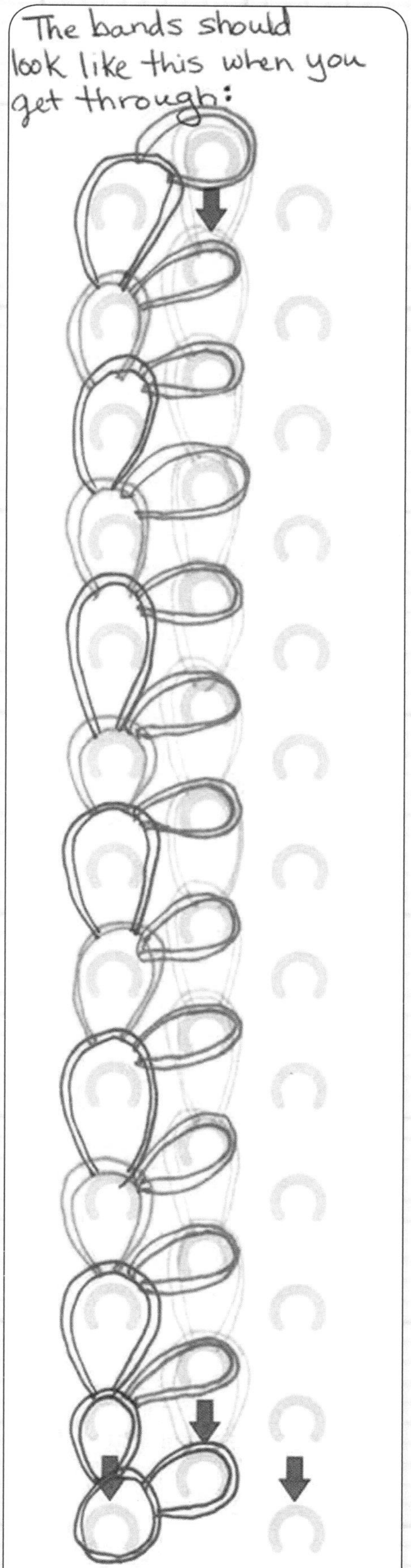
The bands should look like this when you get through:

Step 4: Adding a Loop and a Plastic Connector Clip

Put your hook through the last two looped-back bands—the white and teal colored ones—and pull another white band through them. Then you can add a plastic connector clip to the ends of the newly added white loop to keep it in place. You can now pull the bracelet off the loom. Keep track of the first white loop that you looped back onto its original peg. We need this one for the back of the bracelet in the next step.

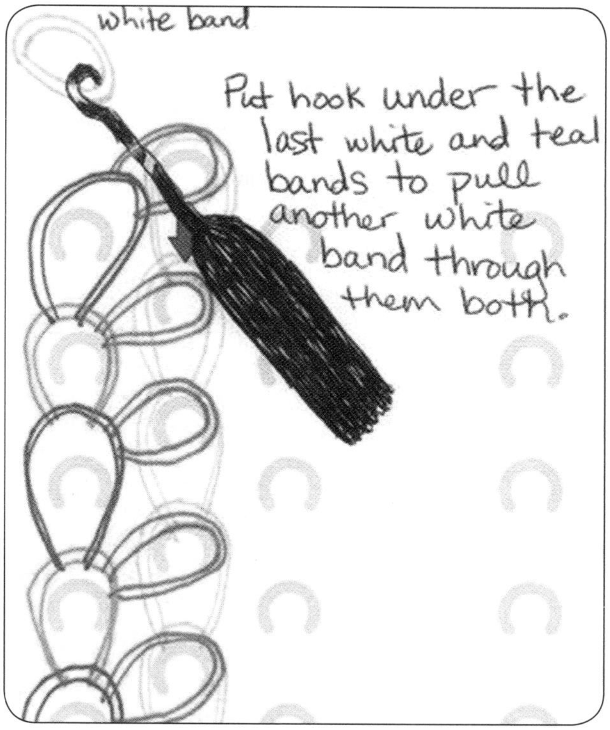
white band
Put hook under the last white and teal bands to pull another white band through them both.

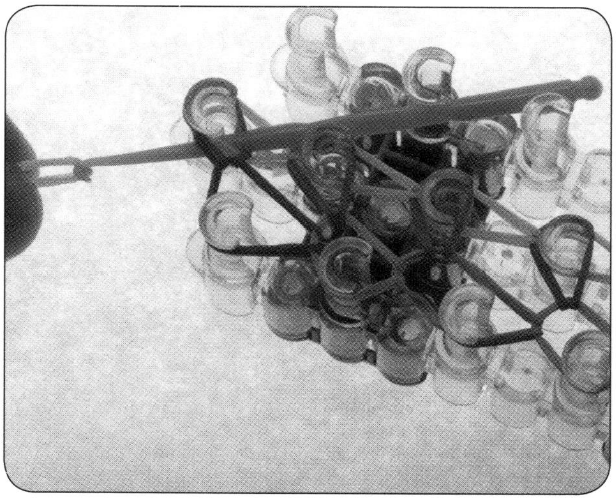

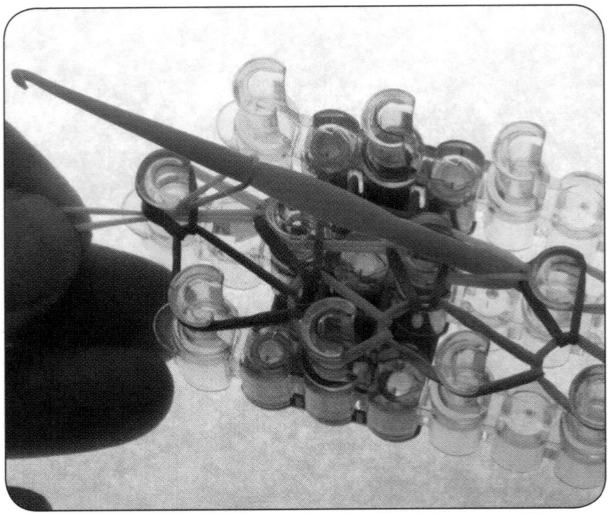

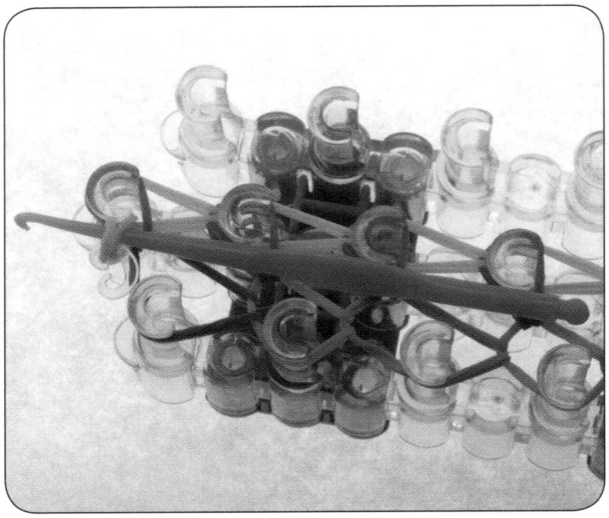

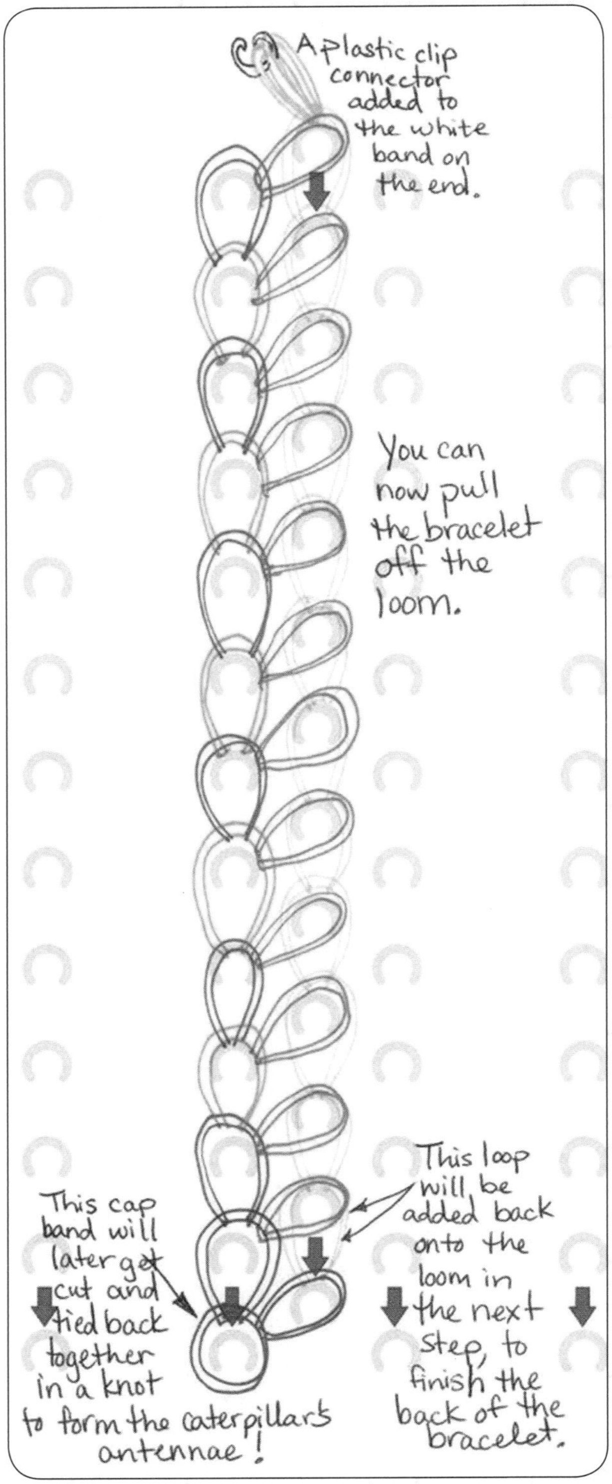
A plastic clip connector added to the white band on the end.
You can now pull the bracelet off the loom.
This cap band will later get cut and tied back together in a knot to form the caterpillar's antennae!
This loop will be added back onto the loom in the next step, to finish the back of the bracelet.

Step 5: Creating the Back of the Bracelet

For the back of the bracelet, you need to add a single row of bands that are the same color as your bracelet band, down one side of the loom. Starting with the loom arrows pointing away from you, place the first band on the pegs closest to you and continue to place the subsequent bands according to the picture. This will be creating the single loop design that is usually the first loop bracelet you learned on the loom. Save the last two pegs for the white loop on our caterpillar bracelet that I told you to keep track of from the previous step. Now flip your loom over so the loom arrows point toward you. Starting from the band immediately after the caterpillar's bracelet loop you placed on the loom, pull the bands up and out and back on their original pegs until you make your way to the end of the loom. You have now completed the back of your bracelet and can pull it off the loom.

For the back of the bracelet, you need to add a single row of bands to the loom, starting with #1
and ending with the white loop on the caterpillar bracelet.
This end gets connected to the other end of the plastic connector clip to join the two ends of the bracelet together.
You can now pull off your bracelet from the loom.
Starting at A and ending at K, pull the bands up and out and back onto their original pegs to create the "single loop" pattern on the back of the bracelet.
This loop attaches here on the loom now

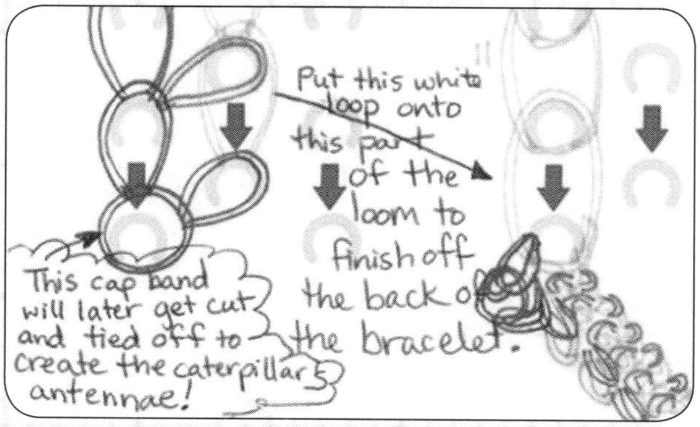
Put this white loop onto this part of the loom to finish off the back of the bracelet.
This cap band will later get cut and tied off to create the caterpillar antennae!

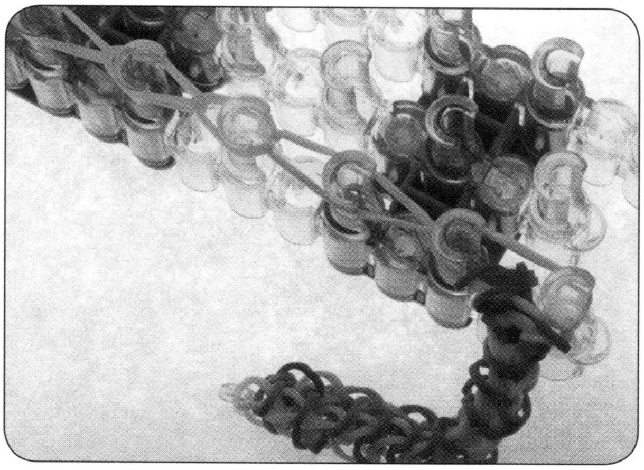

Step 6: Joining the Two Ends of the Bracelet Together

Connect the two ends of the bracelet together using the plastic connector clip already dangling from the other end. Sometimes the back of the caterpillar bracelet gets a little twisted pulling it off the loom. No biggie, just tug on the loop ends with your hook until they untwist themselves.

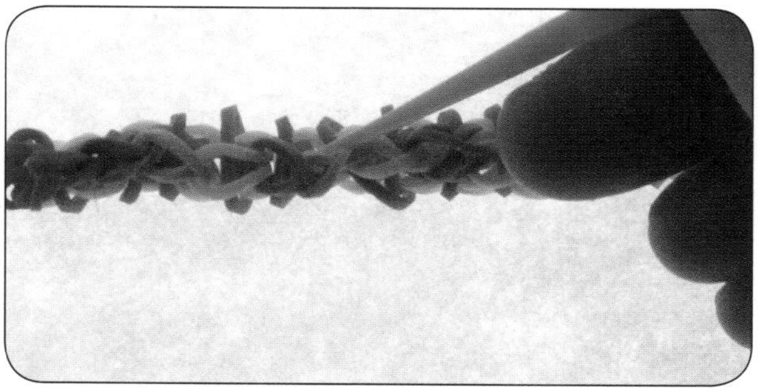

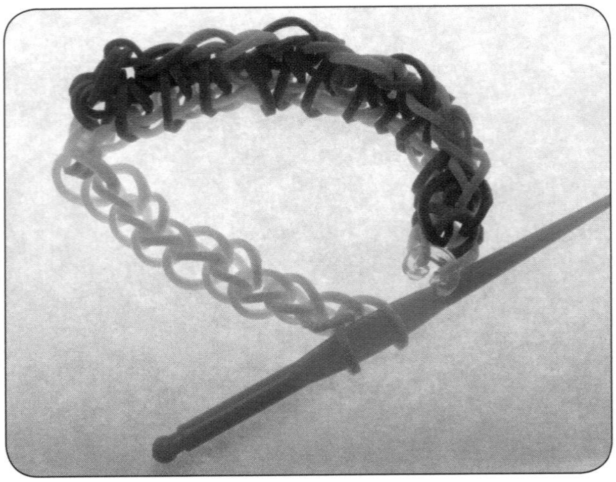

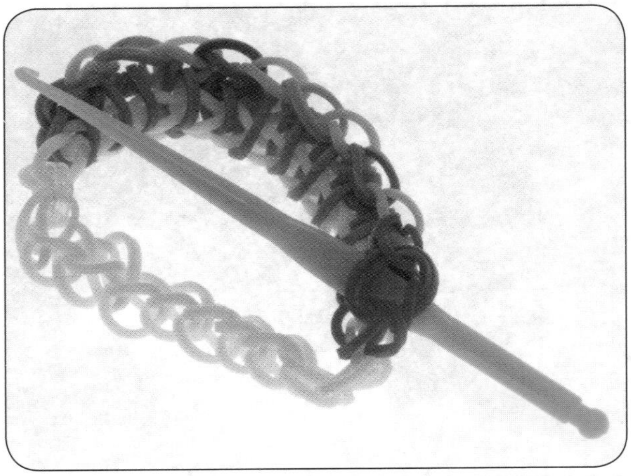

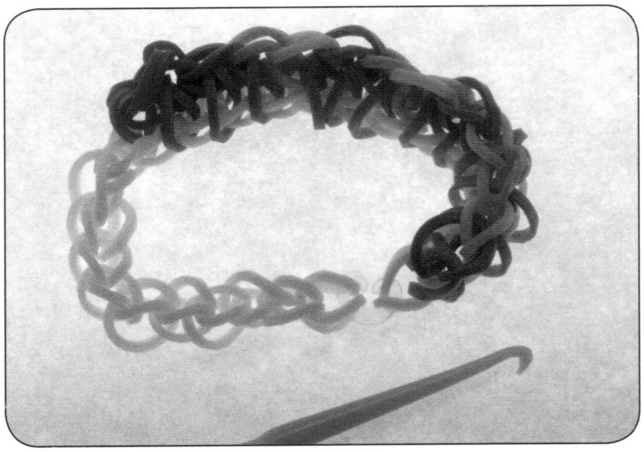

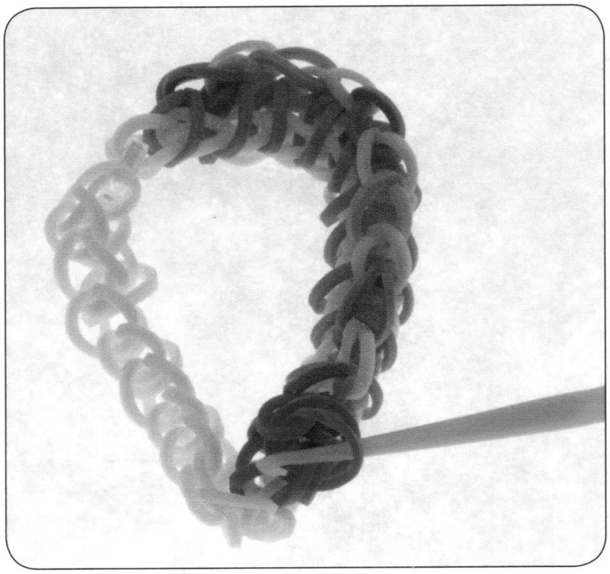

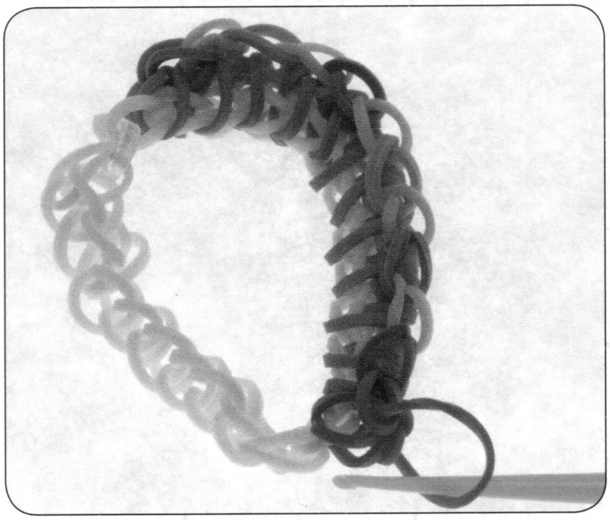

Step 7: Creating the Caterpillar's Antennae

To create the caterpillar's antennae, we need to find the red, doubled-up end-cap loop. It will be the red loop not attached to the white or green bands of the bracelet, only to the other red bands on the bracelet. Using your hook, pull on one of the loops until the other end snugly tightens around the red bands of the caterpillar's head. This is the band you will cut and retie as a knot on top of the caterpillar's head. Tie the knot a few times over to secure it from slipping out over time. You can tie little knots on the ends of the caterpillar's antennas too if you want, or leave them as is for a more streamlined feeler look. The caterpillar bracelet is now complete. Give your caterpillar a name and have fun wearing your fuzzy friend around wherever you go! In the case of the V.H.C., you can add pre-made plastic food charms or create your own out of loom tutorials on the Internet, like I did. Thanks for reading my overly verbose tutorial! I just wanted to make sure nothing was left to question.

Feather Bracelet

By mclare50

(http://www.instructables.com/id/Rainbow-Loom-Feather-Bracelet/)

This is an intermediate level bracelet. Enjoy!

Step 1: Supplies

- Rainbow Loom
- Rainbow Loom hook
- 5 different colors of rubber bands
- Clip

Step 2: Placing the Bands

First, take your base removal hook on the end of your loom and remove the bases. Place the middle row so that all of the rows are next to each other. Take your first band and place it going out from the red arrow sideways. Continue a straight row up the left side of the loom. Once you have finished, take one more rubber band and put it into the middle at the end. Repeat this on the right side so that when you are done, it makes a "frame" around the loom.

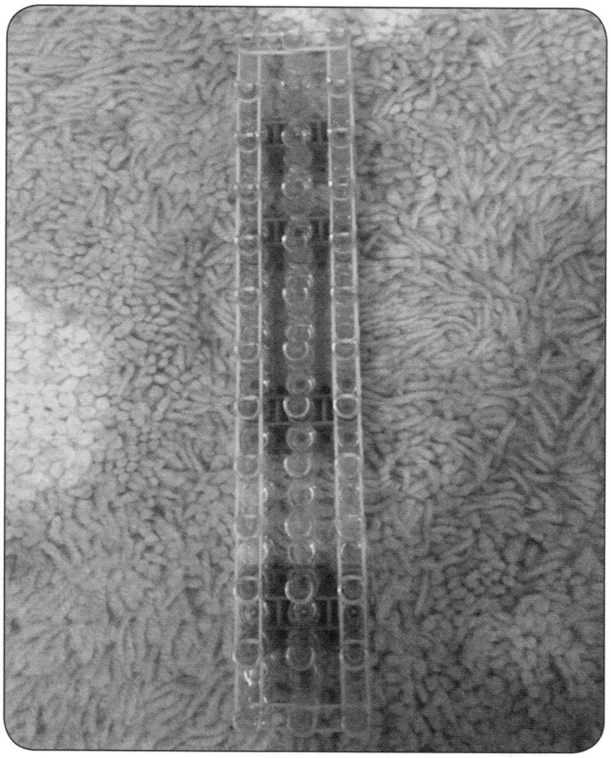

Step 3: Placing the Bands

Now you will start with your next color. Take your second color and put it going forward at the beginning of the loom. Now take another color and place that diagonally from the bottom left peg to the end of the black band. Do this on the right side so that it makes an arrow shape. Take another black band and stretch it forward above that arrow shape, then take a different color and make another arrow. Do this to the end of the loom.

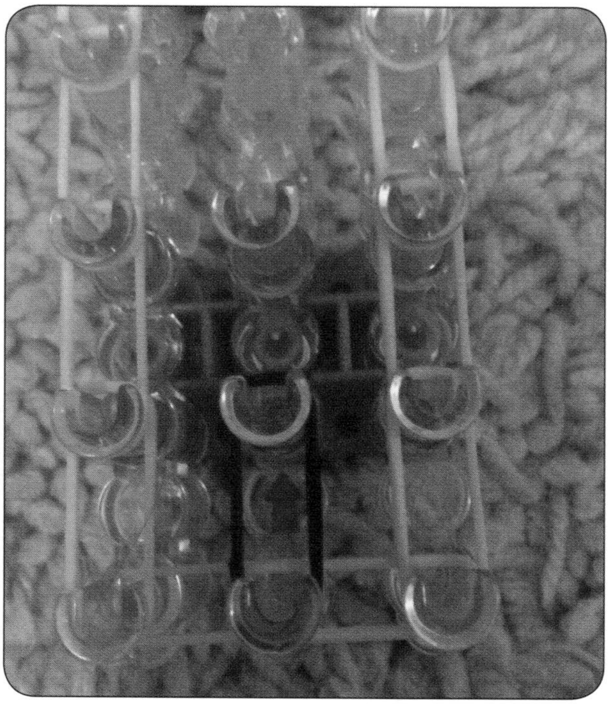

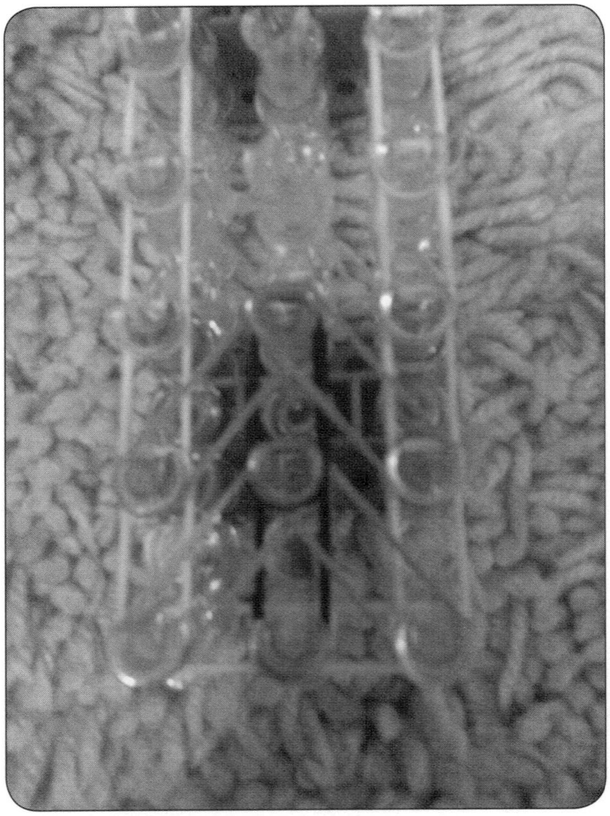

Step 4: A Visual

It should look like the photo when you have finished.

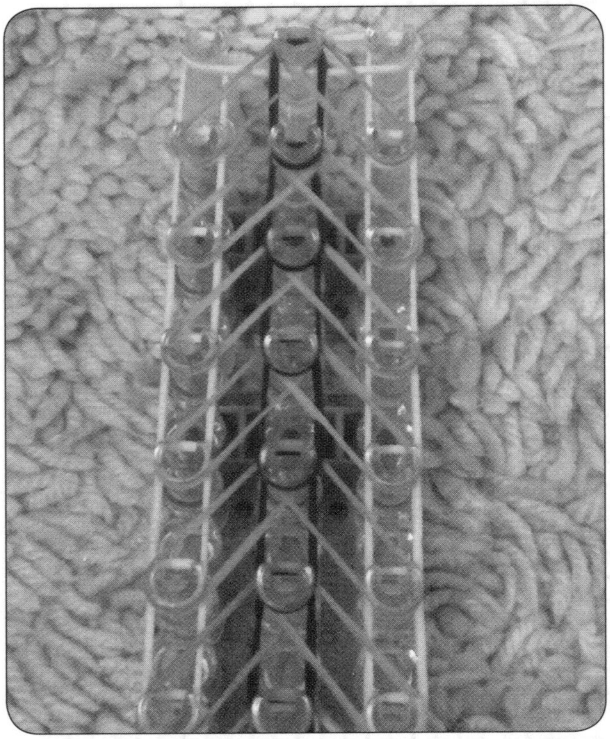

Step 5: V Bands

Now we will place the "V" bands. This color will show up the least. To do this, go back to the beginning of the loom and place a band at the first peg in the middle going out and up diagonally as the picture shows. Do this on the other side to make a V shape. Continue this all the way up the loom.

Step 6: Cap Band

Now we are done placing the bands. Turn the loom over so the arrow is facing you and place a cap band on the first middle peg.

Step 7: Loopin' Time

To start looping, go under all of the bands and take the top yellow band and place it to the left. Do the same with the right band.

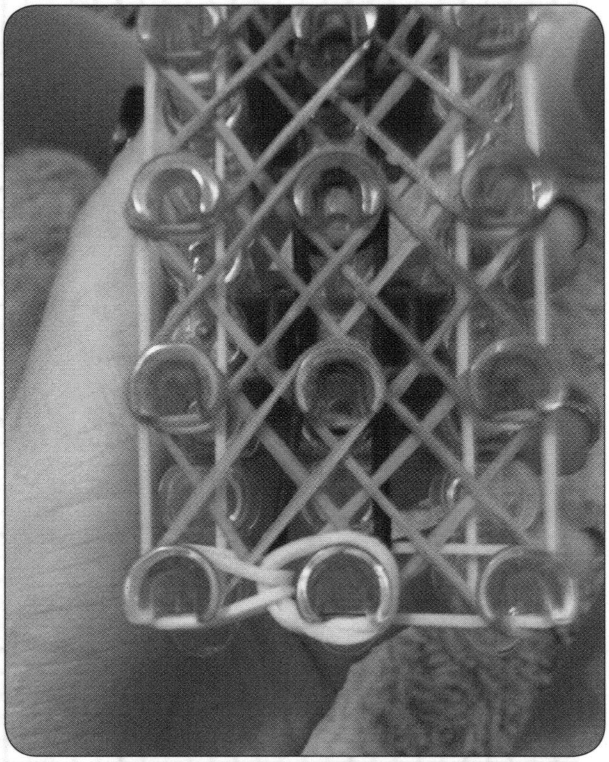

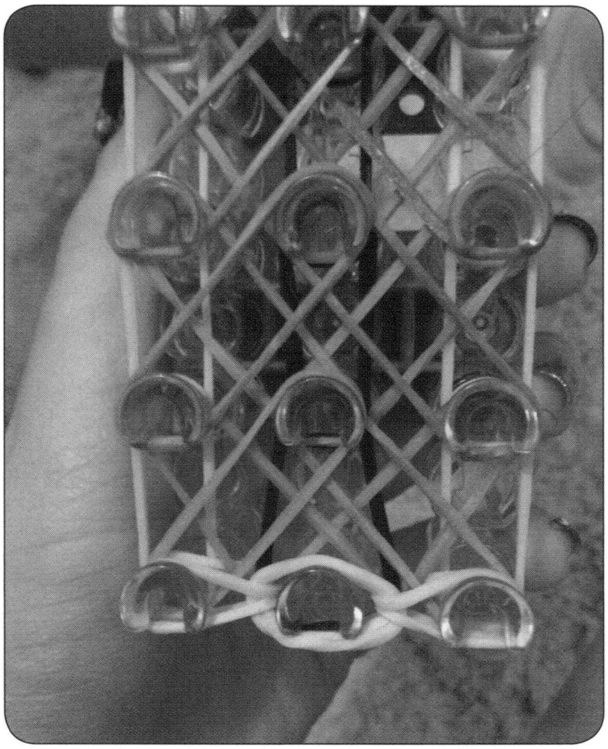

Step 8: Looping the Bands

For this part, you will not get tear drop shapes for most of the bands for this row. Go under the cap band and take the top red. Place the band onto the left peg it came from and do the same on the right. Then take the last band from underneath the cap band (mine is black) and place that forward.

Step 9: Looping the Bands

Now you will take the bands on the bottom sides—mine are green—and loop them onto the middle peg.

Step 10: Looping the Bands

Lastly, take the two side bands and bring them forward.

Step 11: Looping the Bracelet Bands

Now we will start the actual bracelet. Take the two purple bands on each side and bring them to where they started. Take the black in the middle and bring that up to the middle. Then take the two green bands from the sides and bring them to the middle, and take the yellows on the side and bring them forward. Continue this all the way up the loom.

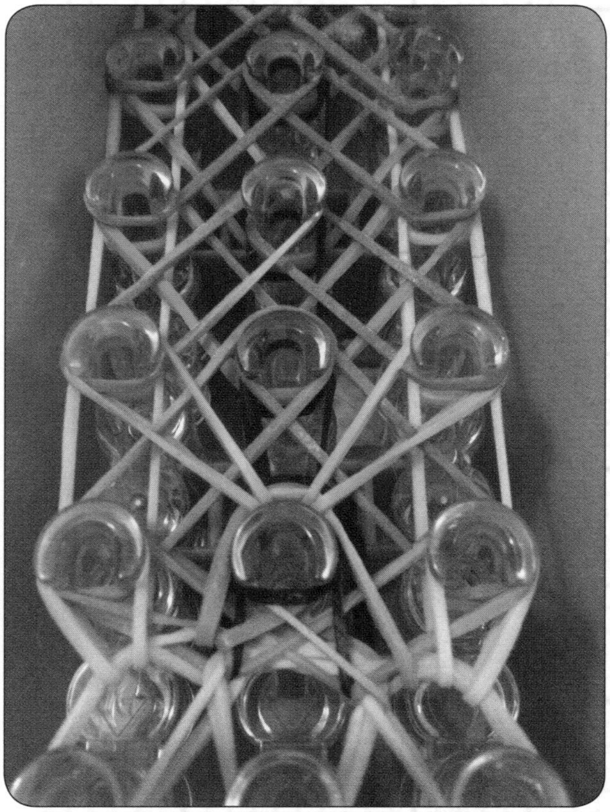

Step 12: Looping the Bracelet Bands

Once you have reached the end, you will see there are two yellow bands going inward. Simply take those and bring them towards the middle.

Step 13: Finish Up

Time to finish! Take your hook and stick it through the last pin with all of the rubber bands on it. Take a yellow rubber band and feed that through to make a loop. Now make an extension doing a single chain. Add a clip and pull your bracelet off the loom.

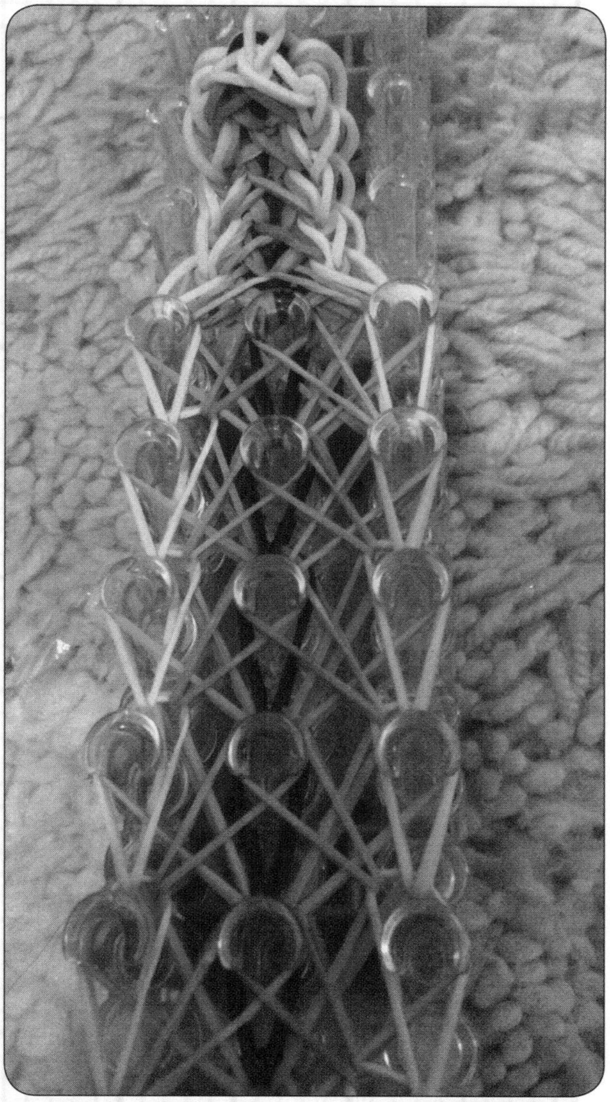

Step 14: Add Clip

Almost done! Take your clip and find the cap band in the other side and attach them.

Step 15: Enjoy!

Enjoy your feather bracelet!

Totem Pole Bracelet

By crazymustacheluver
(http://www.instructables.com/id/How-to-make-Rainbow-Loom-bracelet-Totem-Pole/)

Today I will be showing you how to make a Rainbow Loom Totem Pole.

Step 1: Materials

- S-clip or C-clip
- Rubber bands
- Rainbow Loom
- Hook

Note: You must have your loom in the rectangular position.

Step 2: Placing the Bands for the Base

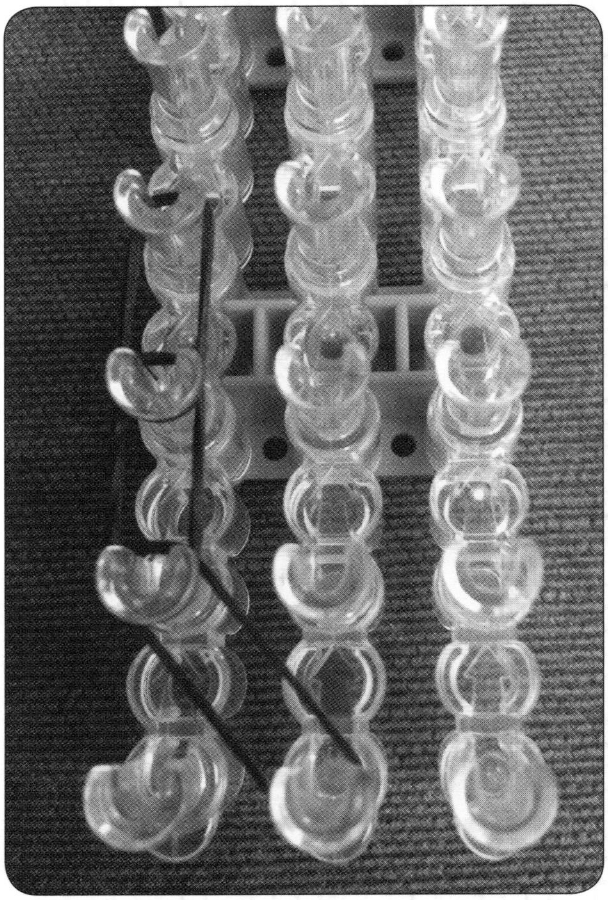

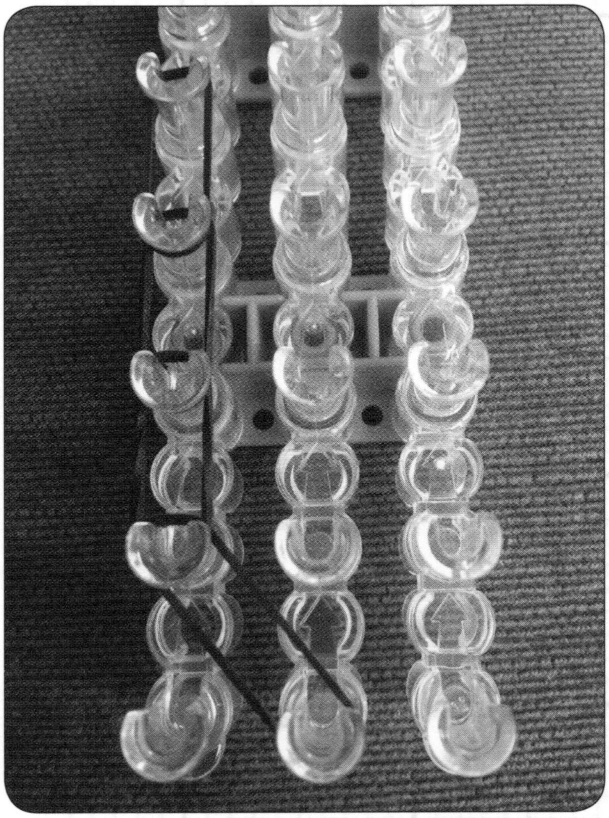

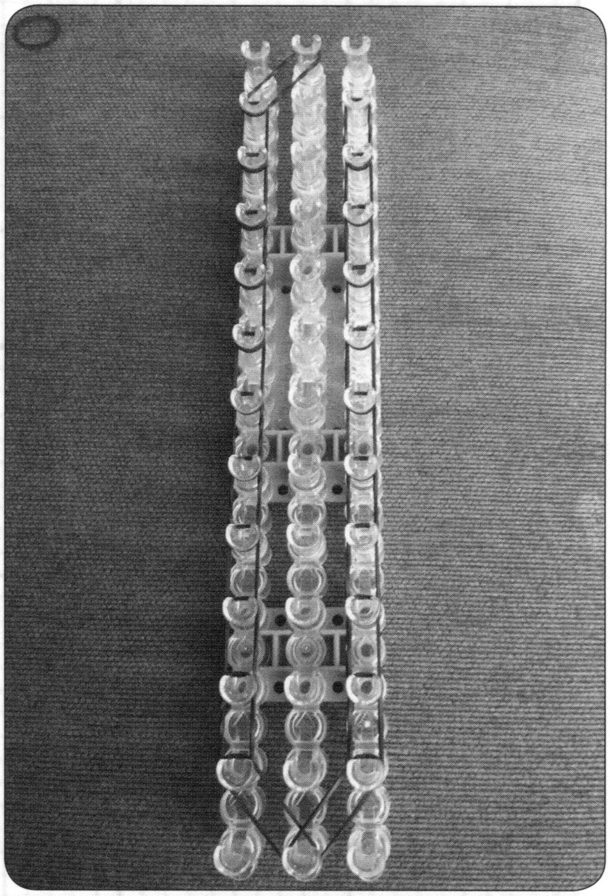

Step 3: Placing Triangles

After this step, turn your loom over.

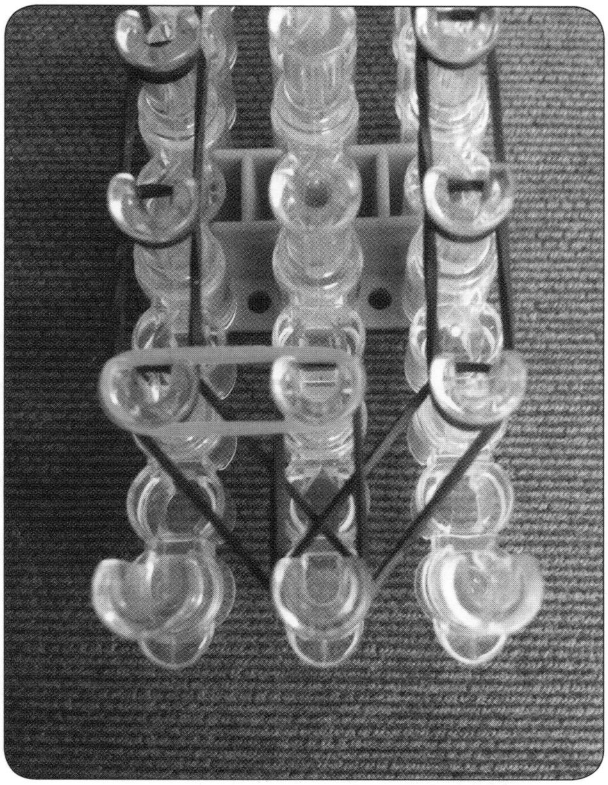

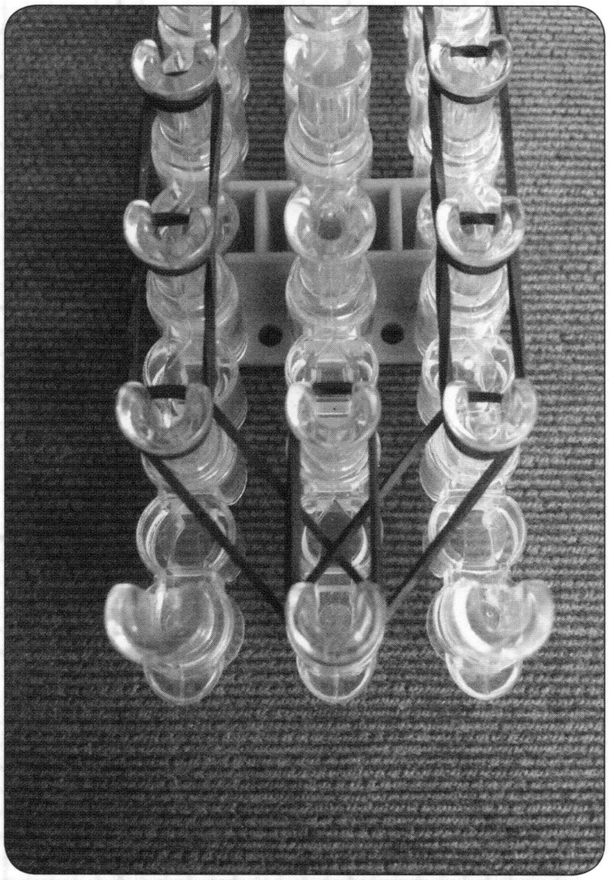

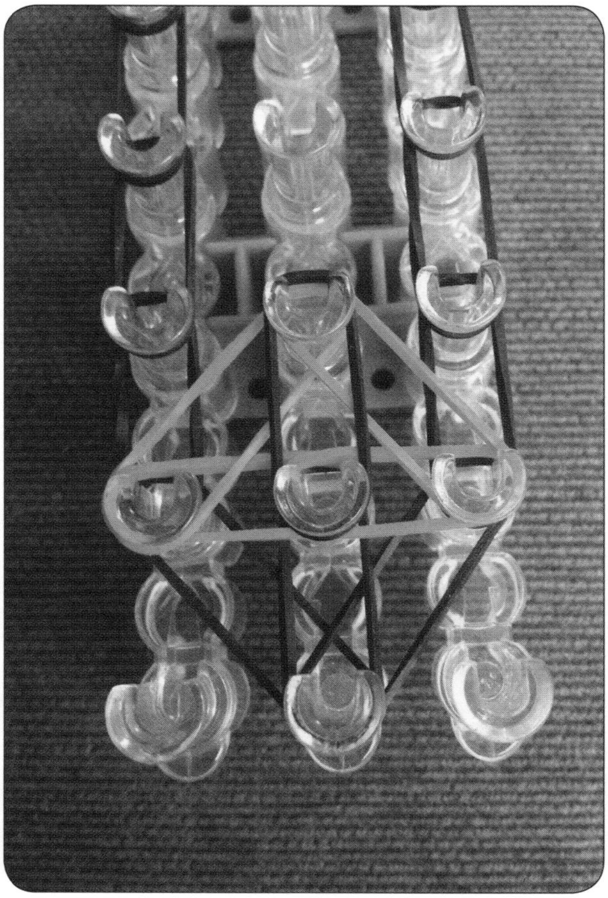

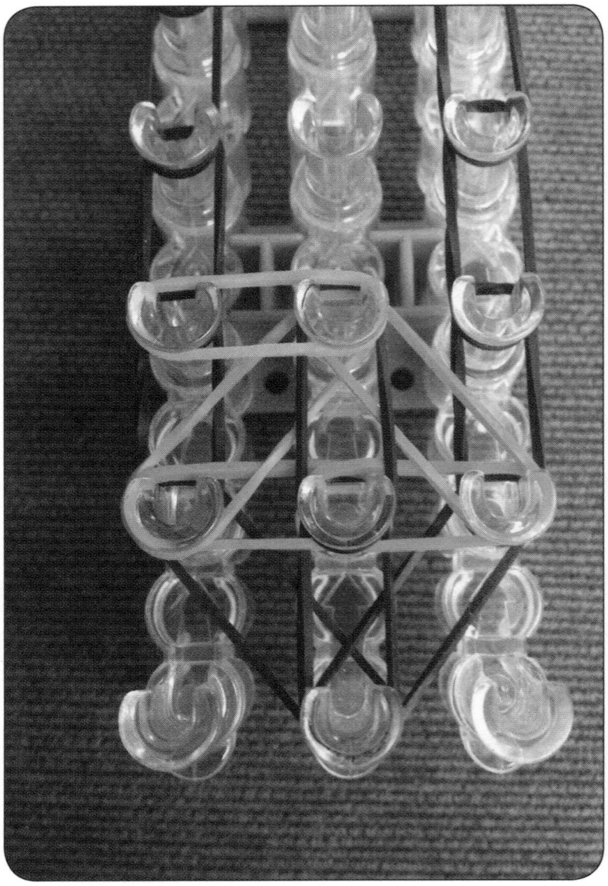

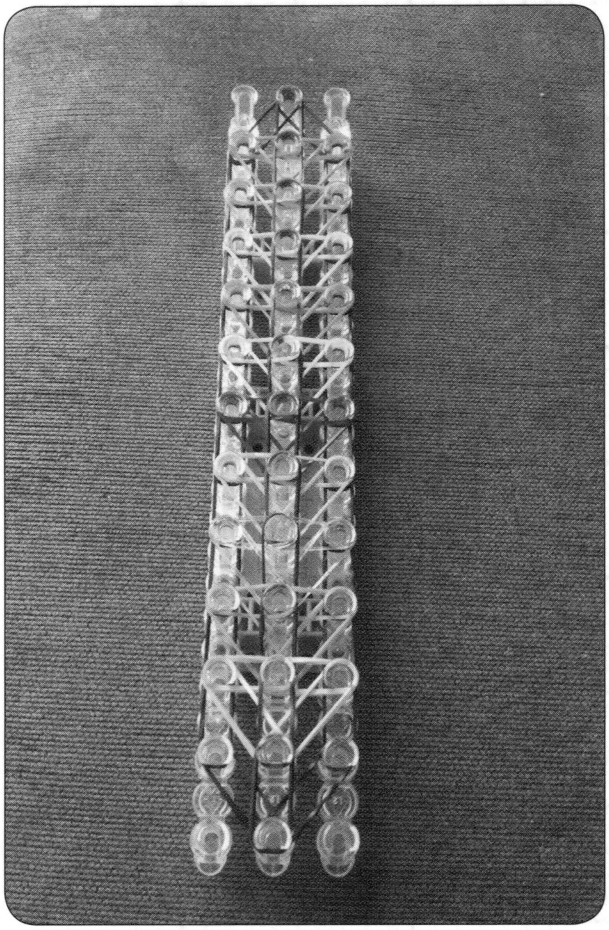

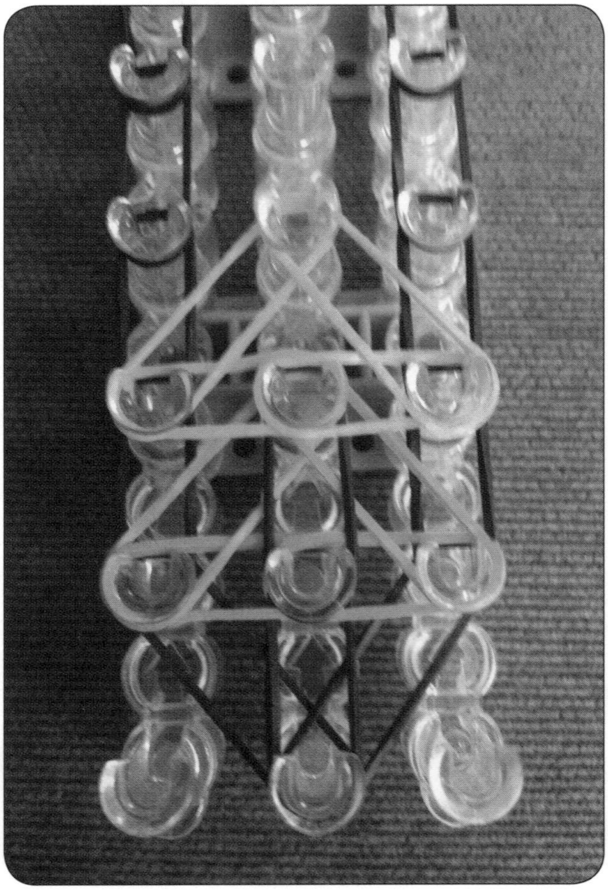

Step 4: Place Cap Band

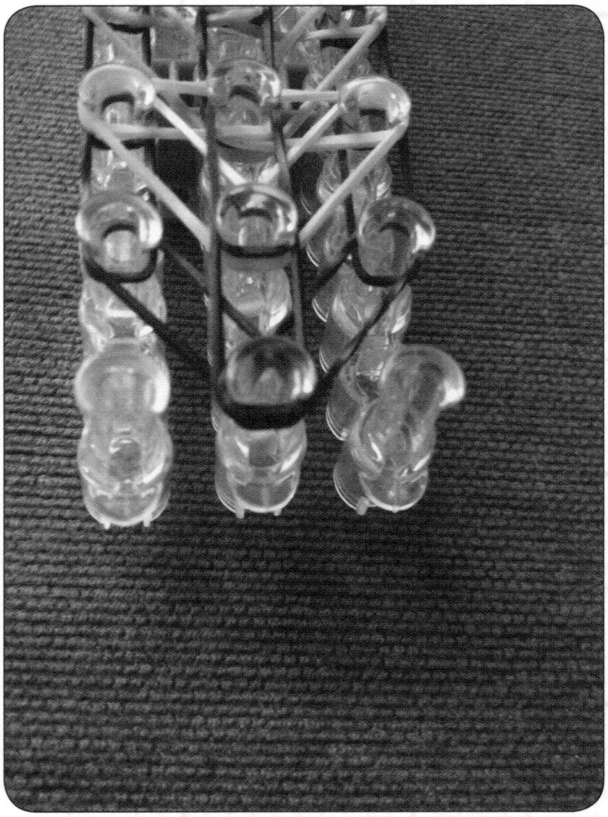

Step 5: Looping

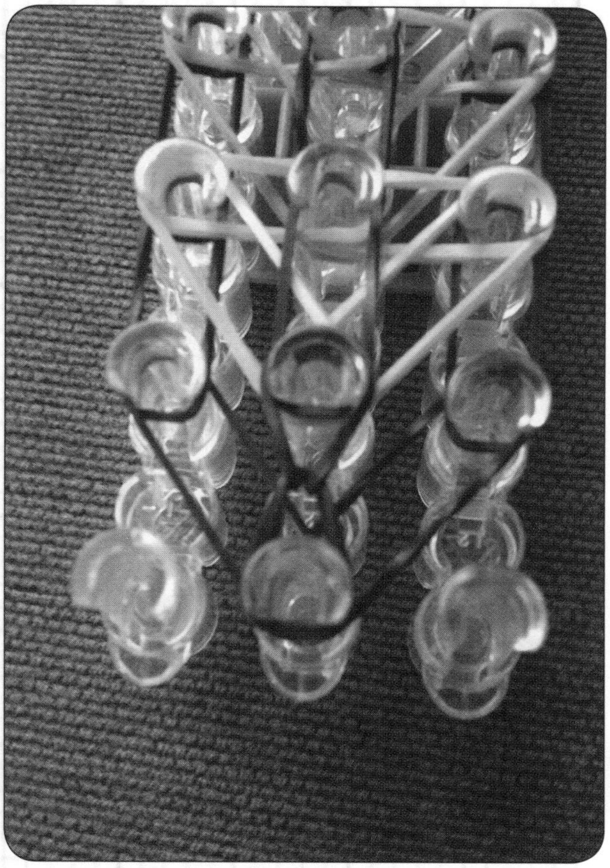

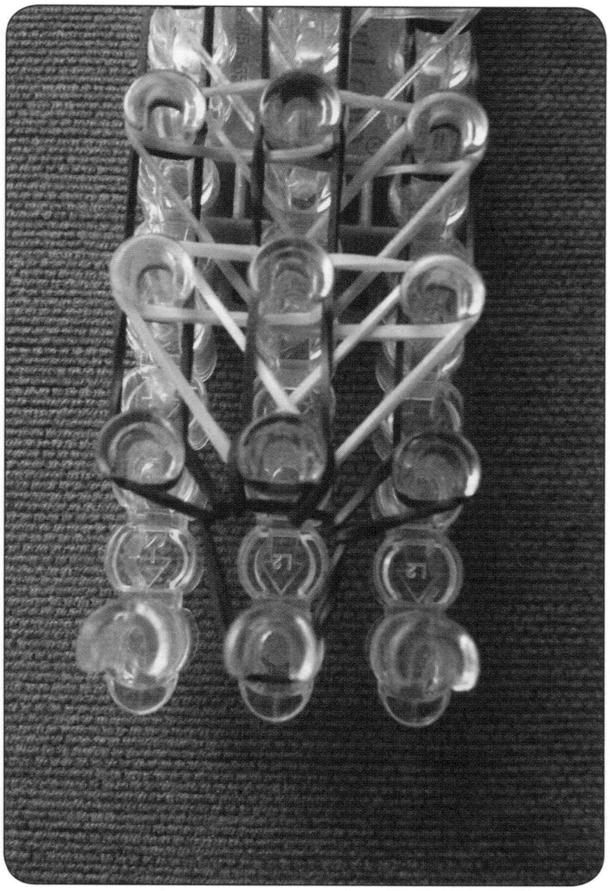

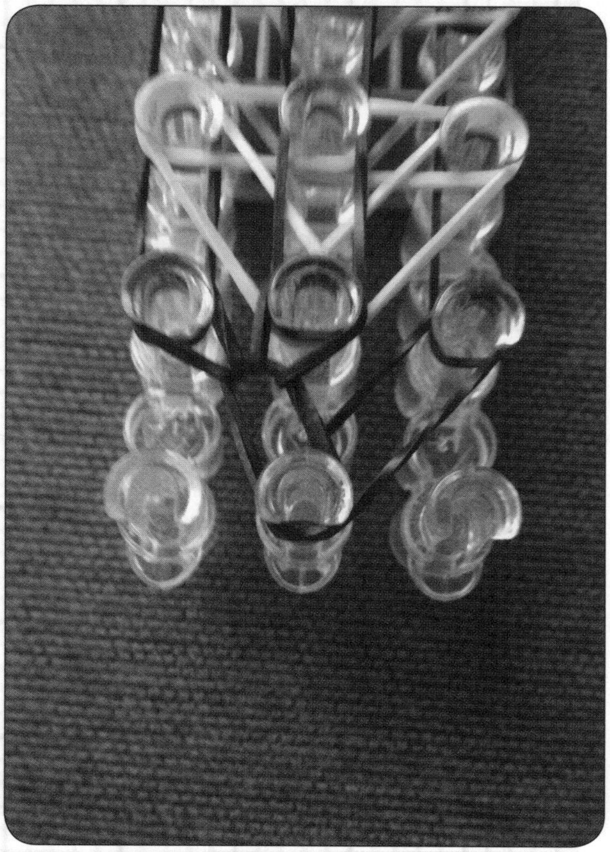

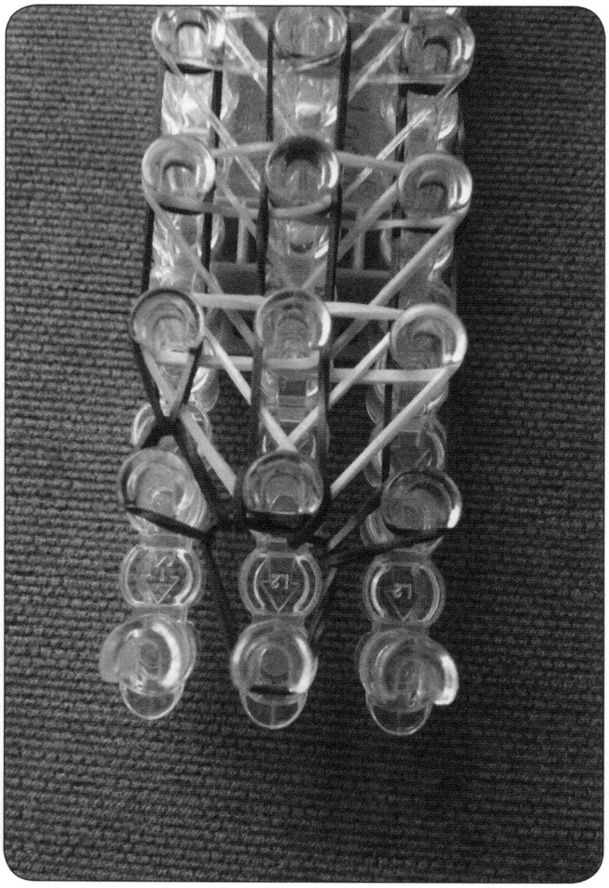

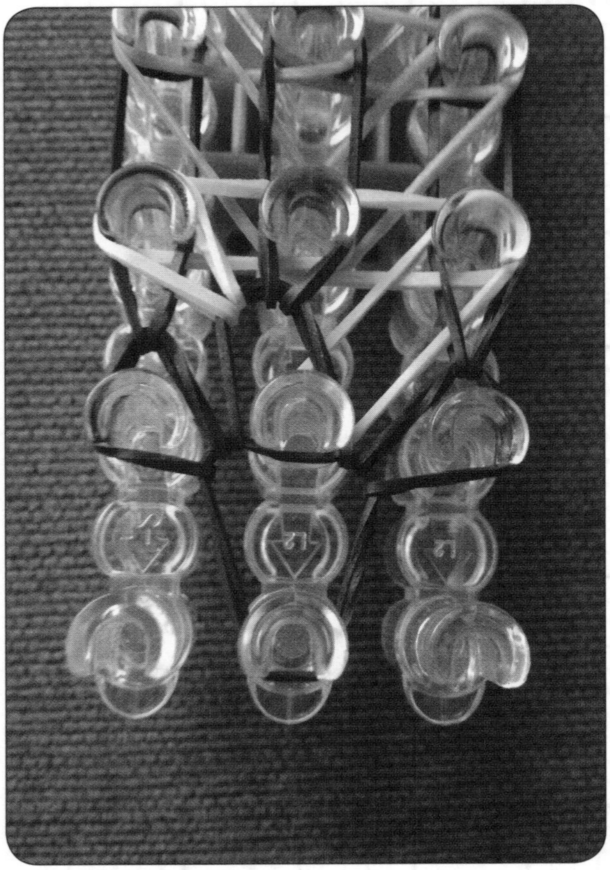

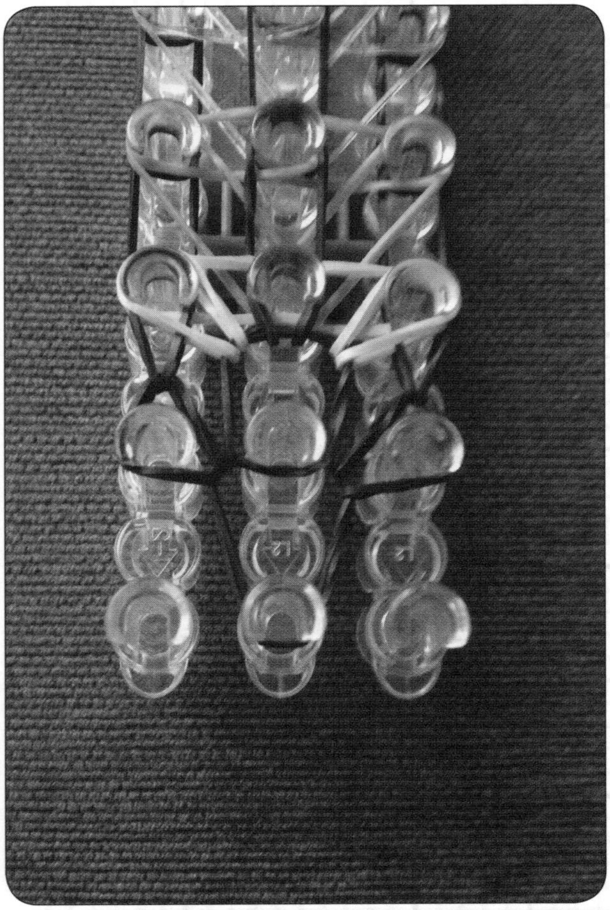

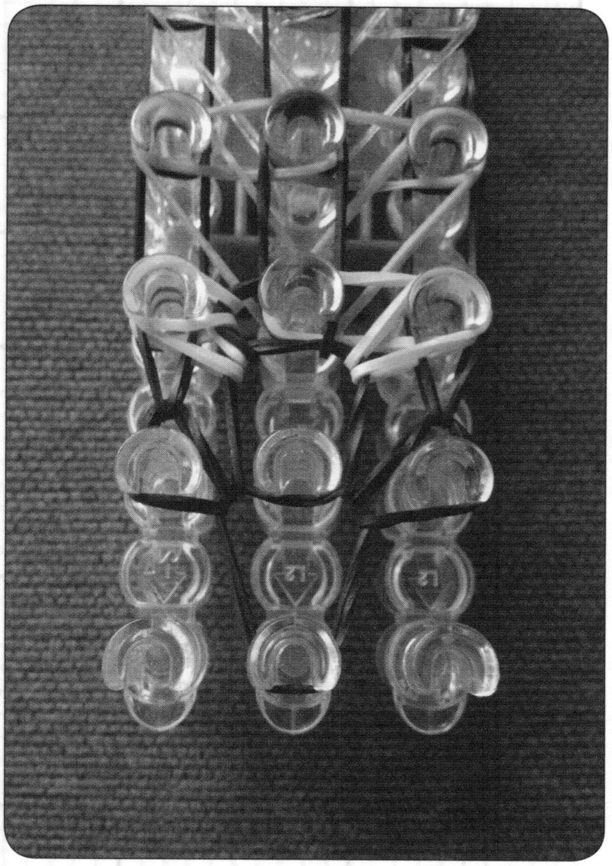

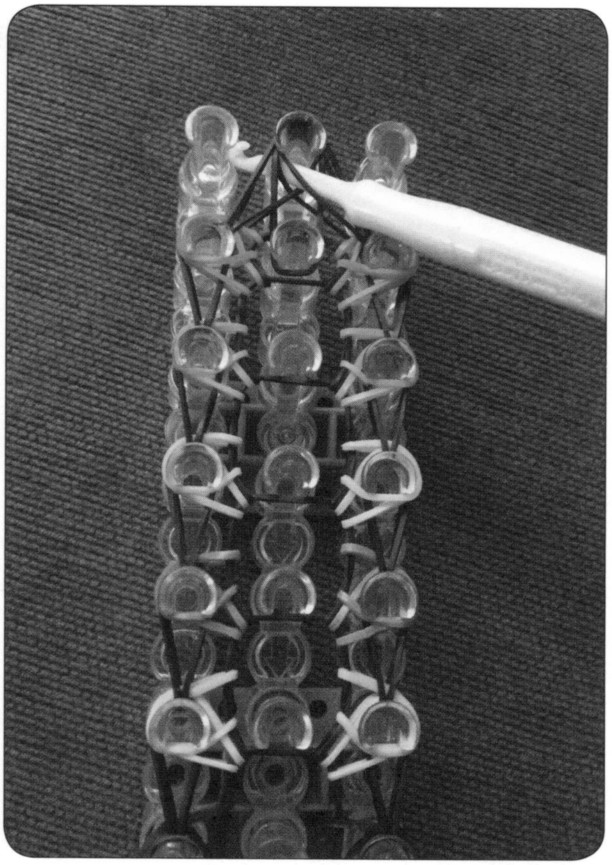

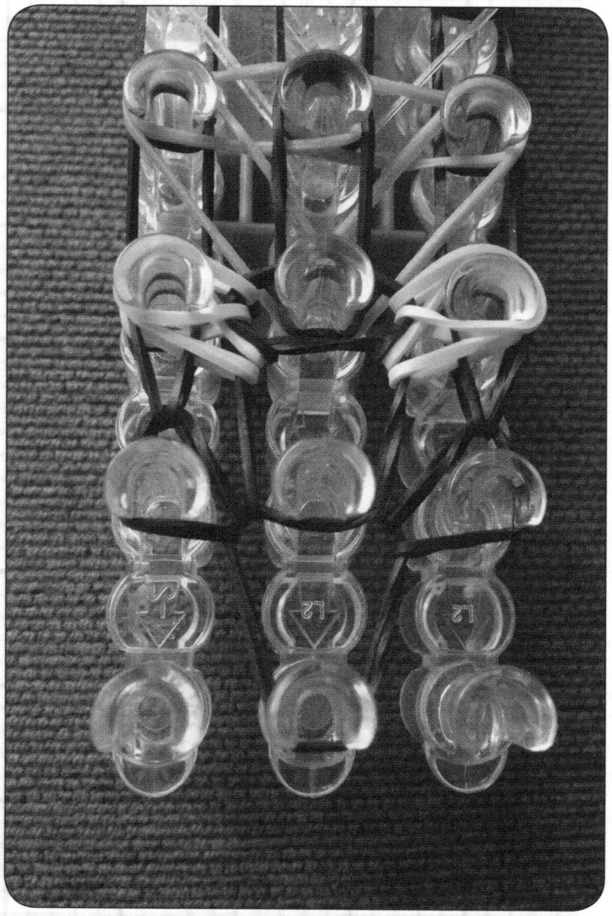

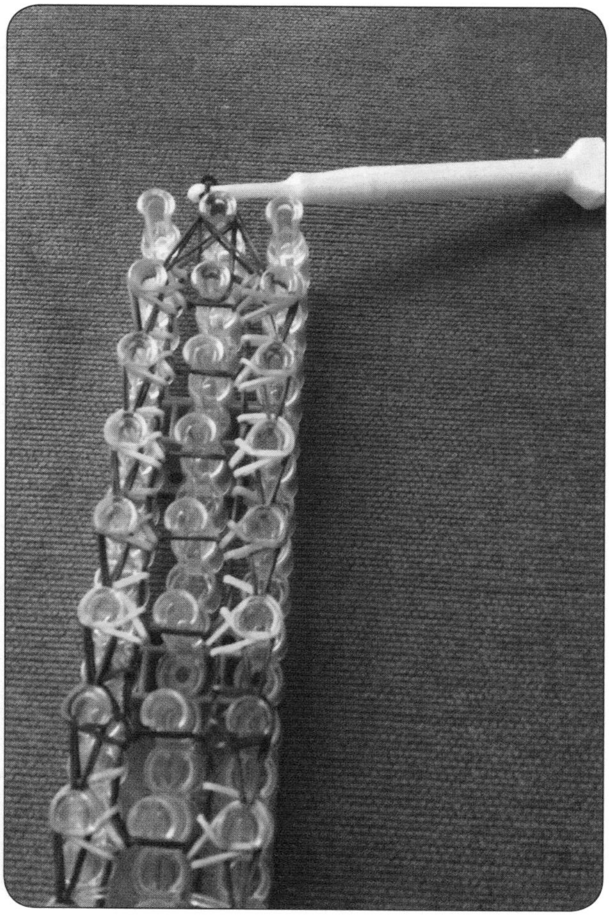

Step 6: Pull Off and Add Extension

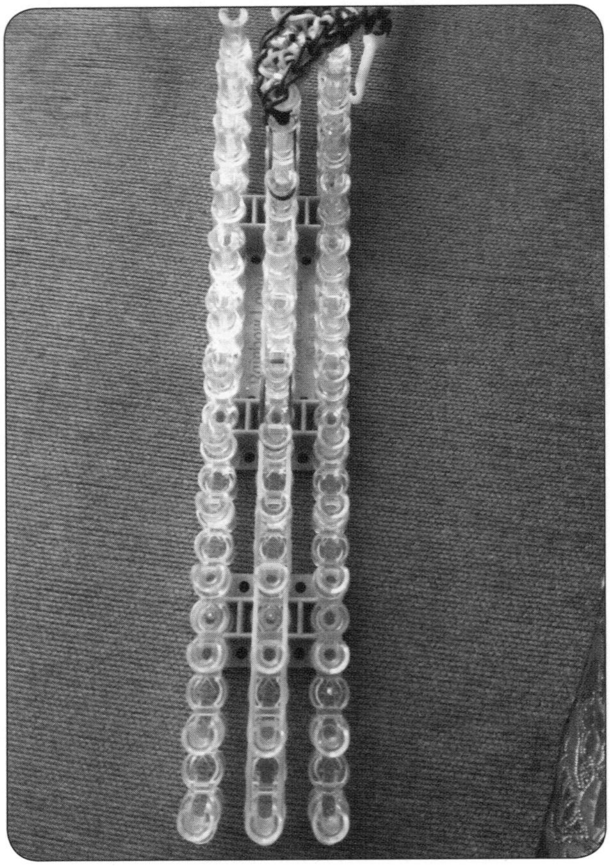

Step 7: Finishing Your Bracelet

Add on your c- or s-clip and any extra rubber bands you need to get it to the right length. Put it on and enjoy!

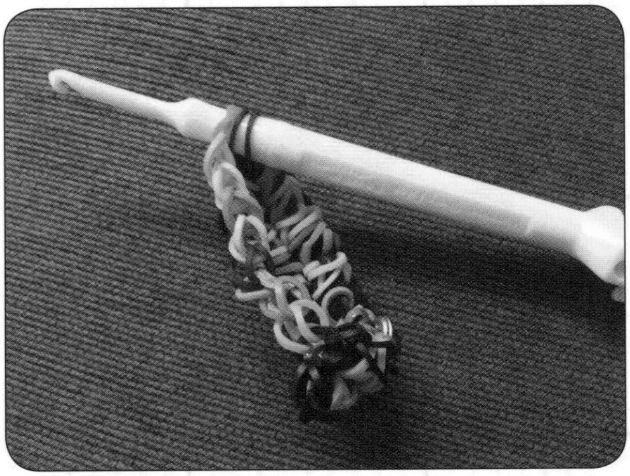

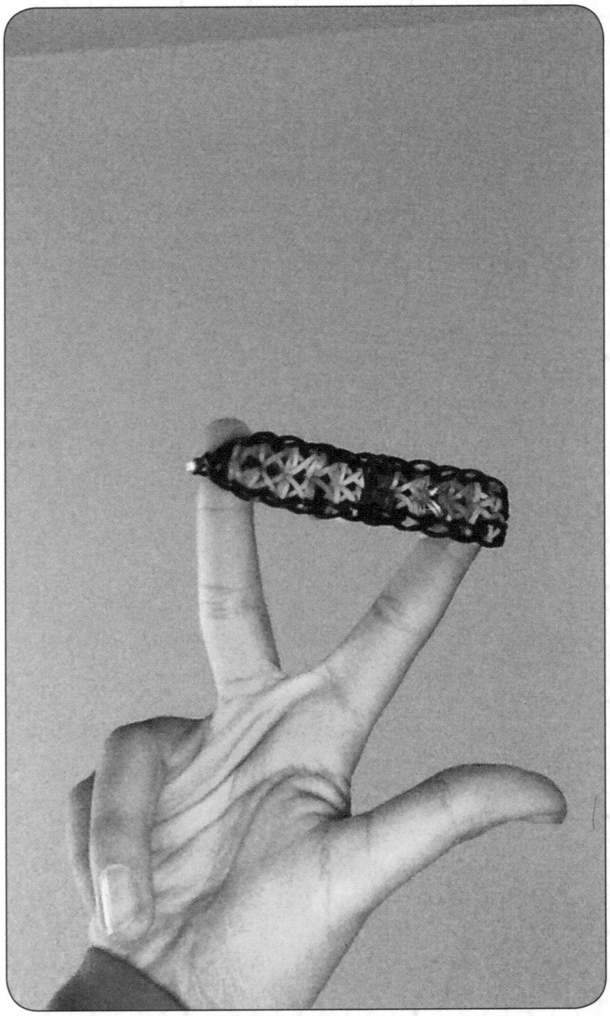

Mustache-Pattern Bracelet

By Rose Winchester

(http://www.instructables.com/id/Mustache-Rainbow-Loom-Bracelet/)

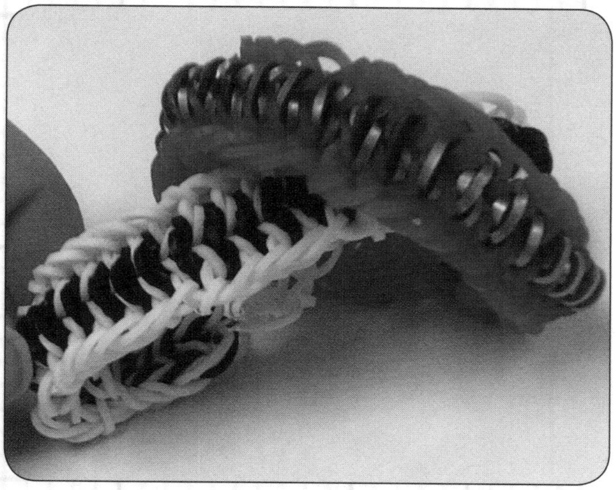

Step 1: Materials

- One strip of pegs from a Rainbow Loom
- Two colors of bands (mine are red for the framing bands and silver for the mustache bands. You will need more than twice the number of framing bands than mustache bands)
- Hook
- Two S-clips (C-clips work just as well)

Step 2: Get Started

We will only be working on the first four pegs. Hook a red band over the first peg and twist it once before looping it over the second peg, so it forms a figure eight between the two. Do the same between the third and fourth pegs. There should be a space between the two bands so that they don't overlap on a peg (see picture). Place a silver band in the same figure-eight pattern between the second and third pegs, bridging the gap between the two red pegs. You should now have one red loop on the first peg, a red and silver on the second peg, a red and silver on the third peg, and a red loop on the fourth peg (see picture). These are the only bands that will be twisted into figure eights. The rest will simply be stretched between pegs without any twists. Place a red band between the first and second pegs, and another between the third and fourth pegs. You should have two red loops over the first peg, two reds and a silver on the second peg, two reds and a silver on the third peg, and two red loops on the fourth peg (see picture).

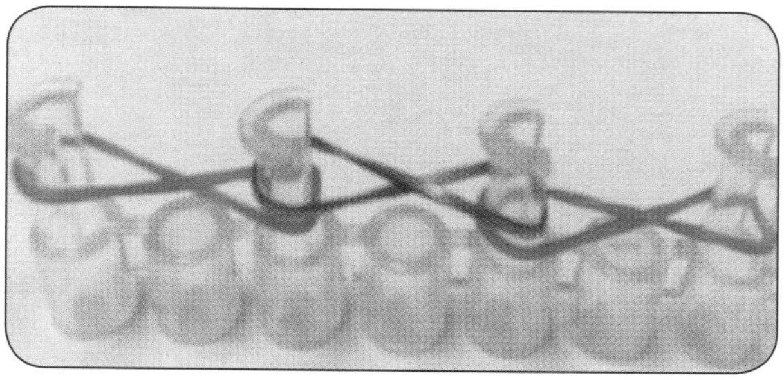

Step 3: Move Loops

As soon as you get three loops on a peg (which you should have on the second and third pegs right now), you want to hook the bottom loop from the outside (not going through the other loops on the peg) and lift it up and over the peg to the other side (see pictures). Always move loops to the same side (I always move mine from the right side of the peg to the left) and your bracelet will begin to form on that side of the peg strip. Once you move the bottom loops from the middle two pegs over, place a silver band between the second and third pegs (no twisting). This will again make you have three loops on the second and third pegs. Take the bottom loops and hook them over to the other side of the pegs. Now place a red band over the first and second pegs, and another over the third and fourth pegs. This will make three loops on all four of the pegs. Continue this pattern: Red on pegs one and two. Red on pegs three and four. Hook third loops over pegs. Silver on pegs two and three. Hook third loops over peg. As the bracelet builds, it will come off the pegs looking like the photo below.

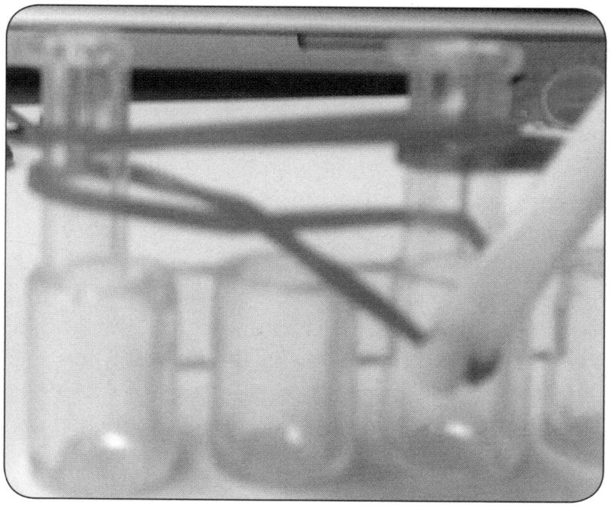

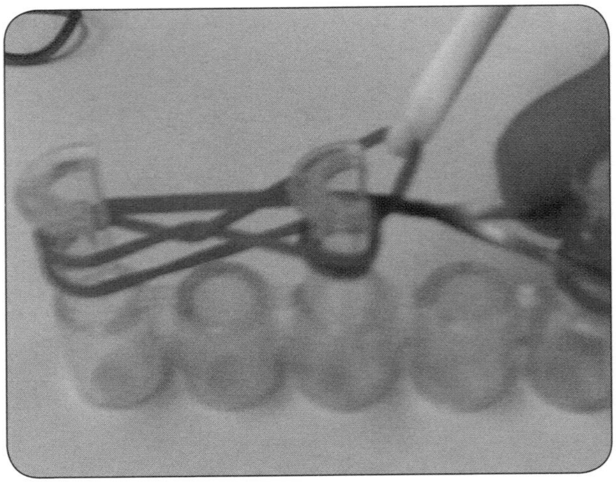

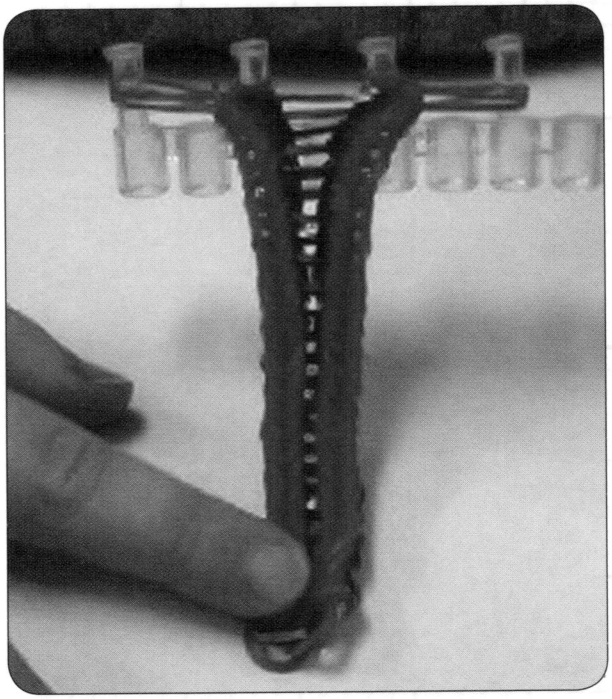

Step 4: Looping

Once you reach the length you want to stretch across the top of your wrist (not around the entire wrist), your bracelet should look like the photo. Hook the two red loops on the first peg over onto the third (in front of the second peg, so they aren't over it). Hook the two red loops on the fourth peg back onto the second (in front of the third peg so they aren't over it). Your bracelet should now only be attached on pegs two and three (see picture). Place your hook through all of the loops on peg two. Use the hook to grab onto a new band and pull it through the loops on the peg (see picture). Make sure to hold the other end of the band until you can thread your hook through both ends, with all the loops from the second peg on the middle of the new band. Hook another band through the ends of the first band and continue this until you have a chain of single bands long enough to complete the circle around your wrist (see picture). Use an S-clip to connect the end of the chain to the other side of the bracelet, forming the loop of the bracelet (see picture). Repeat the process starting from the third peg, forming a chain, and connect your second chain to the other end of the bracelet using your second S-clip (see picture). You should have your patterned part of the bracelet for the top of your wrist connected by two chains of single bands for the underside of your wrist.

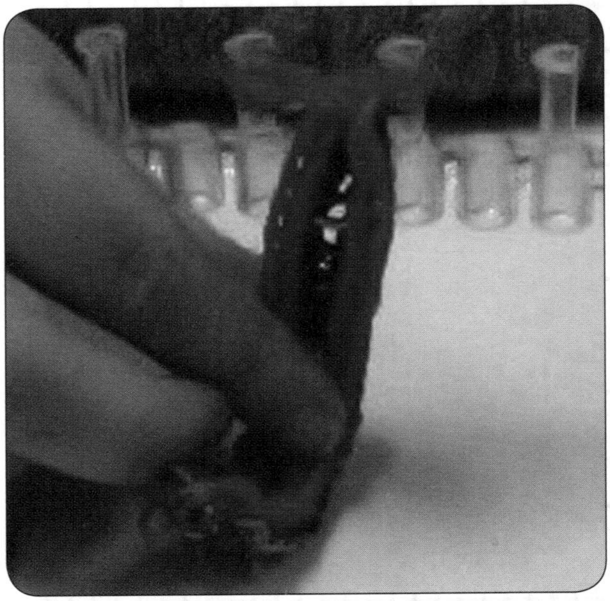

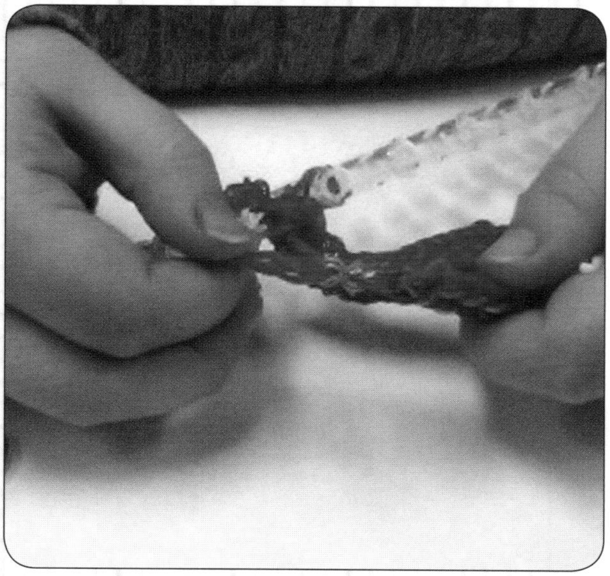

Step 5: Exposing the Mustaches

The outside of your bracelet should have a fishtail pattern (see picture). The mustache pattern is on the inside of the bracelet. However, the bracelet rolls shut to hide them, so we have to peel the sides of the bracelet back to show it (see picture). Flip your bracelet inside out to show the curling side hiding the mustaches. Start at the opposite end from the S-clips.

Run your hook through the inner red band on the right, then go through the inside of the bracelet to hook the inner red loop on the opposite side. This will peel back the curling edges to expose the mustaches (see picture). Hook a new band and pull it through the two loops that are currently over your hooking tool. Repeat this until you have a short, single-band chain on the inside of your bracelet (see picture). After you have about three links in the chain, loop the two ends of the last band over your finger so you can slide your hook out. Use your tool to hook the inner right red band on the top of the bracelet (about five loops farther down from the last one). Before hooking the inner red band on the left top of the bracelet, slip the two loops from your finger onto the hook. You should have the right band from the top, the two bands from the short inner chain, and the left top band all on your hooking tool. Hook a new band through these four loops and make another short chain. Repeat this process for approximately every five loops on the top of the bracelet, slowly uncurling the sides and pulling them back to reveal the mustaches. Once you reach the S-clips, hook through one more set of the top red bands on either side. You should have four loops on your hooking tool. Slide the two closest to the right through the right S-clip, and the two closest to the left through the left S-clip.

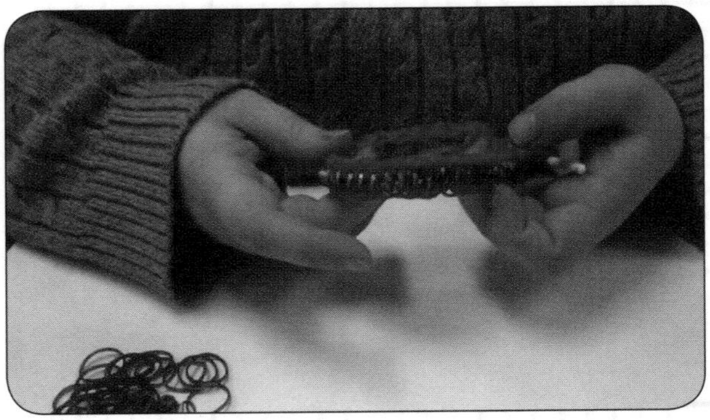

Step 6: You Are Done!

This completes your mustache bracelet! Personally I like the white and black, but you can choose whichever colors you like.

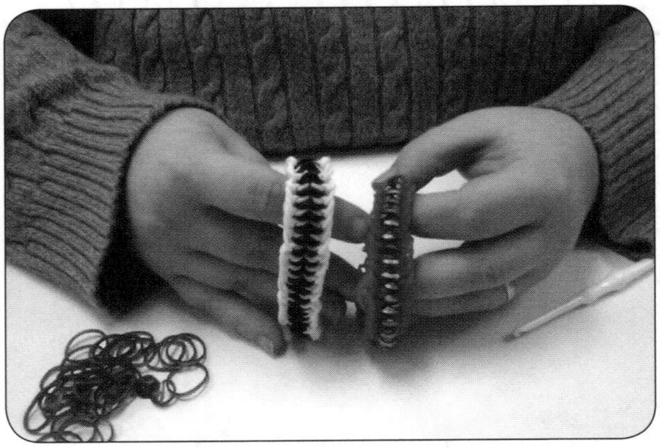

Octaflower Bracelet

By Rainbowloomgirl101
(http://www.instructables.com/id/Octa-Flower/)

Step 1: What You Need

- Rubber bands in colors of your choice
- Rainbow Loom kit or other rubber band loom
- Hook
- C-clip

Step 2: Placing and Looming the Bands!

Place your choice of colored rubber bands on the loom in a pentagon shape. Do this up the loom to the end. Now turn it around and put a cap band on it, then start looping! Loop to one side then the other; do this all the way up the loom to the end. Now you are ready to finish!

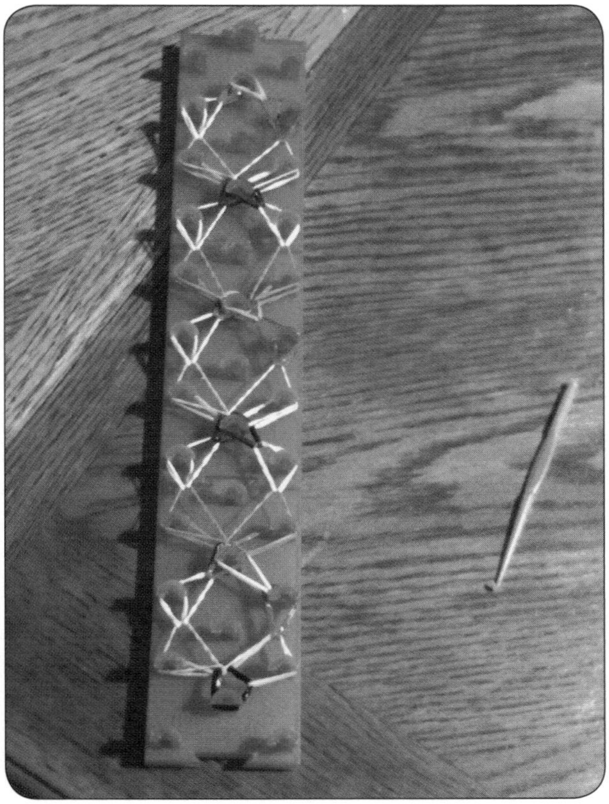

Step 3: Finishing

Take your hook and stick it through all of the rubber bands on the end. Take a rubber band and feed that through to make a loop. Now make an extension doing a single chain. Add a clip and pull your bracelet off the loom and attach the other end to the clip. Now you have your new octaflower bracelet!

Minion Bracelet

By addoaddo

(http://www.instructables.com/id/Minion-Triple-Single-Rainbow-Loom/)

Assemble the minions!

Step 1: Gather Materials

- Rainbow Loom
- Bands in yellow, blue, black, and white
- Rainbow Loom hook
- C- or s-clip

Step 2: Start Your Bracelet

Place loom with the red arrow pointing forward. Place bands as shown. The colors used are nine blue and one black.

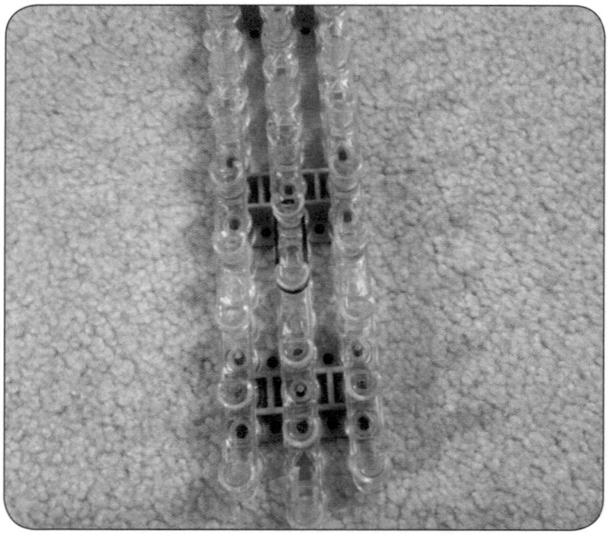

Step 3: Place MORE Bands

Place bands as shown. Colors used are three black and three yellow.

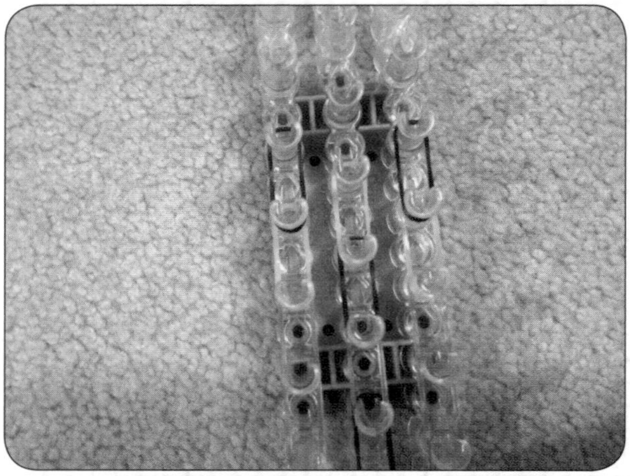

Step 4: Place EVEN MORE Bands

Place bands as shown. The colors used are ten yellow, two white, two blue, and one black.

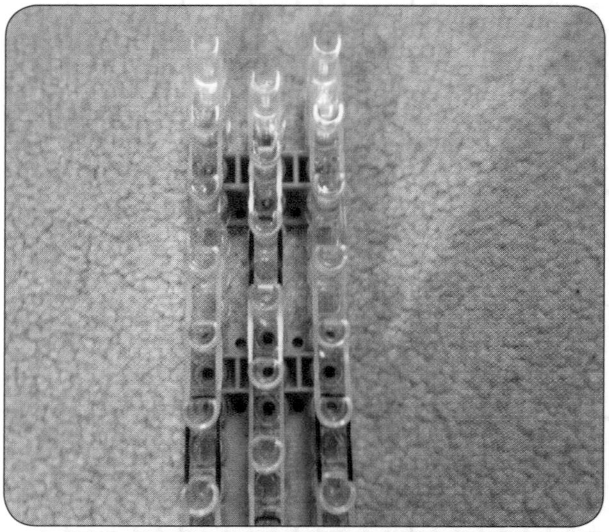

Step 5: Done With Half of Placement!

Well done, you have placed half of the bands!

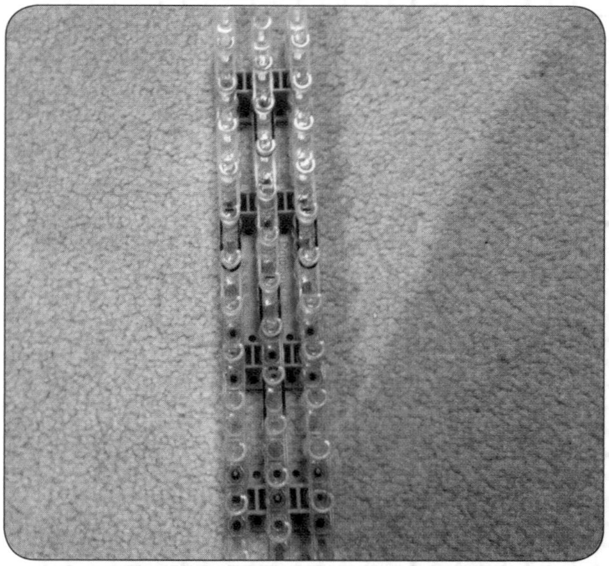

Step 6: Turn Loom Around

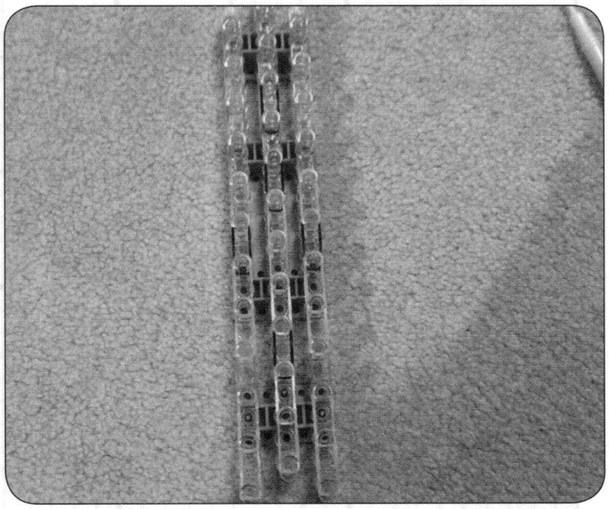

Step 7: Place Bands

Place bands as shown. The colors used are six yellow and one black.

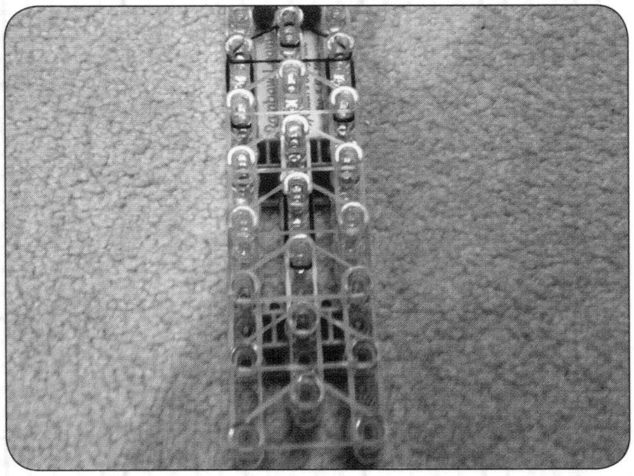

Step 8: Place MORE Bands

Place bands as shown. The color used is five blue.

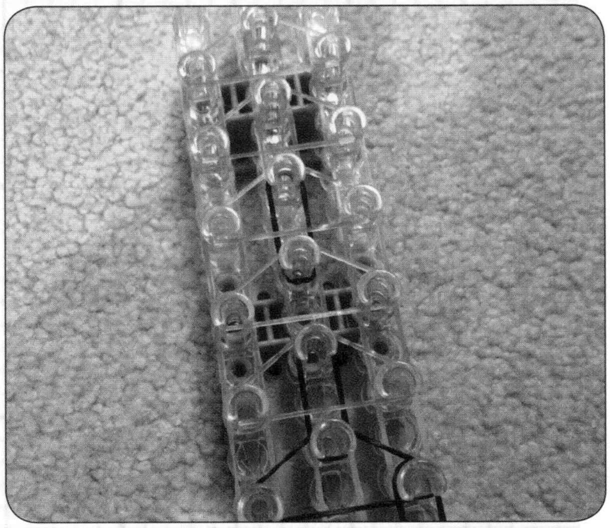

Step 9: Congrats!

You have placed all bands needed! Keep some blue bands handy, as you will need them later.

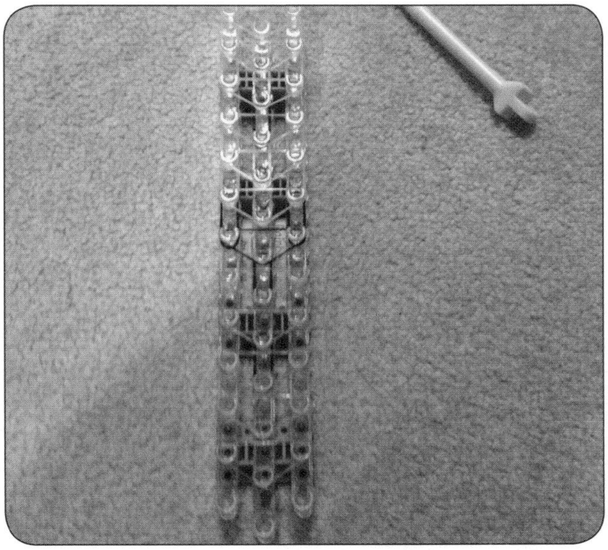

Step 10: Looping!

Loop like a triple single. If you don't know what a triple single is, follow the pictures and go the whole row each time.

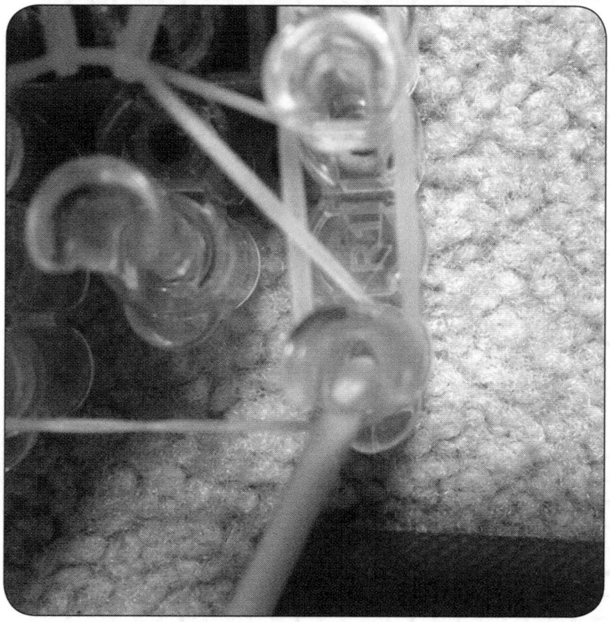

Step 11: Yay!

You have almost completed the minion!

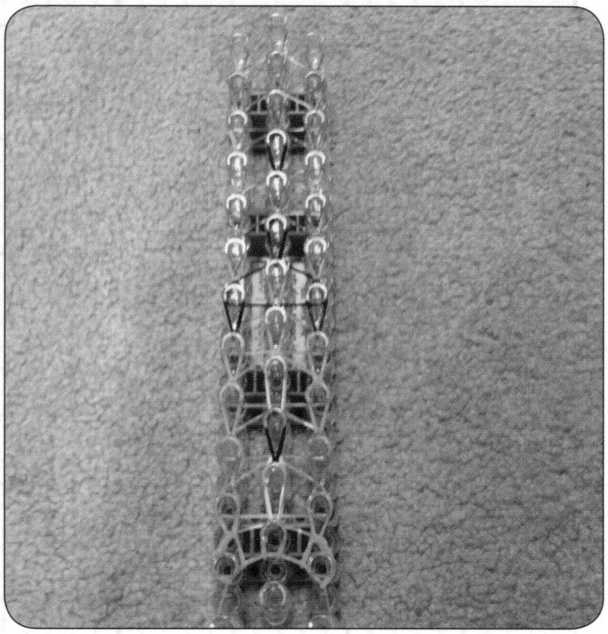

Step 12: Add Cap Band

Follow the picture to add the cap band (has to be blue).

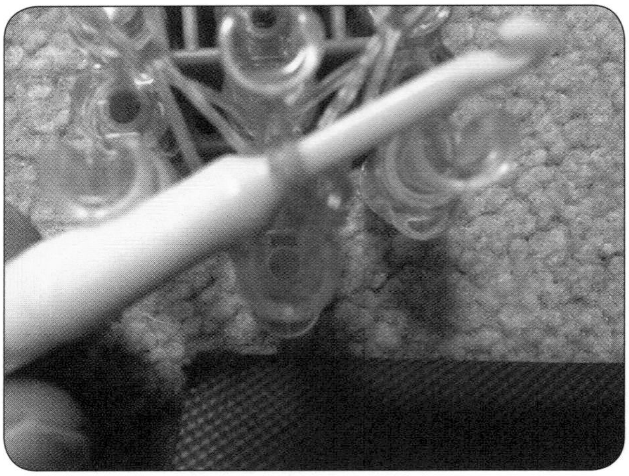

Step 13: Take It Off!

Go on, rip that sucker off, baby!

Step 14: What It Should Look Like

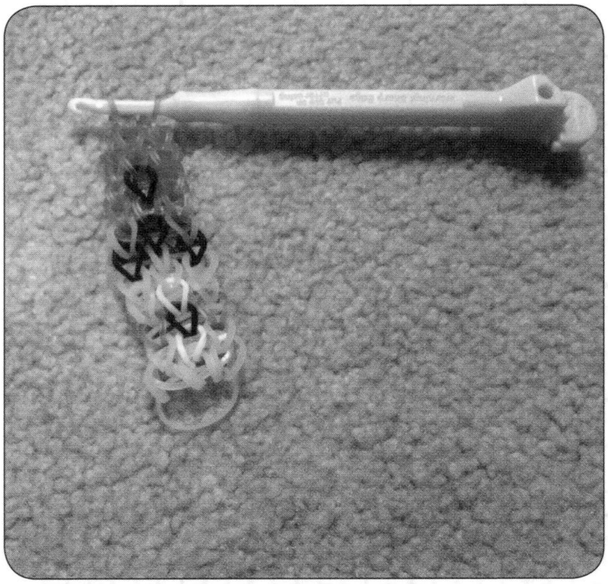

Step 15: Add Extension

Repeat these steps five more times.

Step 16: Extension Added

This is what it should look like.

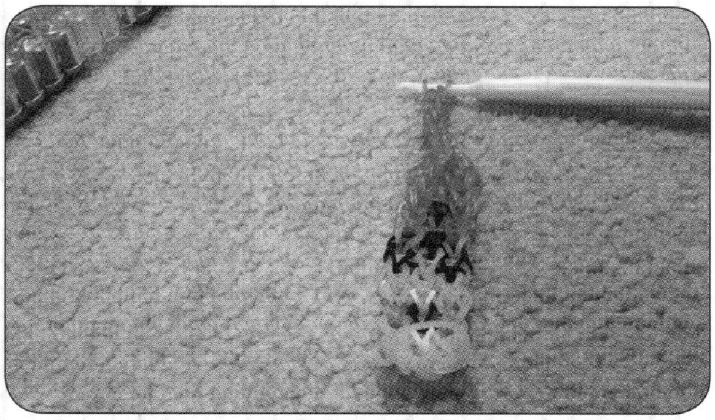

Step 17: Add Clip

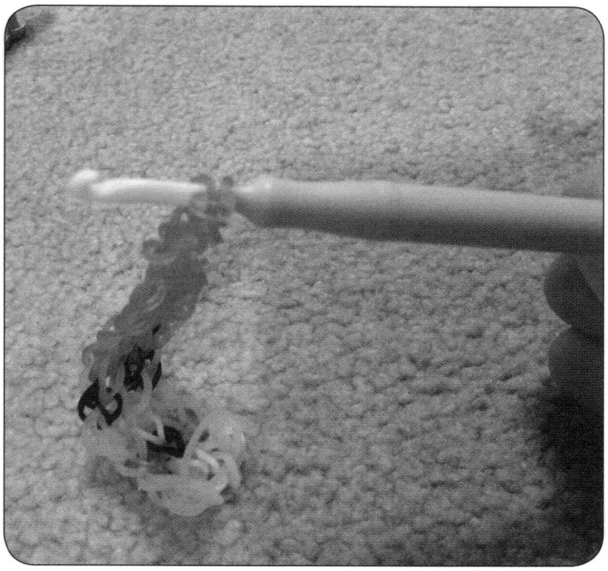

Step 18: You're Done!

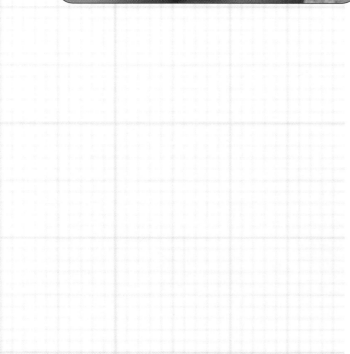

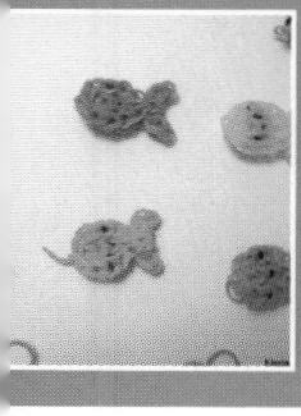

Charms

Goldfish

By Jenny Nguyen (nngân)
(http://www.instructables.com/id/Rainbow-Loom-Goldfish-Charm/)

Step 1: You will need:

- Loom
- Hook
- 39 Rainbow Loom rubber bands, a rubber band for the eyes, and an extra rubber band to hold it all together Rainbow Loom rubber bands in colors of your choice

Step 2: Placing the Bands

Make sure the arrow on your loom is pointing away from you! Place two rubber bands from the bottom middle peg to the right diagonally. Do the same to the left side. Then place two rubber bands from the bottom middle peg forward.

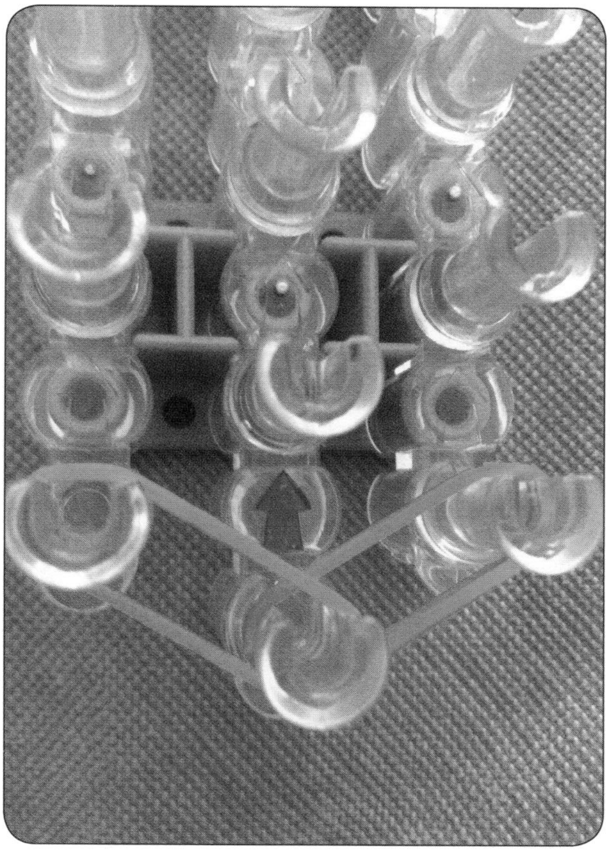

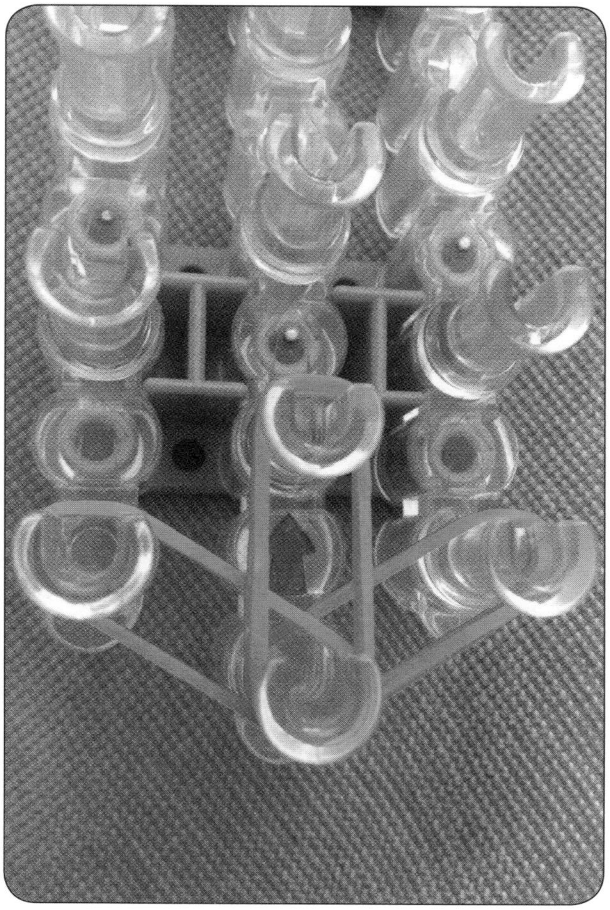

Step 3: Placing the Bands

Then place two rubber bands from the middle forward. Do the same to the left and right. Repeat that! Now place two rubber bands from the left forward. Do the same to the right!

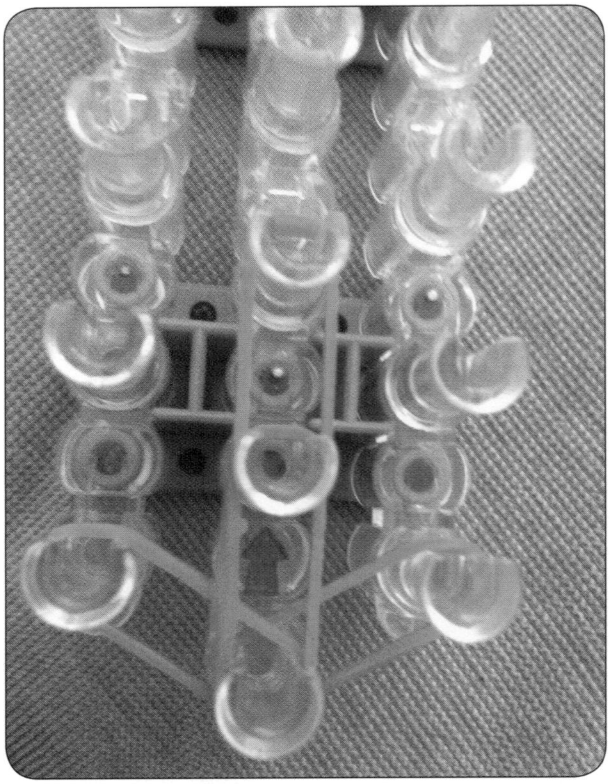

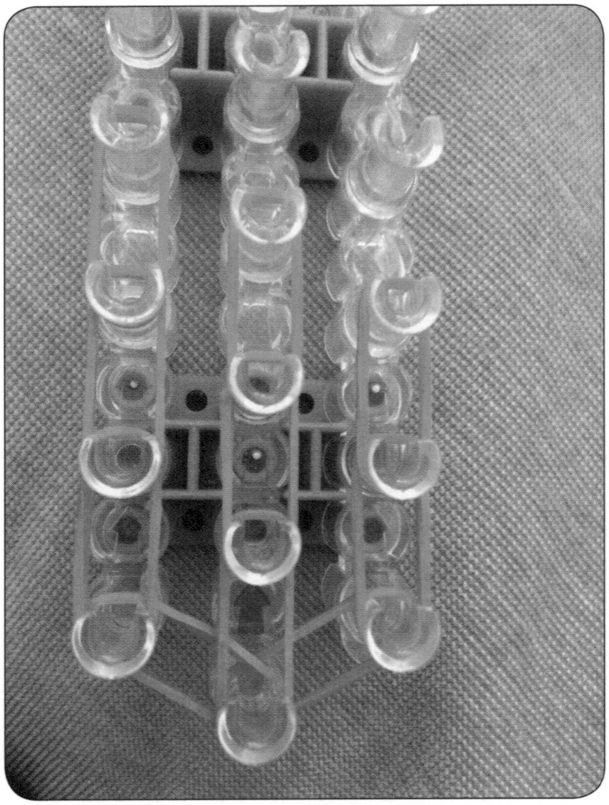

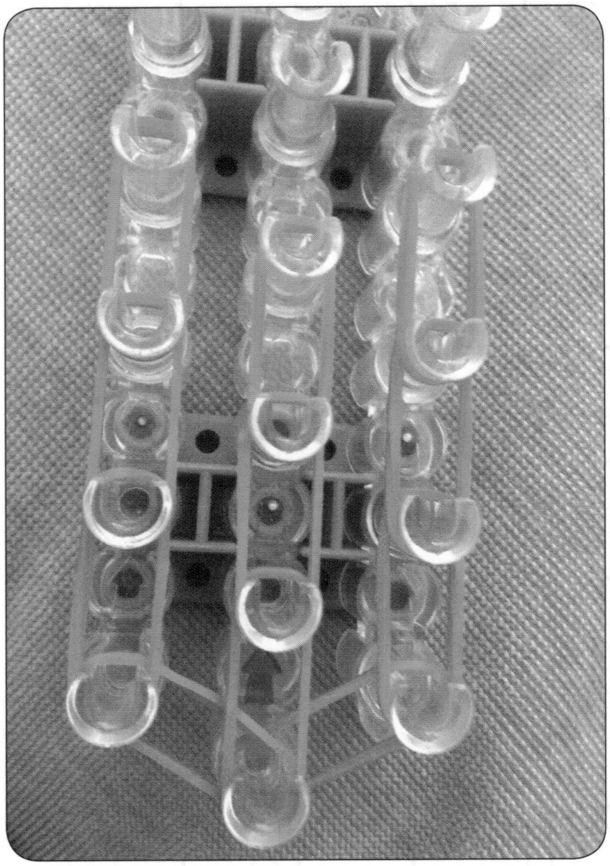

Step 4: Placing the Bands

Now place a single rubber band from the middle forward. Then place a single rubber band from the right to the middle diagonally. Do the same to the left side.

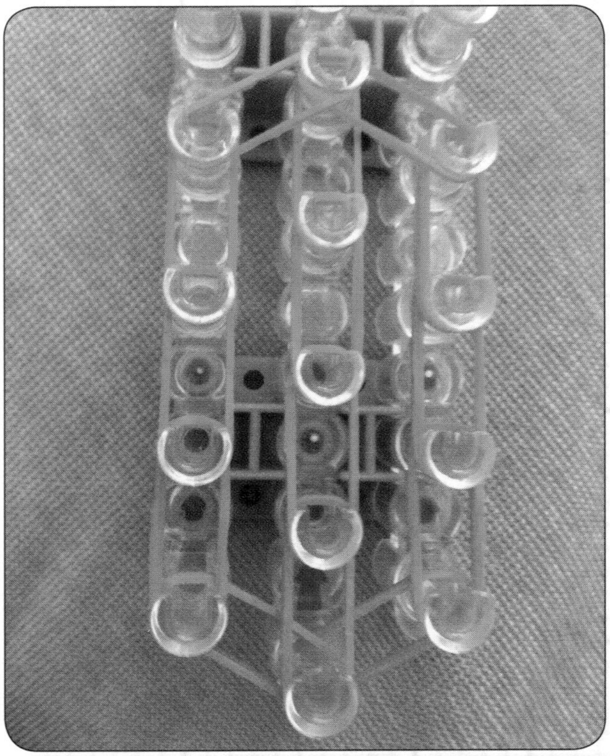

Step 5: Placing the Bands

Now place two rubber bands from the middle to the right diagonally. Do the same to the left side. Then place a single rubber band from the middle forward.

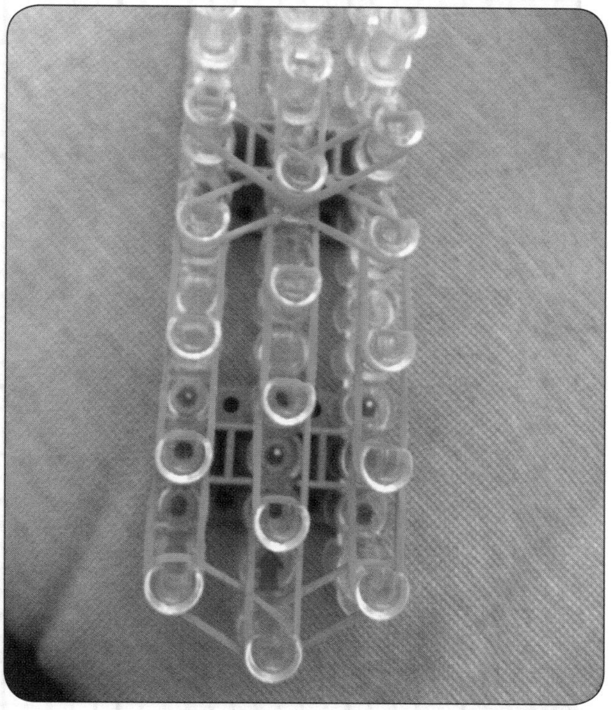

Step 6: Placing the Bands

Now place two rubber bands from the left forward. Do the same to the right side!

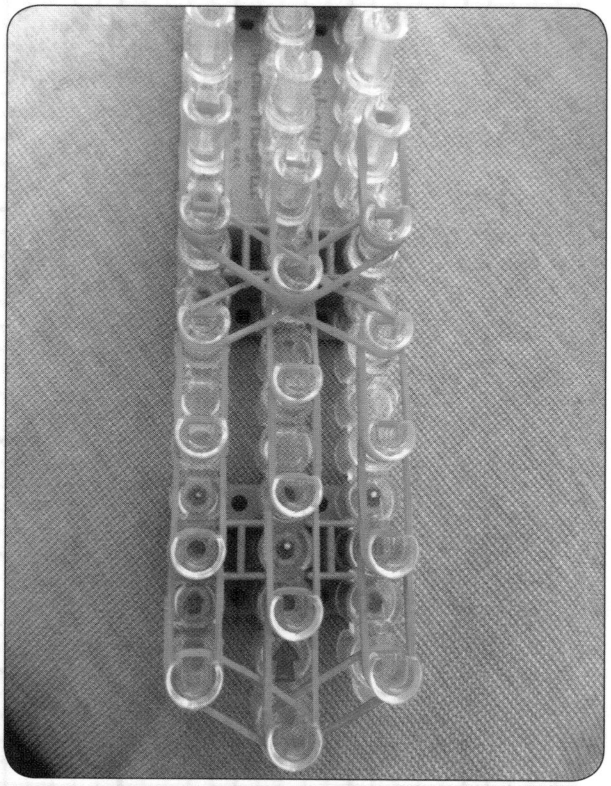

Step 7: The Eyes!

This is optional: Grab a single rubber band and place it on the second bottom peg on the left and stretch it to the right. Then drag the middle of the band to the third peg in the middle row.

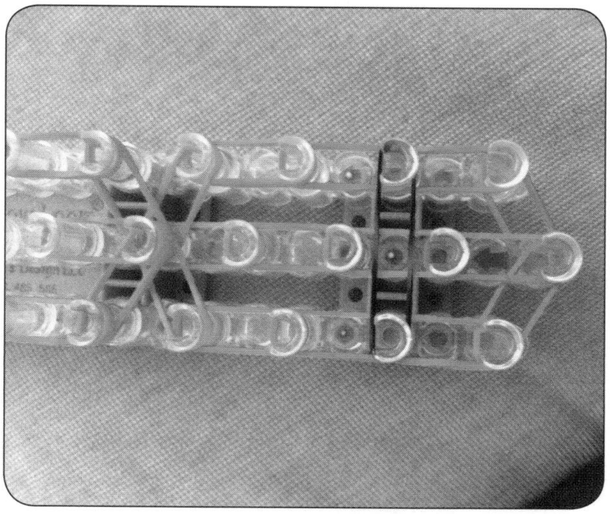

Step 8: Continue the Eyes

Now take two rubber bands and stretch them from the middle of the eyes to form a triangle (look at the pictures) then take a single band and form a figure eight by twisting it. Then place the two holes of the figure eight together to form a stacked O. Then place it below the triangle you placed earlier. Make sure it is also a triangle! See the photos for guidance.

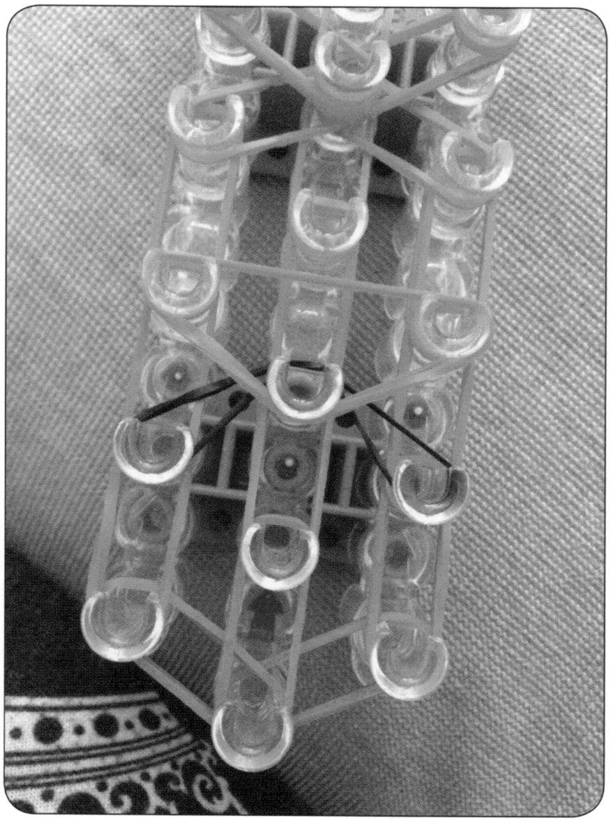

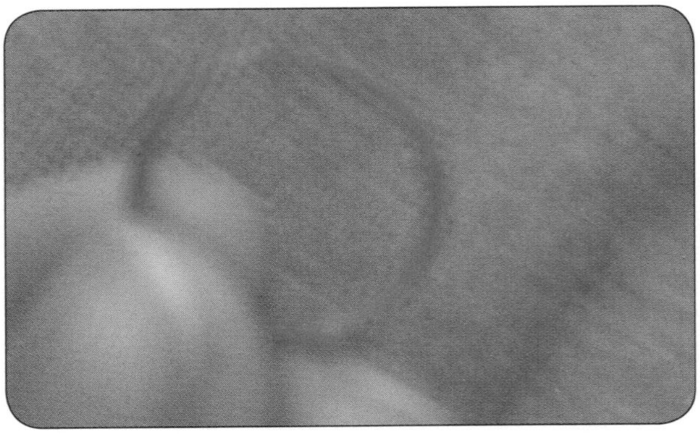

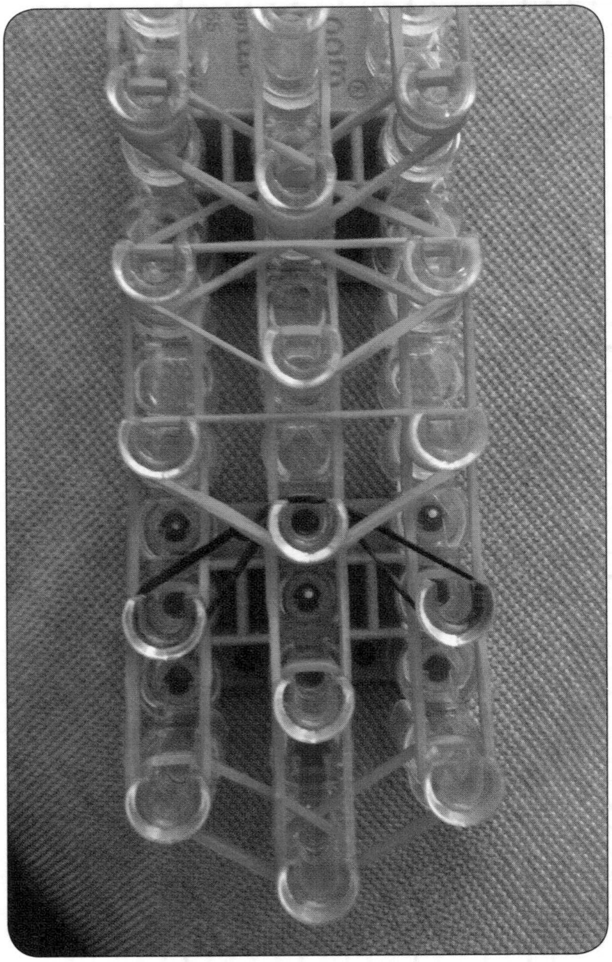

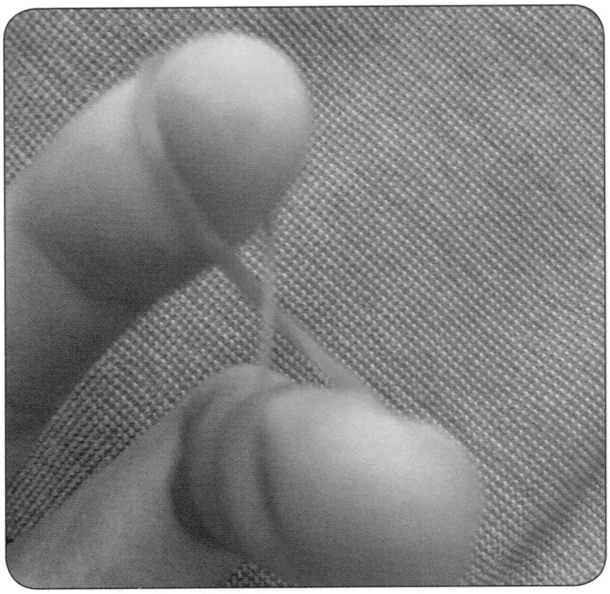

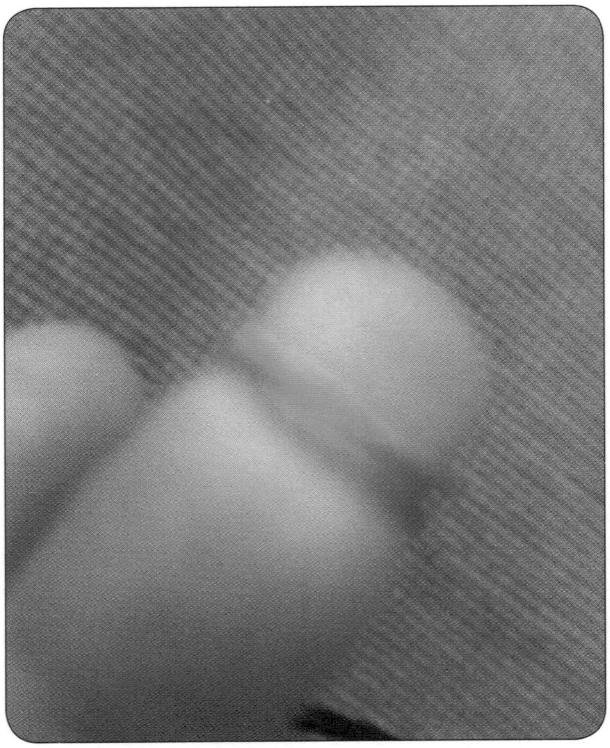

Step 9: Adding More Bands

Now take two rubber bands and place them from the left to right on top of the triangle you just placed. Look at the pictures!

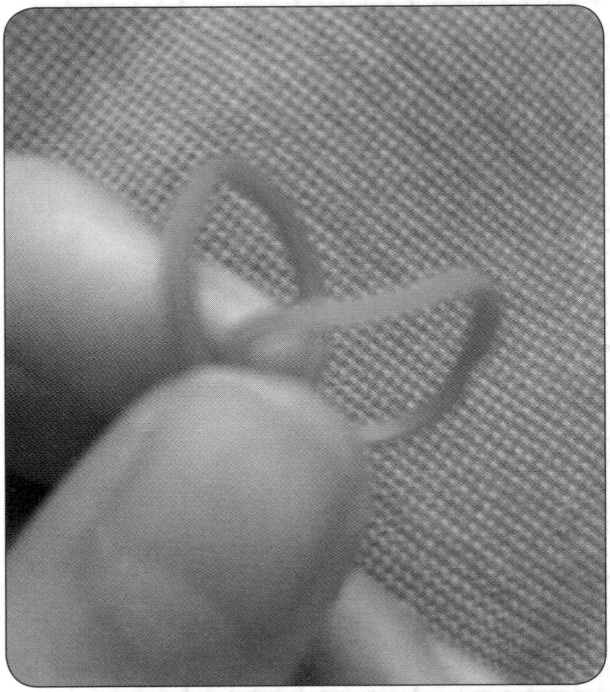

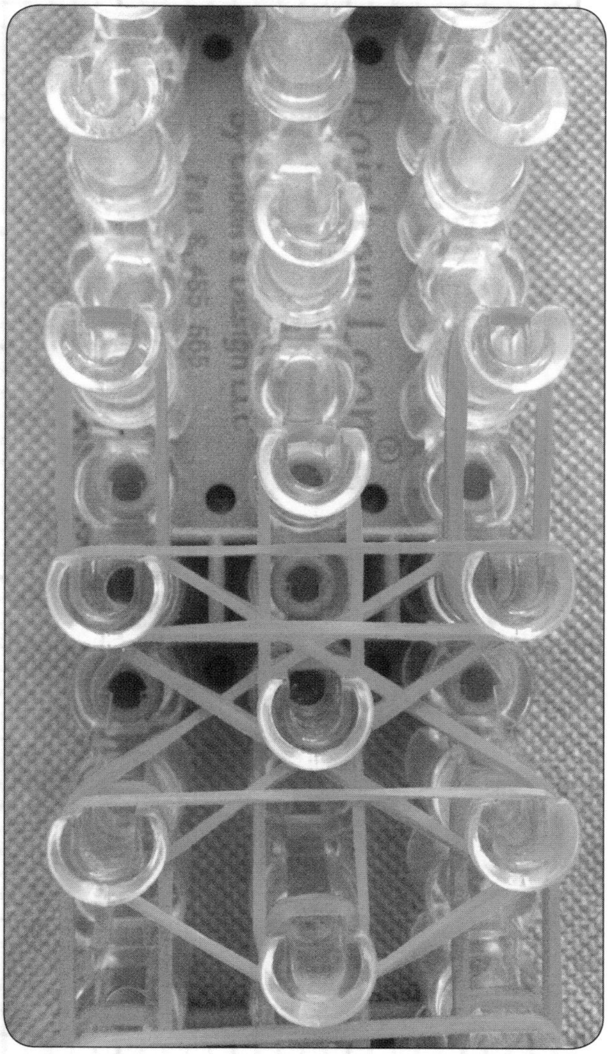

Step 10: More Bands

Now take a single rubber band and twist it two times to have a tripled O. Place it on the top left rubber band. Do the same to the right side!

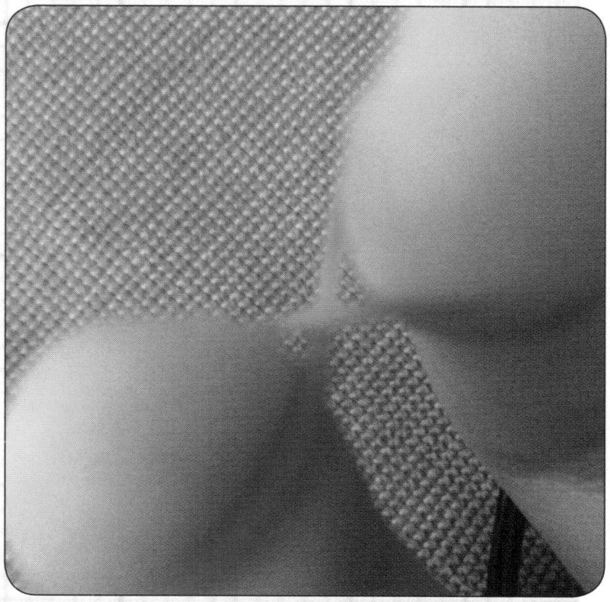

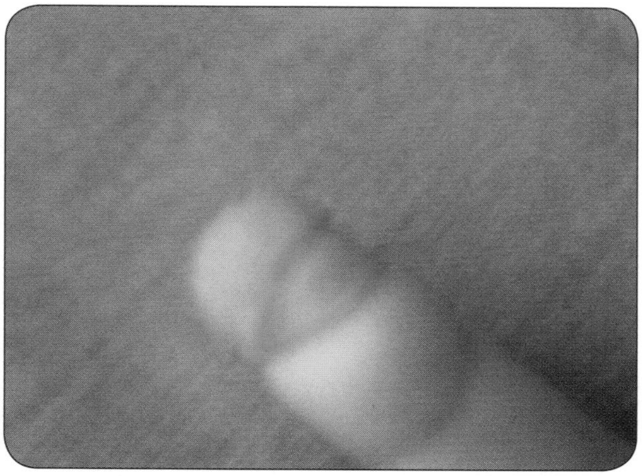

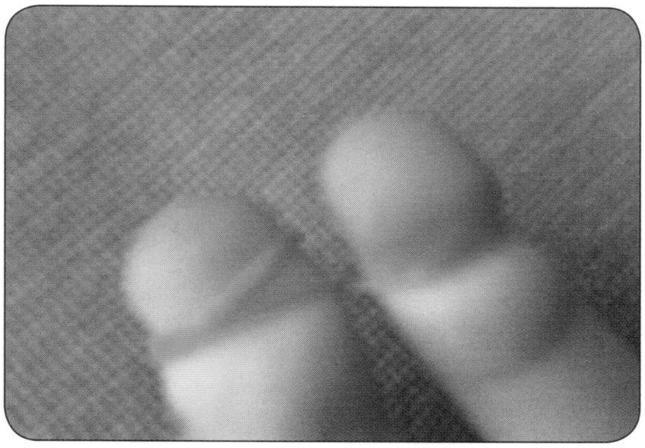

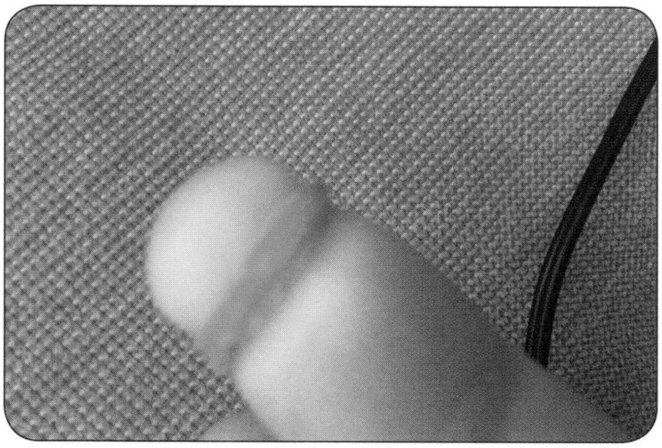

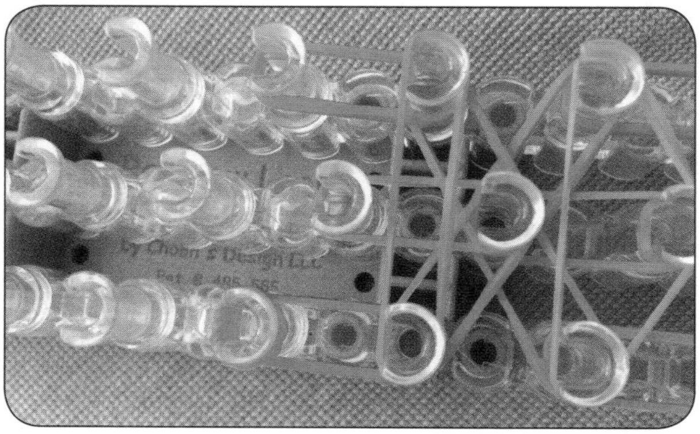

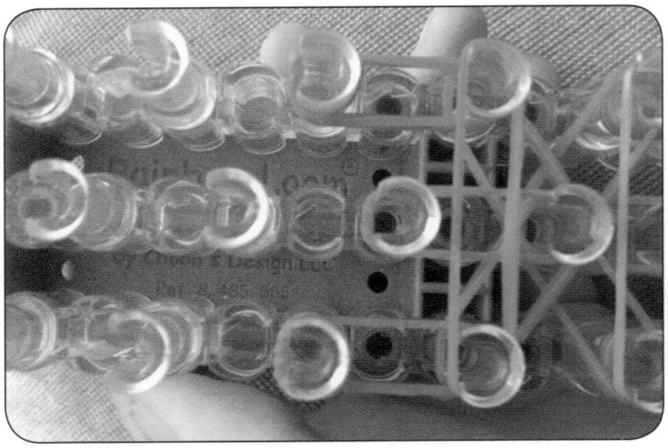

Step 11: Looping the Rubber Bands!

Now flip the loom so that the arrow is pointing at you.

Step 12: Looping

Place your hook in the left cap band and grab the two rubber bands and loop them forward! Then loop the two rubber bands that are in/under the bands you just looped to the middle diagonally. Do the same to the right side.

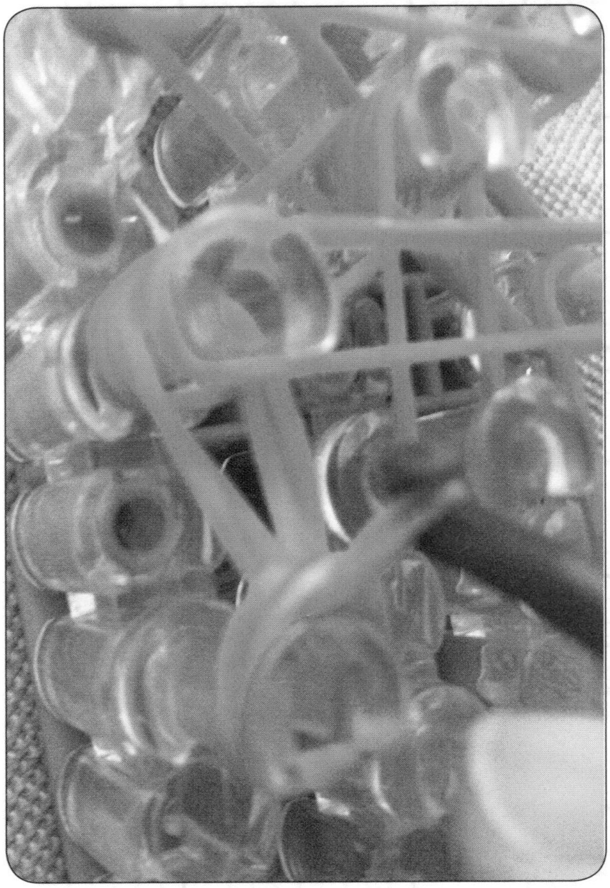

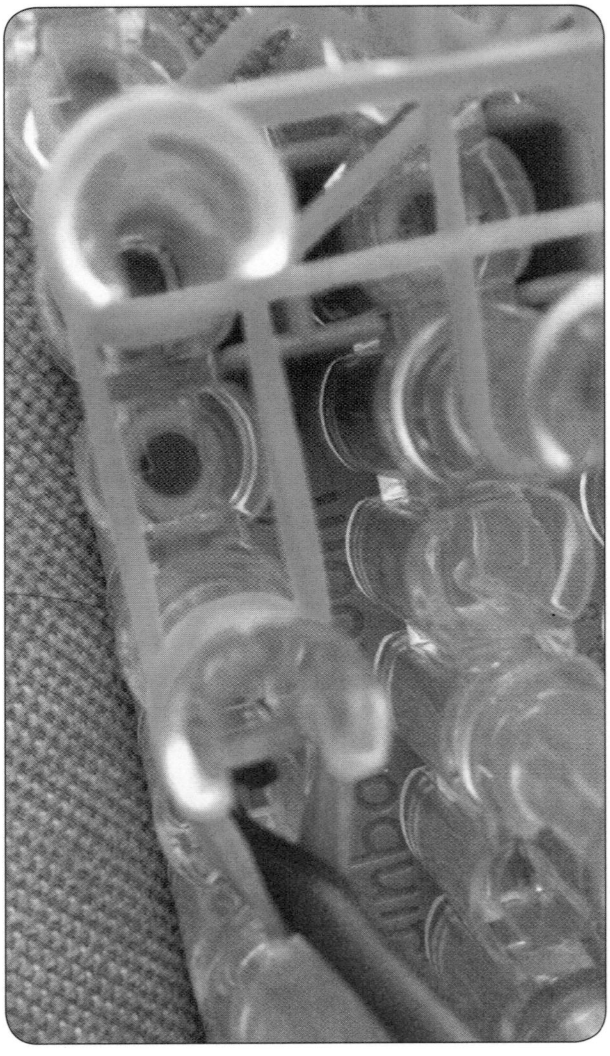

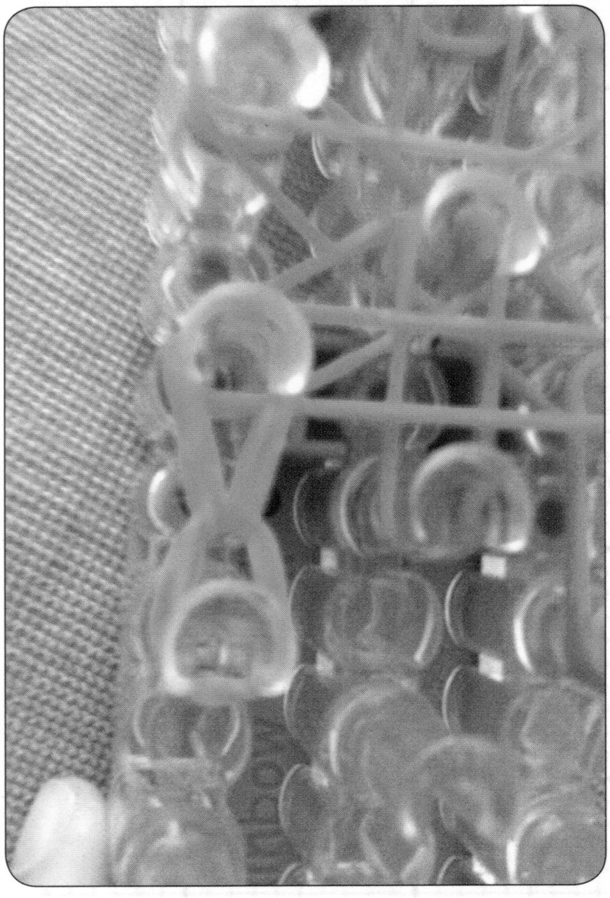

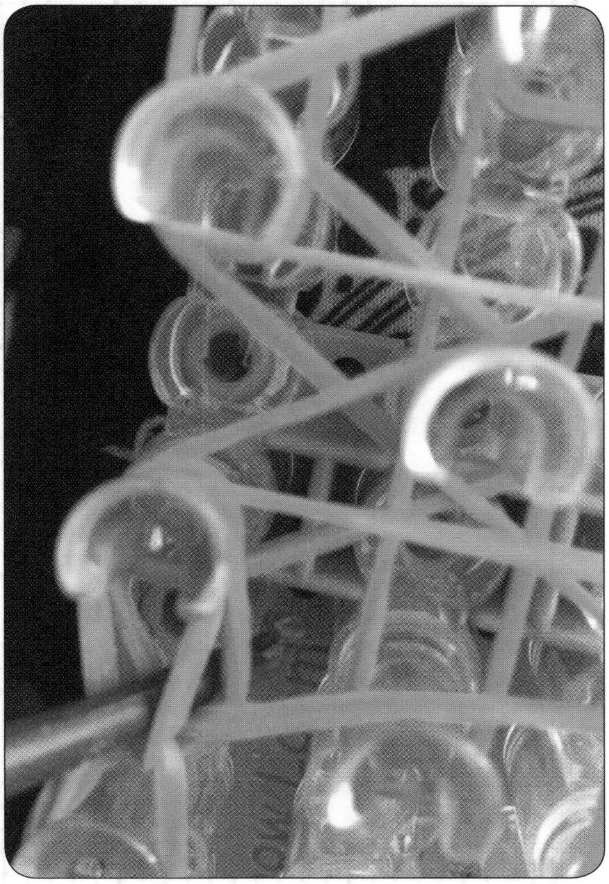

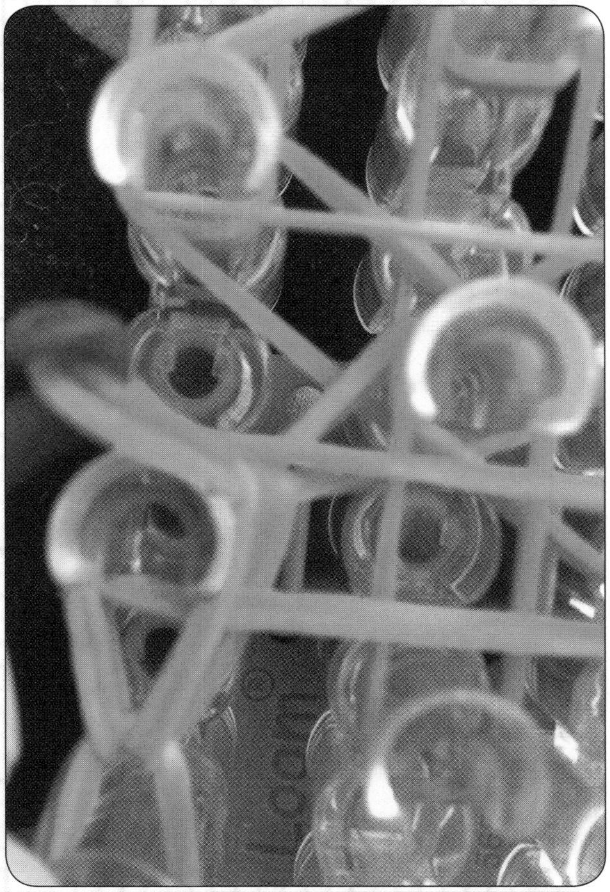

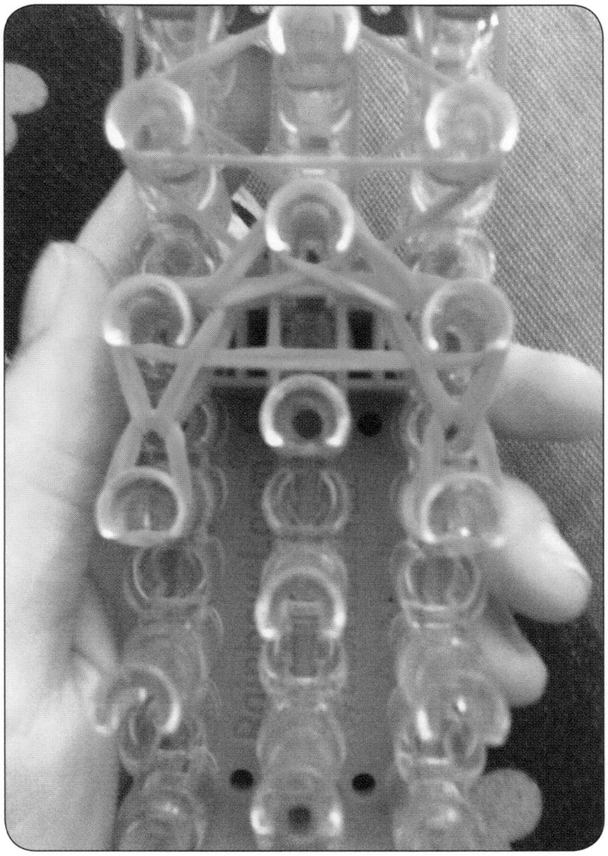

Step 13: Looping

Now loop the middle single band forward!

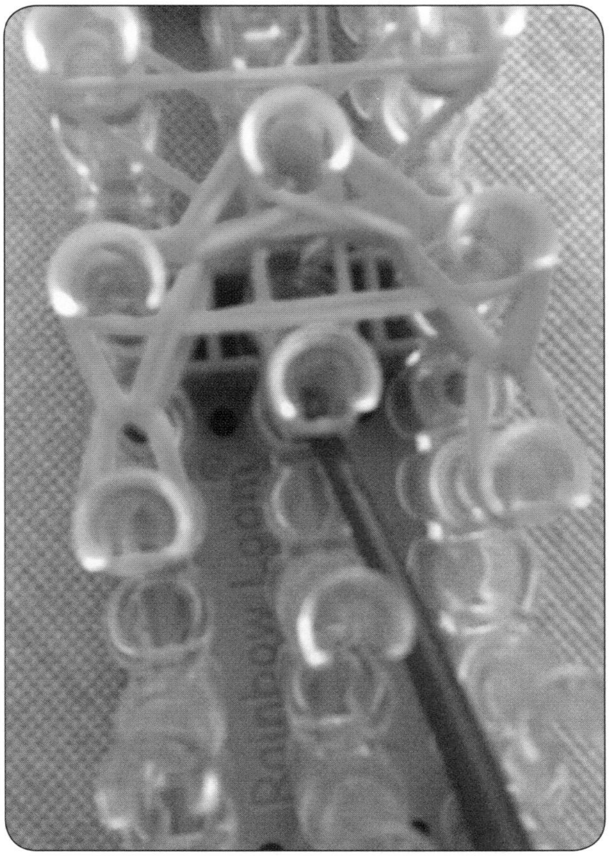

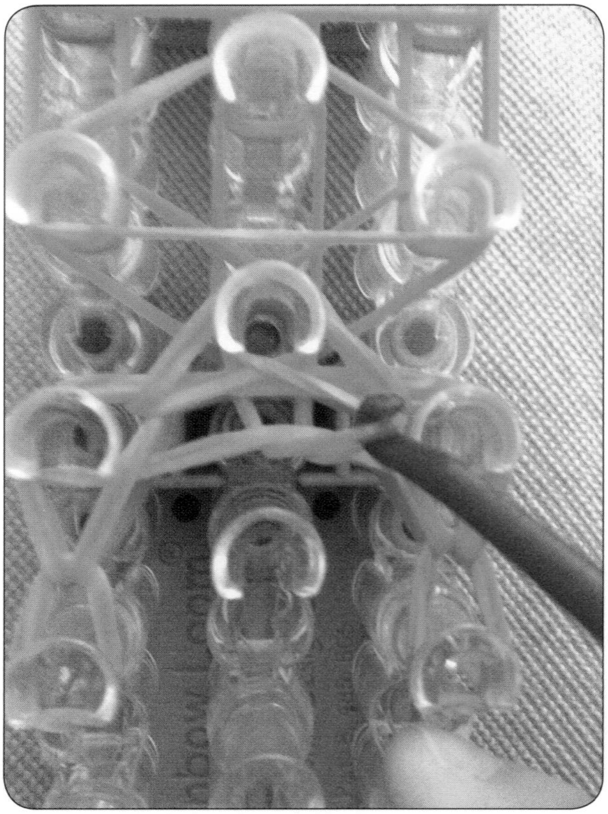

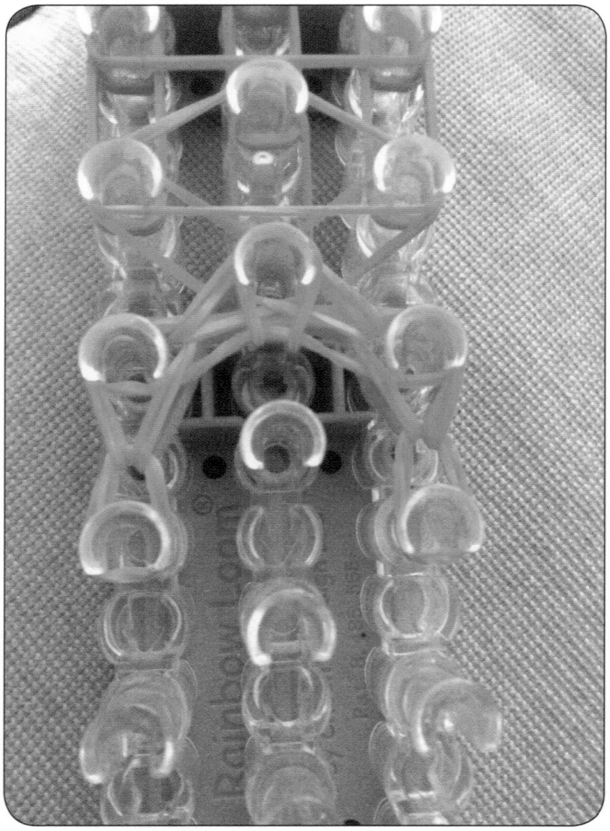

Step 14: Looping

Reach under/in all of the looped bands and loop the top single band to the right diagonally. Now reach back in and pull another single band and loop it to the left diagonally. Loop the last single band forward.

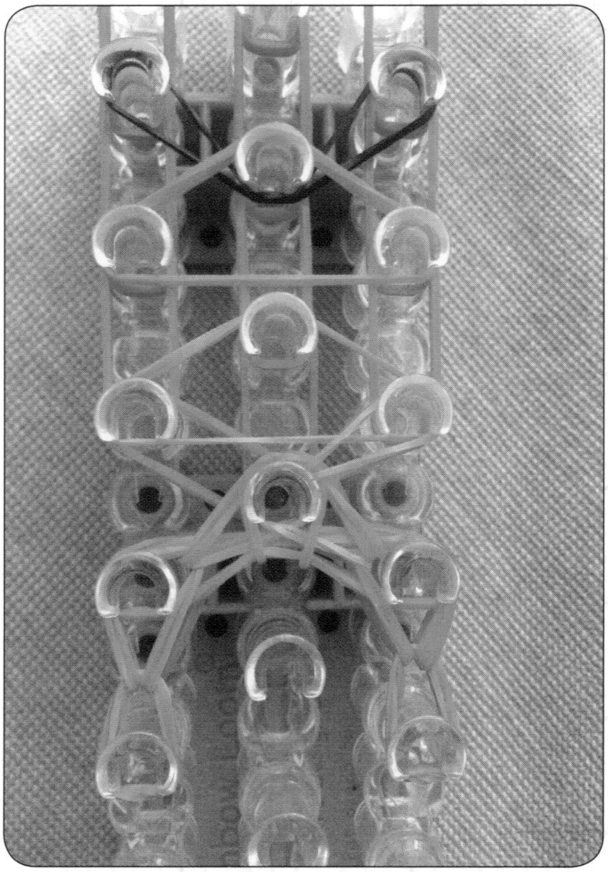

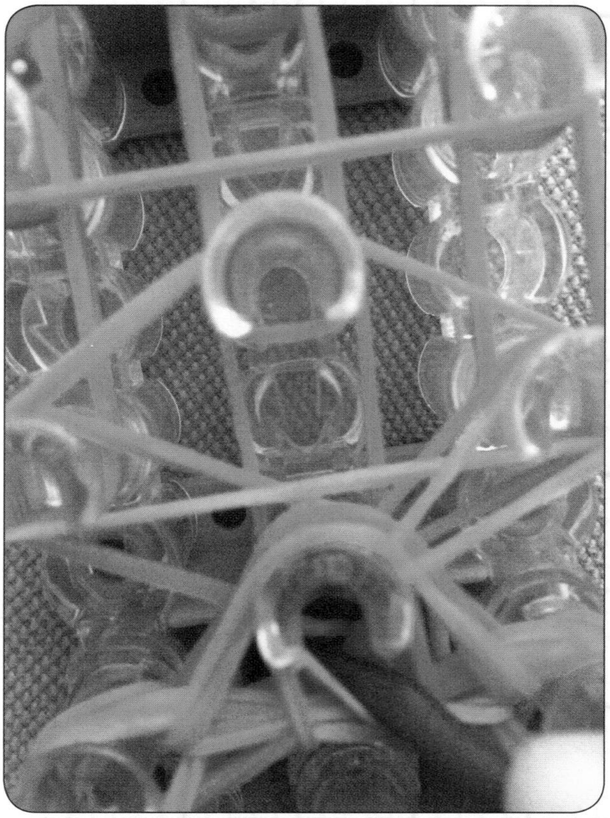

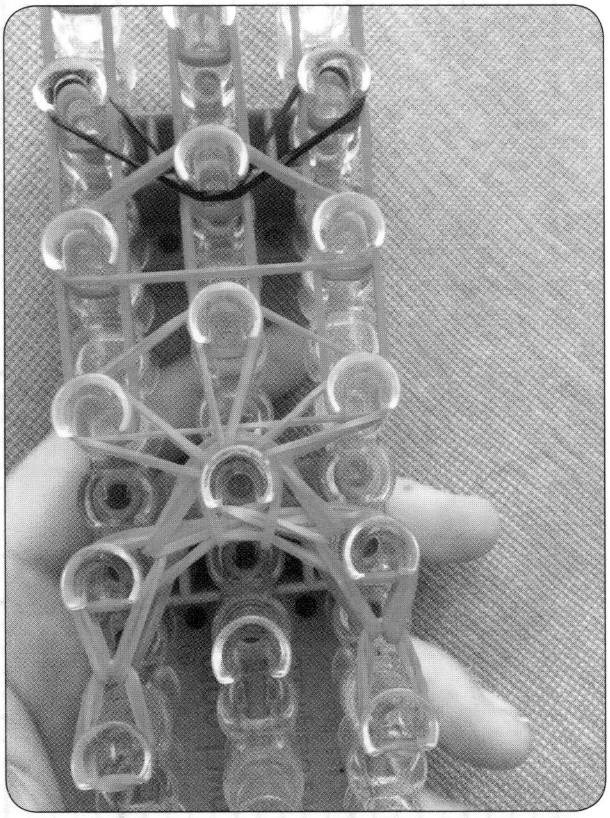

Step 15: Looping

Now loop the right rubber bands forward until you reach the top of the right row. Then loop the last rubber band to the middle diagonally. Do the same to the left side.

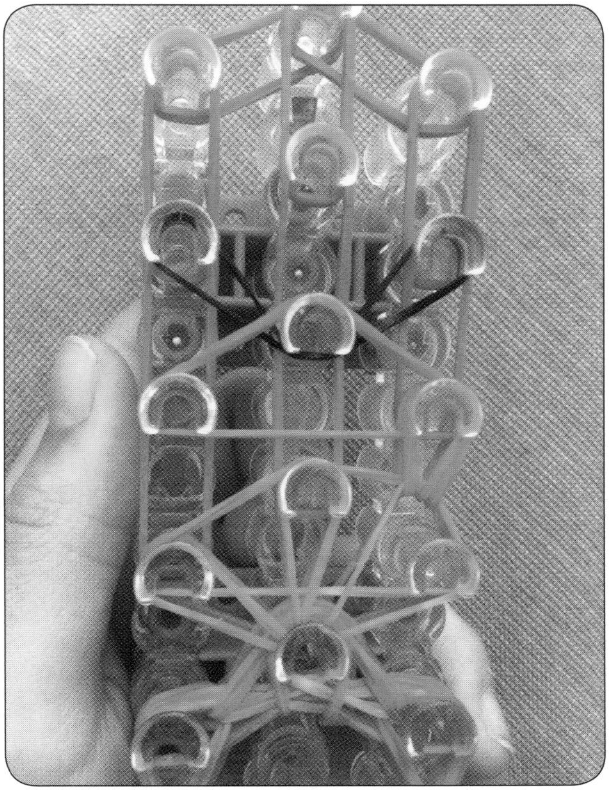

Step 16: Almost Done!

Now loop the rest of the middle row until you reach the top. Then take a single rubber band and knot the top. Then carefully take the charm off the loom. Now you're done!

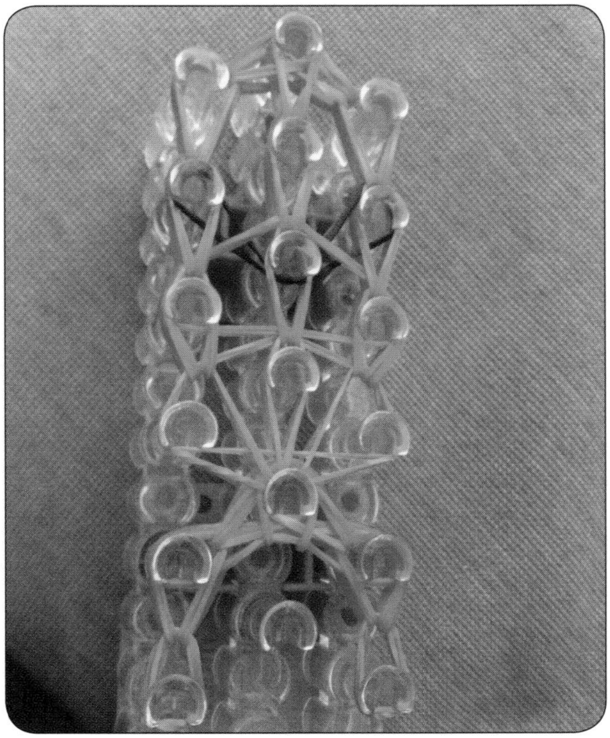

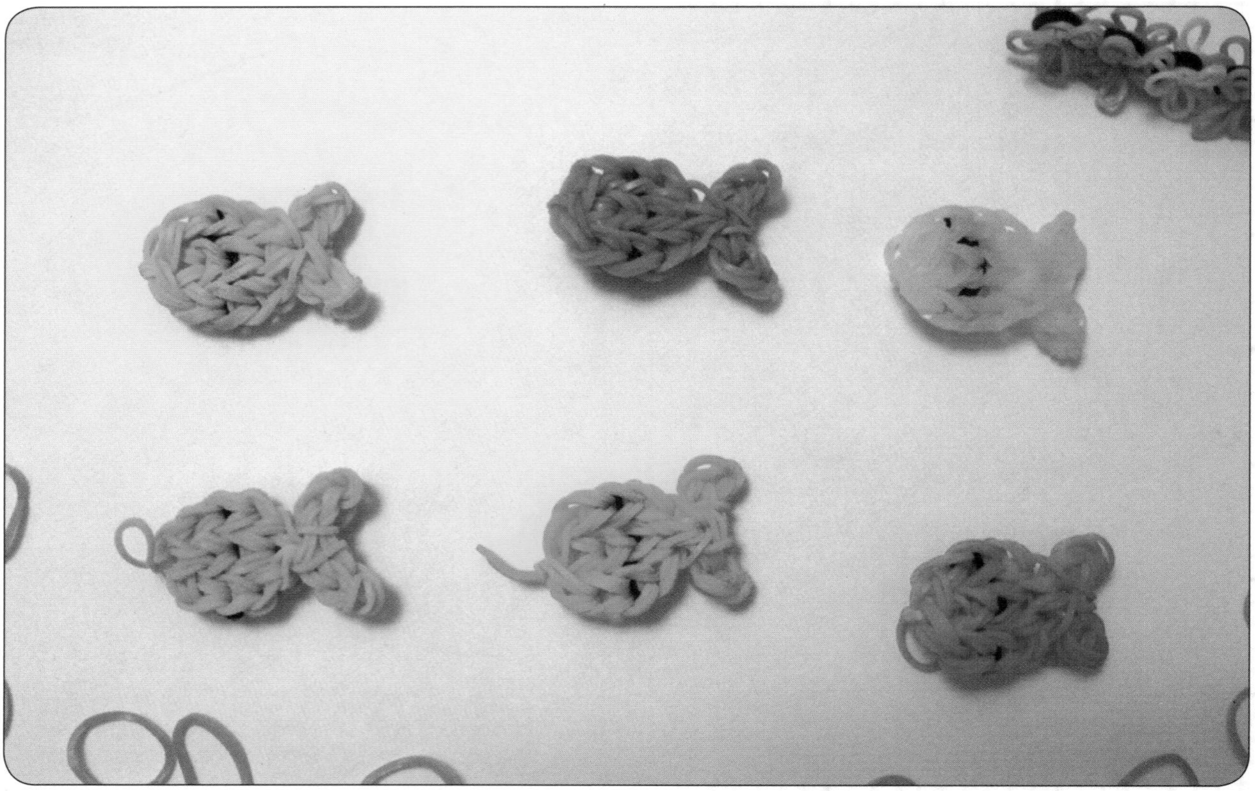

Gingerbread Man

By kawaiilover

(http://www.instructables.com/id/Double-Sided-PersonGingerbread-Person-Bracelet/)

This is a bracelet I really had fun making. It is a bit difficult but worth the time. It is double sided, both a person and a gingerbread person!

Step 1: What You Need

- Rubber bands in colors of your choice
- Rainbow Loom kit or other rubber band loom
- Hook
- C-clip

Step 2: Starting Your Bracelet

Set up your loom so that the arrow is pointing toward you. Lay rubber bands like this, starting from the top down. All bands are doubled except bands going horizontally.

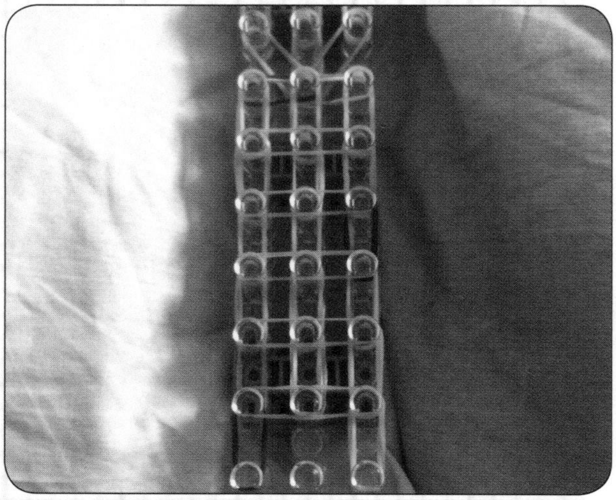

Step 3: The Head

On the head—the pegs three rows down—have a band that is folded in half and placed on horizontally.

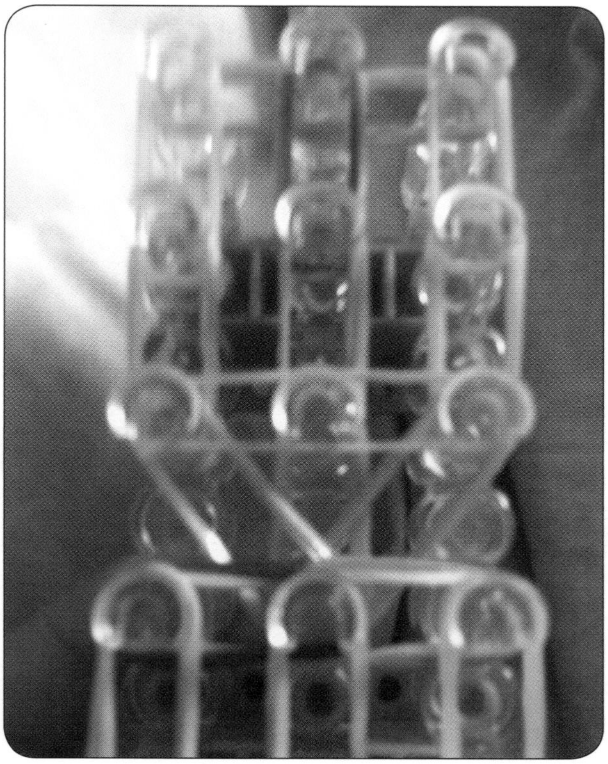

Step 4: Cap Bands

Next, we will make the capping bands on the feet. Take one band per foot and twist it around the feet pegs three times.

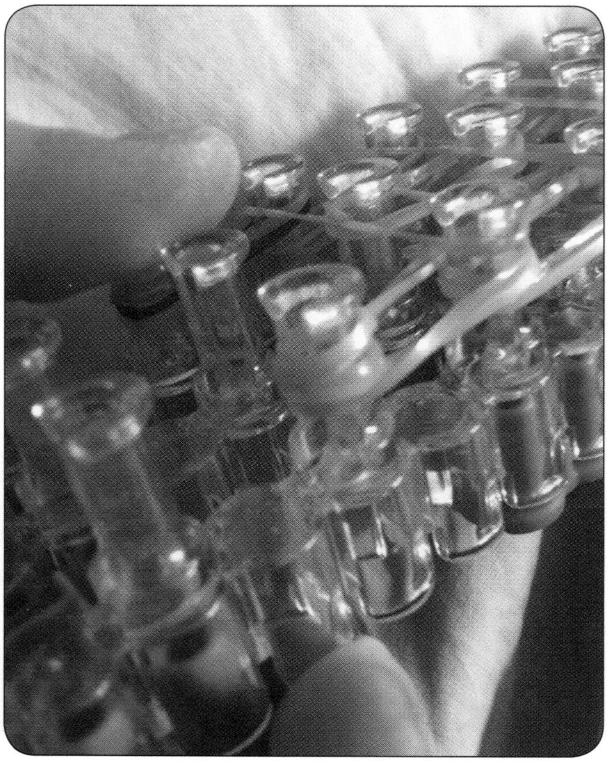

Step 5: Body

Next, we will make the body parts. On the unused bottom nine pegs we will make the arms. Place the bands as shown in the picture, laying them down while the arrow is pointing away from you. Add a double layer of capping bands per arm.

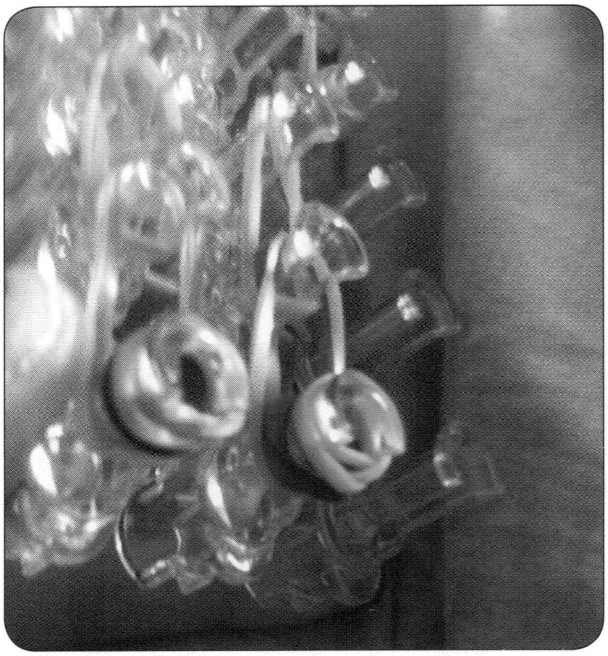

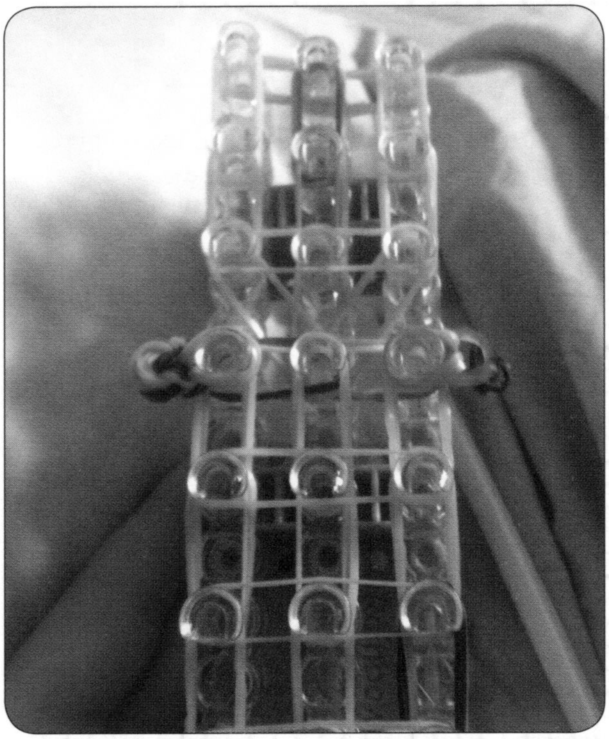

Step 6: Loop Arms

Take the arms and loop them as shown, then place them as shown. Make sure to go under the peg with the arm on it and grab the bottom two bands. Loop them to the peg in the middle. Remember both sides.

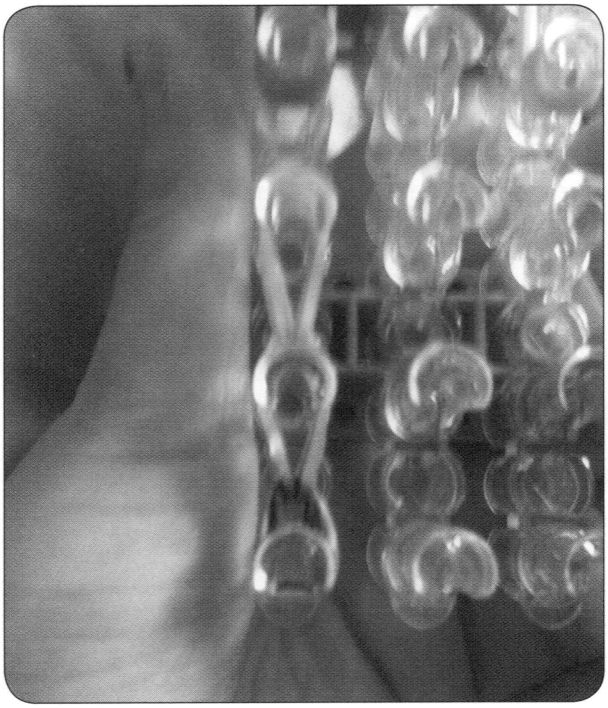

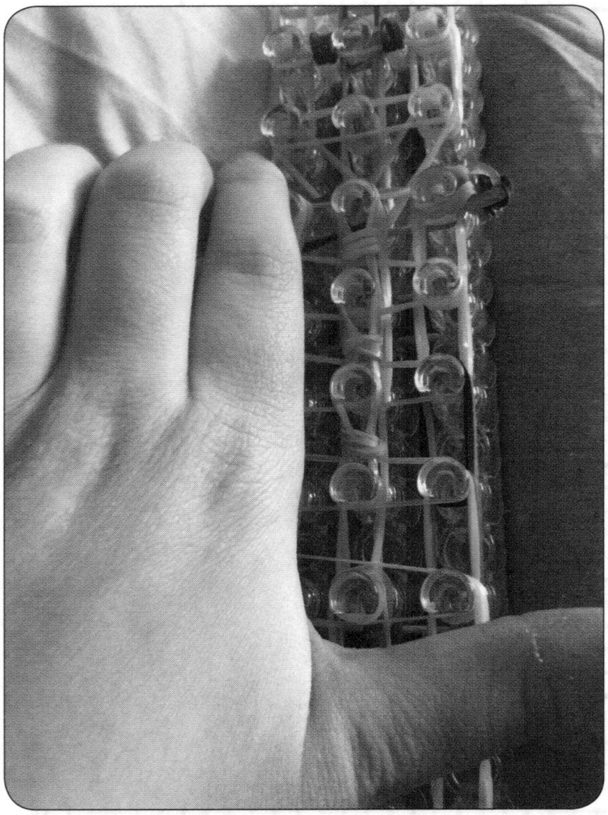

Step 7: Eyes

We will now make the eyes and buttons. For the eyes, take two rubber bands and twist them around your hook so you see three rings per rubber band. Then take one rubber band and pull the two eyes on the band and place the eyes as shown. For the buttons, twist one band around your hook three times so you see three rings, pull the band over two bands, and repeat this two more times. Then place them as shown.

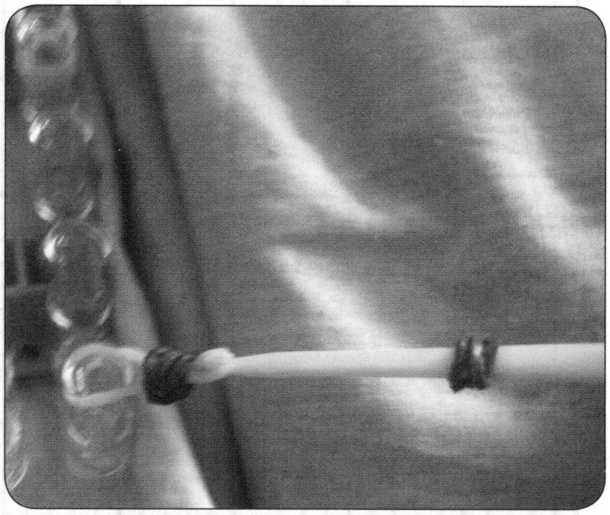

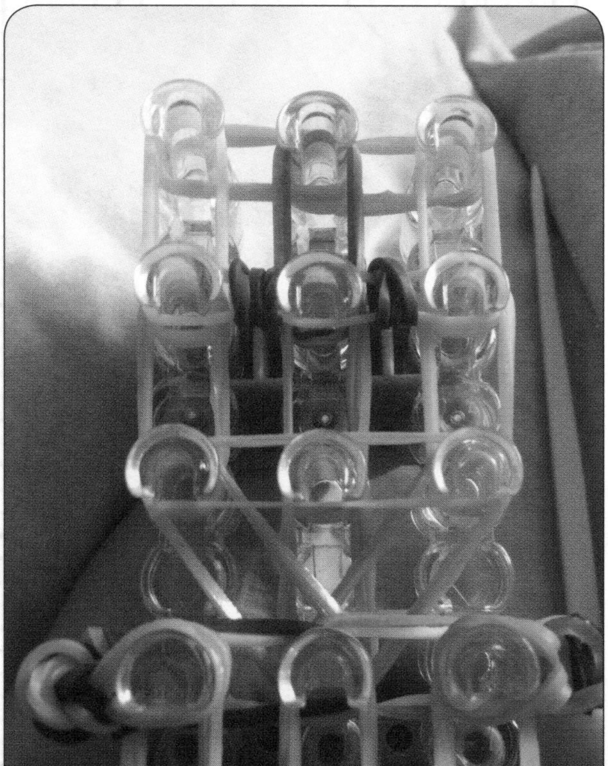

Step 8: Looming

We are now ready to loom! The arrow should point toward you. Starting with the feet, go under all the bands to the bottom two bands and loom up. Continue all the way up to the arms and neck. Loom left to right for all three rows. It should look like the photo.

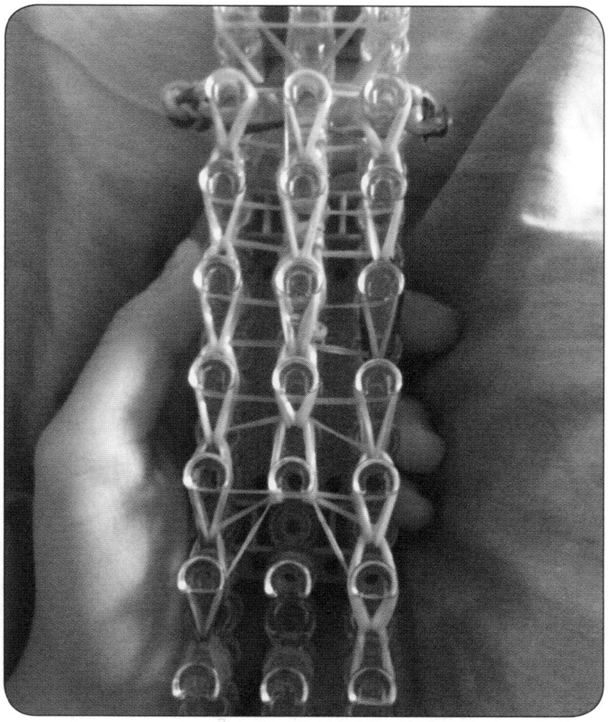

Step 9:

This will be the hardest part. The middle peg of the neck will be where we are now looming. Go under all of the bands until you find the two bands that belong to the left of the head's bands. Pull them through all the bands and loop them onto the slanted peg above it. Repeat these steps on the other two pegs. It should make a tear-drop shape if you have grabbed the correct bands. It should look like the photo.

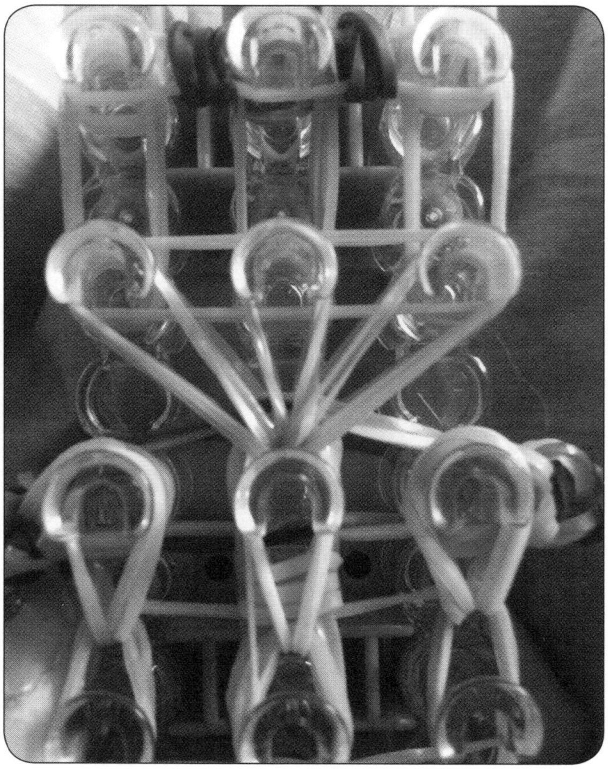

Step 10: Looming

Next, loom from left to right. Going under all the bands grab the bottom two bands and loop forward. Repeat for all rows until you get to the top.

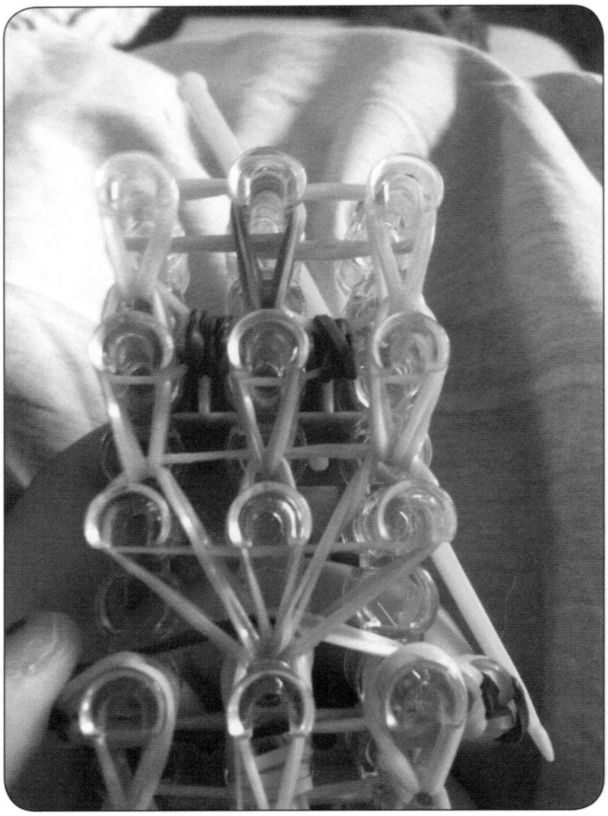

Step 11: Looming

Just like what we just did, go under all the bands and grab the bottom two, then loop them in to the peg to the side of it.

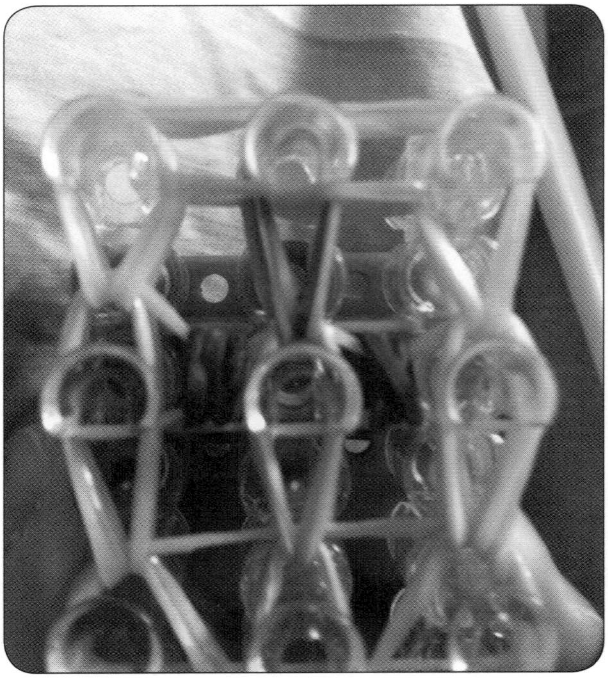

Step 12:

At the top should be the middle peg to which we just finished looming the last of our person, so we need to secure it. Go under all of the bands so the hook is exposed. Grab a band and pull it through all the bands. Pull one end of the band through the other.

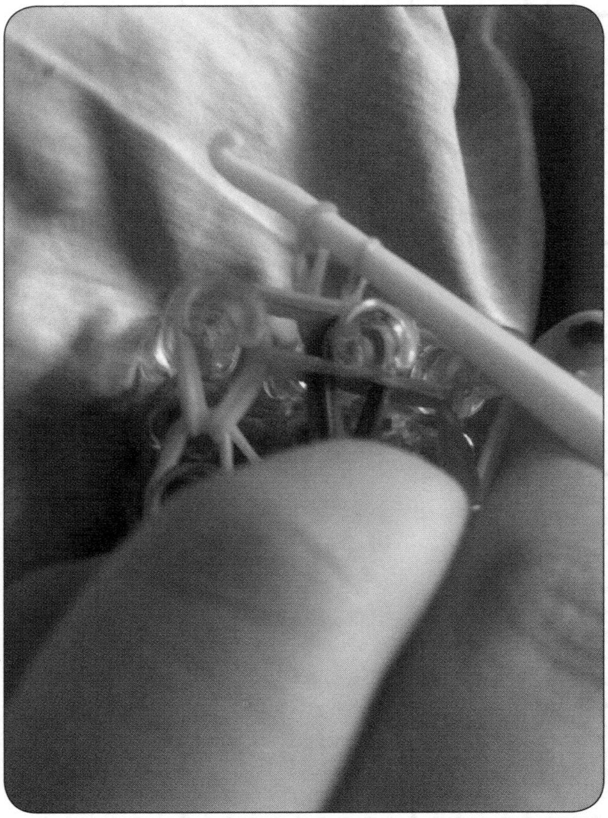

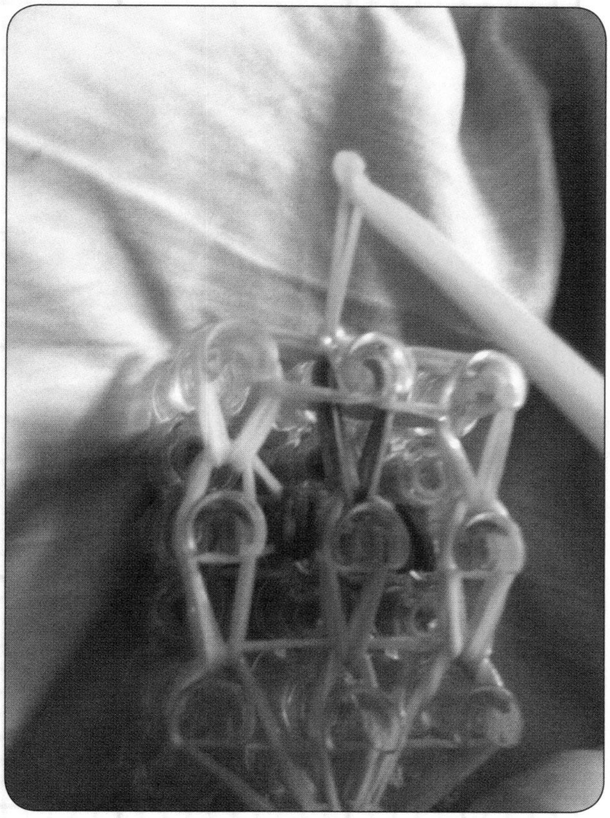

Step 13: Pull It Off

You can now carefully take off the person.

Step 14: Arm Cuffs

We will now make his arm cuffs—just twist a band around each arm until it's tight.

Step 15: Connector

Now, for our connector. On our hook we will make a connector to make a bracelet. First, stick your hook through a place in your person's lower body as shown. Then pull one band through him. Then continue to pull bands through bands to create a single loop chain. Make it as long as needed.

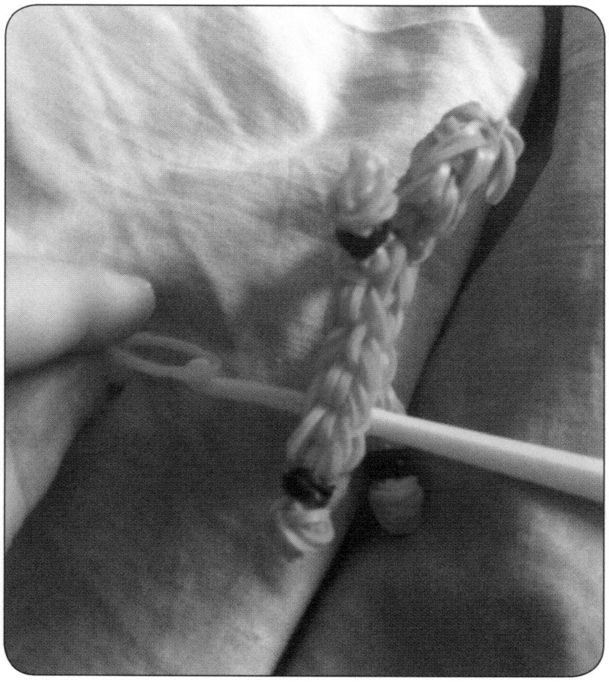

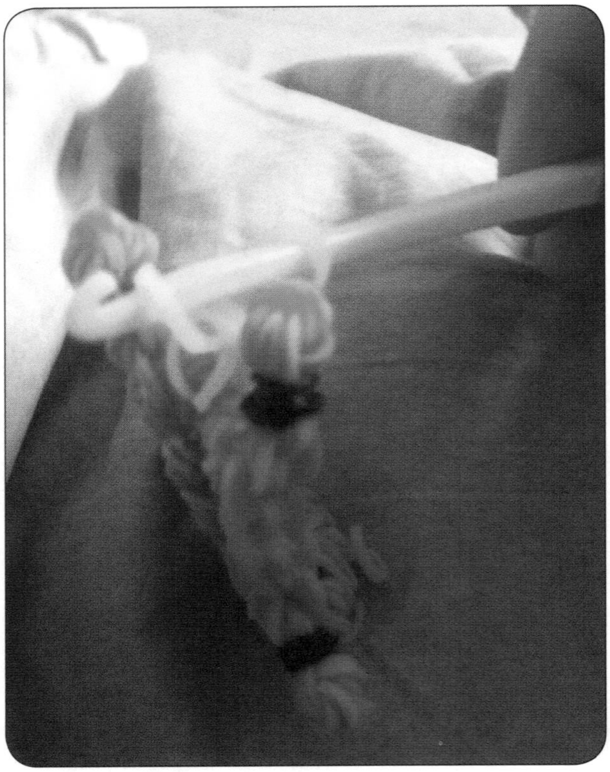

Step 16: Connect Bracelet

Once it is as long as you want, take one of the ends of your rubber band and loop it through the other end. Then tie the loop on the top of the person to the loop of the connector bracelet so it is now one big bracelet.

Step 17: Done!

Your bracelet is now completed! It should look like this photo.

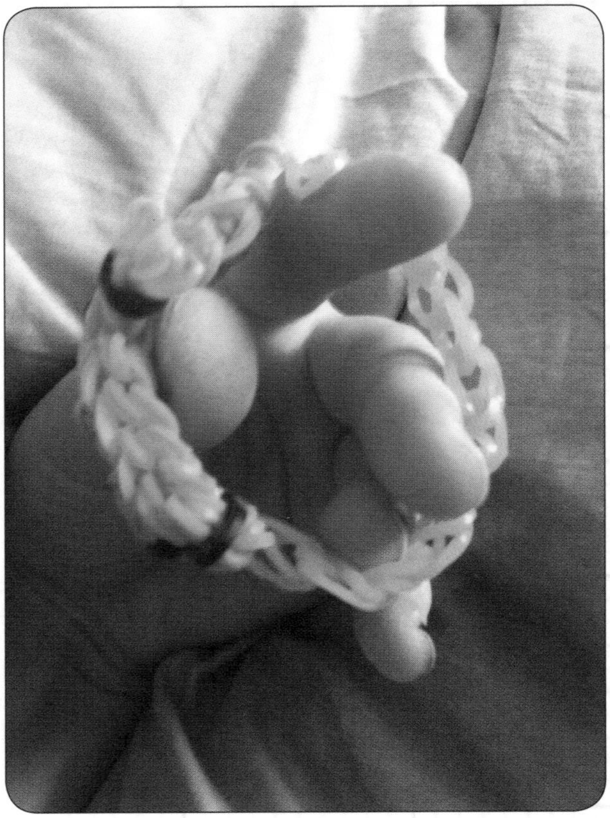

Step 18: Charms

Last but not least, I have made some cute charms for the person/gingerbread person. I've made a butterfly, cross, two flowers, a Christmas wreath, and a candy cane! Don't forget this is reversible!

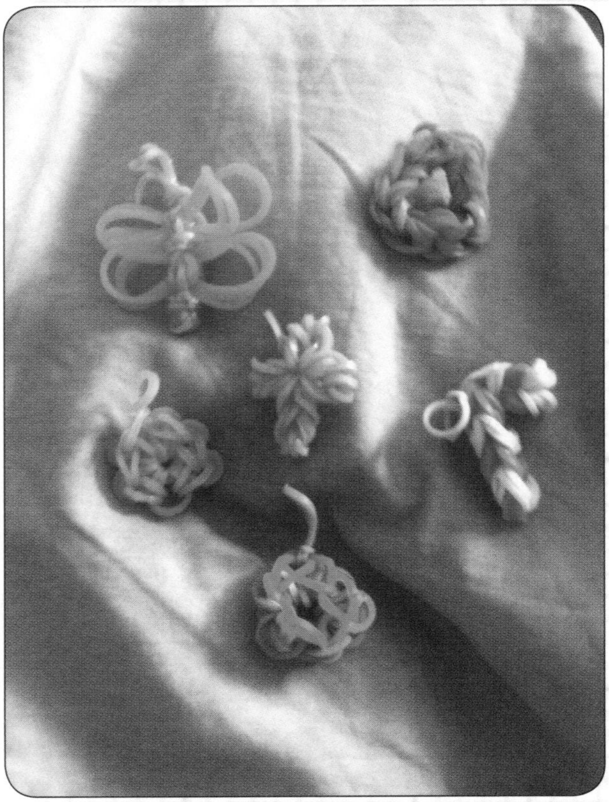

Creeper

By jredmore11
(http://www.instructables.com/id/Minecraft-Rainbow-Loom-Creeper-Charm/)

In this Instructable I will show you how to create a cool Minecraft creeper charm on the Rainbow Loom. You should have a little experience with the Loom to make this charm.

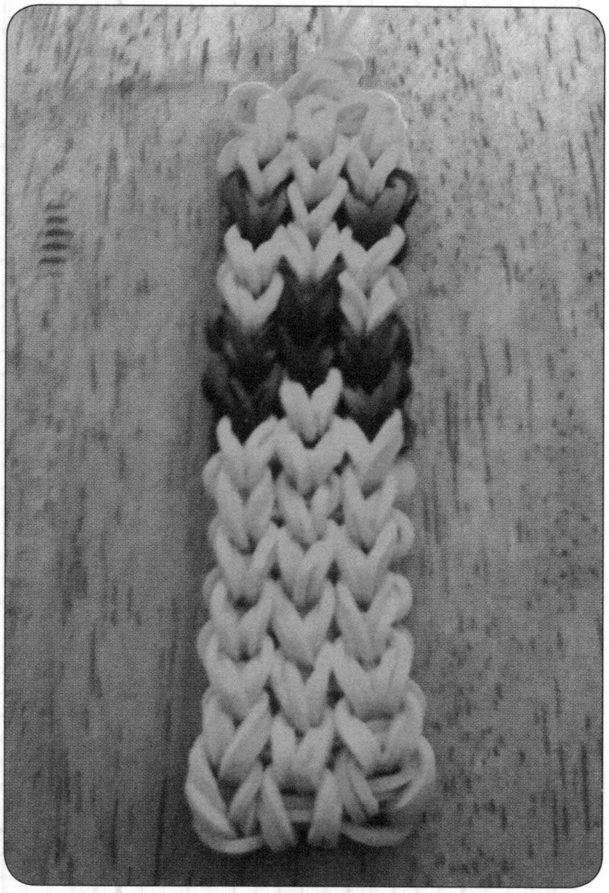

Step 1: Materials

- Rainbow Loom
- A bunch of green bands
- A few black bands
- Hook

Step 2: Note

We will be using all double bands, which means that when you put a band on the loom, you put two instead of one.

Step 3: The Left Side

The pattern for the left side looks like this (G=green and B=black): GGBGGBBGGGGGGG (all double bands).

Step 4: The Center

The pattern for the center looks like this (G=green and B=black): GGGGBBGGGGGGGG (all double bands).

Step 5: The Right Side

The pattern for the right side is the same as the left, so it looks like this (G=green and B=black): GGBGGBBGGGGGGG (all double bands).

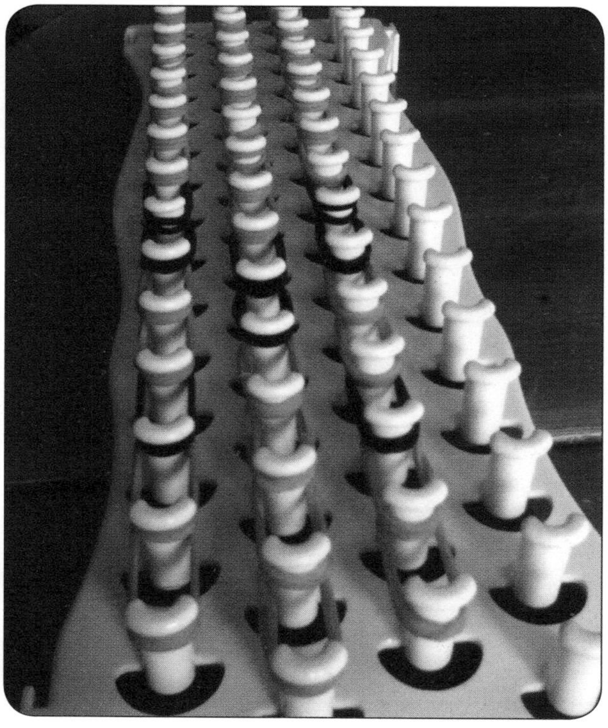

Step 6: Triangles

The triangles (still) are double bands. The first triangle isn't a triangle, it's just a green band connecting R1 and L1 (right 1 and left 1). Then you put triangles the rest of the way down following this pattern (again G=green and B=black): GBBGBBBGGGGGG. The last one (G) should be brought to the bottom of the triangle to make an upside-down V.

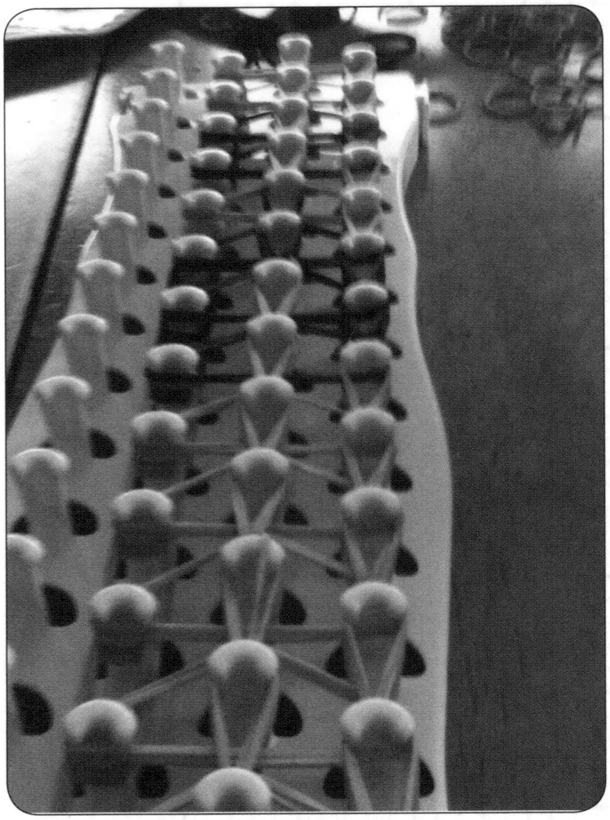

Step 7: Hooking

This is the hardest part of the charm. I go up each row one by one. If you like, you can go all at once.

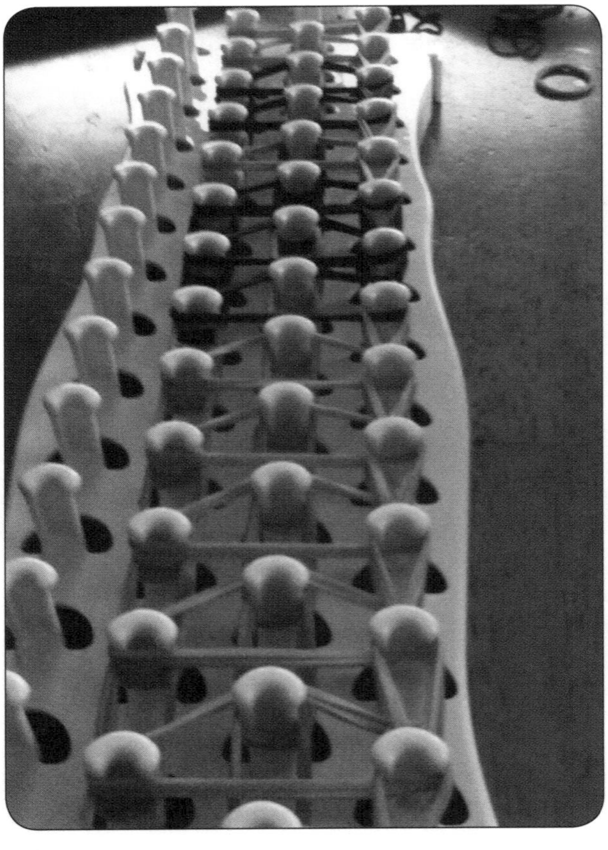

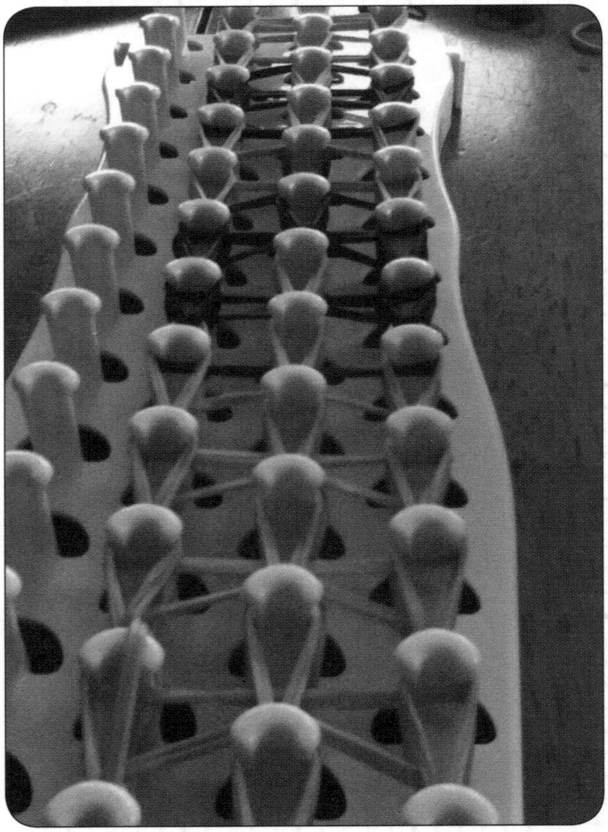

Step 8: Catch Bands

Put your hook through all of the bands. Put a green band on the hook. Pull the hook with the band back though the bands. Pull one of the ends of the bands through the other band. Pull, then repeat for all three rows.

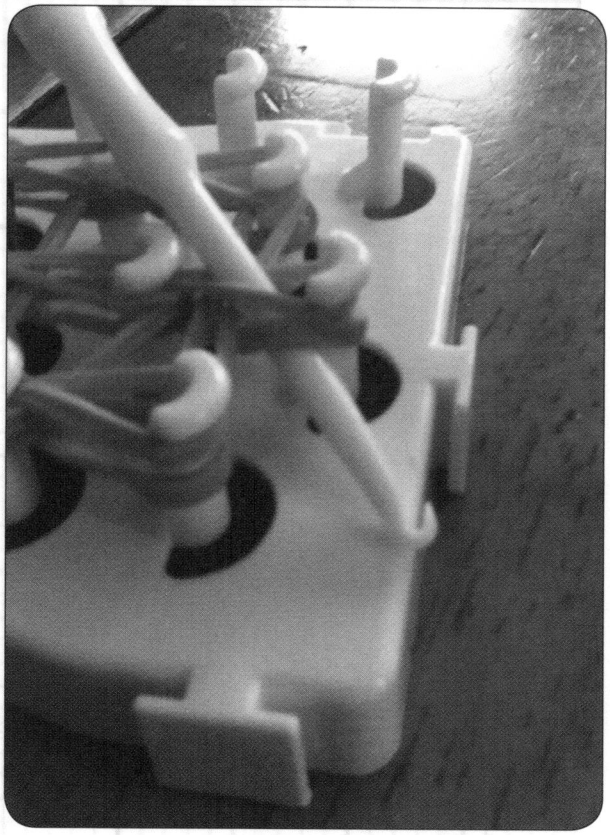

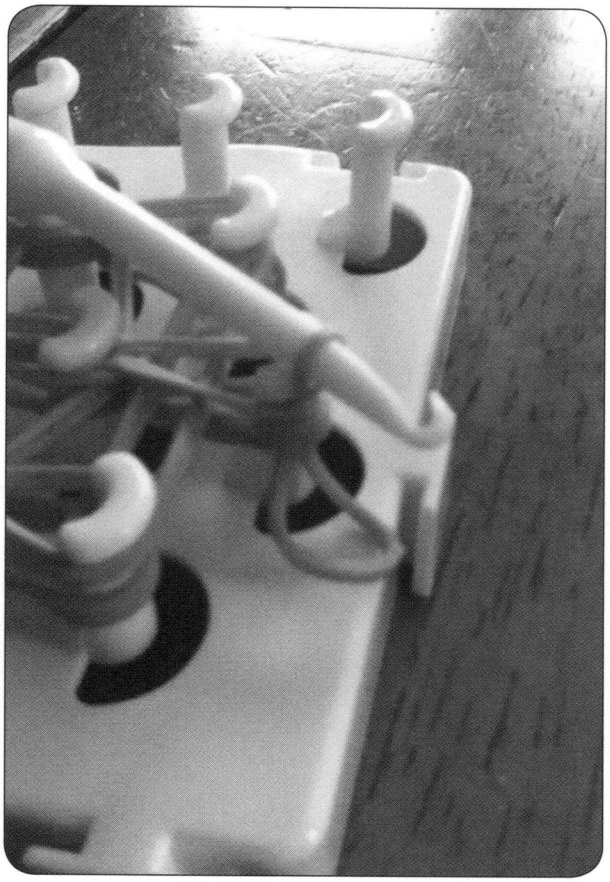

Step 9: The Great Reveal!

Pull the charm off the loom!

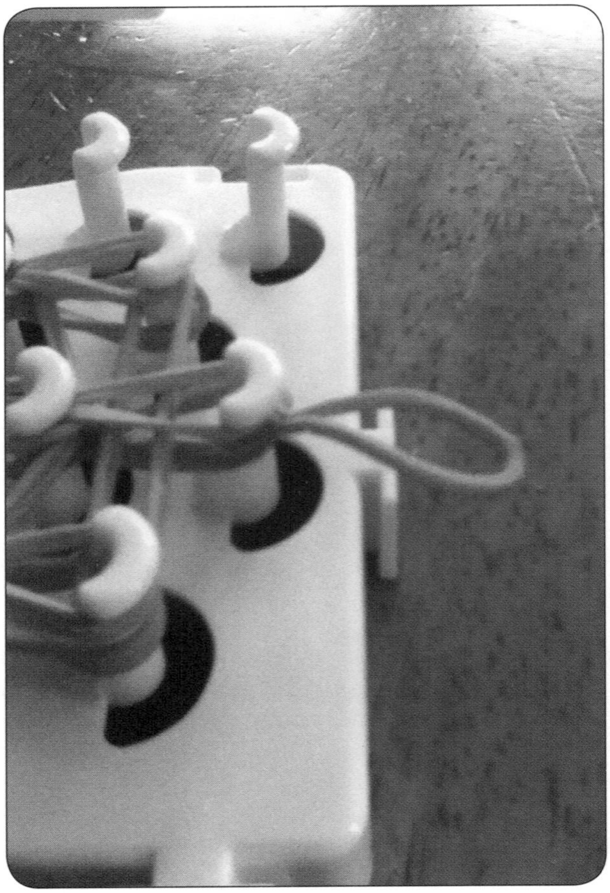

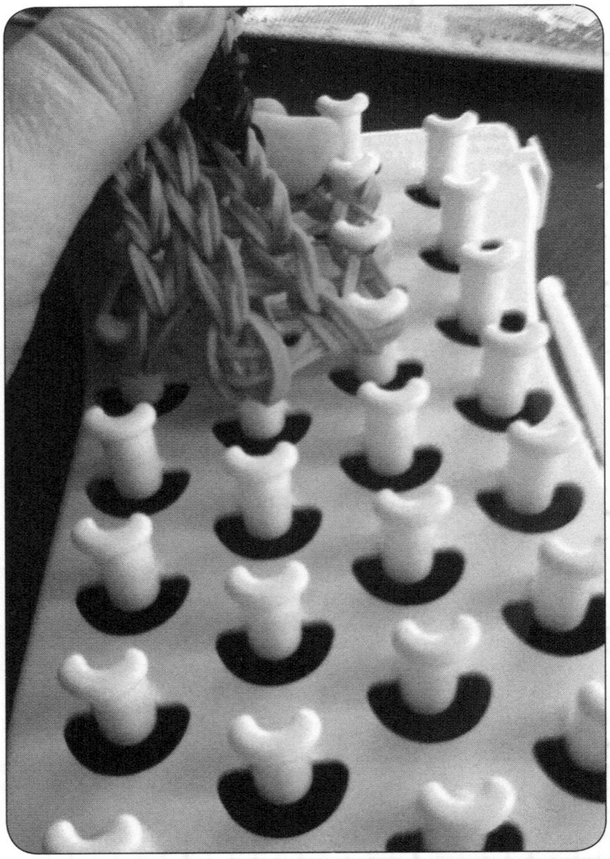

Step 10: Done!

Berry

By Jalynn Newell (Newell_Jaylnn)
(http://www.instructables.com/id/RL-berry-charm/)

These cute little charms can add a dash of fun to a Rainbow Loom bracelet or any kind of bracelet!

Step 1: You Will Need...

- A loom
- A loom hook
- 14 bands of one color
- 1 green band

Step 2: Starting the Berry

Add one band going diagonally to the left.

Step 3: Starting the Berry

Then add one band vertically.

Step 4: Starting the Berry

Then add one diagonally to the right.

Step 5: Add Bands

Add two bands to each row.

Step 6: Add Bands

Add bands diagonally to left and right.

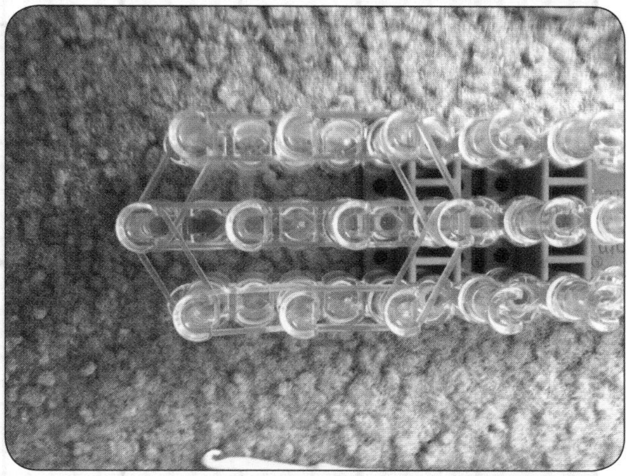

Step 7: Add Triangles

Then add triangles to the middle.

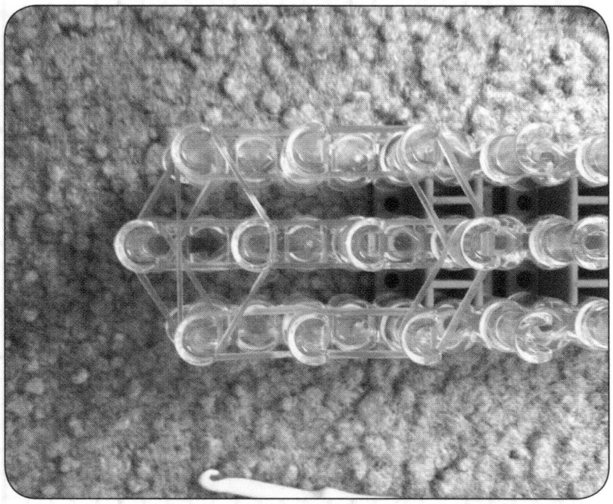

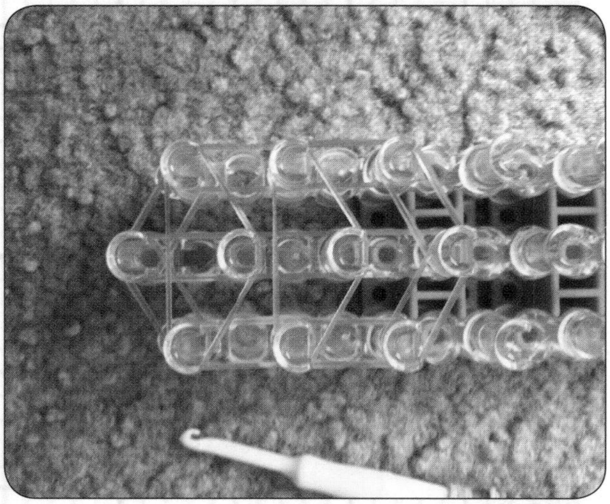

Step 8: Add Cap Band

Fold a band into a cap band.

Step 9: Turn

Turn your loom around.

Step 10: Follow

Follow the way I loop.

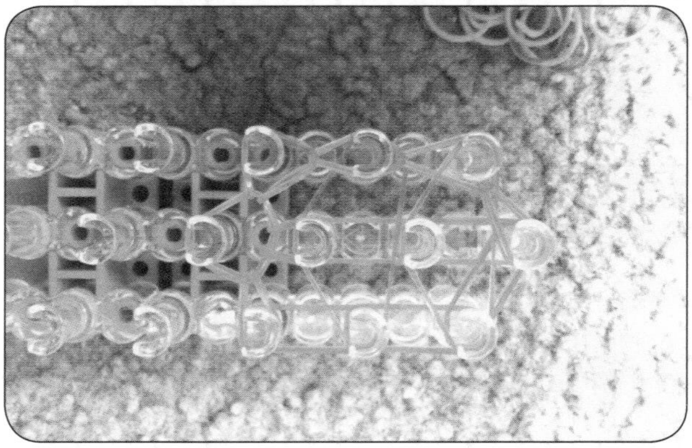

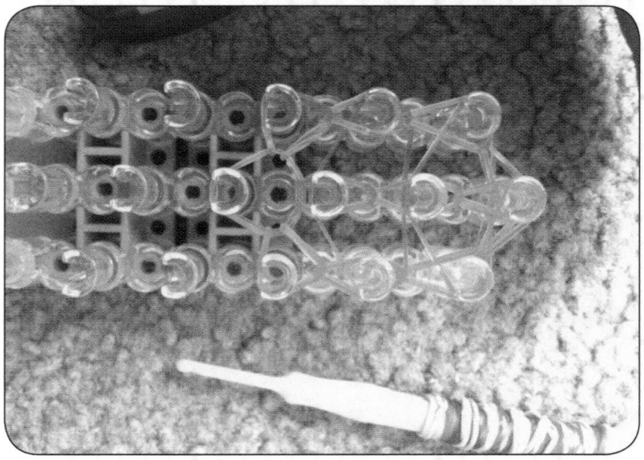

Step 11: Push Hook Through

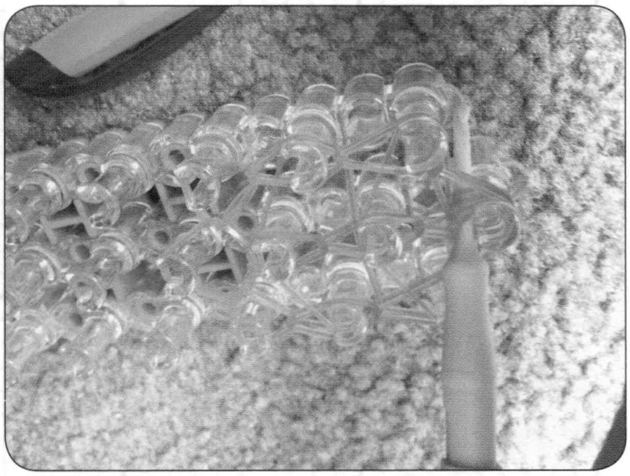

Step 12: Add Slip Knot

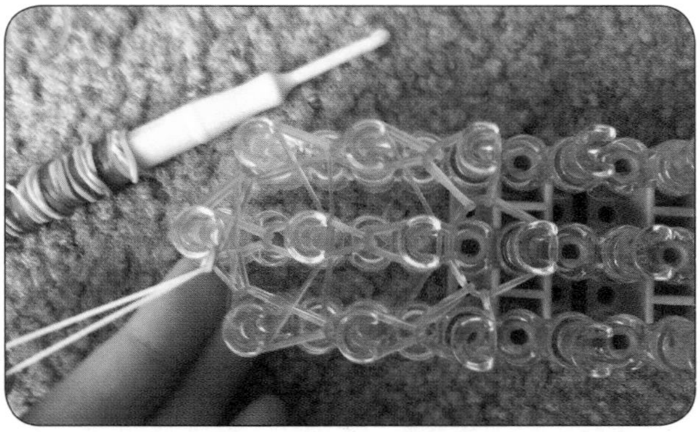

Step 13: Pull

Pull off gently and enjoy.

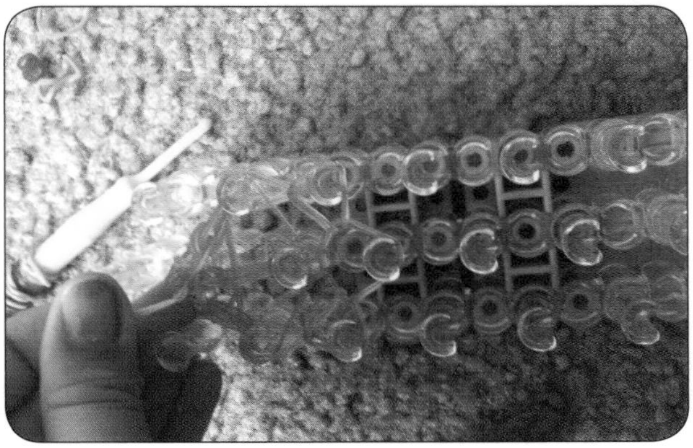

Rose

By estrunk

(http://www.instructables.com/id/Rainbow-loom-Rose-Rings-Or-Charms/)

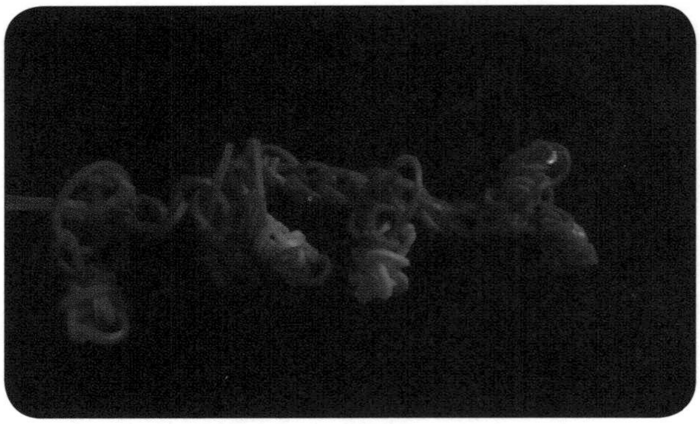

Step 1: Materials

- 4 rose colors
- 2 stem colors
- 1 loom
- 1 Rainbow Loom hook

Step 2: Your Loom

Put the loom so that the middle row is uneven with the outside rows.

Step 3: Lay Your Bands

Lay your rose petal colors first and then your stem colors, just as you would to make a single bracelet.

Step 4: Hook

Hook the bands just like a single bracelet (don't forget to reverse your loom!).

Step 5: Remove

Remove the chain.

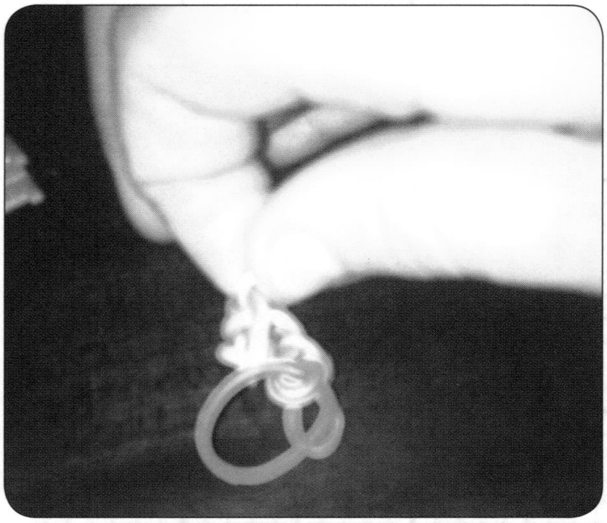

Step 6: Shaping

Follow the pictures and then pull the green tighter until the ends of the pink touch each other.

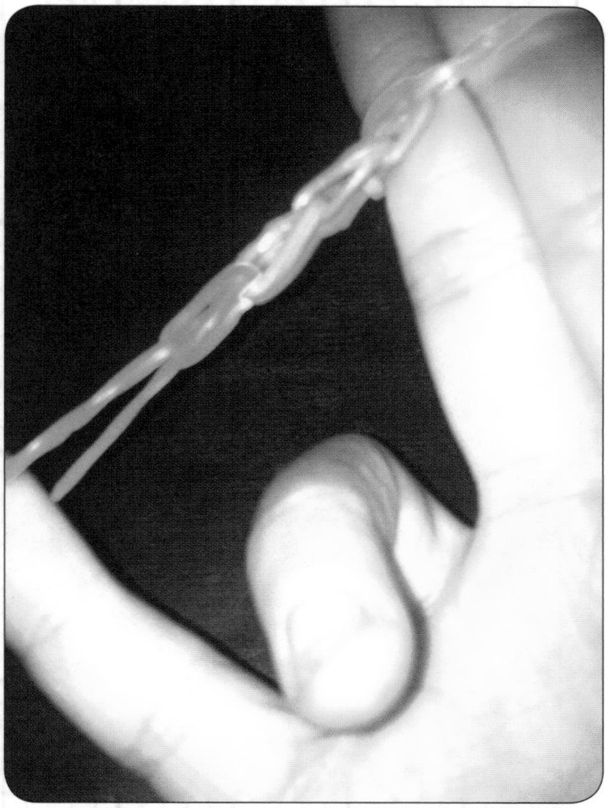

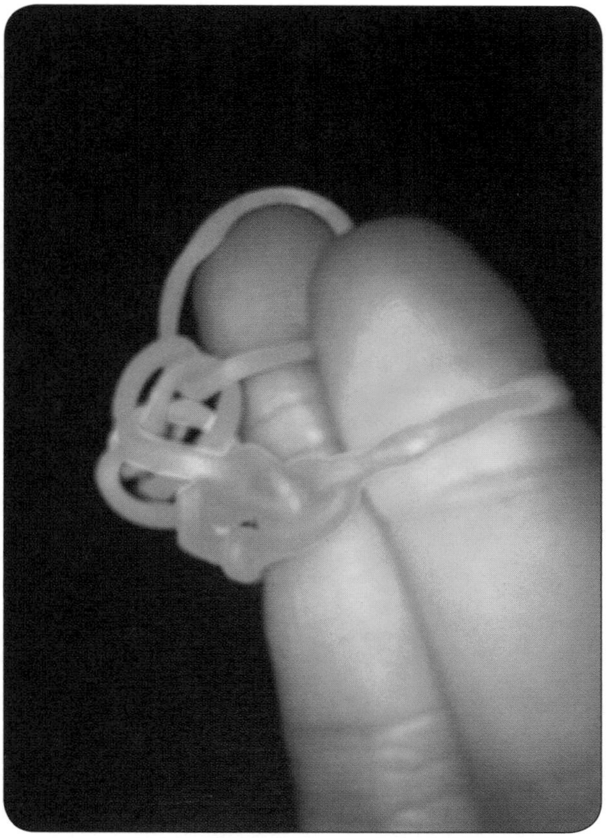

Step 7: Now You're Done

Thanks for trying!

Garden Vegetables

By Erica Robinson (craftpro)
(http://www.instructables.com/id/Rainbow-loom-Vegetable-Garden-Charms/)

These cute little charms are my original designs. They include strawberries, a carrot, a cucumber, a turnip, a tomato, and a green pepper. Please note that to make these, you need to know how to make the starburst. Have fun!

Step 1: What You Need

- Rubber bands in colors needed to make vegetables
- Rainbow Loom kit or other rubber band loom
- Hook
- C-clips

Step 2: The Strawberry, Part 1

The strawberry is all starburst "technology." If you don't know how to starburst, this is going to be hard. Otherwise, it's easy. Starting with the arrow facing up, I start with one band on the middle row going up. Then I go all around and place a cap band on top until it look like an independent starburst. Now, going in the correct backwards order, I hook all the bands back to their original pegs while the cap band holds them in place.

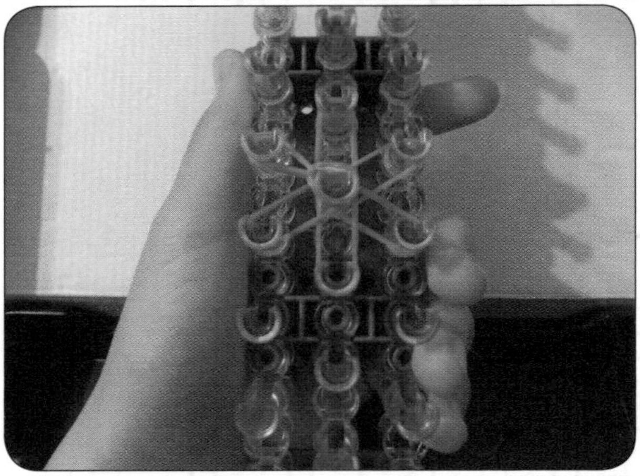

Step 3: The Strawberry, Part 2

To continue, follow the instruction in the boxes.

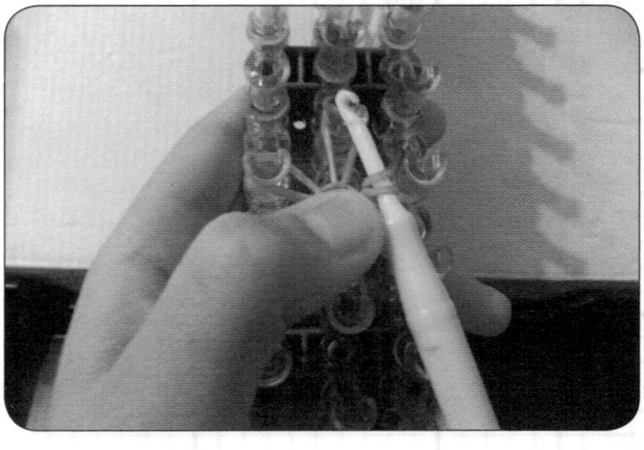

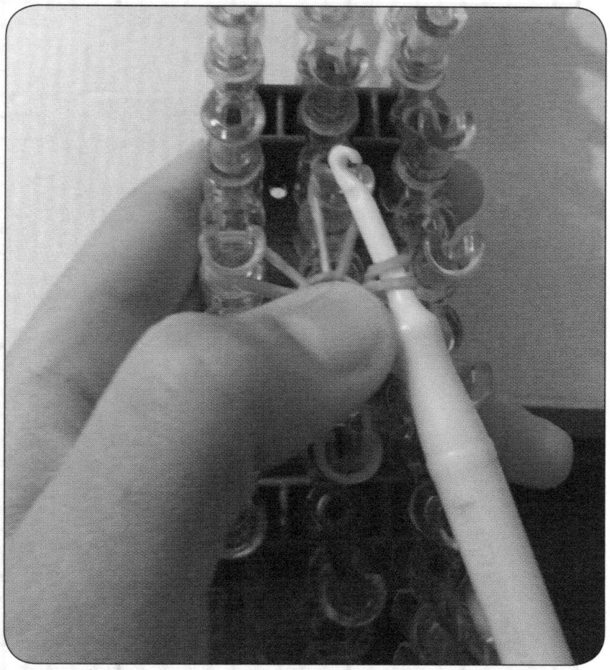

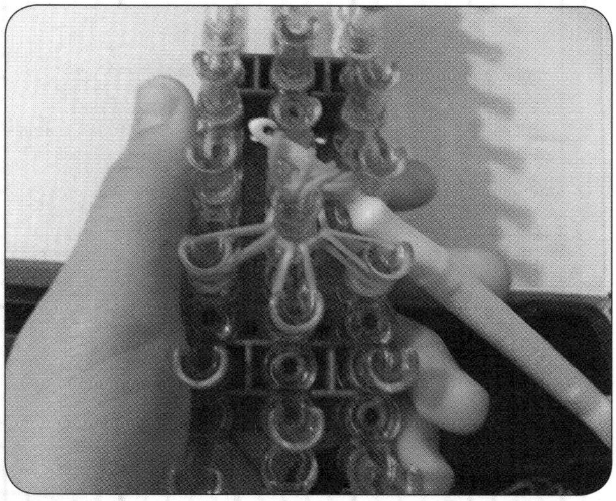

Step 4: The Strawberry, Part 3

Follow the images.

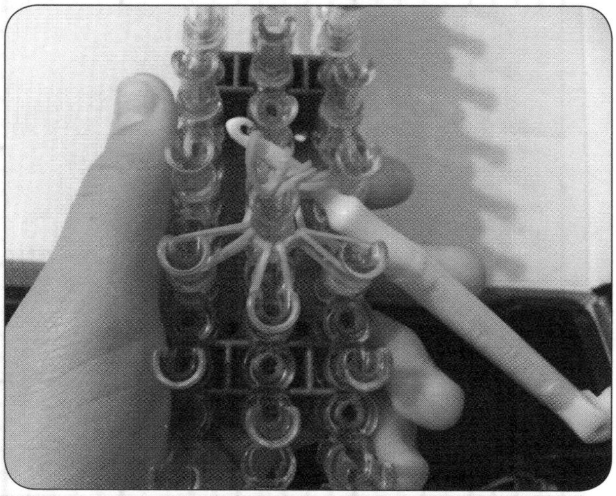

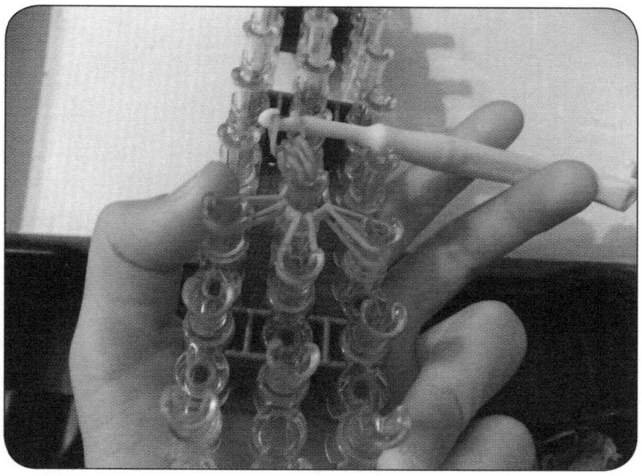

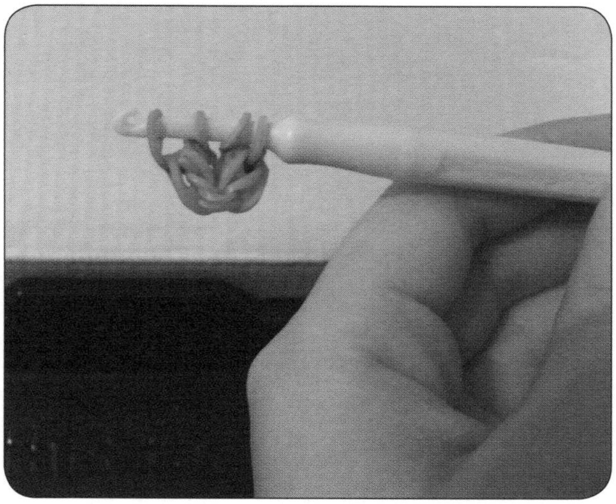

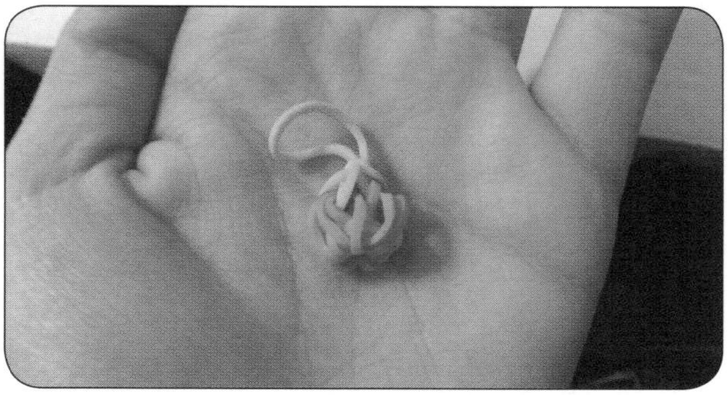

Step 5: Turnip

The turnip is the same as the strawberry, but using purple and white.

Step 6: Tomato and Green Pepper

The tomato and green pepper use similar logic as the strawberry. Refer to the boxes.

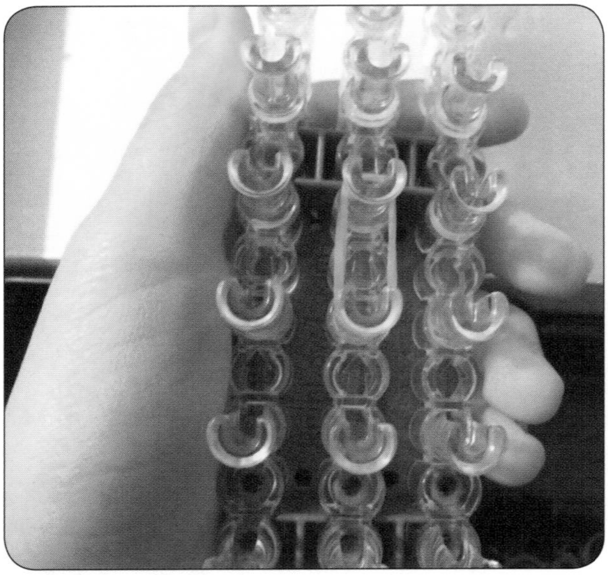

Step 7: Cucumber

Follow the image.

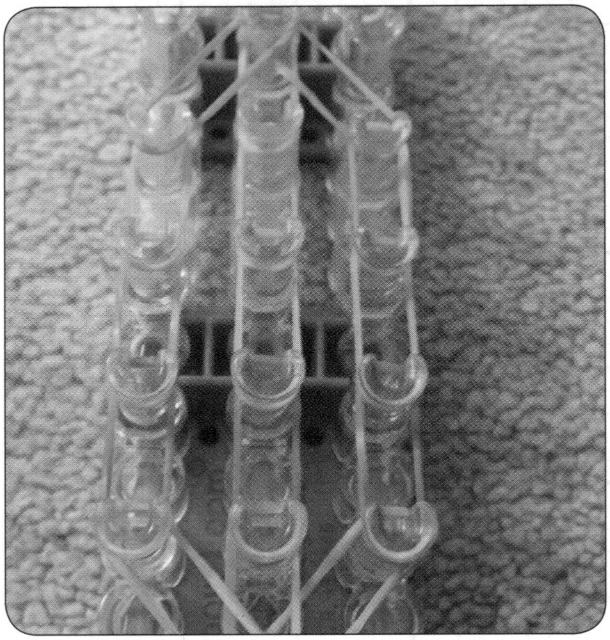

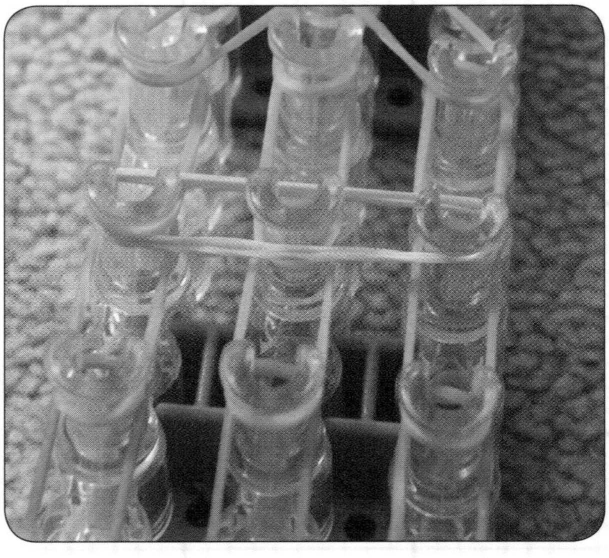

Step 8: Carrot

Follow the images. Put the charms on a Rainbow Loom bracelet, and you're done! Hope you enjoyed!

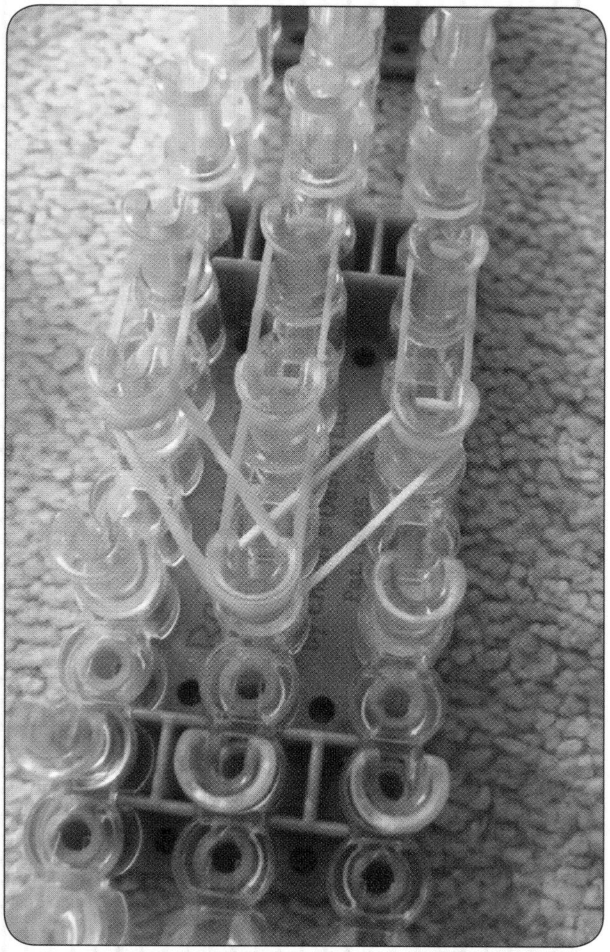

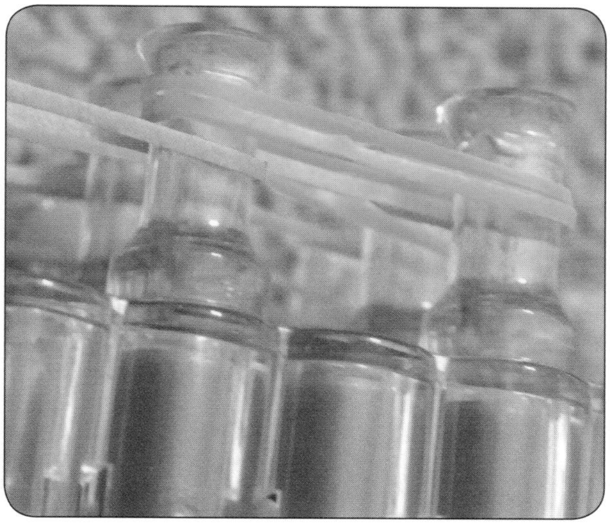

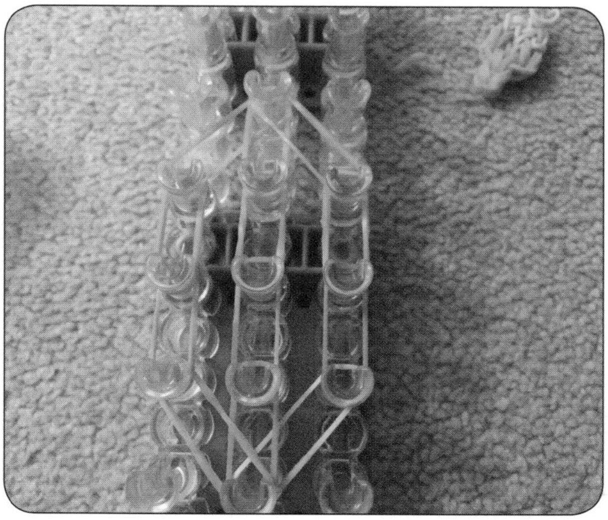

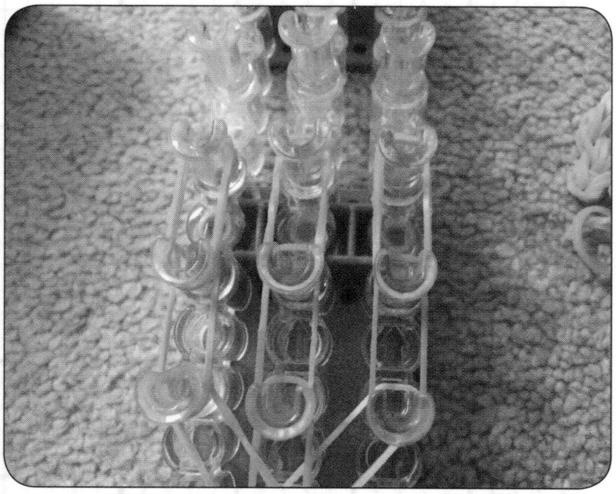

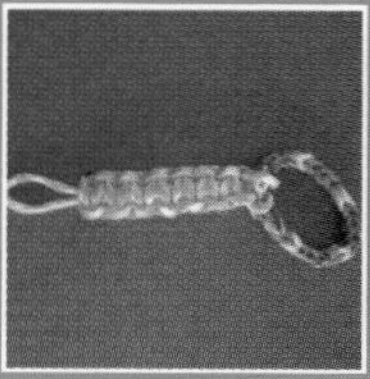

Make Stuff Out of Rainbow Loom Jewelry

Barefoot Sandal

By medwards22

(http://www.instructables.com/id/Rubber-Band-barefoot-sandal/)

Step 1: What You Need

- Rubber bands in colors of your choice
- C- or S-clips

Step 2: First

Make a regular basic bracelet (see page 3).

Step 3: Next

Make a chain to connect the bracelet and toe sections.

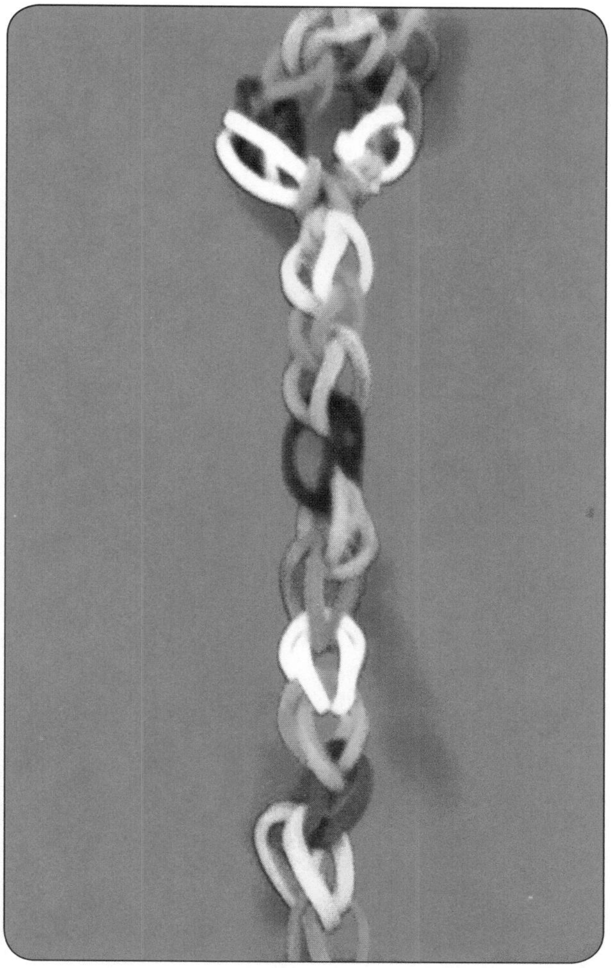

Step 4: Toe Piece

Make a toe piece attached to the chain.

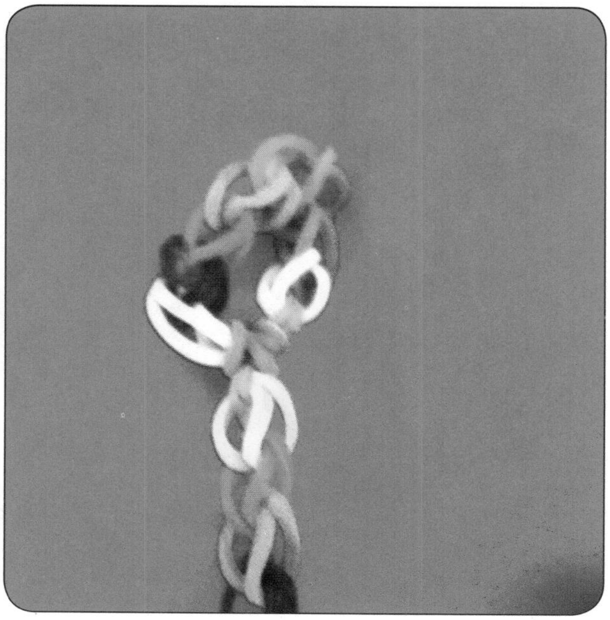

Step 5: Almost Done!

After you have finished the toe piece, you see that it isn't a circle yet. Make a tie-like ending kind of like the one in the picture.

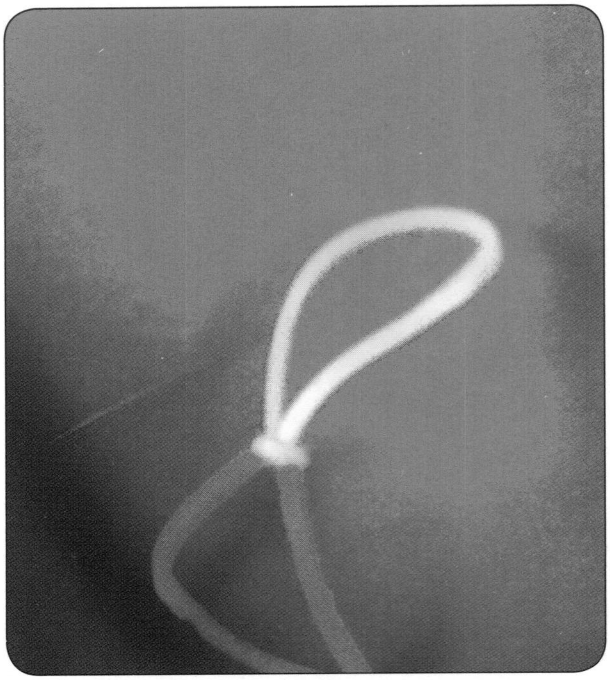

Step 6: A New Sandal!

Wrap the tie around your chain so it looks like the tie I made.

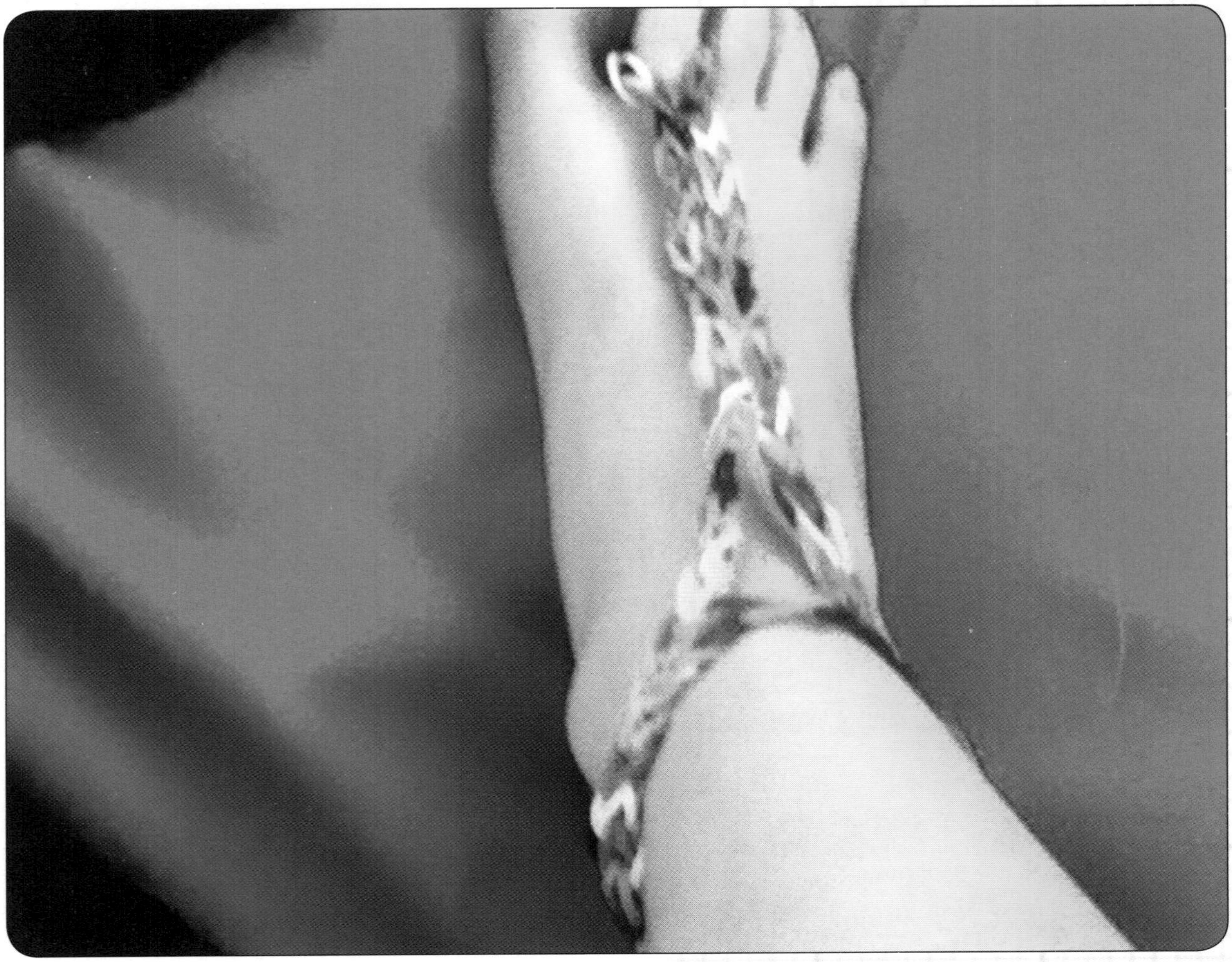

Pencil Décor

By Joann987

This is a cute little cover that goes over your pencil. It is super simple and fun to make. Enjoy!

Step 1: Things You Need

- Rubber bands
- Hook
- C- or S-clip
- Rainbow Loom
- Pencil, preferably NOT a mechanical one

Step 2: Placing Bands

Place your pencil on top of your loom, starting from the bottom to top. Make sure the arrows are pointing away from you. Remove the pencil. Place your bands in a zigzag pattern to however long your pencil is.

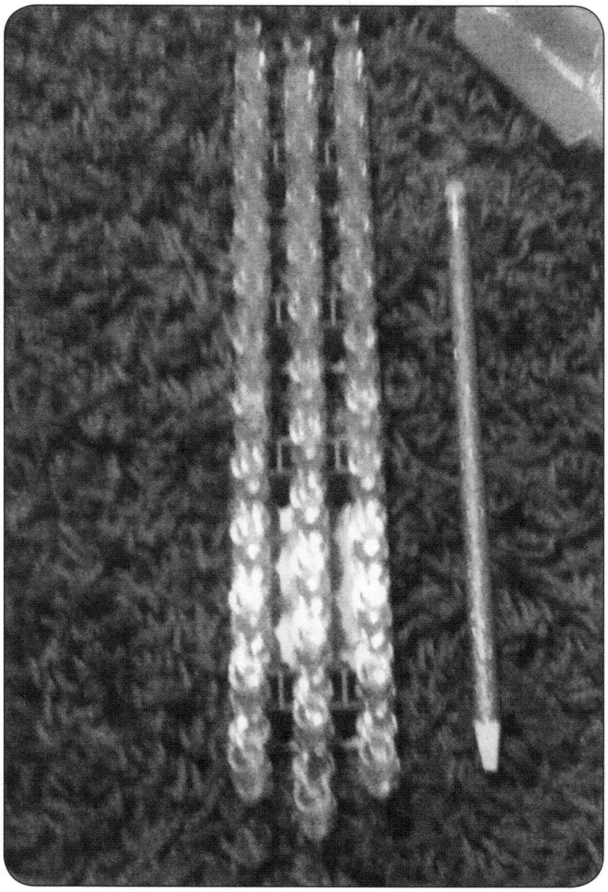

Step 3: Looping Bands

Flip around your loom and place your pencil in between the two pieces of loom. Be gentle though! The pencil should be on top of the bands. Now take your hook and loop the band that is on the second to last peg from where you ended. Loop it back to its original peg. It will be the last band on the peg. Do this all the way down crossing over and on top of the pencil. It is like doing a single chain!

Step 4: Continuing

Now from the third peg bring the two bands over the top. Just flip them over. Stop at the first peg from the beginning. Now, holding the bands at the top, take it off. Twist those bands and put them over the eraser so it is secure. Now, at the part where there is a extra band sticking out, twist it around the pencil three times. Push it down.

Step 5: Done!

It is now secure and finished (if done correctly).

Pencil Holder

By that_star_trek_guy_
(http://www.instructables.com/id/rainbow-loom-pencil-holder/)

Step 1: Holder

Get a paper roll.

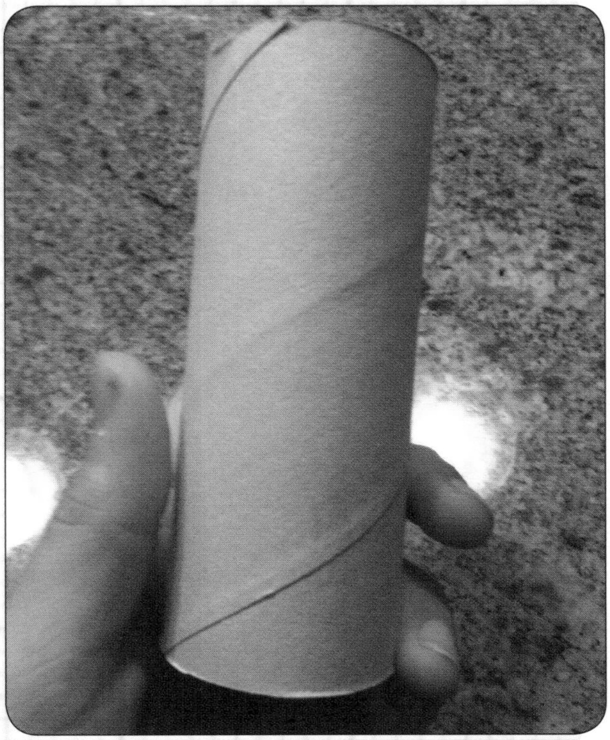

Step 2: Utensils

Get a couple of pens and pencils.

Step 3: Get Some Loomed Bracelets

Make or buy at least fourteen Rainbow Loom bracelets.

Step 4: Plate

Get a paper plate for the bottom.

Step 5: Bottom

Get a Sharpie and trace the bottom of the tub on the middle of the plate. Now cut it out the tube on the middle of the plate.

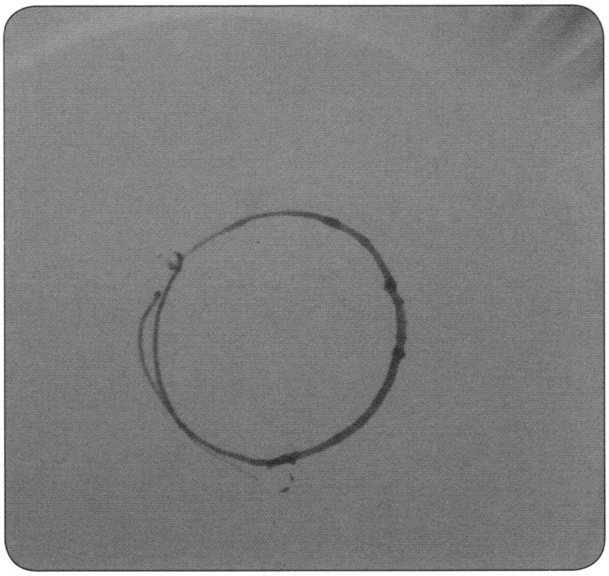

Step 6: Put on the Bracelets

Put the bracelets on the tube.

Step 7: Glue on the Bottom

Step 8: Add Pencils

And you are done!

Paracord Lanyard

By Andrew Fathman (afathman)
(http://www.instructables.com/id/Rainbow-loom-and-paracord-lanyard/)

Carry those keys in style!

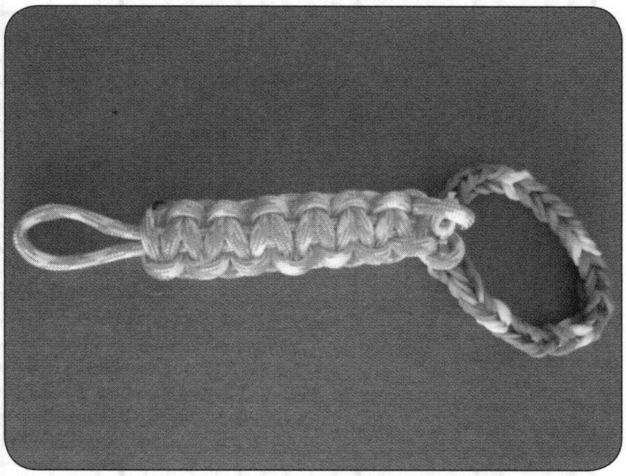

Step 1: Materials

You will need five feet of paracord and a Rainbow Loom bracelet of your choice.

Step 2: Rainbow Loom

I just used a double fishtail (see page 9), but you can use whatever type of bracelet you want! (The freedom is exhilarating!)

Step 3: Paracord

Take five feet or so of your favorite paracord and find the middle. Thread the center through the bracelet and pull it about 5–6 inches down. Then simply perform a cobra weave until you're about an inch from the end, cut the excess, and burn the ends. Now go show off your new hipster/survival accessory!

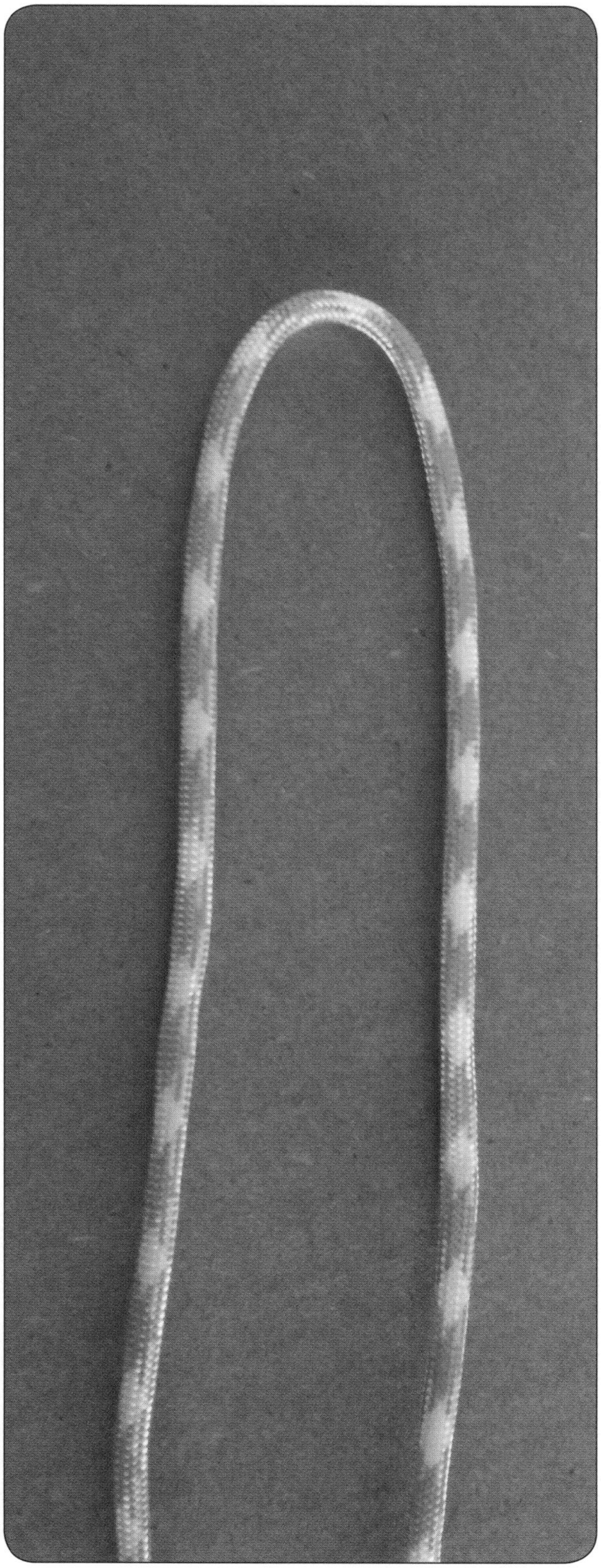

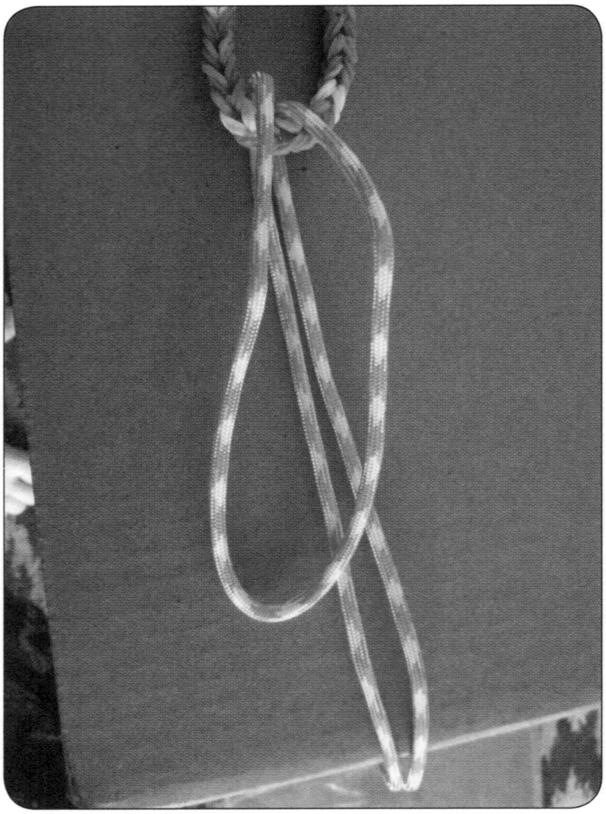

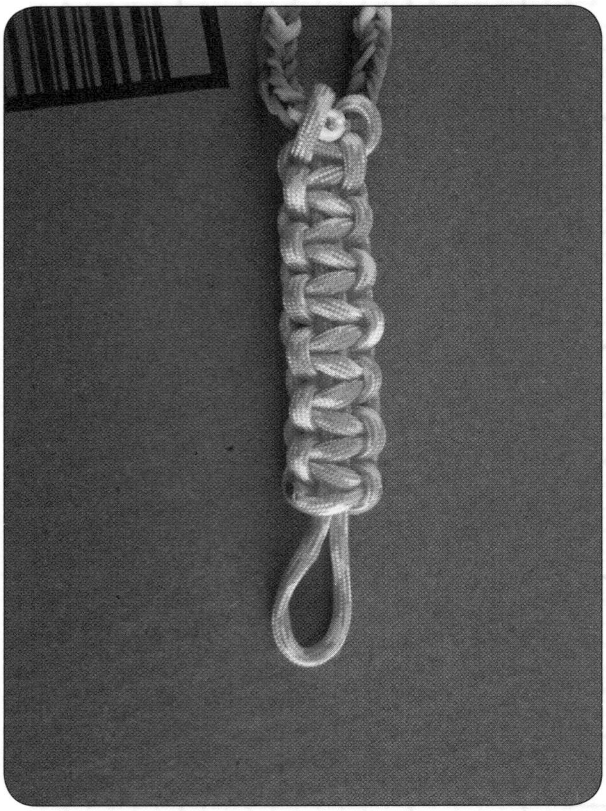

Improv Looming

Fishtail without a Loom

By sydneyhauss

(http://www.instructables.com/id/Fishtail-Loom-Bracelet/)

This will show the few steps to complete a blue and green fishtail loom bracelet (you may use any colors you want).

Step 1: Getting Started

First you will always need to gather your supplies. You will need the items in the photo.

Step 2: Starting Point

Get your two pens in your hand and do exactly what the picture shows. You will basically make an infinity sign with the rubber band.{Insert Images

Step 3: Adding More Bands

Now that you have an infinity sign, put the second color rubber band on top like the picture shows.

Step 4: Three Bands

Now layer the next color on top of the two bands like this.

Step 5: Pulling Over

Now here comes the harder part: pulling the bottom band over the top of the pen like the picture shows.

Step 6: Starting Over

Now you will add a band over everything and pull up the bottom band, which you will keep doing over again.

Step 7: Progress

Your bracelet should soon look like the photo.

Step 8: Pushing Off

Now that you have made your bracelet the size that you want, you'll need to push the bands off of the two pens and hold on to the middle of them.

Step 9: Pulling Two Bands Off

Now you will need to remove the two last bands that were connected to the pens.

Step 10: Adding S- Or C-Clip

I have the C-clips, but some people may have the S-clips. All you do is attach the bands to the clip on both sides.

Step 11: Final Product!

Yes, you have finally finished! This is what it should look like!

Hexafish on a Fork

By Stephanie Larios (lovelyydeath)
(http://www.instructables.com/id/How-To-Make-A-Hexafish-Rubber-band-Bracelet-with-A/)

Step 1: Materials

- Rubber bands in colors of your choice
- S- or C-clip
- Fork
- Pencil (this is used like a Rainbow Loom hook)

Step 2: Begin

Grab your fork and your first rubber band (mine is purple). Slide it through the first tine, pull and twist, then put over second tine, pull and twist, put on third tine, pull and twist one last time, and put on the last tine. You should see what seems like two infinity signs.

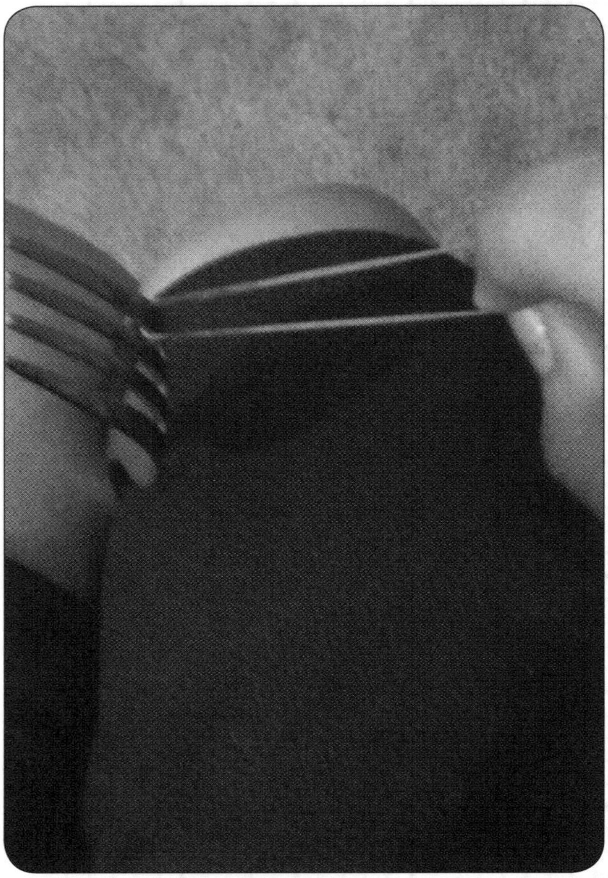

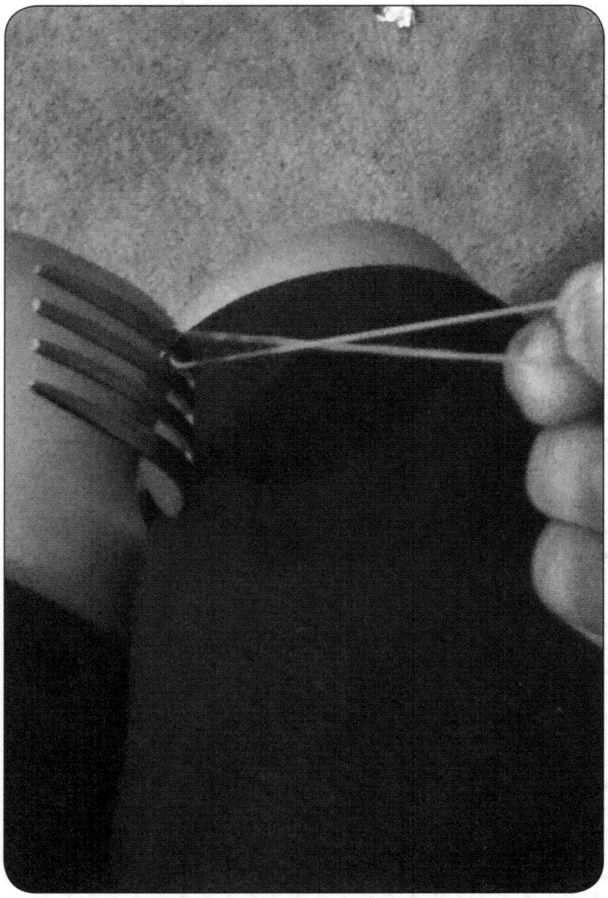

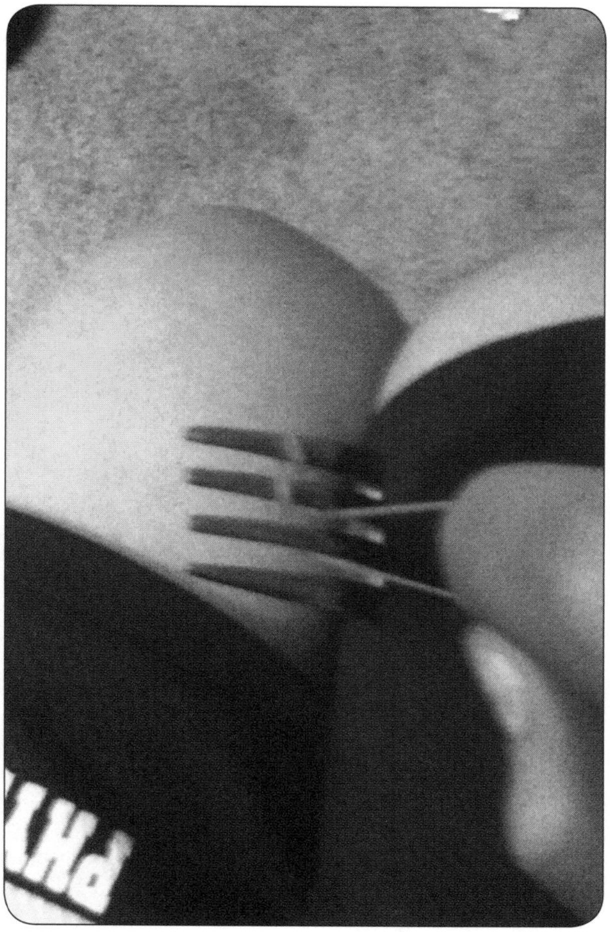

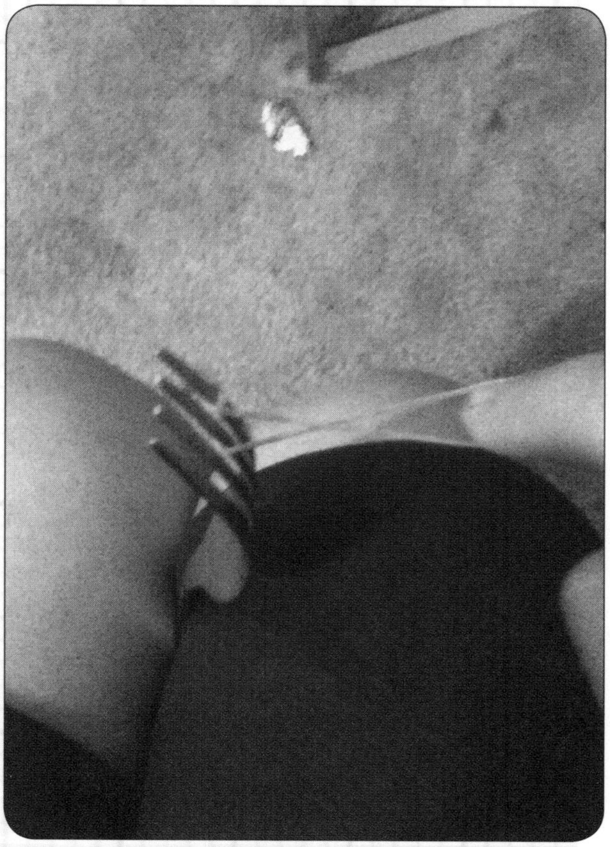

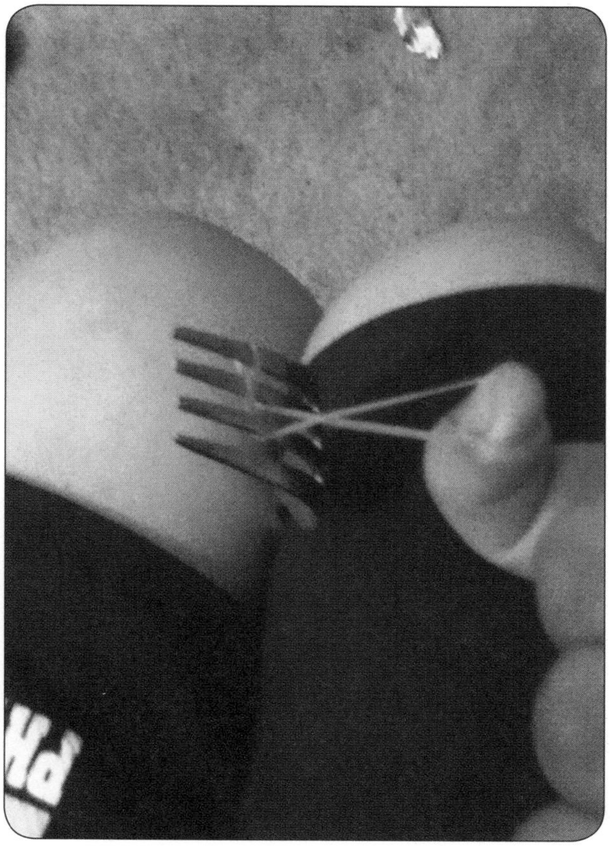

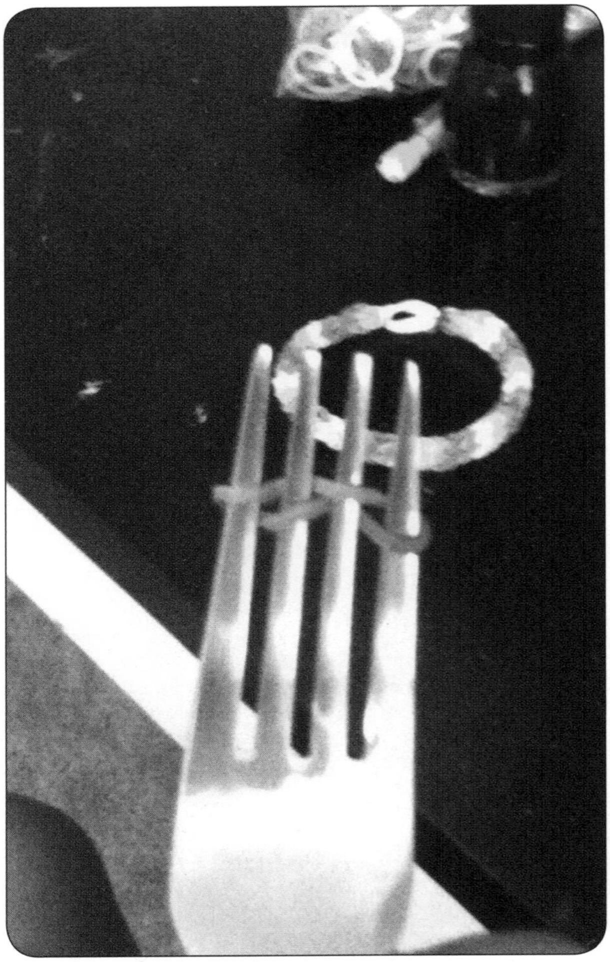

Step 3: Repeat

Repeat what you did in the first step with the next color (mine is still purple).

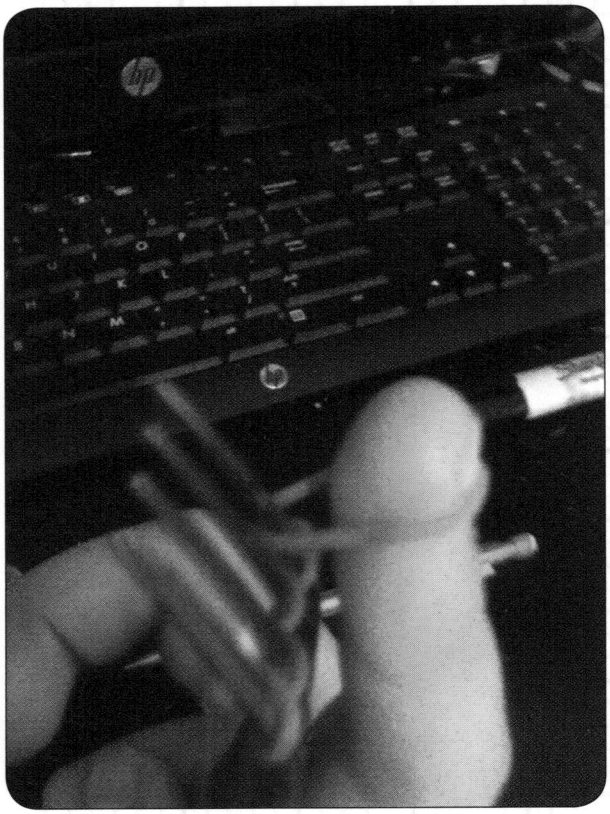

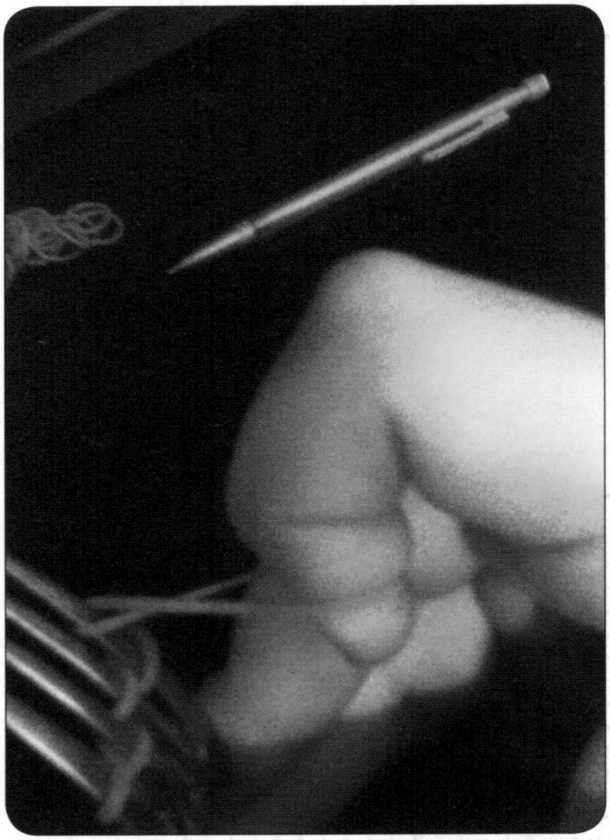

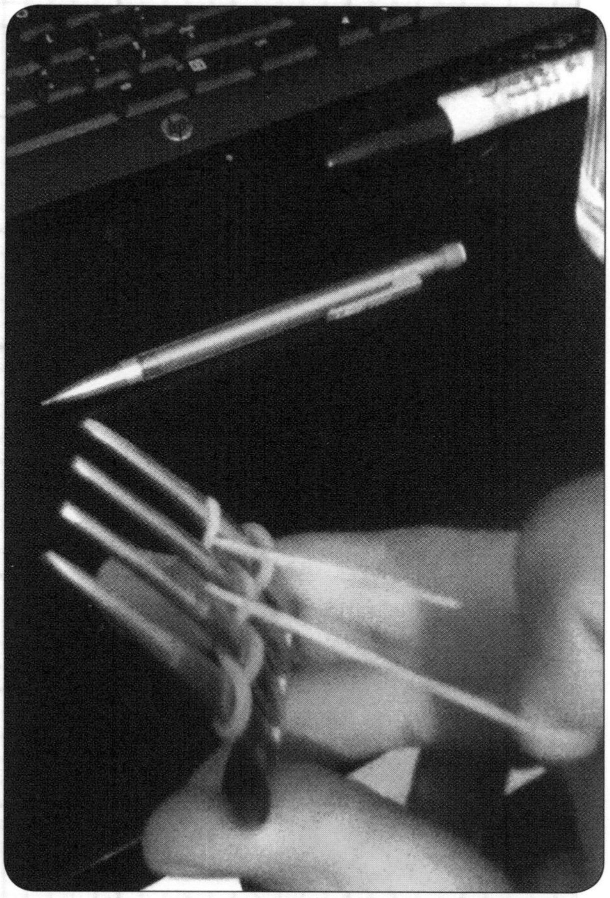

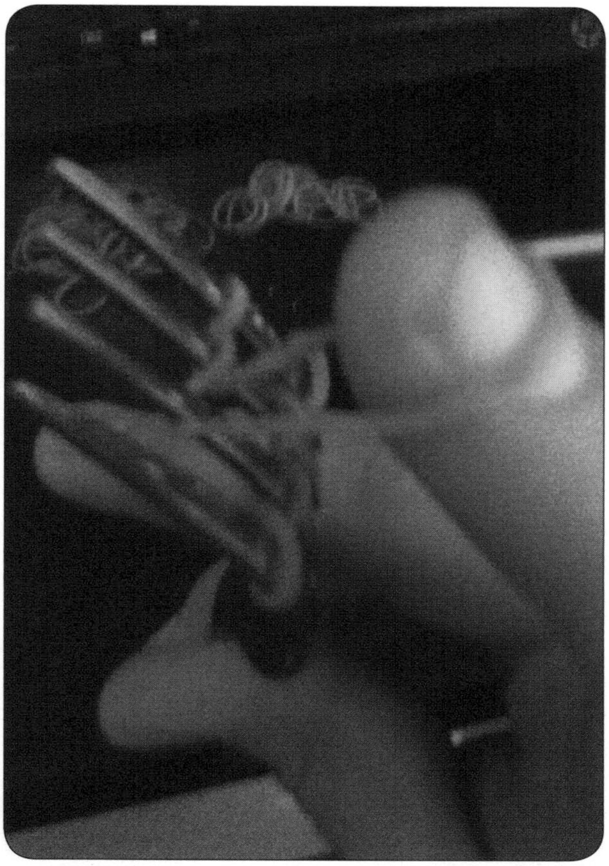

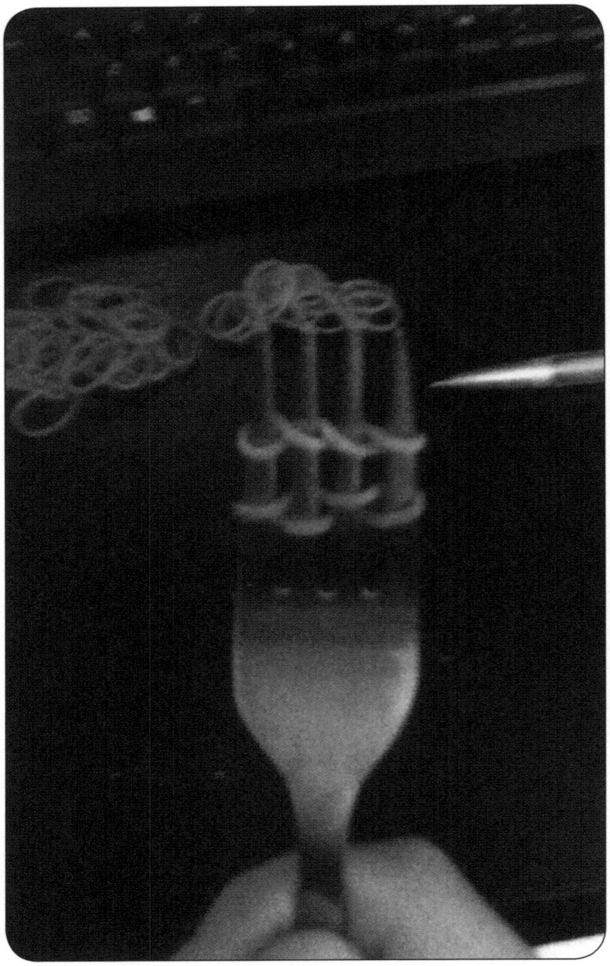

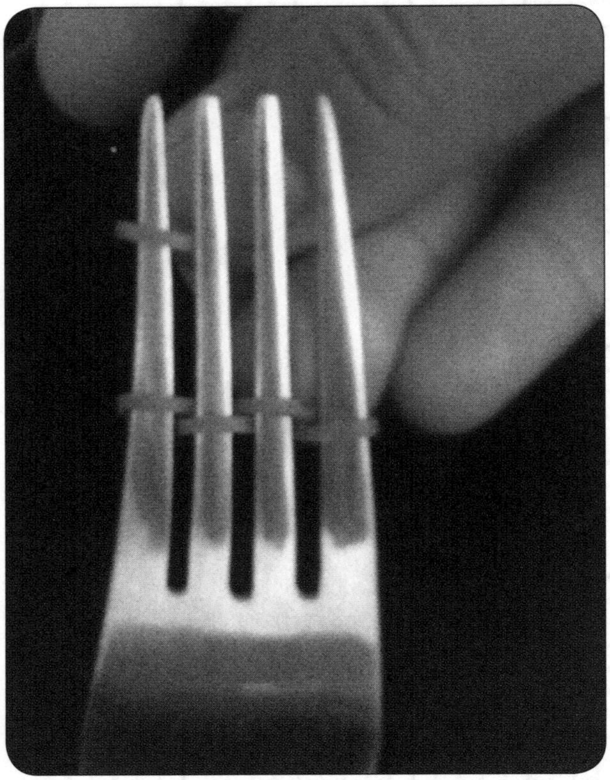

Step 4: Next

Take your pencil (or you can do it with your finger) and pull the first bottom band and put it over the first tine. Pull the second band on the bottom and put it over the second tine. Pull the third band on the bottom and put it over the third tine. Pull the last band on the bottom and put it over the last tine.

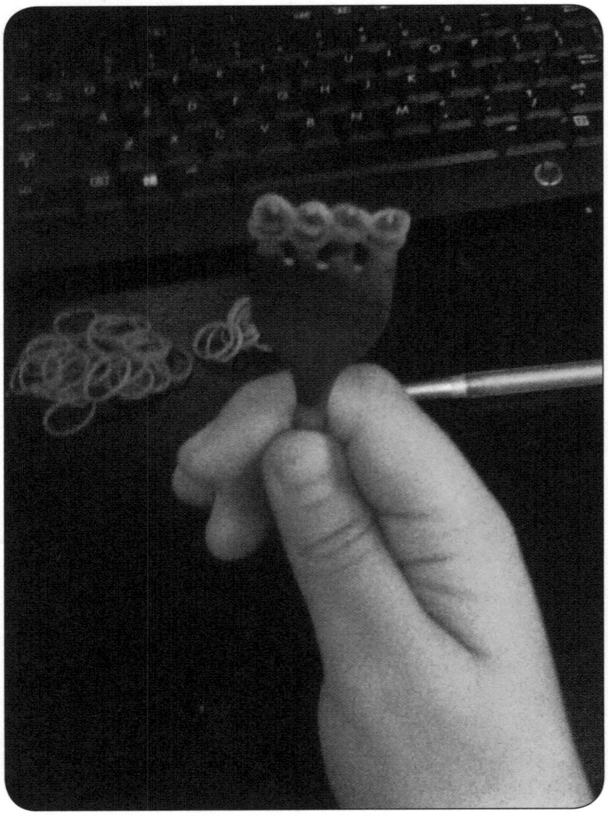

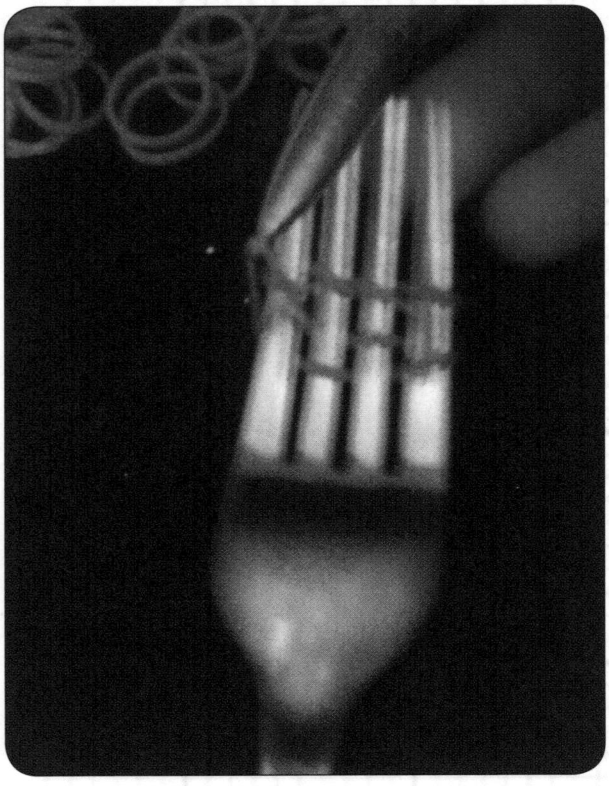

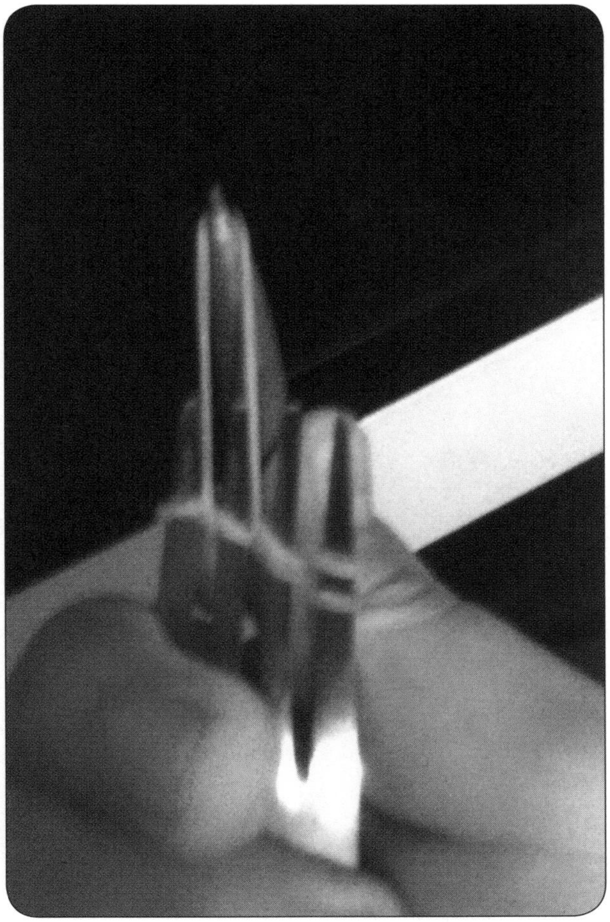

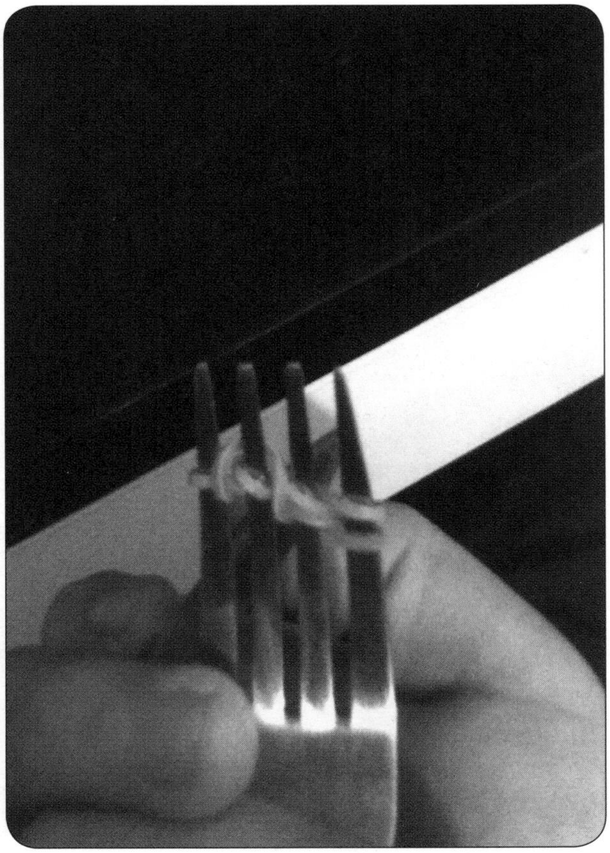

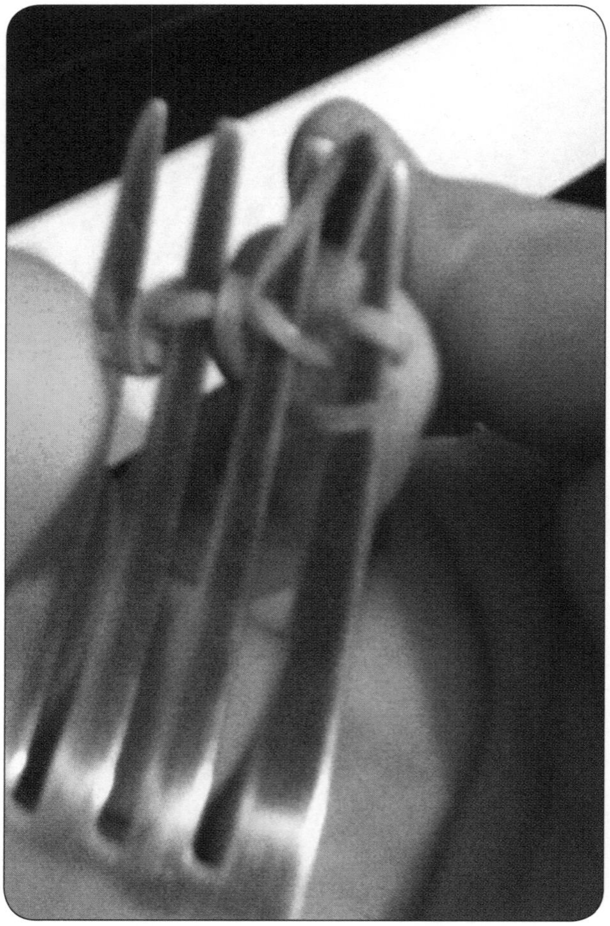

Step 5: It Should Look Like This

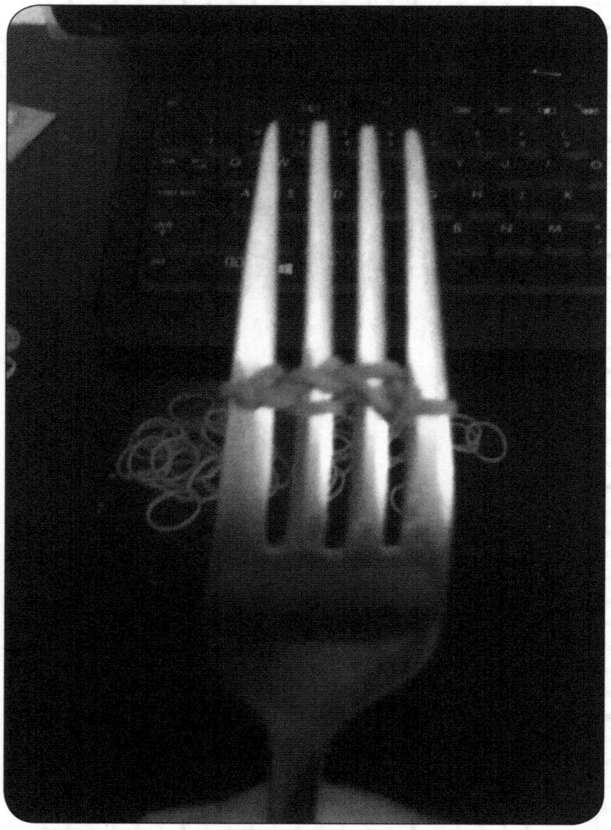

Step 6: Repeat

Repeat steps 2–3 until desired length. You should start seeing the pattern after the first couple of bands.

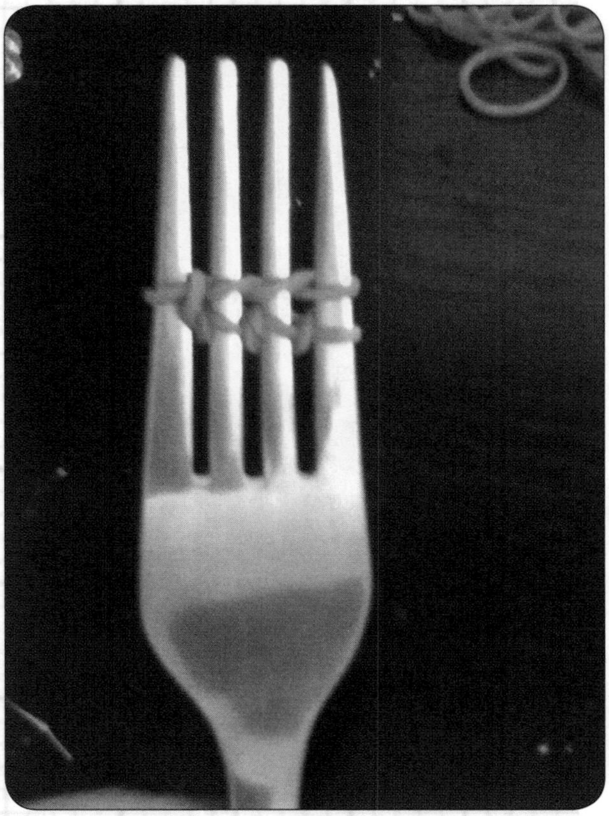

Step 7: Be Sure to Pull

Be sure to pull the back every now and then to see the pattern better.

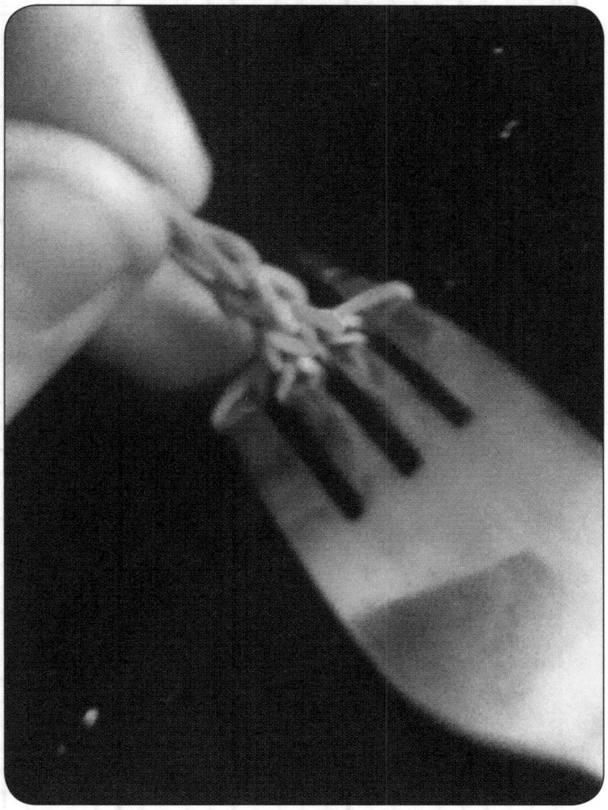

Step 8: Putting on the Clip

While pulling the back you should be able to see two open bands. Pull and insert one side of the S-clip.

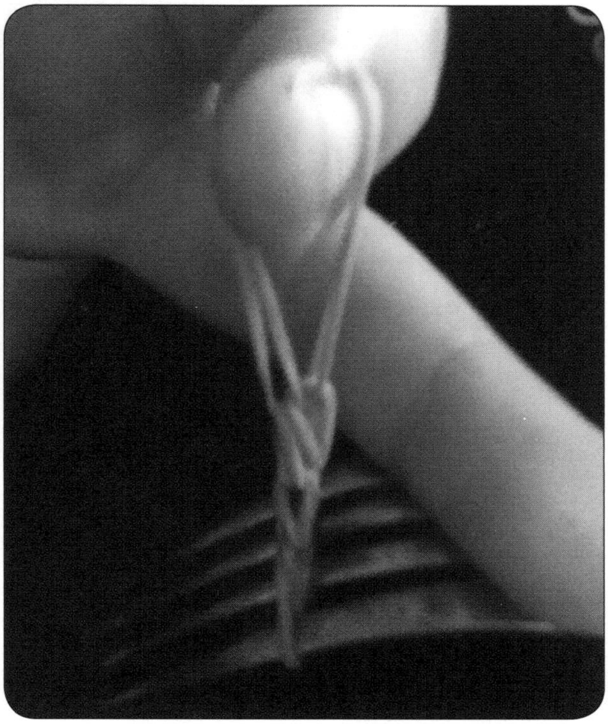

Step 9: Finishing Up

After reaching the desired length, be sure to grab all four bands from the fork, put them all together, and slide in the other side of the S-clip. Now you have your Hexafish Rubber Band Bracelet.

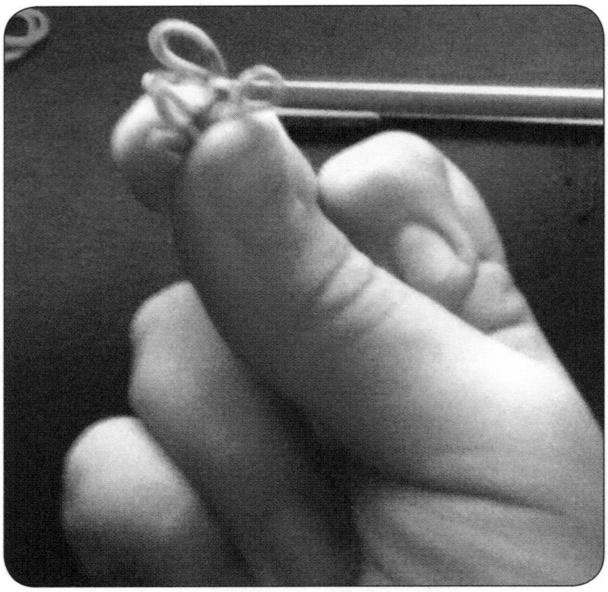

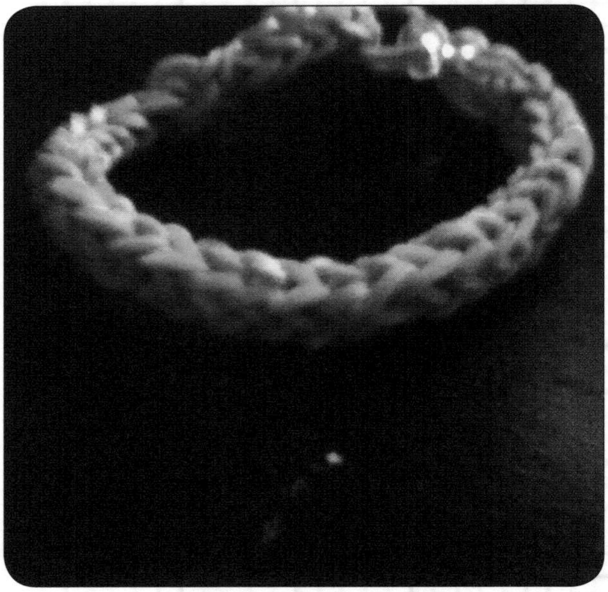

Strappy Hand Bracelet without a Loom

By Yang Ausherman (tofu911)
(http://www.instructables.com/id/Rubber-Band-Slave-Bracelet-no-Rainbow-Loom-needed/)

A few days ago I had some rubber bands but no Rainbow Loom kit. So I thought maybe I'll try a rubber band bracelet that required no tools. Going with this different route, I created this strappy hand bracelet. The concepts used here can create a variety of bracelet styles as shown below.

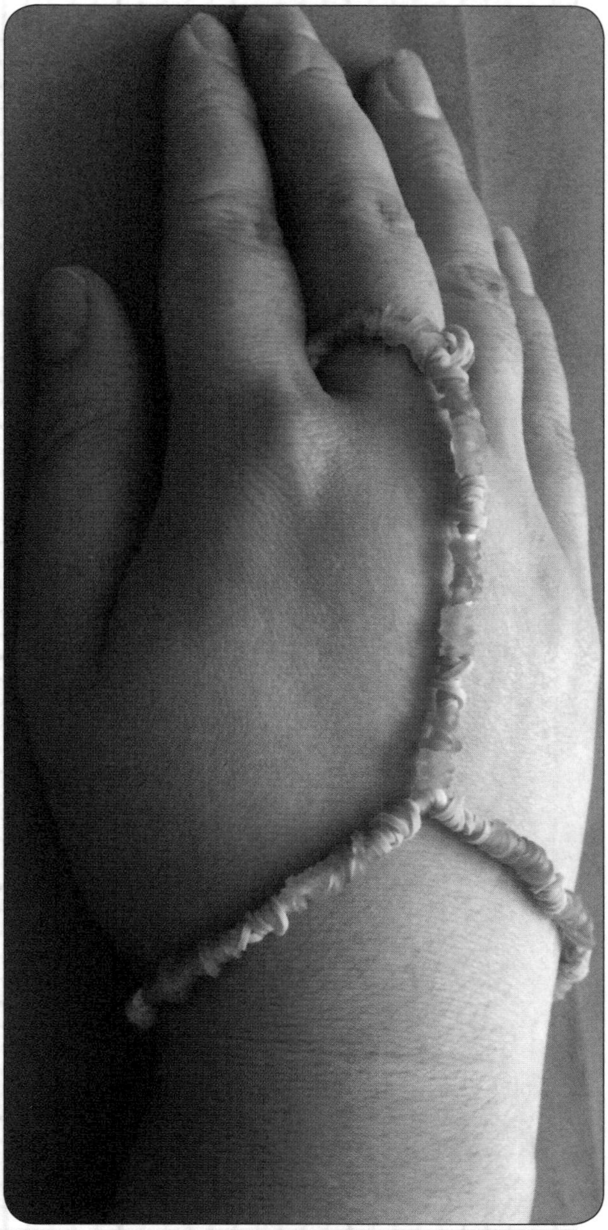

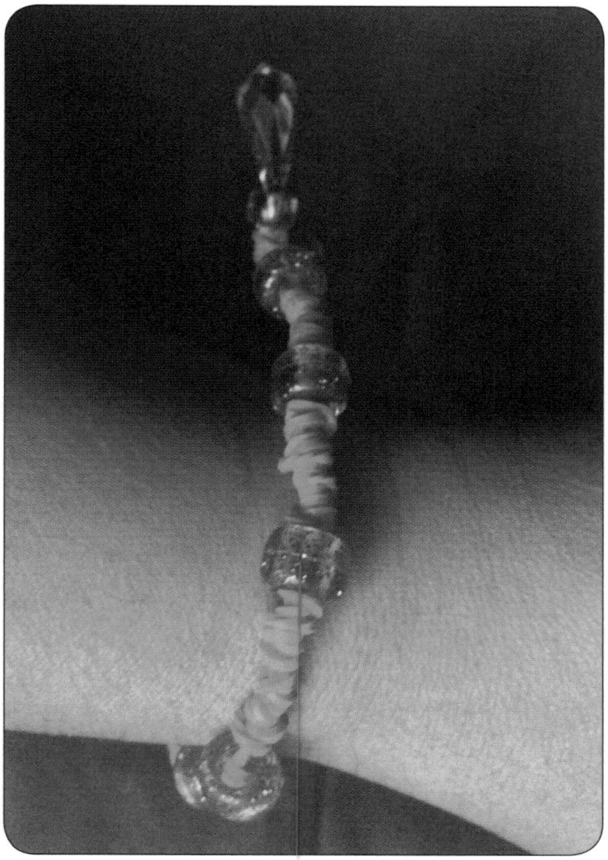

Step 1: White Skeleton

To start all that is needed is rubber bands. You can use whatever colors you want. For my bracelet, I used white, pink, blue, and purple. The white is for the skeleton of the bracelet while the pink, blue, and purple bands are used to create the color beads. To start the skeleton, tie a few rubber bands together end to end. The length should be long enough that it will go around your wrist loosely and about an inch more.

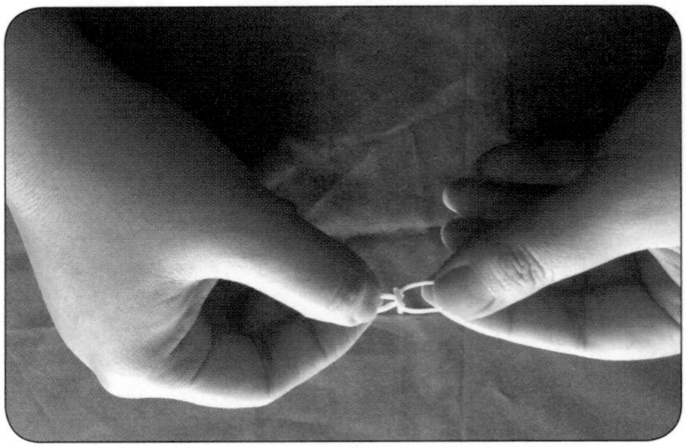

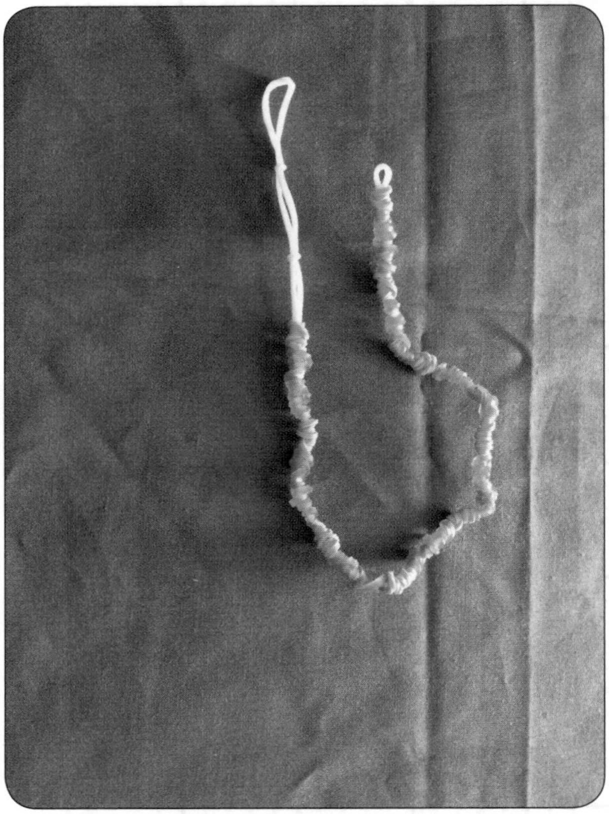

Step 2: Making the Beads

To make the "beads" loop one band (blue, pink, or purple) continuously around the white skeleton band in a small section. Continue to add more bead bands as shown. When the beaded bracelet can loosely fit around your wrist, loop the longer white skeleton through the small white hole on the opposite end of the bracelet until it meets the end of the colored beads as shown in pictures below. Finish the beads so that the length of the skeleton when the bracelet is on will go all the way to the middle finger and loop around it. Add more white bands if necessary.

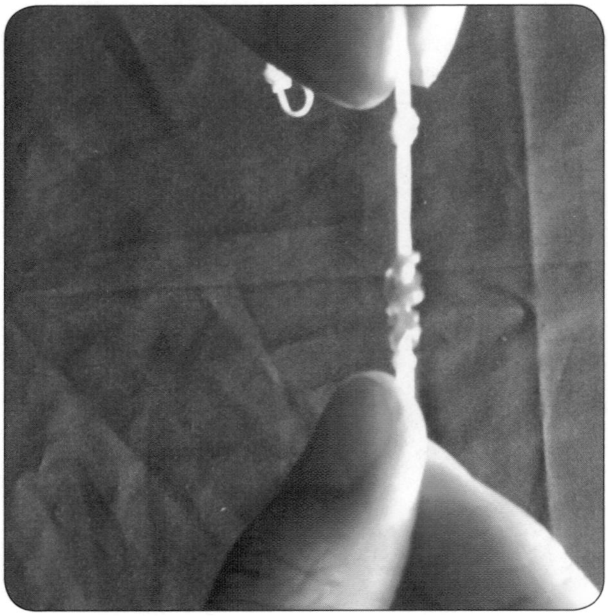

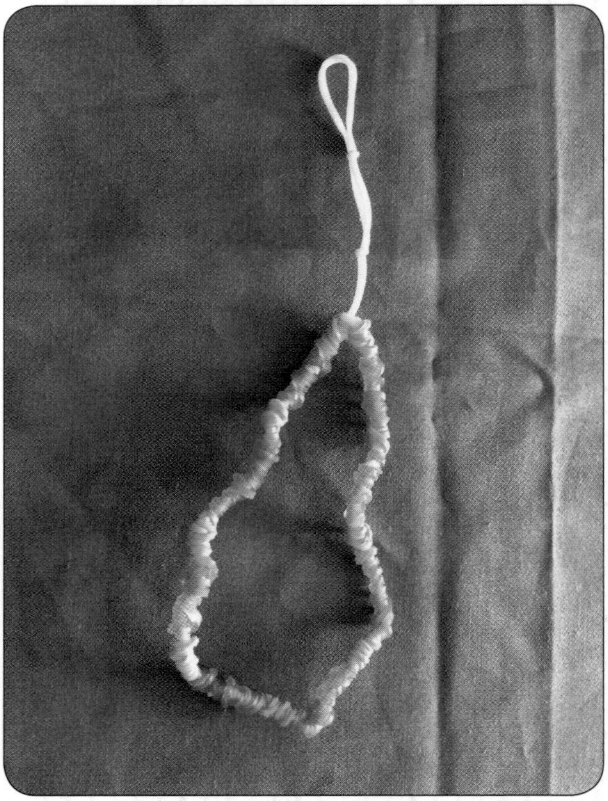

Step 3: Put a Ring on It

On the last portion of the skeleton use a blue band so that it will bend with the beads when tying the loop for the ring. Loop the small blue skeleton hole onto the bracelet so that it creates a small circle large enough to fit your middle finger loosely. Now you have it: your own custom strappy hand bracelet created without any tools. And you have the ability to create endless designs. Your imagination is the limit!

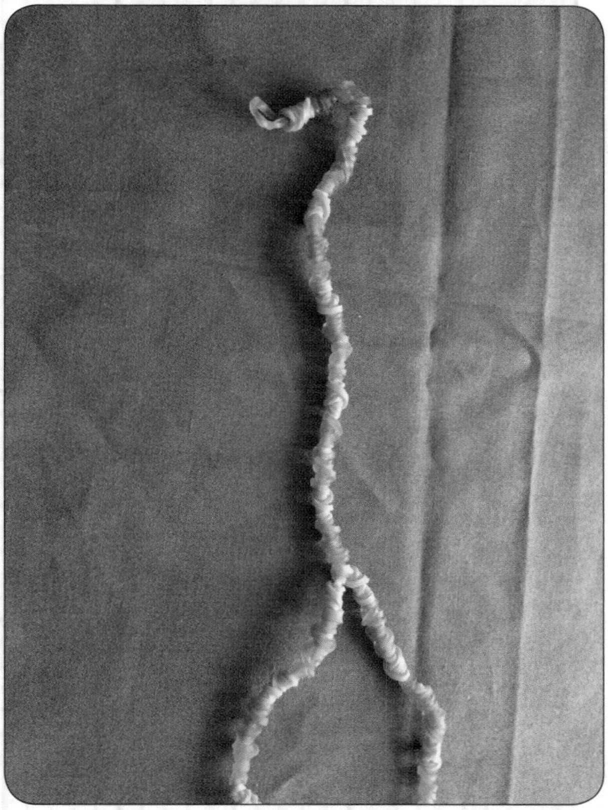

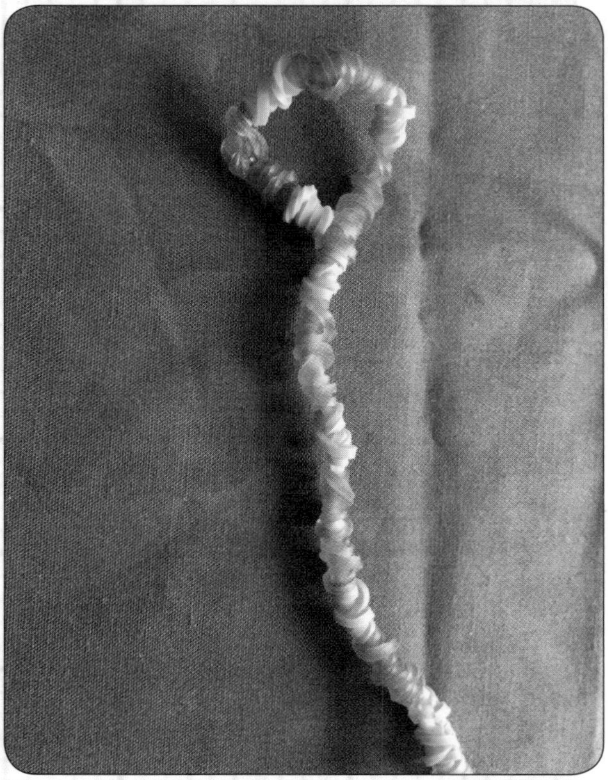

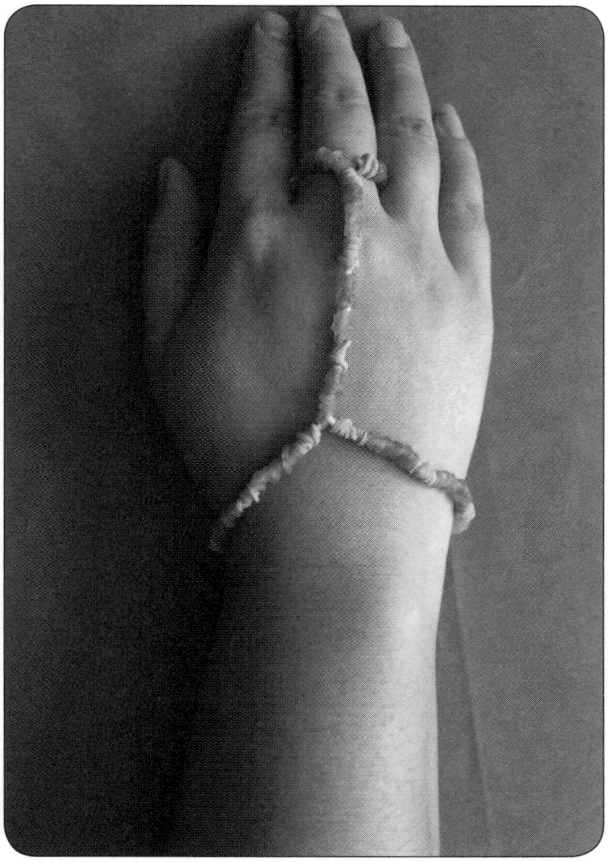

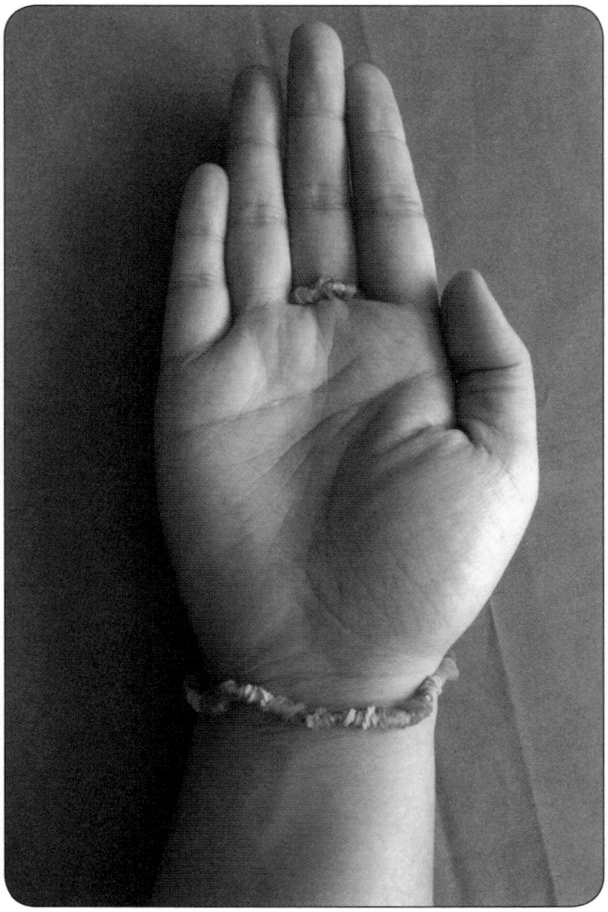

Make Your Own Loom

By imbigman

(http://www.instructables.com/id/Easy-to-Make-Rubber-Band-Loom-and-Bracelet/)

At the height of the rubber band craze, my son decided that he wanted a loom too. Well, at the time, there were none to be found. So it was up to me to make him one. I found a chunk of wood about two feet long and hammered in a bunch of nails. The nails weren't straight, they didn't line up, and it was heavy. However, at the end of that board, I made a circle with the nails and drilled a hole. All the kids in the neighborhood wanted to use that loom, not because of the full size bracelet you can make with it without having to reposition it, but because of the little detail at the end of the board that I added. The kids loved that it made some of the more difficult bracelets easier to do. So I made a pocket version of that little detail. Here is how I made it.

Step 1: Gather Your Materials

I used a chunk of wood that I had lying around (1.5" x 3/4" x 6"); however, just about any size will do. You will also need six pushpins, a pencil, and a half inch drill bit.

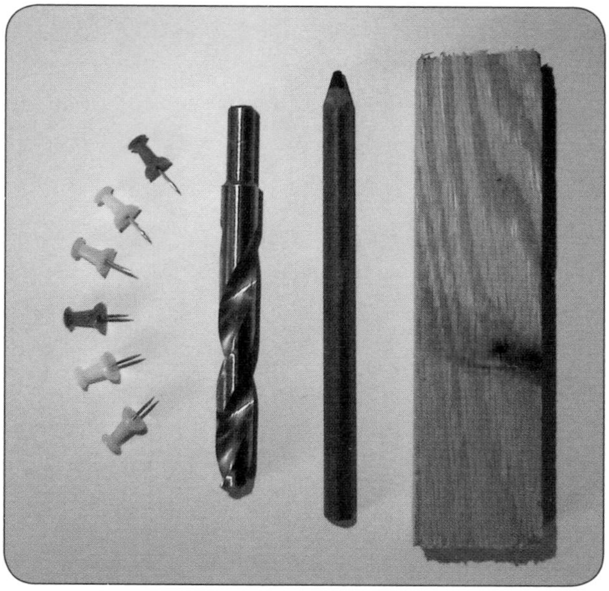

Step 2: Find the Center at One End

Find the center, use your drill bit, and drill a hole.

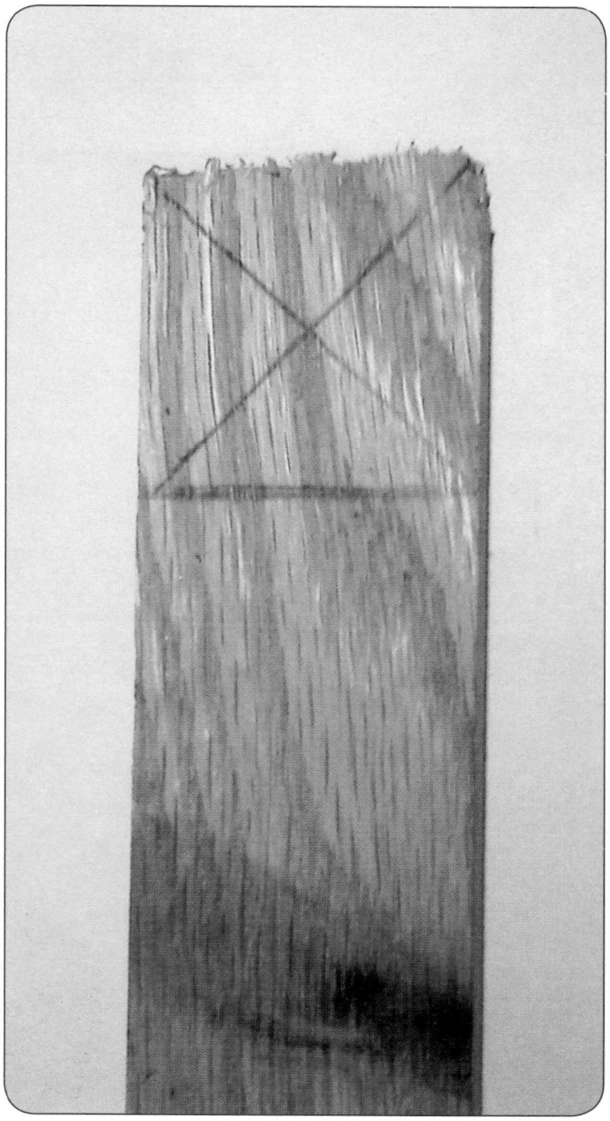

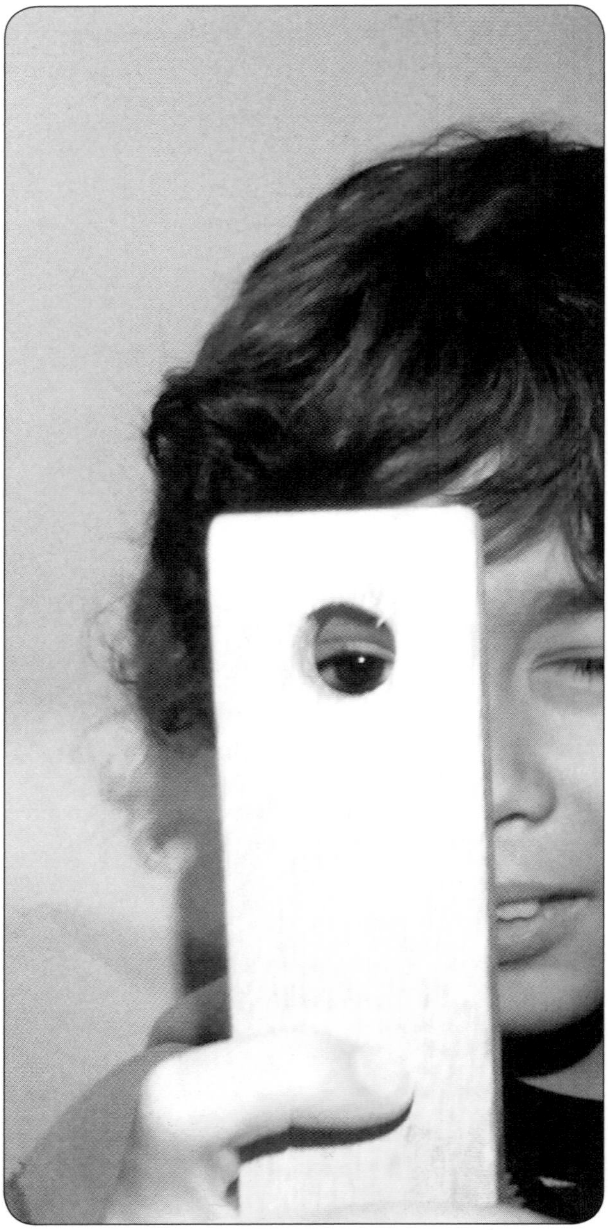

Step 3: Mark with Pencil

With my pencil, I marked where I wanted to place the pins. I didn't measure them out, I just eyeballed this.

Step 4: Pins

Push the pins on your dots. You might need a hammer to put them all the way in.

Step 5: Now for the Bracelet

For this bracelet, we used 25 bands of each color: yellow, brown, and light blue. We also used a crochet hook and the loom we just put together.

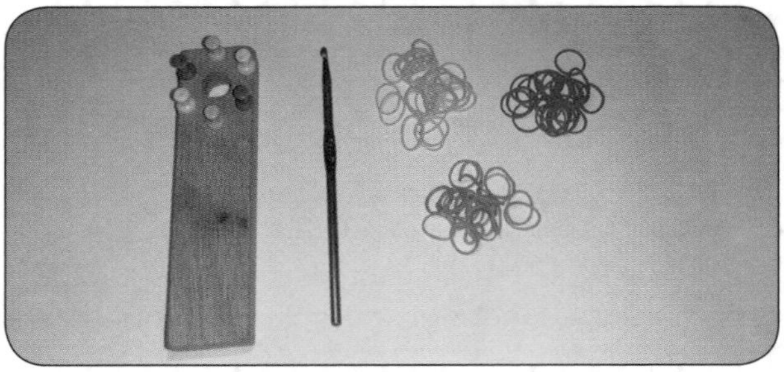

Step 6: Choosing the Pattern and Colors

We started with yellow. We put the first band in a triangle shape pointing up, using three of the pins . Then we placed the second band, of the same color, in a triangle pointing down. After that, we placed blue over top of the yellow, using the same pattern. We flipped the yellow over the blue. Next we placed the brown in the same pattern and flipped the blue over the brown. Continue to do this until you use up your bands or have achieved your desired length.

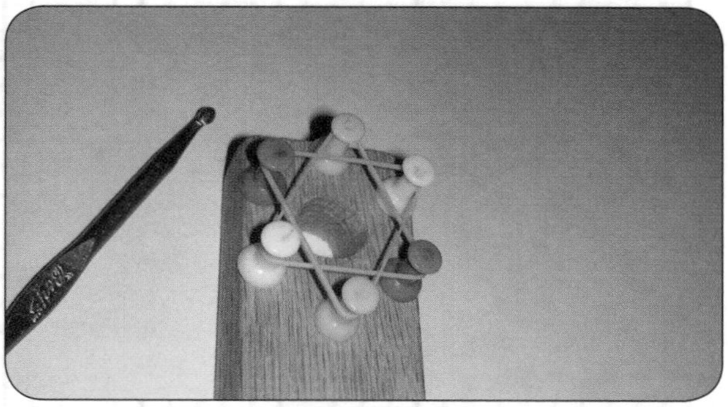

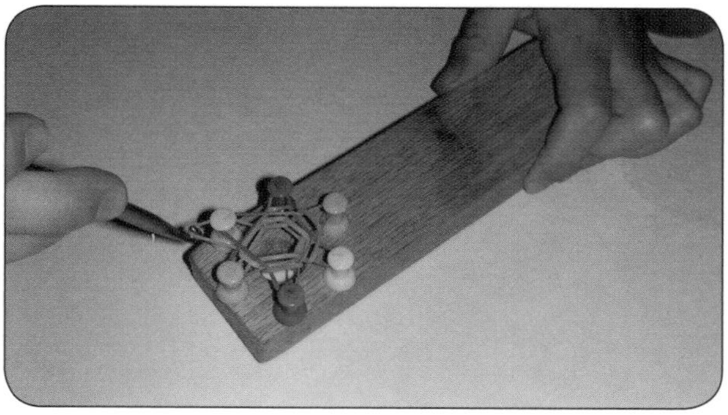

Step 7: Adding the Clip

What I tell the kids to do is pick a pin and take that loop and move it to the opposite side. Do that for the two adjoining pins. Pull the tail out of the hole and add a clip to pull it all together. Remove from loom and attach the other end.

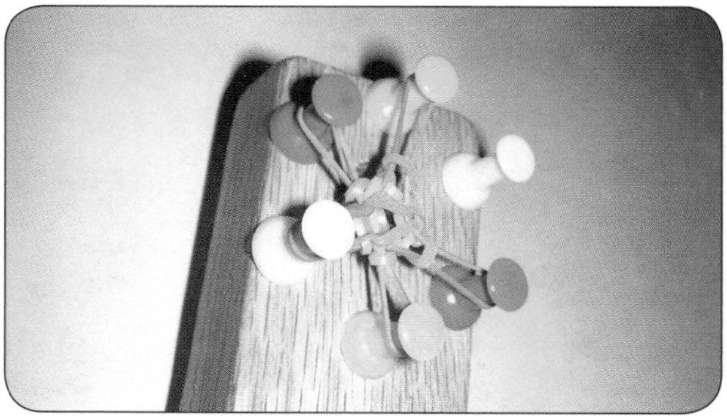

Step 8: Enjoy

This loom can be used with two posts, four posts, or all six. Try different patterns and different styles.

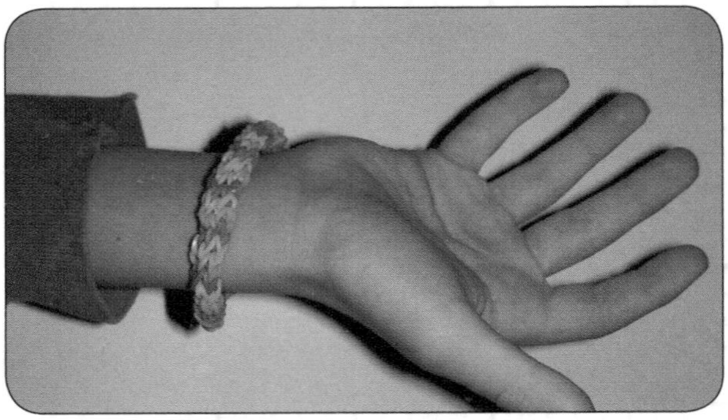

Step 9: First Loom

Thought you might like to see the first loom that I made.

Helpful Tips & Ideas

How to Use the Mini Loom

By Jessy Ellenberger (jessyratfink)

(http://www.instructables.com/id/how-to-use-the-mini-rainbow-loom/)

The Mini Rainbow Loom is a fantastic and portable way to make single Rainbow Loom bracelets. It's super easy to learn, but took me a few minutes to get down, so I thought I would share a tutorial for it!

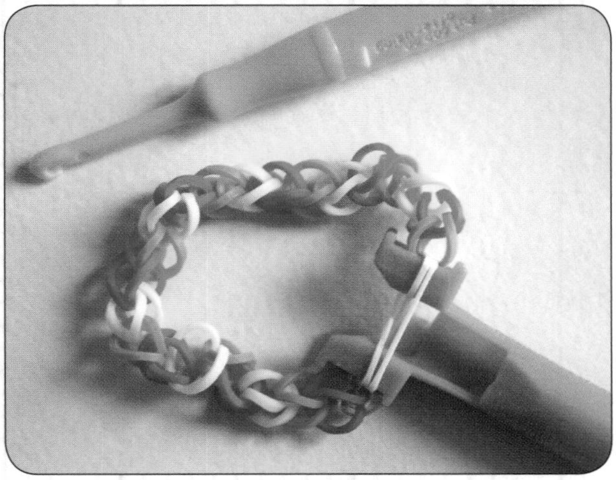

Step 1: What You'll Need

- A Rainbow Loom kit or other rubber band loom (it will come with a mini loom!)
- Rubber bands
- C-clips
- Loom hook or a small crochet hook

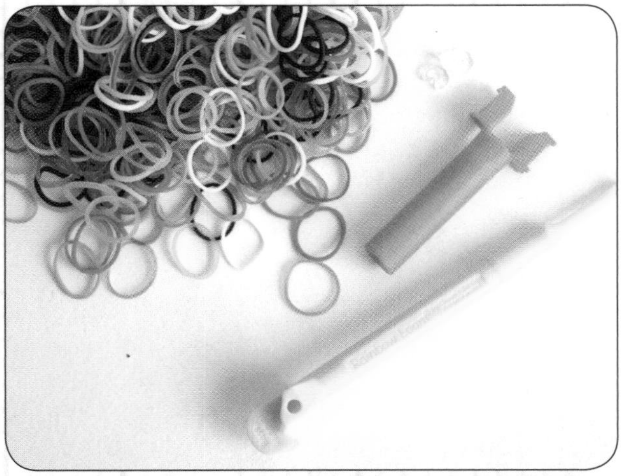

Step 2: Start Your Bracelet

The start of this one takes one band that matches the colors you have in mind for your bracelet. Hold the mini loom so the hooks are facing up and loop the bands around the two loops on one side, then bring it around the other side and loop it over the original hooks again. This will form an X shape. Attach a clip to one side of the band.

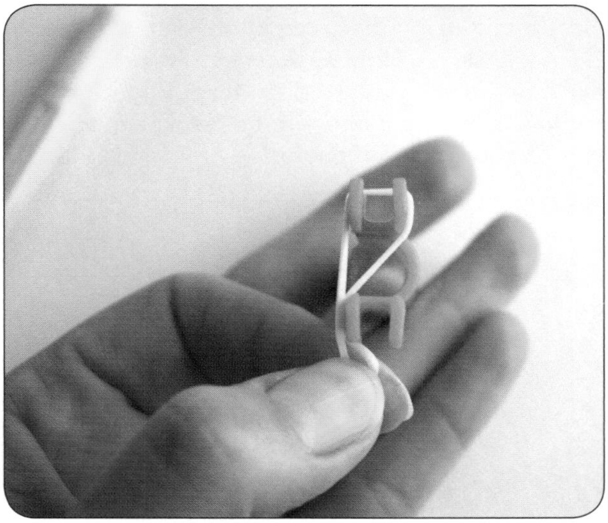

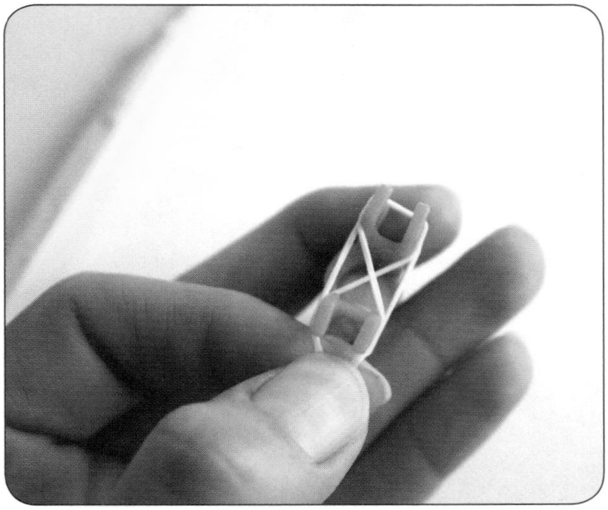

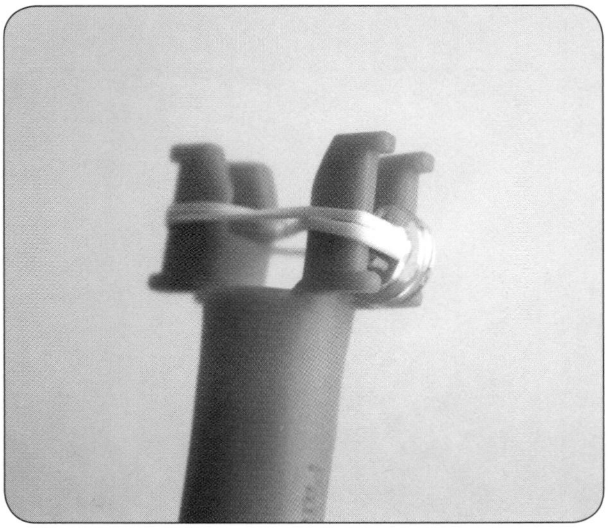

Step 3: Use the Hook to Add Bands

You'll be working on the side without the clip. Hold the mini loom with that side facing up. Slip the hook under the first band and put a band on the end. Pull the hook and band under the first band on the loom. Place both sides of the second band on the hook so it forms a U shape. Now you'll repeat the process over and over—adding a new band by pulling it through the loops of the old one with the hook. See the next step for more detailed photos!

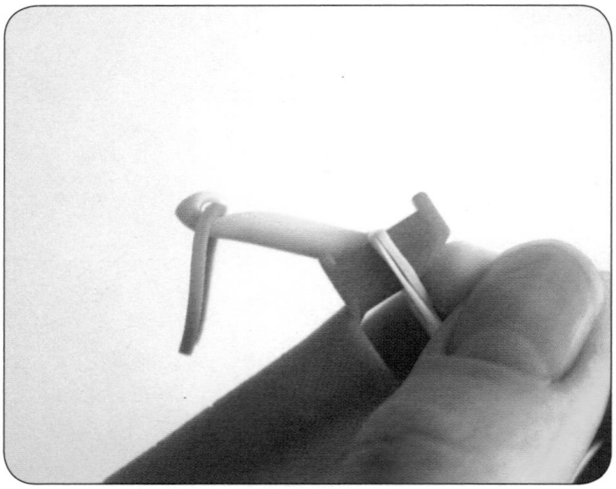

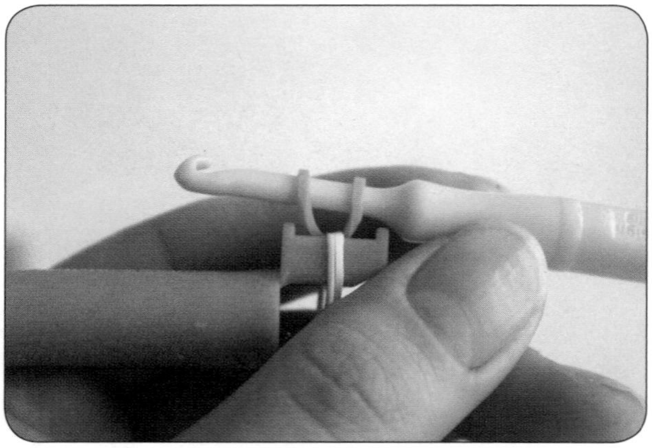

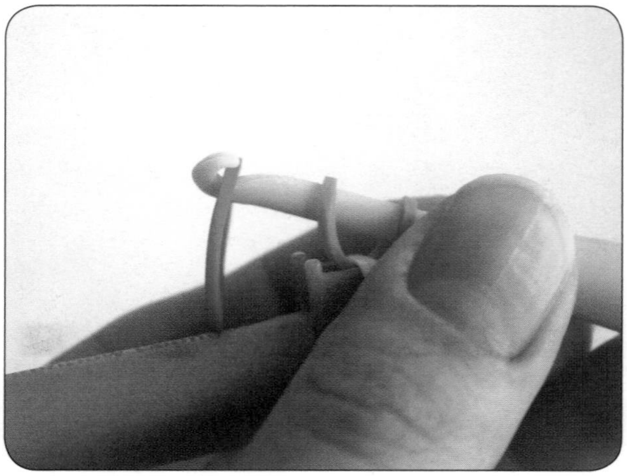

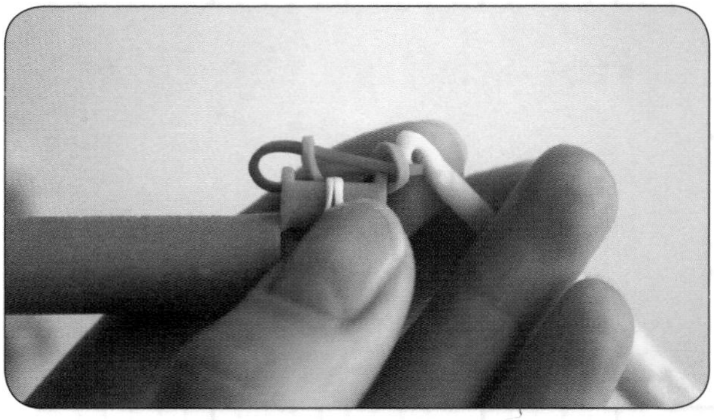

Step 4: Working Efficiently with the Mini Loom

I've included this to show you guys the easiest way to do it. Pull the bands through with the hook facing down so you don't snag the previous band, and always keep the hook facing up when in-between adding bands. This will keep the U shape on the hook while you hunt for your next band.

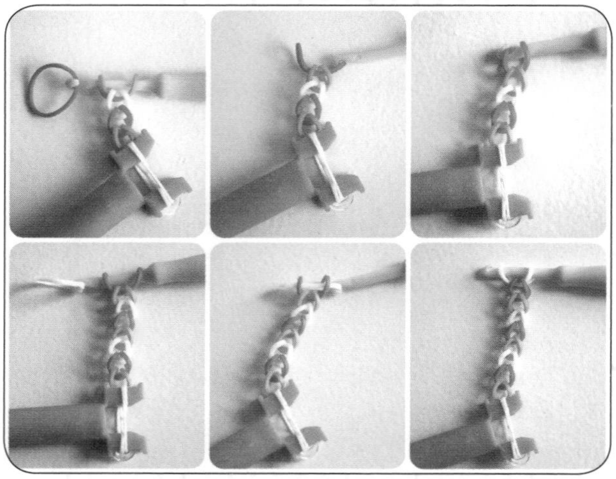

Step 5: Keep on Going Until You're Done!

It took me about five minutes to make a single bracelet that fit my wrist. Once it's long enough, clip both ends of the looped last band to the C-clip you attached at the beginning and pull it off the mini loom.

How to Organize Your Loom Gear

By Katie n Elly
(http://www.instructables.com/id/Organizing-Your-Rainbow-Loom/)

This is a fast and easy way to clean your Rainbow Loom storage if you don't have a dividing box.

Step 1: Starting

Take everything out that you are going to organize.

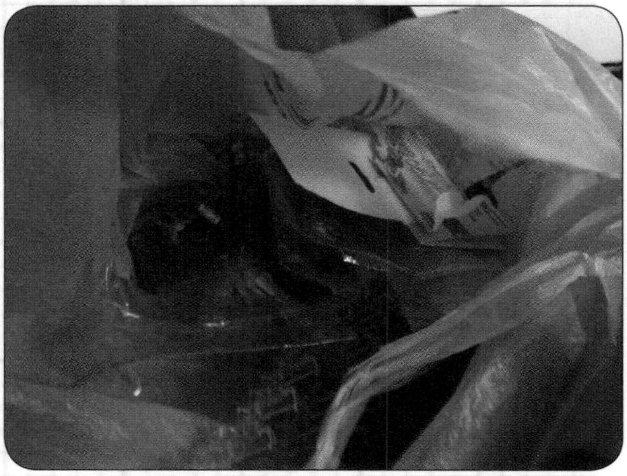

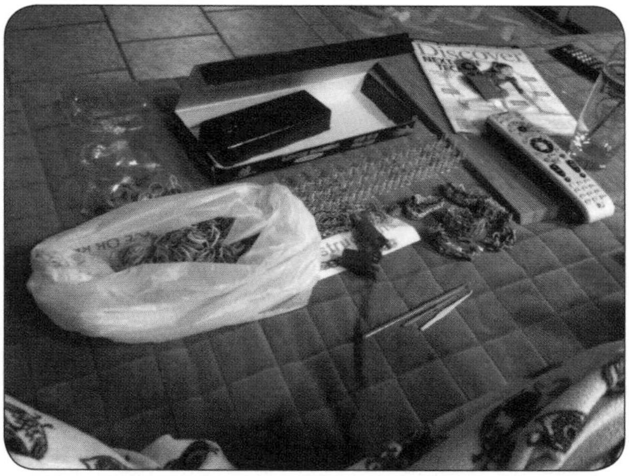

Step 2: Organizing

Start by putting the various colored bands in bags, one bag for each color, then put all your bracelets and hooks plus different contraptions in individual bags.

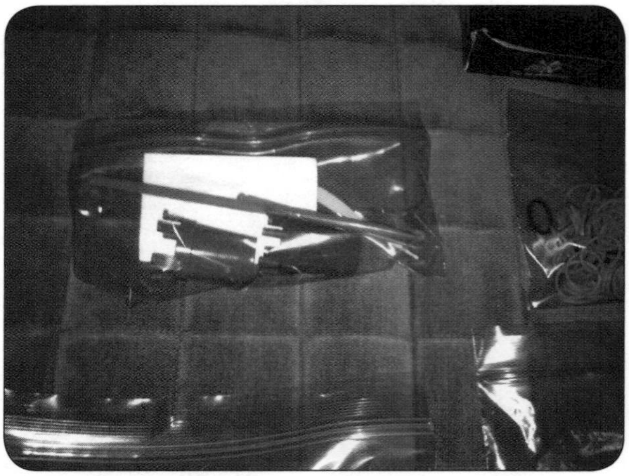

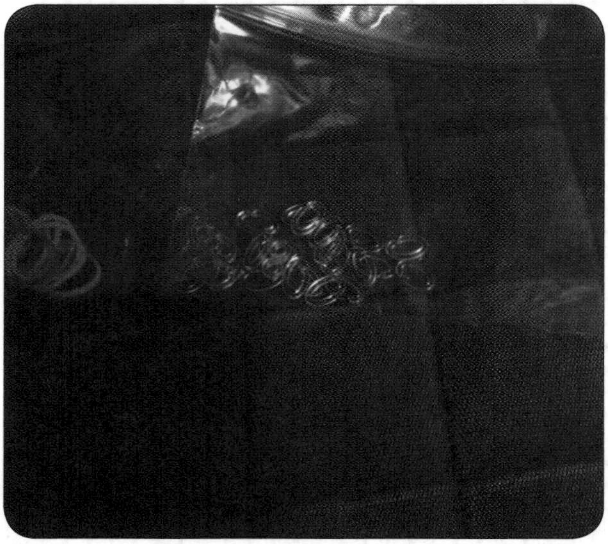

Step 3: Keeping Them Together

Put all the bags in either a box or a bag, then enjoy your clean space!

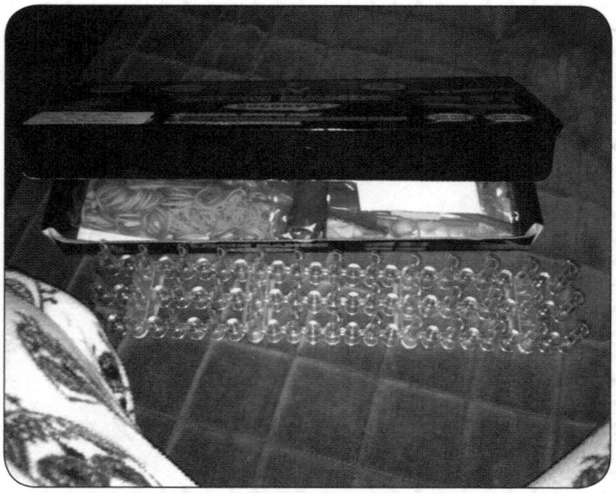

Dress Up Like a Loom

By Jodie and Ryan Sadowsky
(lovethemmadly)
(http://www.instructables.com/id/BE-the-Hottest-Toy-of-The-Year-The-Rainbow-Loom/)

Rainbow Loom is wildly popular in America right now—and especially in my house. My son wanted to BE a Rainbow Loom for Halloween, and we figured out how to do it. You can see the rest of my family's Halloween and few more Rainbow Loom photos here.

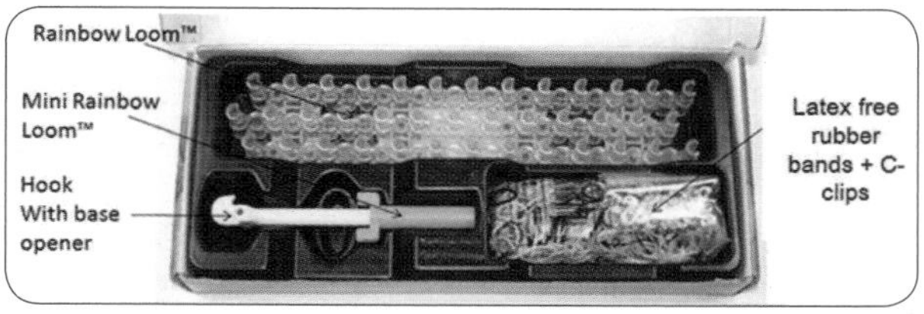

Step 1: Measure and Plan

Take careful measurements of the loom, and the person who will be wearing the costume, to calculate proportionate measurements. Use the height to determine a multiplier between the loom height and the wearer's height. Our loom measures 10 inches long. We wanted the costume to be roughly 36 inches for Ryan so we used a multiplier of 3.6.

Step 2: Test and Cut

We tested a few methods of attaching cups to the cardboard, ultimately deciding to use zip ties and 10-ounce Solo cups for the project. For our method, cut gray posterboard to size (ours is 10 inches by 30 inches). Make one for the front and back. Wrap each with blue duct tape to give the loom's signature blue baseplates. Wrap Saran Wrap around each to give it a shiny plastic look.

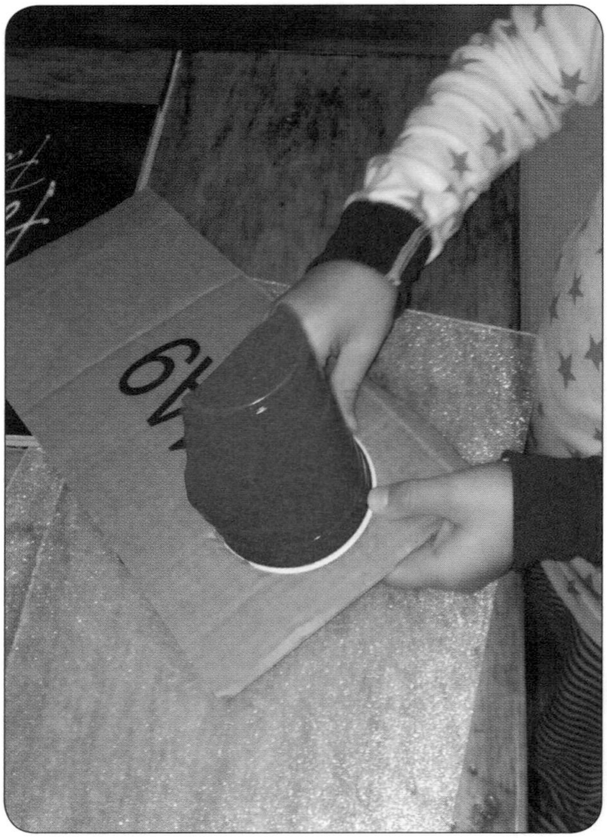

Step 3: Mark and Create

Mark where your cups (pegs) will be. Use a penknife and zip ties to secure 10-ounce clear Solo cups to the poster board in the alternating one-peg/two-peg pattern of the original loom. Then attach front and back together with blue duct tape, making sure that the wearer's head can fit through.

Step 4: Accessorize!

Use giant rubber bands from Staples for bands. Add an upside-down cane for a loom hook tool.